Grief and Trauma Counseling Education:

Preparing Future Counselors

Michelle R. Cox
Azusa Pacific University, USA

A volume in the Advances
in Educational Marketing,
Administration, and Leadership
(AEMAL) Book Series

Published in the United States of America by
IGI Global
Information Science Reference (an imprint of IGI Global)
701 E. Chocolate Avenue
Hershey PA, USA 17033
Tel: 717-533-8845
Fax: 717-533-8661
E-mail: cust@igi-global.com
Web site: http://www.igi-global.com

Copyright © 2024 by IGI Global. All rights reserved. No part of this publication may be reproduced, stored or distributed in any form or by any means, electronic or mechanical, including photocopying, without written permission from the publisher.
Product or company names used in this set are for identification purposes only. Inclusion of the names of the products or companies does not indicate a claim of ownership by IGI Global of the trademark or registered trademark.

Library of Congress Cataloging-in-Publication Data

CIP Pending
ISBN: 979-8-3693-1375-6
EISBN: 979-8-3693-1376-3

British Cataloguing in Publication Data
A Cataloguing in Publication record for this book is available from the British Library.

All work contributed to this book is new, previously-unpublished material.
The views expressed in this book are those of the authors, but not necessarily of the publisher.

For electronic access to this publication, please contact: eresources@igi-global.com.

Advances in Educational Marketing, Administration, and Leadership (AEMAL) Book Series

Siran Mukerji
IGNOU, India
Purnendu Tripathi
IGNOU, India

ISSN:2326-9022
EISSN:2326-9030

MISSION

With more educational institutions entering into public, higher, and professional education, the educational environment has grown increasingly competitive. With this increase in competitiveness has come the need for a greater focus on leadership within the institutions, on administrative handling of educational matters, and on the marketing of the services offered.

The **Advances in Educational Marketing, Administration, & Leadership (AEMAL) Book Series** strives to provide publications that address all these areas and present trending, current research to assist professionals, administrators, and others involved in the education sector in making their decisions.

Coverage

- Academic Administration
- Educational Leadership
- Educational Management
- Enrollment Management
- Governance in P-12 and Higher Education

IGI Global is currently accepting manuscripts for publication within this series. To submit a proposal for a volume in this series, please contact our Acquisition Editors at Acquisitions@igi-global.com or visit: http://www.igi-global.com/publish/.

The (ISSN) is published by IGI Global, 701 E. Chocolate Avenue, Hershey, PA 17033-1240, USA, www.igi-global.com. This series is composed of titles available for purchase individually; each title is edited to be contextually exclusive from any other title within the series. For pricing and ordering information please visit http://www.igi-global.com/book-series/advances-educational-marketing-administration-leadership/73677. Postmaster: Send all address changes to above address. Copyright © IGI Global. All rights, including translation in other languages reserved by the publisher. No part of this series may be reproduced or used in any form or by any means – graphics, electronic, or mechanical, including photocopying, recording, taping, or information and retrieval systems – without written permission from the publisher, except for non commercial, educational use, including classroom teaching purposes. The views expressed in this series are those of the authors, but not necessarily of IGI Global.

Titles in this Series

For a list of additional titles in this series, please visit:
http://www.igi-global.com/book-series/advances-educational-marketing-administration-leadership/73677

Inclusive Educational Practices and Technologies for Promoting Sustainability
Santosh Kumar Behera (Kazi Nazrul University, India) Atyaf Hasan Ibrahim (University of Diyala, Iraq) and Faten Romdhani (Regional Board of Education, Bizerta, Tunisia)
Information Science Reference • copyright 2024 • 310pp • H/C (ISBN: 9798369369555) • US $165.00 (our price)

Inclusivity and Indigeneity in Education for Sustainable Development
Santosh Kumar Behera (Kazi Nazrul University, India) Atyaf Hasan Ibrahim (University of Diyala, Iraq) and Faten Romdhani (Regional Board of Education, Bizerta, Tunisia)
Information Science Reference • copyright 2024 • 297pp • H/C (ISBN: 9798369328026) • US $165.00 (our price)

Global Insights on Women Empowerment and Leadership
Malika Haoucha (University Hassan II of Casablanca, Morocco)
Information Science Reference • copyright 2024 • 315pp • H/C (ISBN: 9798369328064) • US $245.00 (our price)

Exploring Educational Equity at the Intersection of Policy and Practice
José Sánchez-Santamaría (Universidad de Castilla-La Mancha, Spain) and Brenda Boroel Cervantes (Autonomous University of Baja California, Mexico)
Information Science Reference • copyright 2024 • 336pp • H/C (ISBN: 9798369316146) • US $245.00 (our price)

Transformative Intercultural Global Education
Isabel María Gómez Barreto (Universidad de Castilla-La Mancha, Spain) and Gorka Roman Etxebarrieta (Universidad del Pais Vasco, Spain)
Information Science Reference • copyright 2024 • 457pp • H/C (ISBN: 9798369320570) • US $245.00 (our price)

701 East Chocolate Avenue, Hershey, PA 17033, USA
Tel: 717-533-8845 x100 • Fax: 717-533-8661
E-Mail: cust@igi-global.com • www.igi-global.com

Table of Contents

Preface.. xv

Acknowledgement xxiv

Chapter 1
An Overview of the Impact of COVID-19 on Grief 1
Michelle R. Cox, Azusa Pacific University, USA

Chapter 2
Anticipatory Grief: The Pain of What's to Come.. 33
Amy Maturen, Mid America Christian University, USA

Chapter 3
Death Anxiety: The Denial of Our Impermanence.. 57
Aaron Suomala Folkerds, Minnesota State University, Moorhead, USA
Diane Coursol, Minnesota State University, Mankato, USA

Chapter 4
Grief on Pause: Understanding the Concept of Grief Avoidance Behaviors........ 78
Tobi Yvette Russell, Central Michigan University, USA

Chapter 5
When a Balm Aggravates Pain: The Wrong Words to the Bereaved in Grief
and Trauma Counselling 112
Onijuni Olatomide, Obafemi Awolowo University, Ile-Ife, Nigeria

Chapter 6
Children Grieve Too: Offering School-Based Bereavement Support Groups ... 128
Kailey Bradley, Refuge Counseling, LLC, USA
Emily Horton, University of Houston-Clear Lake, USA

Chapter 7
Assisting Teachers With Grieving Students: Strategies for School Counselors 146
Kimberly Tharpe, Azusa Pacific University, USA

Chapter 8
Advancing the Wellbeing of Bereaved People Toward Effective
Rehabilitation 176
  Onijuni Olatomide, Obafemi Awolowo University, Ile-Ife, Nigeria

Chapter 9
Role of a Caregiver: Emotional Tolls of Caregiving 202
  *Diana McCullough, Greater Vision Counseling and Consulting, PLLC,
    USA*

Chapter 10
Planning and Support Systems After the Loss of a Loved One 215
  Joetta Harlow Kelly, Campbellsville University, USA

Chapter 11
Role of Peer Support on Grief and Trauma Counseling During the Pandemic 237
  Megha M. Nair, PES University, India
  Adithi Priyadarshini Prabhu, PES University, India
  Zidan Kachhi, PES University, India

Chapter 12
Self-Care Strategies for Grief Counselors and Caregivers 265
  Ranjit Singha, Christ University, India

Chapter 13
Support Sisters: Life After COVID-19, Cancer, and Caregiving 295
  Michelle R. Cox, Azusa Pacific University, USA

Compilation of References 327

About the Contributors 367

Index 370

Detailed Table of Contents

Preface xv

Acknowledgement xxiv

Chapter 1
An Overview of the Impact of COVID-19 on Grief 1
    Michelle R. Cox, Azusa Pacific University, USA

The COVID-19 worldwide pandemic shed light on gender disparities for mothers who had to work from home, anxiety from use of dating applications, compounded racial disparities, and counselor burn-out. This chapter presents the multifaceted impact of the COVID-19 pandemic on mental health of individuals as well as the counseling profession which will be presented in detail throughout this book. Recommendations are also shared to support the mental health of clients impacted by grief from the COVID-19 pandemic. The recommendations are not only beneficial for practicing counselors and clinicians, but also for students in counselor education related programs, so discussion questions are included at the end of the chapter.

Chapter 2
Anticipatory Grief: The Pain of What's to Come 33
    Amy Maturen, Mid America Christian University, USA

Anticipatory grief is unique from traditional grief as it involves experiencing a loss prior to the loss actually occurring. This form of grief can be experienced by an individual, family members, or both. This grief is not exclusively due to the loss of another person. Anticipatory grief can include loss of dreams, safety, autonomy, marriages, homes, and many others. During the COVID-19 pandemic, the number of anticipatory losses the world faced all at the same time was monumental. Those effects are still affecting many people today. In this chapter, the theory of anticipatory grief will be explored in detail along with the impacts from COVID-19, therapeutic interventions that can be utilized when working with clients and family members and how those implications impact counselors within the field.

Chapter 3

Death Anxiety: The Denial of Our Impermanence.. 57

Aaron Suomala Folkerds, Minnesota State University, Moorhead, USA

Diane Coursol, Minnesota State University, Mankato, USA

This chapter will help counselors and counselor trainees develop the capacity to understand the concept of death anxiety for themselves and for those they serve. Moreover, this chapter will define death anxiety, discuss the history of death anxiety within the helping professions, and provide guidelines for exploring one's own death anxiety and the death anxiety of clients. This chapter will describe terror management theory (TMT) and how the denial of death and death anxiety lies at the heart of human behavior and cultural affiliation. This chapter introduces cultural humility as a foundation for engaging in conversations about death and a model for clinically applying cultural humility is examined. In addition, creative teaching strategies are offered for engaging students in self-reflective learning about death anxiety. Finally, this chapter will provide a foundation to normalize Barbie's question in the blockbuster movie, "Do you guys ever think of death?" (Gerwig, 2023).

Chapter 4

Grief on Pause: Understanding the Concept of Grief Avoidance Behaviors....... 78

Tobi Yvette Russell, Central Michigan University, USA

This chapter reviews the experience of grief that focuses on avoidance. Avoidance can be adaptive in certain situations, including in some cultural practices. However, at other times, avoidance can be maladaptive for the griever. When avoidance is maladaptive for the griever, both physical and emotional concerns can cause long-term difficulties for the grieving process. The purpose of this chapter is to provide the reader with an understanding of grief avoidance behavior. The chapter will describe the common patterns that are seen in grief avoidance behavior, types of experiences leading to grief avoidance behavior, the physical and emotional outcomes of grief avoidance behavior, various assessment tools for grief avoidance behavior and evidence-based treatment for prolonged grief disorders. Dr. Wolfelt created a framework of common patterns of grief avoidance that included: the postponer, the displacer, the replacer, the minimizer, and the somaticizer.

Chapter 5
When a Balm Aggravates Pain: The Wrong Words to the Bereaved in Grief
and Trauma Counselling 112
Onijuni Olatomide, Obafemi Awolowo University, Ile-Ife, Nigeria

The death of a beloved person usually traumatises the bereaved, causing grief.
Remarkably, social supports—family members, friends, religious faithful, clergies,
neighbours, and sympathisers—give available support, rich in physical, social, and
psychological contents. Words are normally used to convey their support during
their visits to the bereaved. However, contrary to expectation that their words would
heal the bereaved, such words could eventually aggravate their grief condition. Not
only could such words emanate from outside of the bereaved—they could also issue
from the bereaved, but producing the same lethality. This chapter provides some of
those aggravating words such as "This is a catastrophe," "Again?" "Just forget about
it," "I know exactly how you feel," and "you should have ...," etc. It similarly offers
systematic steps on how rehabilitative counsellors could assist social support and
the bereaved to acknowledge the dangers inherent in such words, and how to recast
them for desirable therapeutic effect.

Chapter 6
Children Grieve Too: Offering School-Based Bereavement Support Groups ... 128
Kailey Bradley, Refuge Counseling, LLC, USA
Emily Horton, University of Houston-Clear Lake, USA

Children represent an often-forgotten group of mourners. Helping professionals
must be cautious about making assumptions regarding the inherent resilience of
children. Moreover, helping professionals need to avoid minimizing the deleterious
effects of grief on young clients. Grief impacts all children differently. Because
children's grief often manifests differently than adults' grief, bereaved children can
go underassessed and undertreated. Grief support groups in local school settings
can be an efficacious way of supporting bereaved youth. The facilitative nature
of peer support can promote healing through elements of universality and shared
experiences. Due to their developmental level, students may benefit from knowing
a fellow student has navigated something similar. In this chapter, the authors detail
a grief support group model for mental health professionals tending to the unique
mental health needs of bereaved youth.

Chapter 7
Assisting Teachers With Grieving Students: Strategies for School Counselors 146
  Kimberly Tharpe, Azusa Pacific University, USA

The educational setting has provided students with supports in the event of emotional struggles such as grief. Teachers are often the first individual a student seeks for support and some understanding. This chapter involves dividing the content into logical, structured sections that guide educators and counselors through understanding the role of the school, school counselors and teachers when effectively assisting grieving students. Issues of grief associated with the impact of COVID and the school will be addressed. A brief theoretical background examining relational developmental systems (RDS) metatheory as a conceptual framework will be discussed understanding the outcomes of school relationship and connectivity. Additionally, specific strategies for school counselors will be provided, to utilize when assisting teachers with grieving students.

Chapter 8
Advancing the Wellbeing of Bereaved People Toward Effective
Rehabilitation 176
  Onijuni Olatomide, Obafemi Awolowo University, Ile-Ife, Nigeria

Among the inevitable traumatic hazards that people encounter is death of a loved one. A notable reaction to such loss is grief. Individuals in grief could develop a crisis and suddenly start to function with diminished capacity. While some individuals navigate their grieving phase with minimal damage and return to functionality, others lack the requisite resources to manage the phase, leading them to crisis. This latter group needs counsellors to assist them navigate the phase and return to pre-crisis functionality. This chapter provides two-way effective grief and trauma counselling therapies. To social supports, it provides empathic listening, tolerating awkward responses from the bereaved, and observing a task that needs to be done and do it vicariously, etc. To the bereaved, it offers cognitive restructuring, self-monitoring of thoughts and recording, increasing help-seeking behaviours, Premack principle, time out, self-compassion, bibliotherapy, and reinforcement, among other therapies, to manage grief and trauma during bereavement.

Chapter 9
Role of a Caregiver: Emotional Tolls of Caregiving 202
    Diana McCullough, Greater Vision Counseling and Consulting, PLLC,
      USA

The role of a caregiver is a noble and often selfless one, encompassing a wide range of professionals, from counselors and social workers to healthcare providers. Caregivers are at the forefront of offering support, compassion, and assistance to individuals navigating grief and loss. However, it is imperative for counselor educators to recognize that caregiving, while rewarding, also imposes a substantial emotional toll on those who provide this essential support. This chapter aims to explore the profound emotional toll that grief can take on caregivers, shedding light on the emotional turbulence, the self-care challenges they encounter, and the significance of seeking support and supervision. Although not a course taught in higher education or as case studies in the classrooms, students should be able to navigate complex situations that are not so cut-and-dry.

Chapter 10
Planning and Support Systems After the Loss of a Loved One 215
    Joetta Harlow Kelly, Campbellsville University, USA

Loss and subsequent grief are hard. Picking up the pieces after a death while trying to plan a funeral and take care of other responsibilities can leave people feeling a myriad of emotions. Making sure family members of all ages are cared for while dealing with their feelings is difficult on a regular day, but it is even more complicated amid a pandemic. The author of this chapter shares their insights and suggestions, having been through this themselves. Different cultures, ethnicities, religions, socioeconomic status, and developmental factors must also be addressed. COVID-19 affected people in all these areas and placed restrictions on regular practices that may be felt for years. Suggestions for moving on after this scenario are listed to help those affected. Included are suggestions for teachers and counselors to process their feelings and help their students and clients grieve and heal.

Chapter 11
Role of Peer Support on Grief and Trauma Counseling During the Pandemic 237
Megha M. Nair, PES University, India
Adithi Priyadarshini Prabhu, PES University, India
Zidan Kachhi, PES University, India

Peer support happens when people assist one another with information, skills, emotional support, social support, or practical assistance. It is important to understand what peer support is, how it can help an individual, and why it should be encouraged and practiced. The chapter focuses on peer support, especially online peer support that was provided during the covid era for those going through grief and trauma. The chapter's goal is to gather as much research and data regarding peer support for grief and trauma counseling during the COVID-19 pandemic. It aims to enlighten the importance of peer groups and the types of peer group support that exist. The chapter will enable future counselors to understand the isolation aspect of grief and trauma and provide guidance to individuals to get the necessary peer support.

Chapter 12
Self-Care Strategies for Grief Counselors and Caregivers 265
Ranjit Singha, Christ University, India

This chapter analyzes the significance of self-care within the bereavement counselling and caregiving fields, focusing on its capacity to avert burnout and sustain professional effectiveness. Alongside case studies demonstrating the successful application of self-care practices, this chapter examines techniques for efficient time management, establishing boundaries, and cultural sensitivity. Addressing practitioners' ethical obligations and emphasizing the need for continuous dedication to one's welfare are critical points of emphasis. Making self-care a priority cultivates resilience and enables professionals to deliver empathetic and enduring assistance to individuals requiring care.

Chapter 13
Support Sisters: Life After COVID-19, Cancer, and Caregiving 295
Michelle R. Cox, Azusa Pacific University, USA

Those who lost loved ones to illness other than COVID-19 during the pandemic may have experienced feelings of confusion, isolation, and loneliness. Losing a spouse during the COVID-19 pandemic was a phenomenon. As society feared the coronavirus, some individuals fought deadly cancer diseases. Victims of cancer may not have received the proper and due medical care during the pandemic due to limited hospital beds, priority of care given to COVID-19 patients, or there may have been reduced medical staff. The author shares her personal story about her connection to group of women who met each other after the loss of their husbands to cancer during the COVID-19 pandemic. This chapter reviews the benefits of creating support groups after the COVID-19 pandemic, and counseling implications of how grief support counseling groups are proven to be compassionate, encouraging, resourceful, comforting, and life changing.

Compilation of References 327

About the Contributors 367

Index 370

This book is dedicated to caregivers across the world who fought with their loved ones who lost their lives in their battles against cancer and other diseases, while the world focused its attention on the COVID-19 Pandemic. I see you....

And of course...I dedicate this book to my beloved husband Sammy. You were my inspiration throughout the writing of this book. God has sustained me through my grief because I realize you were God's precious gift to me for over 25 years. You were the best husband I could have ever imagined, and I hope you know how much I've always loved you. Thanks for taking great care of me. Rest in Peace Sweetheart!

Preface

OVERVIEW OF THE BOOK

The editor was inspired to publish the book *Grief and Trauma Counseling Education: Preparing Future Counselors* as a result of the COVID-19 pandemic and the loss of her husband. She includes her own detailed personal experience of grief while caring for her husband who was diagnosed with pancreatic cancer in the midst of the worldwide COVID-19 pandemic. As a counselor educator for over 20 years, the editor recognized the value of application with lessons on grief counseling theories and strategies for students. There are very few textbooks focusing on grief counseling, but none that present it from the perspective of a counselor educator during her own recovery from the death of her spouse during a monumental pandemic. The authors of the book present tools to inform mental health practitioners on supporting clients to navigate various grief processes.

Grief is an experience that everyone will encounter. However, supporting or losing a loved one during a worldwide pandemic is a phenomenon which has led to trauma for some individuals. By May 2024, over 7 million deaths related to the novel COVID-19 worldwide pandemic were estimated (Worldometer, 2024; Beer, 2020), and many patients died of other life-threatening illnesses, such as cancer, during the COVID-19 pandemic. In fact, in 2020 it was reported that over 10 million people died of cancer globally, according to the World Health Organization (WHO, 2022). The world experienced hardships such as agreeing to stay-at-home orders and masking mandates, suffering from the COVID-19 disease, or missing important celebrations. These hardships may have led to an increase in depression, anxiety, sleep disorders, and stress (Costa et al., 2022). However, caregivers who lost their loved ones during the COVID-19 pandemic to non-related COVID-19 diseases, may have experienced trauma to unnoticed competition for care with patients diagnosed with COVID-19 infections, which should warrant the attention of the mental health profession.

Some caregivers witnessed their loved ones take a back-seat to patients who suffered from COVID-19 infections. The COVID-19 pandemic prevented some caregivers from accompanying their loved ones to treatments. Some caregivers and family members were prevented from being with their loved ones as they took their last breaths. Family members of the deceased were restricted from typical funerals due to COVID-19 restrictions. The impact of the pandemic caused trauma to many caregivers who may have felt they were navigating the healthcare system alone during the COVID-19 pandemic, and some lacked the physical comfort from friends or family members due to stay-at-home orders which they otherwise would have received if it were not for a worldwide pandemic (Mentor et al., 2023). There are different forms of grief, and the COVID-19 pandemic may have impacted clients' grief compounding it with additional layers of disorders such as post-traumatic stress disorder (PTSD) and complicated grief (Costa et al., 2022; Diolaiuti et al., 2021).

Not only did individuals suffer from complications to grief such as PTSD, some may have suffered from racial trauma as a result of not receiving adequate healthcare during the COVID-19 pandemic due to their minoritized group membership (Carter 2007; CDC, 2021). Minoritized individuals, such as the editor, may have not received proper medical care due to implicit bias interwoven through the healthcare industry.

Client experiences of frustrations through their grief during and after the COVID-19 pandemic are presented in this book to bring attention to life changing events that must be addressed by mental health professionals. Not only were lives lost during the COVID-19 pandemic impacting healthy grief processes, but it even changed the landscape of social interaction. The use of dating applications increased during the COVID-19 pandemic due to social distancing and has led to an increase in depression as well as psychological distress as people experience rejection from being left-swiped on dating applications (Holtzhausen et al., 2020). These experiences are important to understand in order to meet the challenges of clients post-COVID-19. The worldwide pandemic changed the way counselors and counselors in training have been taught to provide grief counseling.

Preparing Counseling Professionals

Grief and Trauma Counseling Education: Preparing Future Counselors is a powerful tool useful to counseling trainees and mental health professionals to support clients through grief and trauma. The central theme of the textbook is grief and trauma during the COVID-19 pandemic. Counseling strategies to support caregivers and those who suffered loss are uniquely presented. Topics such as anticipatory grief, death anxiety, grief avoidance, and support systems are discussed within the book. There is also a focus on special populations such as clients in rehabilitation and children. Finally, a chapter is devoted to self-care for counselors who also experience counselor burn-out while supporting clients who are experiencing grief.

Additionally, recommendations for public health policy legislation based on lack of proper medical care during the pandemic, and supporting caregivers are also included in this book.

Target Audience

The target audience that will benefit from this book includes individuals who provide mental health support for clients suffering from grief including, but not limited to counselors, school counselors, educational counselors, rehabilitation counselors, therapists, social workers, and psychologists.

This textbook is recommended to be adopted by college level programs to prepare future counselors. Suggested college programs include but are not limited to psychology, social work, clinical mental health counseling, clinical rehabilitation counseling, marriage couple and family counseling, counselor education and supervision, and school counseling. Classroom discussion questions are included at the end of each chapter which is useful in classroom settings to deepen understanding through group discussions and self reflections.

Policy makers who have the responsibility to improve a failed healthcare system for caregivers and patients who were deprived of adequate healthcare during the Covid-19 pandemic, would also benefit from the readings of this book to support new and existing legislation.

Importance of Each Chapter

The chapters contained in this book have relevance and inform the reader about different aspects of counseling education after the various forms of grief and trauma after the COVID-19 pandemic. Each chapter was carefully selected due to unique perspectives and contemporary research on grief and trauma uncovered since the COVID-19 pandemic. Each chapter also provides discussion questions useful in counselor education program classes.

An Overview of the Impact of COVID-19 on Grief

This chapter introduces the various complexities that occurred during and after the COVID-19 worldwide pandemic and impacts a needed shift in how counseling professionals meet the needs of clients who suffer from grief. The chapter sheds light on gender and racial disparities as well as access to medical care. It also presents new issues which have increased the needs for mental health support. The increase of mental health services have contributed to a shortage of counselor professionals which can lead to counselor burn-out. The chapters of the book were written in response to the current issues of grief and trauma which have surfaced after the COVID-19 pandemic are briefly introduced in this book overview.

Anticipatory Grief: The Pain of What's to Come

Anticipatory grief involves experiencing a loss prior to the loss actually occurring and can include loss of dreams, safety, autonomy, marriages, homes, and many others. The COVID-19 pandemic, increased the number of anticipatory losses, so understanding the effects of anticipatory grief are important for counselors and counselor trainees as presented in this chapter. The theory of anticipatory grief is described and explored in detail. Therapeutic interventions that can be utilized when working with clients and family members and how those implications impact counselors within the field are also described.

Death Anxiety: The Denial of Our Impermanence

Death anxiety is a concept defined and presented in this chapter as the author assists both counselors and counselor trainees to understand the history of death anxiety and guidelines to support the needs of clients who suffer from it. The COVID-19 pandemic was unexpected and some individuals experienced anxiety as they contemplated the world ending and led to thoughts of mortality. Death anxiety is explored on a deeper level, as the reader is guided to self-reflect on personal experiences. The cultural impact of death anxiety is examined and strategies to engage counseling trainees are presented.

Grief on Pause: Understanding the Concept of Grief Avoidance Behaviors

Some people lost their loved ones to the COVID-19 disease or other life-threatening diseases during the COVID-19 pandemic. Knowing that a loved one may die is a process that could result in grief avoidance in response to the discomfort of realizing death. This chapter reviews the experience of grief avoidance that could influence both physical and emotional concerns leading to long-term difficulties for the grieving process. The chapter provides readers with the conceptualization of grief avoidance behavior and describes common patterns associated with it.

When a Balm Aggravates Pain: The Wrong Words to the Bereaved in Grief and Trauma Counselling

When someone loses a loved, often family, friends, and coworkers do not know what to say to comfort the griever. Readers of this chapter will be informed on the words that contribute to aggravated pain of grief to the griever, and words that can provide healing. The chapter introduces some common aggravating words and offers systematic steps on how counselors can provide social supports to grievers as a way to acknowledge the dangers inherent in such words.

Children Grieve Too: Offering School-Based Bereavement Support Groups

During the COVID-19 pandemic, adults attempted to understand the crisis occurring across the world. Adults tried to make sense of isolation, stay-at-home orders, and other COVID-19 pandemic restrictions. As the death toll rose, adults experienced stress or anxiety. Children are a population that may have been forgotten as they mourned the death of loved ones or even grieved personal losses to important events. The authors of this chapter argue that mental health professionals have made assumptions regarding the inherent resilience of children, and their grief can go underassessed and undertreated. Grief support groups are encouraged in school settings and the author presents an efficacious way of supporting bereaved youth. Presented is a grief support group model for mental health professionals tending to the unique mental health needs of youth who suffer from grief.

Assisting Teachers with Grieving Students: Strategies for School Counselors

This chapter describes the mental health supports needed in educational settings for students experiencing grief that can be implemented by teachers. Teachers are often the first individuals students seeks seek out for support and understanding. Guidance is presented to school counselors to inform educators to affectively provide support to grieving students. Issues of grief associated with the impact of the COVID-19 pandemic within schools are presented and addressed in this chapter. The chapter also presents specific strategies for school counselors to utilize when assisting teachers supporting grieving students.

Advancing the Wellbeing of Bereaved People toward Effective Rehabilitation

This chapter focuses on the response to grief for clients who are undergoing rehabilitation counseling. Rehabilitation counselors are expected to provide social supports to clients to return them to pre-bereavement functionality after the death of a loved one to accelerate the healing of individuals in grief and trauma. In this chapter, the author discusses how grief can form a crisis, such as loss after the COVID-19 pandemic, can cause clients to function with diminished capacity. Clients in rehabilitation may grieve differently, and navigate their grieving phase with minimal damage and return to functionality, while others may lack the requisite resources to manage the phase, leading them to crisis. Through this chapter, readers learn affective grief and trauma counseling therapies and skills of empathic listening, tolerating awkward responses from the bereaved, and observing a task that needs to be done and do it vicariously. The chapter also presents cognitive restructuring, self-monitoring of thoughts and recording, increasing help-seeking behaviors for clients who are grieving.

Role of a Caregiver: Emotional Tolls of Caregiving

Caregivers provide support to loved ones who are ill at home. Duties may consist of attending doctors' appointments, housework, or simply companionship. Commonly, caregivers are provided with direction and resources from medical professionals. However, the COVID-19 pandemic complicated that process and many caregivers were left to care for loved ones while navigating instructions on their own due to hospital restriction which would not allow them to accompany their loved ones to medical visits. Caregivers also encompass a wide range of professionals, from counselors and social workers to healthcare providers. The chapter presents the substantial emotional toll on those who provide this essential support and sheds light on the emotional turbulence, self-care challenges, and the significance of seeking support and supervision.

Planning and Support Systems After the Loss of a Loved One

The COVID-19 pandemic placed restrictions on usual practices such as planning or caregiving at home. Grief varies based on the relationship of the deceased, and those who suffered loss during the COVID-19 pandemic may feel their loss is unique. In this chapter, the author shares different types of loss and supports for clients who may benefit from support systems based on the relationship they had with the deceased. Suggestions are presented to identify and develop support systems such as support groups, to assist clients in healing after a loss by presenting aspects of wellness. The author discusses coping mechanisms for grievers as well as cultural implications.

Role of Peer Support on Grief and Trauma Counseling During the Pandemic

Peer support can be affective for those who experience grief, particularly after the COVID-19 pandemic. Peer support offers an exchange of assistance members with information, skills, emotional support, social support, or practical assistance. The chapter stresses the importance of understanding for purpose of peer support, as well as how it should be encouraged and practiced. The chapter focuses on the online peer support which will enable future counselors to understand the isolation aspect of grief and trauma from the COVID-19 pandemic and provide guidance in how to connect clients to peer support.

Self-Care Strategies for Grief Counselors and Caregivers

Self-care is an important and expected professional expectation for counselors to avoid counselor burn-out and vicarious trauma. This chapter analyzes the significance of self-care as it relates to bereavement counseling and caregiving. Case studies are presented, demonstrating the successful application of self-care practices, and an examination of techniques for time management, establishing boundaries, and increasing cultural sensitivity. Making self-care a priority cultivates resilience and enables professionals to deliver empathetic and enduring assistance to individuals requiring care, particularly after the COVID-19 worldwide pandemic that has caused a shortage of mental health professionals.

Support Sisters: Life after COVID, Cancer, and Caregiving

After the loss of her husband from cancer during the COVID-19 pandemic the author was compelled to share her personal story which connected her with a group of women who also loss their husbands to cancer during the COVID-19 pandemic. They initially met through a support group but continued their friendship years after their losses. This chapter reviews the benefits of creating support groups after the COVID-19 pandemic, and presents counseling implications of how grief support counseling groups are proven to be compassionate, encouraging, resourceful, comforting, and life changing.

Impact on Counseling Education

It is the intent that the book informs counselors, social workers, school counselors, rehabilitation counselors, psychologists, counselor educators, and future counselors to support clients who have experience grief as a result of the COVID-19 pandemic. Grief has been complicated due to experiences of loss during the COVID-19 pandemic and requires new approaches to treating clients who may suffer additional mental issues such as complicated grief, grief avoidance, and racial trauma (Costa et al., 2022; Diolaiuti et al., 2021). The COVID-19 pandemic has also impacted the realities of individuals with fear of the future, causing grief to those who may have suffered losses of celebrations such as child births, graduations, and proms. The COVID-19 pandemic has also increased use of dating applications which could lead to an increase of mental health issues such as psychological distress and depression (Holtzhausen et al., 2020). These experiences have increased the need for mental health services, leading to a shortage of mental health practitioners. As a result, some mental health practitioners are experiencing counselor burn-out which requires focus on self-care planning and interventions (Ko & Lee, 2021). This book will support these needs and hopefully prepares the industry for any future pandemics that may arise.

Michelle R. Cox
Azusa Pacific University, USA

REFERENCES

Beer, T. (2020). November's grim COVID-19 totals: More than 4.3 million infections and 37,000 Americans killed. *Forbes.*https://www.forbes.com/sites/tommybeer/2020/12/01/novembers-grim-COVID-19-totals-more-than-43-million-infections-and-37000-americans-killed/?sh=2b94405f6acb

Carter, R. T. (2007). Racism and psychological and emotional injury: Recognizing and assessing race-based traumatic stress. *The Counseling Psychologist*, 35(1), 13–105. 10.1177/0011000006292033

Center for Disease Control and Prevention (CDC). (2021). *Racism and Health.* CDC. https://www.cdc.gov/minorityhealth/racism-disparities/index.html

Costa, A. C. D. S., Menon, V., Phadke, R., Dapke, K., Miranda, A. V., Ahmad, S., Essar, M. Y., & Hashim, H. T. (2022). Mental health in the post COVID-19 era: Future perspectives. *Einstein (Sao Paulo, Brazil)*, 20, eCE6760. 10.31744/einstein_journal/2022CE676035584448

Diolaiuti, F., Marazziti, D., Beatino, M. F., Mucci, F., & Pozza, A. (2021). Impact and consequences of COVID-19 pandemic on complicated grief and persistent complex bereavement disorder. *Psychiatry Research*, 300, 113916. 10.1016/j.psychres.2021.11391633836468

Holtzhausen, N., Fitzgerald, K., Thakur, I., Ashley, J., Rolphe, M., & Winona, S. (2020). Swipe-based dating applications use and its association with mental health outcomes: A cross-sectional study. *BMC Psychology*, 8(1), 22. 10.1186/s40359-020-0373-132127048

Ko, H., & Lee, S. M. (2021). Effects of Imbalance of Self- and Other-Care on Counselors' Burnout. *Journal of Counseling and Development*, 99(3), 252–262. 10.1002/jcad.12372

Mentor, K., Pandanaboyana, S., & Sharp, L. (2023). Systematic review of caregiver burden, unmet needs and quality-of-life among informal caregivers of patients with pancreatic cancer. *Supportive Care in Cancer*, 31(1), 74. 10.1007/s00520-022-07468-736544073

World Health Organization (WHO). (2022). *Cancer.* WHO. https://www.who.int/news-room/fact-sheets/detail/cancer

Worldometer (2024). *Coronavirus cases and deaths*. Worldometer. https://www.worldometers.info/coronavirus/

Acknowledgement

To my children, HannahJo, Israel, Terrance, and Aaron. Your dad loved you so much. Each of you were his pride and joy. Continue his legacy…never forget who you are. I love each of you. To my daughters-in-law, grandchildren, parents, sisters, brothers-in-law, nieces and nephews, and my extended family and friends…I appreciate all of the times you listened to me talk about the memories and the loss of my beloved through my grief. It helped me heal. Thank you for supporting and encouraging me though the writing of this book.

To my Support Sisters (Laura, Carol, and Crystal). Although we met only a shorty time after the passing of our husbands, we understood each other's pain and loneliness, as if we were sisters. I value the support, company, and love that we've shared through our journeys in what appears to be a new world for us. Thank you for giving me permission to share your stories in this book. We have each other to lean on.

Finally, to my loving husband, Sammy, who is in his eternal rest. You were my best friend, confidant, encourager, cover, protector, provider, life- coach, and counselor. I miss you baby. Thank you for all of the wonderful years of love that even strangers noticed. We were indeed "the power couple". I know you are glorifying God in heaven and I'll see you again in our spiritual bodies that will never decay nor disease. I'll always love you…

Chapter 1
An Overview of the Impact of COVID–19 on Grief

Michelle R. Cox
https://orcid.org/0000-0002-2083-3582
Azusa Pacific University, USA

ABSTRACT

The COVID-19 worldwide pandemic shed light on gender disparities for mothers who had to work from home, anxiety from use of dating applications, compounded racial disparities, and counselor burn-out. This chapter presents the multifaceted impact of the COVID-19 pandemic on mental health of individuals as well as the counseling profession which will be presented in detail throughout this book. Recommendations are also shared to support the mental health of clients impacted by grief from the COVID-19 pandemic. The recommendations are not only beneficial for practicing counselors and clinicians, but also for students in counselor education related programs, so discussion questions are included at the end of the chapter.

INTRODUCTION

In May 2019, the world had a common enemy…COVID-19. People panicked and not only was there a scarcity of face masks which left many people surfing the web to learn how to construct do-it-yourself masks, but there were also shortages of toilet paper and paper towels, as people hoarded supplies in fear of running out of them. Individuals tried to make themselves comfortable at home during mandated stay-at-home orders. Such panic had never been witnessed at such a magnitude by the generation who experienced the worldwide pandemic. Over 100,000 lives were

DOI: 10.4018/979-8-3693-1375-6.ch001

Copyright © 2024, IGI Global. Copying or distributing in print or electronic forms without written permission of IGI Global is prohibited.

lost due to COVID-19. Not only did people suffer the loss of family and friends due to COVID-19 infections, but some lost loved ones during the pandemic to other medical conditions and diseases because they could not access adequate medical attention. Grief was suffered during the monumental COVID-19 pandemic, and lives would be forever changed.

The COVID 19 pandemic was not expected, therefore mental health clinicians were not prepared for the psychological impact on individuals. The pandemic fractured the normalcy most people were accustomed to at home. With COVID-19 stay-at-home orders, families had to quickly shift to working from home, and because schools and colleges were closed, students learned remotely. There was an increase in the incidences of depression, anxiety, stress, panic disorder, obsessive-compulsive disorder, somatic symptoms, sleep disorders, insecurity about the future, fear of contracting the disease, fear of the negative economic effects due to the pandemic, and uptick of suicide reports (Costa et al., 2022).

Due to social distancing restrictions during the pandemic, dating was transformed and there was an increase in use of dating applications. The COVID-19 pandemic fueled the use of online dating through dating applications as people sought companionship, which has continued to be a popular form of meeting people. As long as the popularity of online dating continues to rise, it is expected that the number of clients seeking mental health counseling who utilize online dating will continue to increase as well (Gibson, 2021; Ali & Bloom, 2019). Dating application users have reported anxiety from factors such as changes in routines, virtual education, and financial insecurity. According to the National Institute of Health (NIH), some users have reported self-esteem issues due to rejection that occurs on dating applications in high numbers (NIH, 2022; Konings et al., 2023; Ali & Bloom, 2019).

Mental health needs have increased due to the impact of the COVID-19 pandemic which has led to a shortage of mental health professionals. During the COVID-19 pandemic, in-person mental health services were provided by phone or virtually the rough video conferencing platforms known as telemental health which has now become a more commonly used approach to providing services (Lee et al., 2023). The shortage is not only due to the demand, but for other reasons such as lack of funding and the number of mental health professionals retiring (Phillips, 2023). According to the American Psychological Association (APA), baby boomers are retiring during a time when the public has an increase in mental health needs. It is possible more clinicians will leave the profession from exhaustion or fatigue. The demand for mental health services can also cause counselor burnout (APA, 2022). The COVID-19 pandemic had a profound effect on individuals including mental health professionals, and those who provide support must also be supported. Some clinicians may have also suffered from grief after losing loved ones during the COVID-19 pandemic.

An Overview of the Impact of COVID-19 on Grief

Grief is defined by the American Psychological Association (APA) as anguish experienced after significant loss, usually the death of a beloved person. Grief often includes physiological distress, separation anxiety, confusion, yearning, obsessive dwelling on the past, and apprehension about the future (APA, 2024). Individuals suffered from grief during the COVID-19 pandemic for various reasons. Individuals experienced grief due to the death of a loved one infected by COVID-19 or from a death unrelated to COVID-19. Some people suffered from loss of friendships or even important events such as graduations. Canceled milestone events as a result of the COVID-19 pandemic can contribute to psychological distress (Flesia et al., 2023).

This chapter introduces the multifaceted impact of the COVID-19 pandemic on mental health of individuals which impact the counseling profession which will be presented in the following book chapters. Counseling recommendations are shared at the end of each chapter as well as discussion questions. The recommendations and discussion questions are not only beneficial for active clinicians, but also for students in counselor education related programs.

THE IMPACT OF COVID-19 ON FAMILIES

The COVID-19 pandemic impacted relationships as couples had to be inventive to keep their marriages healthy while access to restaurants, and hotels were restricted. Weekend getaways were transformed to watching television together and finding entertainment in social media. Married couples commonly derive more closeness from dating, which promotes self-expansion and relationship satisfaction (Harasymchuk, et al., 2021; Garcia et al., 2019), but the COVID-19 pandemic interfered with the common ways couples kept their relationships strong.

Marriages and Gender Roles

Couples had to adjust to working from home or remote work. Some jobs already allowed for flexibility to remote work and were confined to typical work hours. However, there was a gender disparity with an increase of the total workload of women who worked from home. Increase in domestic work fell on women, with the responsibilities of supervising children who couldn't not attend school. Men are more likely than women to evaluate working from home positively when they are able to disconnect from work and neglecting this reality can turn remote work into a false solution for reconciling work and family life for women (Moreno-Colom et al., 2022); but during the COVID-19 pandemic, not only were women expected to fulfill their work duties from home, but they also were expected to provide daycare, prepare lunches, and maintain other domestic work during the workday.

It's possible increased responsibilities during the pandemic could have increased stress with women.

Prior to the pandemic, maintaining work boundaries contributed to healthy professional and private lives. A lack of work boundaries for a job that wasn't confined to regular work hours could add stress to a marriage. It can also physically, mentally, and emotionally separate parents from their children, whether young or old (Kossek, 2016; Finzi-Dottan & Berckovitch Kormosh, 2018). A study conducted in Mexico revealed a decline in new marriages and divorces during the COVID-19 pandemic, which suggests a demographic variance between middle-class and high-income responders. Divorce rates recovered faster than marriage rates after stay-at-home orders ended (Hoehn-Velasco et al., 2023). People may not have found filing for divorce during the COVID-19 pandemic an ideal time.

Working from home also required work boundaries with colleagues, as email messages and phone calls could be received any time of the day. People had to learn to maintain work boundaries by separating themselves from the smartphones or computers at the end of each day. Couples had to intentionally and thoughtfully balance work, marriage, and family by respecting and prioritizing the marital and family relationships over careers (Määttä & Uusiautti, 2012; Orellana, 2021; Finzi-Dottan & Berckovitch Kormosh, 2018). However, in some cases, strategies to balance life became impossible as responsibilities collided at home through stay-at-home orders. Working from home while supporting children who were not in school due to the pandemic, blurred the boundaries.

Children/Students

The COVID-19 pandemic also impacted the lives of students. Children had to attend school from home through virtual classes which impacted the availability for parents to be able to manage work from home while ensuring their children were connected to their classes. Some students missed important events and celebrations of milestones such as proms and graduation ceremonies. College students were disappointed because the pandemic collided with college life as many college students returned home due to college closures and were required to complete synchronous virtual classes. As a result of the COVID-19 pandemic, roughly 50% of college students experienced severe mood disorders which required urgent attention and support from society, families, and colleges (Hu et al., 2022).

People with working access to broadband service worked from home during the COVID-19 pandemic, but school work boundaries were challenging to maintain. Some students were feeling the anxiety from the COVID-19 infection rates, unreliable internet service from home, and separation from their peers, which resulted in numerous student requests for clarification of program requirements. Anxiety was high and being at home increased depression and isolation. According to Runkle et al. (2023), the pandemic was associated with increased reports of stress and anxiety, abuse, substance abuse, and isolation among young people. Students, whether they were children or young adults, suffered from lack of social interactions with their peers as a result of the pandemic. The use of social media during the pandemic resulted in conflicting results depending on the reasons for using it. Using social media for the purpose of connecting with others attenuates the negative effect of social media use on well-being. Increased feelings of social connectedness is associated with less negative effects on well-being (Midgley et al., 2022). Social media use was an approach to connect with others, and some may have found benefit in it.

DATING AND ROMANCE

Use of online dating applications increased as a result of the COVID-19 pandemic. Social distancing and the fear of being infected by the virus boosted the number of people using the online dating applications (Gibson, 2021). Although the use of dating applications has become popular over the past decade, the COVID-19 pandemic caused a surge in use as people looked for other ways to meet people while maintaining social distance. According to Pew Research (2023), about 53% of people surveyed report having ever used a dating site or app, compared with 37% of those ages 30 to 49, 20% of those 50 to 64 and 13% of those 65 and older. Dating applications are commonly used to connect with others and is a common use on social interactions. If a user wants to connect with someone on the application after reviewing the profile of that user, the response is to right swipe the smartphone screen. If there is no interest in interacting with someone after reading a profile, the user will left-swipe.

The use of dating applications has been shown to impact the mental health of the users due to feelings of rejection, or being ghosted when all communication is cut-off from someone they have connected to or interacted with interacting on the dating application. Daily users and those who used dating applications for more than a year have reported anxiety and depression from use of dating applications compared to those who did not use dating applications. Additionally, it is suggested that dating application users are an at-risk population, and further research into the effects and mediators of effects of dating application use on the mental health and psychological wellbeing of users is warranted, particularly regarding the role of motivation and validation-seeking in its use. (Holtzhausen et al., 2020). Some users have also been impacted by rejection that occurs on the applications in high numbers so self-esteem has taken a negative hit (NIH, 2022; Konings et al., 2023; Ali & Bloom, 2019).

PSYCHOLOGICAL DISTRESS

The COVID-19 pandemic was a time of panic, uncertainty, and loneliness. The World Health Organization (WHO), comprised of the world's leading health experts who coordinate responses to worldwide health emergencies, reported that in the first year of the pandemic, there was a global prevalence of anxiety and depression (WHO, 2022). According to the Pew Research (2022) Center, four out of 10 adults living in the U.S. during the COVID-19 pandemic experienced high levels of psychological distress. The COVID-19 pandemic also may have exacerbated psychological distress that was already diagnosed prior to the pandemic. People were concerned about spreading the virus, the economy, and about the future (Holiwa et al., 2021) while some were even confined to their homes through stay-at-home orders.

Social Isolation

Following COVID-19 restrictions to protect from COVID-19 infections may have contributed to isolation for certain demographical groups. Cancer patients who are younger aged, female, unmarried, current smokers, were more likely to experience social isolation during the COVID-19 pandemic (Hathaway et al., 2022). Those practicing more COVID-19 risk mitigation behaviors reported more perceived daily life change due to the COVID-19 pandemic, and were more likely to report higher social isolation (Hathaway et al., 2022). Potentially, patients recognized the need for physical support, but were forced to follow COVID-19 stay-at-home orders and restrictions. Isolation and social distancing restrictions may have contributed to distress and anxiety for families who did not have an opportunity to say goodbye to their loved ones who died during the COVID-19 pandemic.

Terminal Illness

There was a loss of lives due to COVID-19 infectionsc, but others lost their lives due to other health issues. Medical care and treatments were not as accessible for those diagnosed with terminal diseases as they were prior to the pandemic due to hospital restrictions and social distancing requirements (Voo et al., 2020).Trying to care for a loved one within the chaos of the COVID-19 pandemic is unforgetful. Losing a close relative as a consequence of terminal cancer may trigger Post Traumatic Stress Disorder (PTSD) in the bereaved individual. PTSD is a mental health condition manifested by a traumatic event that is experienced or witnessed, and which is triggered by the flashbacks or uncontrollable thoughts of the event (Kristensen et al., 2012). During the COVID-19 pandemic, family members were separated from loved ones and couldn't be near their bedsides. Remembering the

An Overview of the Impact of COVID-19 on Grief

isolation of the loved one, not having access to treatment, or experiencing medical mishaps can lead to uncontrollable thoughts of the events.

Prolonged Grief Disorder

Approximately one in 10 bereaved adults develop prolonged grief disorder (PGD), which involves intense symptoms of grief that last for more than six months after the loss, separation distress, intrusive thoughts, and feelings of emptiness or meaninglessness (Selman et al., 2020). Not only did terminally ill patients and their families encounter trauma from the diagnosis, but they also suffered from fighting the disease during a worldwide pandemic. Trauma can also be experienced through terminal diagnosis or loss of a loved one from a terminal disease, which could lead to prolonged grief disorder.

It's common for people to hope their family and friends who are experiencing grief will get through it quickly so that they can return to what society considers normal. It may be assumed that there is an appropriate and inappropriate length of time to grieve, so people who exceed this expected time may not experience healthy grief. On the contrary, grief may seem as if it will never end, particularly a spouse, parent, or child, and the survivors may experience an ongoing adjustment to life without the deceased for possibly a lifetime. According to the APA (2022), prolonged grief occurs when intense feelings of grief persist, and the symptoms are severe enough to prevent those experiencing it from continuing with their lives. Symptoms might include a preoccupation with thoughts of the deceased, or challenges with everyday activities with the loss occurring at least a year prior to the diagnosis for adults or six months for children and adolescents. Grief can be triggered several years after the death of a loved one which is normal as long as the survivors are able to function through life. Grief may be considered prolonged for some and depends on the relationship with the deceased. Having intruding thoughts immediately after the death of a loved one should be expected, but if the thoughts are prolonged and impact everyday life, the survivor may be suffering from prolonged grief disorder. At least three symptoms must have occurred each day for the six months prior to the diagnosis of prolonged grief disorder (APA, 2022):

- Identity disruption (such as feeling as though part of oneself has died).
- Marked sense of disbelief about the death.
- Avoidance of reminders that the person is dead.
- Intense emotional pain (such as anger, bitterness, sorrow) related to the death.
- Difficulty with reintegration (such as problems engaging with friends, pursuing interests, planning for the future).
- Emotional numbness (absence or marked reduction of emotional experience).

- Feeling that life is meaningless.
- Intense loneliness (feeling alone or detached from others).

Grief is expressed in different ways and may be more severe depending on the depth of the relationship one had with the deceased (Rosenblatt, 2017). For example, the survivor may have lost more than a husband, because the deceased could have also held the roles of best friend, co-parent, or may have been married to the survivor for more than 50 years. However, social norms may dictate what is considered normal. According the (APA, 2022), bereavement lasting longer than might be expected based on social, cultural, or religious norms, is a consideration for a diagnosis of prolonged grief disorder. Prolonged grief disorder is much more common than previously thought and appears significantly impactful for a considerable or large proportion of people experiencing grief (Wilson et al., 2022).

The normalization of grief is complicated considering variances of cultural practices of grief and bereavement. There are strong cultural differences in how people grieve, and some people cycle into and out of intense grieving, even for years after a death. It may be common in some cultures to move in and out of intense grief with the movement governed by what they do to control emotions and what they encounter that reminds them of their loss (Rosenblatt, 2017). Examination of cultural differences is an important consideration in the identification of prolonged grief.

Racism and Systemic Oppression

Racism often results in grief because victims undergo loss of hope when perpetrators of their victimization get away with it, leaving a major flaw in the justice system (Afuape & Kerry Oldham, 2022; APA, 2017; Douglas, et al., 2021). Black Americans have been subjected to a history of lynching, limited access to healthy and fresh foods, redlining of housing, and other forms of discrimination and institutional racism, that leads to a lack of trust. The systemic oppression and a history of atrocities against Black Americans shaped the mistrust of the American systems that lead to trauma which has also contributed to a mistrust of the mental health profession.. Trauma is complicated and other words used to describe it are hurt, damage, injury, anguish, and agony. However, the APA (2023a) describes it as an emotional response to a terrible event like an accident, rape, or a natural disaster like the COVID-19 pandemic, and includes reactions such as unpredictable emotions, flashbacks, strained relationships, and even physical symptoms like headaches or nausea. Black Americans were still subjected to trauma from the COVID-19 pandemic while experiencing racial trauma.

An Overview of the Impact of COVID-19 on Grief

Black American parents often have "the talk" with their children, particularly with sons when they are young. "The talk" is a specific type of racial socialization message that many Black parents have with their children about how to safely conduct themselves when interacting with police officers and other individuals in positions of power (Anderson et al., 2022), and this message may have been amplified during the COVID-19 pandemic. However, during the COVID-19 pandemic, Black Americans were lynched by White police officers, such as George Floyd and others (Cox, et al.. 2023). Although Black parents try to protect their children from harm, trauma may be experienced from those families as they are continually made aware that their children may not come home after running into altercations with law enforcement.

According to the Center for Disease Control and Prevention (CDC) (2021), racial and ethnic minority groups, throughout the United States, experience higher rates of illness and death across a wide range of health conditions, and systemic racism in the medical industry was also prevalent during the COVID-19 pandemic. For example, high proportions of non-injury deaths among children, adolescents, and young adults that were coded to ill-defined causes in 2020 and might suggest that some COVID-19 deaths were missed due to timely access to medical care (Pathak et al., 2021).

Post-Traumatic Slave Syndrome (PTSS) is a term that was coined by Dr. Joy DeGruy (2017), and describes the Black Americans experience. Black Americans who have suffered trauma from ongoing racism and institutional racism can be multigenerational trauma from continued oppression with a lack of opportunity to heal from it. PTSS is the result of mistrust in mental health service systems as well (Alang, 2019). Ongoing systemic racism can lead to trauma but can be compounded by a worldwide crisis, such as COVID-19.

Asian Americans experienced discrimination during and after the COVID-19 pandemic after former President Donald Trump made statement about the origination of the virus from China. Anti-Asian American hate crimes spiked in the U.S., with nearly 1900 hate crimes against Asian Americans reported by victims, and around 69% of cases were related to verbal harassment (Hans et al., 2023). Victimization of hate crimes can also lead to psychological distress for Asian Americans.

Counseling Recommendations

The COVID-19 pandemic increased anxiety and depression worldwide as people worried about contracting the virus, financial impact, and the future. Interventions that empower individuals to better accept and cope with disruption to daily life, such as mindfulness training, could mitigate negative mental health consequences from the impact of the COVID-19 pandemic as an everyday routine (Holiwa et al., 2021).

Although it's important to recognize the stages of grief of those who are suffering from terminal illnesses' it's also important to identify and assess the distinct features of caregiver grief with people who are caring for a terminally ill person (Waldrop, 2007). Surviving family members may find the validation of their feelings reassuring if they understand their feelings aren't unique. Directing those suffering from loss to support groups to discuss similar experiences may prove helpful through the grief process. Surviving family members may not understand they are experiencing stages of distress as grief, especially while they are still engaged in caregiving responsibilities, and should be assured that what is happening is normal (Waldrop, 2007). Practitioners can educate surviving family members who normalize their feelings of grief and feel validated.

Caregiving for terminally ill patients during the COVID-19 pandemic may have led to anxiety, particularly for those who competed for medical attention with caregivers of COVID-19 infected patients. Consideration of the wellbeing of the patient's caregiver as well as clinical intervention should also be assessed throughout the care continuum (Mitchell et al., 2022). This is particularly critical in cases when the caregiver is the household provider and is responsible for a multitude of household duties.

Advocacy is a term usually taught in the school counseling programs, and is defined as supporting or pleading a cause for someone (Meyers, 2014). Counselors are expected to support their clients and protect them from harm. It is a professional ethical responsibility for counselors who support patients, but it became a personal responsibility for caregivers to support and protect their loved ones through illnesses and medical treatment that could be life-threatening during the pandemic.

The counseling ethics of the American Counseling Association (ACA) requires counselors to advocate for their clients at even societal levels to address potential barriers and obstacles that inhibit their growth and development (ACA, 2014). Counselors must be aware of perpetual systemic racism and how it can impact the mental health of clients. Clients who are victims of systemic racism may have experienced additional layers of racism during the COVID-19 pandemic. Mental health professionals should seek continuing education courses or workshops to learn the current approaches to assessing race-based traumatic stress injury (Carter, 2007).

Interestingly, counseling interventions to protect individuals from becoming victims of systemic racism are scarce, and leave some minoritized individuals feeling they are responsible for eliminating it. The dismantling of systemic racism should not be the responsibility of the victims, but is society's responsibility to dismantle. Therefore, it is a problem that must be addressed first by stopping the perpetrators of it within the system and legislation that support it. Counselors are expected to advocate for the clients they serve (ACA, 2024), so the best intervention is systems change agency. Counselors can commit to dismantling racism from within the profession and within educational settings. These efforts might include the following: reporting implicit as well as explicit bias in schools (Cox et al., 2017); engaging in organized actions to dismantle barriers that exclude racialized students from participating in graduate education (Leigh et al., 2023); supporting the adoption of anti-racist counselor training curriculum within professional counseling associations; and developing leadership pathways that include people of color at the state, regional, and national levels, and counseling programs and organizations can acknowledge a racist history, commit to undo a racist history and legacy by institutionalizing efforts to diversify the profession (Hannon et al., 2023).

Currently there is a destructive movement to remove offices of diversity, equity, and inclusion (DEI) offices on college campuses when college leadership should attend to creating and maintaining diversity-centered institutional structures to protect minoritized students (Parker III, 2024). Counselors can push back on the efforts by contacting their U.S. members of congress to protect and support minoritized students. Advocacy is an ongoing work towards ending systemic racism.

To support clients who suffer from anxiety, grief, or stress as a result of the COVID-19 pandemic, it is important to educate clients of behavioral strategies that can be followed for coping with stress. This can be done by implementing psychological intervention services that offer mental health support applications, regular monitoring for mental health illnesses, and provide early support (Costa et al., 2022).

Recommending group discussions to help employees openly talk about how the pandemic is affecting their work and to identify factors that cause stress and work together to identify solutions (Costa et al., 2022). Research has revealed interventions targeting resilience against distress and mental health of parents at the time of pandemics in the future might focus on reducing loneliness while working from home and within social distancing and stay-at-home orders (Mikocka-Walus et al., 2021). During pandemics, it would benefit clients to encourage working together to complete tasks and to include those who may be isolated and alone.

Clients who use online dating applications could suffer from anxiety or low self-esteem due to rejection, although dating applications may be beneficial for others (Ali & Bloom, 2019).

It is important to address online dating in counseling to determine if the use of online dating is directly linked to presenting problems. If the client wishes to address how online dating may interplay with presenting problems, counselors should be certain interventions are appropriate for the client. Counselors should utilize the tasks with clients who are looking for relationship partners rather than a casual encounter (Ali & Bloom, 2019). It's possible the underlying issue with the client may not be due to the use of dating applications, but may surface after using them.

Online dating application users would benefit from realistic expectations in their romantic interactions on dating applications. Mental health professionals should inform their clients about the ways in which online dating applications shape interactions. Clients should also be educated on the prevalence rates of individuals being ghosted on dating applications to rationalize ghosting experiences and to shape their expectancies with the odds of being ghosted to empower them to not attribute the ghosting experience to their own romantic experiences (Konings et al., 2023). Online dating may be beneficial for clients who are lonely or have limited opportunities of meeting people in person. However, mental health professionals should educate clients on the realities and expectancies of being ghosted or left swiped in the online dating world.

The COVID-19 pandemic caused considerable social and emotional distress for cancer patients who required immediate care and treatment (Alexander et al., 2022). It was unusual to be required to have special permission to even escort my husband to his treatments, blood transfusions, and surgeries. Evidence shows family members are important in the delivery of patient centered care such as advocacy, mobility, emotional support, and transitions to critical care. It is necessary for hospitals to relax no visitor policies, which can occur with PPE monitoring and community prevalence of the disease (Munshi & Razak, 2021). During the COVID-19 pandemic, hospitals were inundated with COVID-19 patients, and there was a shortage of doctors and medical staff. Prolonged delays to cancer treatment may have resulted in deadly consequences for many cancer patients during the COVID-19 pandemic. The potential for tragic outcomes in the future for these pancreatic cancer patients highlights the urgency of timely healthcare decisions in the future should another pandemic occur (Alexander et al., 2022).

COVID-19 IMPACT ON GRIEF

Dr. Elisabeth Kubler-Ross was a medical doctor and psychiatrist who studied the dying. She identified the stages of grief as denial and isolation, anger, bargaining, depression, and acceptance (Kübler-Ross, 1997). In the first stage of grief, there is denial following the diagnosis which is usually used as a buffer to allow an opportunity to mobilize and line up defenses (Kübler-Ross, 1997). For example, a patient may not immediately accept a cancer diagnosis after it is received leading him to seek a second medical opinion. Denial is a temporary defense of grief and does not always increase distress. In some cases, the patient might fight stress levels off as they seek hope in an alternative medical opinion. In the second stage of grief, the denial response is usually replaced with anger which can be projected to anyone or anything. The third stage of bargaining may occur when people plead for healing or more time. At this stage most bargaining is made to God. The fourth stage of grief is depression, when the illness can no longer be denied and the patient or loved one begins to experience evidence of the illness such as required surgeries, weakness, or more symptoms, leading to a stoic or numbness that is noticed about the patient at this stage. The final stage of grief is acceptance when the patient or loved one begins to work through the reality of the diagnosis (Kübler-Ross, 1997). Realizing death can finally be accepted by the terminally ill patient, as well as the caregiver or family member.

The grief process is not isolated to those who are dying. Loved ones of those dying or have died, may also progress through the stages of grief. Anxiety, hostility, depression, trouble concentrating, remembering, and getting things done are a few of the experiences of the caregiver who is caring for a loved one who is suffering from terminal illness (Waldrop, 2007). The stages of grief are not always clearly visible and it's unclear how the COVID-19 pandemic may have impacted the grief process. Valliani et al. (2022) suggests some may have experienced several losses during this COVID-19 pandemic which could have included the inability to meet loved ones, be with them at time of death, or mourn when they died, and these losses can also occur simultaneously which might substantially complicate the grief process and delay a person's capability to adapt, heal, and recover.

Complicated Grief

Caregivers are responsible for the care of their loved ones, and in some cases, this is round-the-clock care which does not leave much available time to grief the upcoming loss of the loved one. According to (Rolbiecki et al., 2020), the burden of caregiving to terminally ill patients presents numerous challenges both physically and mentally that can affect how the caregiver copes after a family member dies. Bereaved cancer caregivers who are distressed during active caregiving and after death are at risk for prolonged or complicated grief. The COVID-19 pandemic added another layer of grief by altering the mourning process. The suddenness of loss, the social isolation, and the lack of social support from COVID-19-related death are risk factors for complicated grief (Khoury et al., 2022). Research reveals there is a positive association between symptoms of complicated grief and posttraumatic stress disorder (PTSD). PTSD symptoms predicts complicated grief reactions at a subsequent time point, but not vice versa, so targeting PTSD symptoms may hinder later development of complicated grief (Glad et al., 2022).

During the COVID-19 pandemic, hospitals created policies restricting the number of patient visitors. However, in some cases, patients were not able to receive any visitors at all, particularly at the onset of the pandemic when there wasn't much known about it other than patients dying from it or requiring ventilators. Unfortunately, terminally ill patients from diseases which were not COVID-19 related, suffered alone due to the pandemic which was not customary. Additionally, family members were restricted from visiting their loved ones whether they were battling the COVID-19 disease or not. Patients who were COVID-19 infected were separated from other patients in hospitals, but the policy restrictions applied to all, so patients who died from diseases such as cancer, died alone as if they had COVID-19, but at any other time they would have been with family. Unfortunately, cancer patients were casualties.

Healthcare professionals' own attitudes may affect the end-of- life care given to dying individuals and their families; but Recognizing death as part of life and thinking about death itself are social coping strategies (Ruíz, et al., 2021). Research informs us that increases in psychological well-being, spirituality, and death acceptance can be learned through college courses. Courses that engage students in the whole person, rather than only the intellect or through a service-learning component, fosters greater wisdom and psychosocial growth than regular sociology or religion courses (Ardelt, 2020). Death is a natural occurrence, so it is baffling that it is not discussed more in various academic programs, particularly those which provide a service to patients.

Spirituality

Individuals who value faith rely on religious resources to construct meaning in coping with terminal diagnosis. Redemption of suffering are prominent in the process of their grief with varieties of despair to hope, from grief to consolation, from being alone to being in community, and from loss of control to spiritual surrender (Hall et al., 2020).

Clinicians may reinforce beliefs about the effects spirituality can have on healing. Effective counseling incorporates mind, body, and spirit in healing. Research suggests there is religious and spiritual value in counseling, and counselors are taught to investigate the spirituality of the clients they serve (Sutton et al., 2016). The counseling profession has stressed more advocacy for marginalized populations, while also recognizing the religious values of counselors. To ignore the faith of patients is like ignoring the gender. Unfortunately, counselors are more likely to value the importance of addressing spirituality in sessions than they are to actually use faith as an intervention (Scott et al., 2016). Spirituality can be a source of meaning in the lives of some clients, therefore, counselors have an ethical responsibility to recognize and respect the spirituality of the client and the impact it may have on healing (ACA, 2014). For example, Christians may recognize the power of healing through faith which the Bible defines as "the substance of things hoped for and the evidence of things unseen." They can't see what is happening inside of a loved

An Overview of the Impact of COVID-19 on Grief

one's body, but they believe that the body is being healed. Believing in healing is not enough, but they also had to believe without doubt which was the challenge while disbelieving we heard from doctors that was contrary to what they believed. It's important to include spirituality in counseling, if it is of value to the client. Counselors are taught how spirituality influences clients' decisions.

Counseling Recommendations

Patients with a diagnosis of terminal illness should be supported through the grieving process by working on the meaning of the illness for their identity and improving psychosocial environments to minimize discrimination and facilitate hope (Gökler-Danışman, et al. 2017). It is also important to have understanding of real-time patient thoughts and feelings as soon after diagnosis as possible with full patient consent (Emanuel, et al., 2017). One impactful intervention is providing an invitation to send pictures for the patient's room, which patients could enjoy daily. For unresponsive patients, these pictures humanize them by allowing staff to see images of patients with the loved ones who would typically be at their bedside (Burke et al., 2021).

Not only are patients grieving after receiving a diagnosis of terminal illness, but it's important to support family as well. Communication between patients, families, and healthcare teams at the end-of-life or through caregiving at home remains critically important during times of limited in-person visitation such as what occurred during the COVID-19 pandemic. Low-quality communication creates profound distress on the families and the patients which may impact the quality of dying and bereavement (Feder et al., 2021).

After the loss of a loved one, caregivers and family members need ongoing support. Routine public health screening of all people who are bereaved should be conducted at six months after the death so early intervention can hopefully prevent prolonged grief from developing or in assessing the effects of ongoing serious and impactful grief (Wilson et al., 2022). Clinicians should develop effective treatment strategies and formulate good treatment plans to target complicated grief by helping the bereaved cope with their posttraumatic stress reactions to hinder the development of complicated grief (Glad et al., 2022). Psychological assessments, grief counseling, and mental health support are needed by families of patients who died from COVID-19, but arguably for those who died of other illnesses during the COVID-19 Pandemic. These services must be essential components of any comprehensive public health response to the pandemic (Khoury et al, 2022).

Psychological flexibility, such as allowing clients to remain in contact with unwanted private events of distressing thoughts, feelings, sensations, and memories, without attempts to change, avoid, or eliminate them. Providing space to process these thoughts should be considered as a psychological resource in people experiencing the loss of a loved one, particularly during COVID-19 pandemic that imposed restrictions to saying goodbye to a dead loved one (Diolaiuti et al., 2021). Professionals might support clients in creating a souvenir book to give relatives in order to let them know that their loved one is supported and accompanied (Diolaiuti et al., 2021).

Healthcare professionals should also assess their own personal attitudes towards death. The concept of dignified death is linked to humanization of healthcare, death should be approached from a naturalistic perspective by healthcare professionals, and academic institutions (Ruíz, et al., 2021). Attendance in growth courses may inoculate students against increased stress and may contribute to greater wisdom, psychological well-being, spirituality, and death acceptance (Ardelt, 2020).

Legislation is needed to support caregivers of cancer patients, however most people don't understand the overwhelming amount of pressure devoted to caregiving to those who are terminally ill, unless they experience it. It may take walking in the shoes of a caregiver to understand the overwhelming stress that is experienced. Most caregivers don't have formal healthcare training, so they should not be expected to provide adequate care at home, particularly when they are working to keep the lights on at home. Research informs us there is a need for better clinical communication, briefings for informal caregivers, and help with navigating health systems (Chong et al., 2023).

COVID-19 AND BEREAVEMENT

Following the death, loneliness, sadness, and tears usually increase by the family member, with overwhelming responses triggered by unforeseen visual or auditory reminders of the person (Waldrop, 2007). The family member may be inundated with caring for the patient that she or he doesn't have the time to shed tears, so after the death, reminders of the deceased triggers an overwhelming sense of grief and tears may then flow. Caregiving itself can also have a lasting emotional toll for caregivers after patient death (Mah et al., 2022). Living after the death of a loved one can be daunting as the family tries to adjust to life after the death of the loved one. Sleep disturbances may have begun during end-stage care, but may continue after the death (Waldrop, 2007). The family member may have difficulty focusing as they try to adjust to the absence of the loved one, but grief during a worldwide pandemic may also lead to trauma. **Trauma of COVID-19 Infections**

People were dying at the hospitals at monumental rates. It was reported at that time 37,000 people died of COVID-19 and 3.4 million were infected by the end of November 2020 (Beer, 2020). Many hospital morgues couldn't contain all of the bodies, so they kept them in mobile morgues. Research indicates spousal caregivers' mental and emotional resources are exhausted over time and can contribute to depression. The COVID-19 pandemic restricted caregiving support and limited it to whoever lived under the same roof, so responding to overwhelming grief while the world focused on the pandemic, may have created feelings of loneliness and isolation when support was needed.

The personality of trauma survivors may affect the extent to which they seek social support, their perceived receipt of social support, and the extent to which they benefit from social support. It's natural for trauma survivors to have a desire to talk about the experience of the trauma. Trauma survivors may not recognize the benefit of social support or may not know where to turn to for it. A positive support system allows the trauma survivor to share thoughts and feelings about the event, as well as responses to them.

A Covid-Funeral

Most people don't understand how to process grief, and it is unfathomable considering grief is something most will experience within their lifetime. Responses to someone who has suffered a loss may be uncomfortable because grief support is not usually taught unless one receives training in an education program. In fact, the words to describe the experiences of loss are misunderstood. Mourning is the external expressions of loss that we see such as attending a funeral. Worden (2018) describes mourning as a process that happens when a bereaved person comes to terms with the loss. Bereavement is what we experience immediately after a loss such as taking time off from work, but that event may have a socially accepting ending. Grief is an internal experience of emotional feelings through a loss. Grief is a process that can last a lifetime.

Typical responses to someone who is grieving are avoidance, sending bereavement cards, or even calling and stumbling over words. One of the worst things a person can say to someone grieving the death of a spouse is "you'll get over it". It's common for people to assume the bereaved will get over grieving someone as if there is an expiration date. Memories don't go away like that. There will always be something that reminds the bereaved of their loved ones or even triggers crying spells.

Grief is a process of adjusting to a new life, but the love remains existent. It's interesting how planning funerals only postpones the processing of grief. According to Kübler-Ross (1997), the first few days after the death of a loved one may be filled with busy work, funeral arrangements and visiting relatives. There is a void and emptiness felt after the funeral, and it's at that time family members of the deceased need comforting the most. People grieving a recent loss of a loved one need family and friends to allow them to share and ventilate (Kübler-Ross, 1997).

Grief counseling allows the client to process normal grief through sharing memories or feelings. It assists clients with coping through the loss. However, grief therapy is reserved for those who experience abnormal or complicated grief from high level distress such as not anticipating the death, having young children to raise alone, having a highly dependent relationship with the deceased, lack of supportive social networks, or a trauma related death (Worden, 2018).

Counseling Recommendations

There may be feelings of discomfort in supporting the bereaved and it's likely because people don't know what they could say to make the person who is grieving feel better. They should not focus so much on what they might say to relieve those grieving from pain. There really isn't anything that is said that is going to take away the pain. The best way people can support those who are grieving is by allowing them to talk, cry, or scream if necessary (Kübler-Ross, 1997).

Providing an atmosphere of support to someone who is grieving the death of a loved one can simply be accomplished by providing a listening ear leading to crying, but crying is very therapeutic. People are naturally uncomfortable seeing people cry around them. Most people relate crying to sadness and therefore try to avoid making people cry. In fact, there are many benefits to crying. Crying detoxifies the body, it improves mood, and provides healing. Crying in grief is also healthy. (Gračanin et al., 2014).

Allowing those who are grieving space to talk about the deceased helps them to heal, so family and friends who want to support them should prepare themselves for crying. Counselors should understand this form of healing well. Crying is healthy and helpful, so counselors should work to identify the source of pain to begin the healing process. Generally, people are uncomfortable with seeing others cry, but crying becomes a place of normalcy for those who are experiencing healthy grief.

Some clients may experience complicated grief in which they are unable to carry on with normal life activities such as work, school, or maintain healthy relationships. They may feel their lives have no meaning or purpose without their loved ones in it. This should not be confused with normal grief in which the grieved continue to talk about the deceased. For example, when a widow talks about her deceased husband for years after his death, she might be labeled as someone who has complicated grief. When in fact, talking about the deceased is part of the grief process; If more people understood the process of grief and the comfort of memories that may trigger tears, they might provide more support to those who are grieving. Grief is a lifelong process of adjustment that will never end as long as the griever has memory of the loved one. Everyone will experience grief on some level, and the closer the person is to the deceased, the more difficult the adjustment.

An Overview of the Impact of COVID-19 on Grief

Finding support after trauma from a loss of a loved one from terminal illness is one of the most challenging experiences one can have, but the support received from others after the trauma is impactful. Receiving positive social support after a trauma can lead to better adjustment to the trauma (Kristensen et al., 2012). Support for extended family members and friends may be even less common. Spouses and children of the patients received more social support than other relatives which may be the result of a society that holds strong norms for perceptions of trauma as only being needed for immediate family members. Lack of social support could predispose trauma survivors to secondary traumatic stress (Kristensen et al., 2012).

Secondary traumatic stress, otherwise known as compassion fatigue, is a set of reactions from working with trauma survivors and mirrors symptoms of PTSD, characterized by feelings of helplessness, confusion, isolation, numbness or avoidance, and persistent arousal in those who interact with traumatized individuals (Sprang et al, 2019).

COUNSELOR BURNOUT

The COVID-19 pandemic resulted in the shut-down of movie theatres, shopping malls, and restaurants. Political divides formed due to the decisions to shut down establishments made by local governments. Many people were concerned about being exposed to the virus, but in a country that relied and supported a strong economy, there was concern that shut-downs would result in a devastating economic downturn. Businesses were the livelihood for some families, so shutting them down could have been financially destructive. Choosing safety over the economy was the conflict that contributed to the major political divide.

Many people were dying but loss of life would have had an impact on revenue for businesses anyway. However, not having restaurants and movie theatres also impacted the self-care of counselors who were expected to support those who experience mental health issues and crises during the COVID-19 pandemic. Counselors had to adapt to changes brought by the pandemic to continue their counseling services, and the adaptation to online practices caused professional changes such as lack of confidentiality as clients received counseling from home and technology glitches with virtual counseling (Tuna & Avci, 2023). These changes may have impacted counselors' mental health. Counselor burn-out may be the result of exhaustion caused by the COVID-19 pandemic leading to a deterioration in their own personal lives.

According to the American Counseling Association's code of ethics, counselors should engage in self-care activities to maintain and promote their own emotional, physical, mental, and spiritual well-being to best meet their professional responsibilities (ACA, 2014). Failure to sufficiently attend appropriate ongoing self-care activities can have significant consequences for the practitioner's personal and professional functioning to include experiencing symptoms of burnout and compassion fatigue that could result in problems with professional competence (Barnett & Homany, 2022).

During the COVID-19 pandemic, counselors played an important role in protecting patients from the risk of contagion COVID-19 and in ensuring the protection of their loved ones. However, the pandemic limited their ability to provide expected care leading to maintenance, increase or decrease of self-care and contributions to self-care behaviors. Self-care behaviors such as healthy eating, exercise, engaging in a hobby, relaxation, time spent with a supportive person, and talking online with friends and family, have had mental health benefits during stressful environments such as the COVID-19 pandemic and stay-at-home orders and negative affect can play an adaptive role during times of stress by facilitating self-care (Disabato, 2022).

Caregivers were also exposed to disrupted lives which increased anxiety levels and reacted in different ways in their performances of providing self-care and contribution to patients' self-care behaviors because their ordinary daily lives were disrupted (De Maria et al., 2022). The burden of providing care to the patients weas placed on the caregivers due to stay-at-home orders and limited care provided by hospital staff due to overcrowding of patients. During the COVID-19 pandemic, caregivers helped their loved one maintain the stability of chronic conditions at home by ensuring the regular provision of medicines and supervising their intake, and maintaining contact with the patients' family physicians. This was particularly important because it reduced the need to use healthcare services that were overburdened by the treatment of COVID-19 patients (De Maria et al., 2022). However, the self-care provided by the caregivers were challenging particularly if they were not supported in providing their own self-care.

Self-care was an important responsibility for counselors and counselor educators, but it became even more important during the COVID-19 pandemic. Self-care is important for medical professionals such as counselors and social workers who support cancer patients and their families. It requires a commitment to creating and maintaining activities that pour into them, so that they can pour out into others. Counselors were expected to support clients in crisis, but the pandemic created a shortage of counselors due to the enormous need for therapy. People were confined to their homes during the stay-at home order and were having melt-downs. Counselors became overwhelmed while trying to support others. Without self-care, counselors would experience counselor burn-out which occurs when they are emotionally drained from caring for their clients (Ko & Lee, 2021; Plath & Fickling, 2022). Counselors are like pitchers. Counselors pour into their clients, but if the pitcher is not replenished, there is nothing to pour out. Self-care became an important practice during the COVID-19 pandemic in which counselors longed for the replenishment of the emotional support, which is metaphorically described as pouring back into an empty pitcher.

A communitarian approach to self-care involves creating and actively utilizing a competence constellation of engaged colleagues who assess and support each other on a regular basis based on a created self-care plan that integrates independent self-care activities. The role of the communitarian approach is to promote ongoing wellness and maintain clinical competence while preventing burnout and problems with professional competence (Barnett & Homany, 2022). The support from colleagues can be a resourceful tool to ensure the self-care plan is met. This can be accomplished through weekly meetings within the unit of clinical colleagues.

Examples of Self-Care

- Regular appointments at the hair salon
- Working out at the gym
- Fate nights
- Managing or lowering case load
- Personal therapy
- Taking walks
- Yoga or Mindfulness exercises
- Visiting friends and family
- Reading

Counseling Recommendations

To alleviate counselor burnout, peer support is recommended. Most psychologists said they have sought peer consultation or support to manage burnout, that they were able to practice self-care, and that they have been able to maintain a positive work-life balance (APA, 2022).

Maintaining equilibrium between self-care and other care has been reported by helping professionals' especially counselors. By strengthening their cognitive emotion regulation capacities, and enrolling in specific programs such as Mindfulness training and life skills training counselors to manage their own mental health and avoid counselor burnout (Sandhu & Singh, 2021).

CONCLUSION

The COVID-19 pandemic changed the way counseling professionals support clients because the isolation due to restrictions led to sychological distress. Counselors must be prepared to support clients who may be suffering from trauma or complicated grief as a result of the COVId0-19 pandemic. However, counselors must also apply exercise self-care so they do not experience counselor burn-out. Further chapters within this book will provide details of the impact of the COVID-19 pandemic on clients who suffered grief and how the mental counseling profession should address grief as it relates to school counseling, peer support, trauma, caregiving, and support groups.

Discussion Questions

1. What impact might the COVID-19 pandemic have on the trauma of non-COVID 19 terminally ill patients and their families?
2. When does the grief process begin for a caregiver of a partner diagnosed with cancer or other life-threatening disease?
3. How do you respond when someone cries? Why do you think discussions of death are uncomfortable for people?
4. Why do you feel it's important to assess the long-term impact COVID-19 pandemic may have had on family members of those who died during the pandemic?
5. What would be the consequences on the mental health profession if counselors do not prevent burnout when there is a shortage of counselors?

REFERENCES

Afuape, T., & Kerry Oldham, S. (2022). Beyond "solidarity" with Black Lives Matter: Drawing on liberation psychology and transformative justice to address institutional and community violence in young Black lives. *Journal of Family Therapy*, 44(1), 20–43. 10.1111/1467-6427.12369

Alang, S. M. (2019). Mental health care among blacks in America: Confronting racism and constructing solutions. *Health Services Research*, 54(2), 346–355. 10.1111/1475-6773.1311530687928

Alexander, A., Fung, S., Eichler, M., Lehwald-Tywuschik, N., Uthayakumar, V., Safi, S.-A., Vay, C., Ashmawy, H., Kalmuk, S., Rehders, A., Vaghiri, S., & Knoefel, W. T. (2022). Quality of Life in Patients with Pancreatic Cancer before and during the COVID-19 Pandemic. *International Journal of Environmental Research and Public Health*, 19(6), 3731. 10.3390/ijerph19063731353294416

Ali, S., & Bloom, Z. D. (2019). Creative approaches to address online dating in counseling. *Journal of Creativity in Mental Health*, 14(1), 81–93. 10.1080/15401383.2018.1535922

American Counseling Association (ACA). (2014). *2014 ACA Code of Ethics*. ACA. https://www.counseling.org/Resources/aca-code-of-ethics.pdf

American Psychological Association (APA). (2017). *Stress in America: The state of our nation*. APA. https://www.apa.org/news/press/releases/2017/11/lowest-point

American Psychological Association (APA). (2022). *Increased need for mental health care strains capacity*. APA. https://www.apa.org/news/press/releases/2022/11/mental-health-care-strains

American Psychological Association (APA). (2023a). *Trauma*. APA. https://www.apa.org/topics/trauma

American Psychological Association (APA). (2024). *Grief*. APA. https://www.apa.org/topics/grief#:~:text=Grief%20is%20the%20anguish%20experienced,and%20apprehension%20about%20the%20future

Anderson, L. A., O'Brien Caughy, M., & Owen, M. T. (2022). "The Talk" and Parenting While Black in America: Centering Race, Resistance, and Refuge. *The Journal of Black Psychology*, 48(3–4), 475–506. 10.1177/00957984211034294

Ardelt, M. (2020). Can wisdom and psychosocial growth be learned in university courses? *Journal of Moral Education*, 49(1), 30–45. 10.1080/03057240.2018.1471392

Barnett, J. E., & Homany, G. (2022). The new self-care: It's not all about you. *Practice Innovations (Washington, D.C.)*, 7(4), 313–326. 10.1037/pri0000190

Beer, T. (2020). November's grim COVID-19 totals: More than 4.3 million infections and 37,000 Americans killed. *Forbes.*https://www.forbes.com/sites/tommybeer/2020/12/01/novembers-grim-COVID-19-totals-more-than-43-million-infections-and-37000-americans-killed/?sh=2b94405f6acb

Burke, C., Hampel, S., Gholson, K., Zhang, P., & Rufkhar, B. (2021). COVID-19 family support team: Providing person and family centered care during the COVID-19 pandemic. *Journal of Social Work in End-of-Life & Palliative Care*, 17(2–3), 158–163. 10.1080/15524256.2021.192212634057887

Carter, R. T. (2007). Racism and psychological and emotional injury: Recognizing and assessing race-based traumatic stress. *The Counseling Psychologist*, 35(1), 13–105. 10.1177/0011000006292033

Center for Disease Control and Prevention (CDC). (2021). *Racism and Health.* CDC. https://www.cdc.gov/minorityhealth/racism-disparities/index.html10.1007/s00520-022-07468-7

Costa, A. C. D. S., Menon, V., Phadke, R., Dapke, K., Miranda, A. V., Ahmad, S., Essar, M. Y., & Hashim, H. T. (2022). Mental health in the post COVID-19 era: Future perspectives. *Einstein (Sao Paulo, Brazil)*, 20, eCE6760. 10.31744/einstein_journal/2022CE676035584448

Cox, J. M., Toussaint, A., Woerner, J., Smith, A., & Haeny, A. M. (2023). *Coping while Black: Comparing coping strategies across COVID-19 and the killing of Black people.* NCBI. https://www.ncbi.nlm.nih.gov/pmc/articles/PMC10132418/

Cox, M. R., Bledsoe, S., & Bowens, B. (2017). Challenges of Teacher Diversity Training. *The International Journal of Diversity in Education*, 17(2), 1–15. 10.18848/2327-0020/CGP/v17i02/1-15

De Maria, M., Ferro, F., Vellone, E., Ausili, D., Luciani, M., & Matarese, M. (2022). Self-care of patients with multiple chronic conditions and their caregivers during the COVID-19 pandemic: A qualitative descriptive study. *Journal of Advanced Nursing*, 78(5), 1431–1447. 10.1111/jan.1511534846083

DeGruy. (2017). *Dr. Joy DeGruy: Post Traumatic Slave Syndrome.* DeGruy. https://www.joydegruy.com/

Diolaiuti, F., Marazziti, D., Beatino, M. F., Mucci, F., & Pozza, A. (2021). Impact and consequences of COVID-19 pandemic on complicated grief and persistent complex bereavement disorder. *Psychiatry Research*, 300, 113916. 10.1016/j.psychres.2021.11391633836468

Disabato, D. J., Aurora, P., Sidney, P. G., Taber, J. M., Thompson, C. A., & Coifman, K. G. (2022). Self-care behaviors and affect during the early stages of the COVID-19 pandemic. [Supplemental]. *Health Psychology*, 41(11), 833–842. 10.1037/hea000123936107666

Douglas, R. D., Alvis, L. M., Rooney, E. E., Busby, D. R., & Kaplow, J. B. (2021). Racial,\ ethnic, and neighborhood income disparities in childhood posttraumatic stress and grief: Exploring indirect effects through trauma exposure and bereavement. *Journal of Traumatic Stress*, 34(5), 929–942. 10.1002/jts.2273234643296

Emanuel, L., Johnson, R., & Taromino, C. (2017). Adjusting to a Diagnosis of Cancer: Processes for Building Patient Capacity for Decision-Making. *Journal of Cancer Education*, 32(3), 491–495. 10.1007/s13187-016-1008-326960311

Feder, S., Smith, D., Griffin, H., Shreve, S. T., Kinder, D., Kutney, L. A., & Ersek, M. (2021). "Why couldn't I go in to see him?" Bereaved families' perceptions of end-of-life communication during COVID-19. *Journal of the American Geriatrics Society*, 69(3), 587–592. 10.1111/jgs.1699333320956

Finzi-Dottan, R., & Berckovitch Kormosh, M. (2018). The spillover of compassion fatigue into marital quality: A mediation model. *Traumatology*, 24(2), 113–122. 10.1037/trm0000137

Flesia, L., Adeeb, M., Waseem, A., Helmy, M., & Monaro, M. (2023). Psychological Distress Related to the COVID-19 Pandemic: The Protective Role of Hope. *European Journal of Investigation in Health, Psychology and Education*, 13(1), 67–80. 10.3390/ejihpe1301000536661755

Garcia-Rada, X., Sezer, O., & Norton, M. I. (2019). Rituals and Nuptials: The Emotional and Relational Consequences of Relationship Rituals. *Journal of the Association for Consumer Research*, 4(2), 185–197. 10.1086/702761

Gibson, A. F. (2021). Exploring the impact of COVID-19 on mobile dating: Critical avenues for research. *Social and Personality Psychology Compass*, 15(11), e12643. 10.1111/spc3.1264334899975

Glad, K. A., Stensland, S., Czajkowski, N. O., Boelen, P. A., & Dyb, G. (2022). The longitudinal association between symptoms of posttraumatic stress and complicated grief: A random intercepts cross-lag analysis. *Psychological Trauma: Theory, Research, Practice, and Policy*, 14(3), 386–392. 10.1037/tra000108734398627

Gökler-Danışman, I., Yalçınay-İnan, M., & Yiğit, İ. (2017). Experience of grief by patients with cancer in relation to perceptions of illness: The mediating roles of identity centrality, stigma-induced discrimination, and hopefulness. *Journal of Psychosocial Oncology*, 35(6), 776–796. 10.1080/07347332.2017.134038928609249

Gračanin, A., Bylsma, L. M., & Vingerhoets, A. J. (2014). Is crying a self-soothing behavior? *Frontiers in Psychology*, 5(502). 10.3389/fpsyg.2014.0050224904511

Hall, M. E. L., Shannonhouse, L., Aten, J., McMartin, J., & Silverman, E. (2020). The varieties of redemptive experiences: A qualitative study of meaning-making in evangelical Christian cancer patients. *Psychology of Religion and Spirituality*, 12(1), 13–25. 10.1037/rel0000210

Han, S., Riddell, J. R., & Piquero, A. R. (2023). Anti-Asian American Hate Crimes Spike During the Early Stages of the COVID-19 Pandemic. *Journal of Interpersonal Violence*, 38(3-4), 3513–3533. 10.1177/08862605221107056356571278

Hannon, M. D., White, E. E., & Fleming, H. (2023). Ambivalence to action: Addressing systemic racism in counselor education. *Counselor Education and Supervision*, 62(2), 108–117. Advance online publication. 10.1002/ceas.12264

Harasymchuk, C., Walker, D. L., Muise, A., & Impett, E. A. (2021). Planning date nights that promote closeness: The roles of relationship goals and self-expansion. *Journal of Social and Personal Relationships*, 38(5), 1692–1709. 10.1177/026540 7521100043634121791

Hathaway, C. A., Bloomer, A. M., Oswald, L. B., Siegel, E. M., Peoples, A. R., Ulrich, C. M., Penedo, F. J., Tworoger, S. S., & Gonzalez, B. D. (2022). Factors associated with self-reported social isolation among patients with cancer during the COVID-19 pandemic. [Supplemental]. *Health Psychology*, 41(4), 311–318. 10.1037/hea000117235324248

Hoehn-Velasco, L., Balmori de la Miyar, J. R., Silvario-Murillo, A., & Sherajum, M. F. (2023). *Marriage and divorce during a pandemic: the impact of the COVID-19 pandemic on marital formation and dissolution in Mexico*. NCBI. https://www.ncbi .nlm.nih.gov/pmc/articles/PMC10088673/

An Overview of the Impact of COVID-19 on Grief

Holtzhausen, N., Fitzgerald, K., Thakur, I., Ashley, J., Rolfe, M., & Pit, S. W. (2020). Swipe-based dating applications use and its association with mental health outcomes: A cross-sectional study. *BMC Psychology*, 8(1), 22. 10.1186/s40359-020-0373-132127048

Hu, K., Godfrey, K., Ren, Q., Wang, S., Yang, X., & Li, Q. (2022). The impact of the COVID-19 pandemic on college students in USA: Two years later. *Psychiatry Research*, 315, 114685. 10.1016/j.psychres.2022.11468535872401

Khoury, B., Barbarin, O., Gutiérrez, G., Klicperova-Baker, M., Padakannaya, P., & Thompson, A. (2022). Complicated grief during COVID-19: An international perspective. *International Perspectives in Psychology : Research, Practice, Consultation*, 11(3), 214–221. 10.1027/2157-3891/a000055

Ko, H., & Lee, S. M. (2021). Effects of Imbalance of Self- and Other-Care on Counselors' Burnout. *Journal of Counseling and Development*, 99(3), 252–262. 10.1002/jcad.12372

Konings, F., Sumter, S., & Vandenbosch, L. (2023). It's not You, it's Me: Experiences with Ghosting on Mobile Dating Applications and Belgian Emerging Adults' Self-Esteem. *Sexuality & Culture*, 27(4), 1328–1351. 10.1007/s12119-023-10065-3

Kossek, E. E. (2016). Managing work–life boundaries in the digital age. *Organizational Dynamics*, 45(3), 258–270. 10.1016/j.orgdyn.2016.07.010

Kristensen, T., Elklit, A., & Karstoft, K.-I. (2012). Posttraumatic Stress Disorder after bereavement: Early psychological sequelae of losing a close relative due to terminal cancer. *Journal of Loss and Trauma*, 17(6), 508–521. 10.1080/15325024.2012.665304

Kübler-Ross, E. (1997). *On death and dying: What the dying have to teach doctors, nurses, clergy, and their own families (reprint ed.).*

Leigh, O. K. T., Clemons, K., Robertson, A., Placeres, V., Gay, J., Lopez, P. C., Mason, E. C., Ieva, K. P., Lane, E. M. D., & Saunders, R. (2023). Antiracist school counseling: A consensual qualitative study. *Journal of Counseling and Development*, 101(3), 310–322. 10.1002/jcad.12477

Määttä, K., & Uusiautti, S. (2012). Seven Rules on Having a Happy Marriage Along With Work. *The Family Journal (Alexandria, Va.)*, 20(3), 267–273. 10.1177/1066480712448997

Mah, K., Swami, N., Pope, A., Earle, C. C., Krzyzanowska, M. K., Rinat, N., Hales, S., Rodin, G., Breffni, H., & Zimmermann, C. (2022). Caregiver bereavement outcomes in advanced cancer: Associations with quality of death and patient age. *Supportive Care in Cancer*, 30(2), 1343–1353. 10.1007/s00520-021-06536-834499215

An Overview of the Impact of COVID-19 on Grief

Meyers, L. (2014). *Advocacy in action.* CT Counseling. https://ct.counseling.org/2014/04/advocacy-in-action/

Midgley, C., Lockwood, P., & Thai, S. (2022). *Can the social network bridge social distancing? Social media use during the COVID-19 pandemic.* Research Gate. https://www.researchgate.net/publication/363794377_Can_the_social_network_bridge_social_distancing_Social_media_use_during_the_COVID-19_pandemic

Mikocka-Walus, A., Stokes, M., Evans, S., Olive, L., & Westrupp, E. (2021). Finding the power within and without: How can we strengthen resilience against symptoms of stress, anxiety, and depression in australian parents during the COVID-19 pandemic? *Journal of Psychosomatic Research*, 145, 110433. 10.1016/j.jpsychores.2021.11043333812660

Mitchell, H.-R., Kim, Y., Llabre, M. M., & Ironson, G. (2022). Four-symptom model of medical-related posttraumatic stress among adult cancer patients. [Supplemental]. *Health Psychology*, 41(7), 492–501. 10.1037/hea000118735587888

Moreno-Colom, S., Borràs Català, V., Cruz Gómez, I., & Porcel López, S. (2023). The Experience of Remote Work during Lockdown in Catalonia: A Gender Perspective. *Revista Española de Investigaciones Sociológicas*, 183, 77–98. 10.5477/cis/reis.183.77

Munshi, L., Evans, G., & Razak, F. (2021). The case for relaxing no-visitor policies in hospitals during the ongoing COVID-19 pandemic. *CMAJ : Canadian Medical Association Journal = Journal de l'Association Medicale Canadienne, 193*(4), E135–E137. https://doi.org/10.1503/cmaj.202636

National Institute of Health (NIH). (2022). *Mental health.* NIH. https://COVID-19.nih.gov/COVID-19-topics/mental-health

Omid, S., Alarcon, S. V., Vega, E. A., Kutlu, O. C., Olga, K., Chan, J. A., Vera, K., Harz, D., & Conrad, C. (2022). COVID-19's Impact on Cancer Care: Increased Emotional Stress in Patients and High Risk of Provider Burnout. *Journal of Gastrointestinal Surgery*, 26(1), 1–12. 10.1007/s11605-021-05032-y34027579

Pamela, N., Alberth, A. G., Tell, E. J., & Jansen, T. (2023). Policies to Sustain Employment Among Family Caregivers: The Family Caregiver Perspective. *Journal of Applied Gerontology*, 42(1), 3–11. 10.1177/07334648221125635536114013

Parker, E. T., III. (2024). What's lost in dismantling DEI offices? *Inside Higher Ed.* https://www.insidehighered.com/opinion/views/2024/02/19/whats-lost-dismantling-dei-offices-opinion#

Pathak, E. B., Garcia, R. B., Menard, J. M., & Salemi, J. L. (2021). Out-of-Hospital COVID-19 Deaths: Consequences for Quality of Medical Care and Accuracy of Cause of Death Coding. *American Journal of Public Health. American Journal of Public Health*, 111(S2, Supplement 2), S101–S106. 10.2105/AJPH.2021.30642834314208

Pew Research Center. (2022). *At least four-in-ten U.S. adults have faced high levels of psychological distress during the COVID-19 pandemic*. Pew Research Center. https://www.pewresearch.org/short-reads/2022/12/12/at-least-four-in-ten-u-s-adults -have-faced-high-levels-of-psychological-distress-during-covid-19-pandemic/

Pew Research Center. (2023). *Key findings about online dating in the U.S.* Pew Research Center. https://www.pewresearch.org/short-reads/2023/02/02/key-findings -about-online-dating-in-the-u-s/

Phillips, L. (2023). A closer look at the mental health provider shortage. *Counseling.* https://www.counseling.org/publications/counseling-today-magazine/article -archive/article/legacy/a-closer-look-at-the-mental-health-provider-shortage

Rolbiecki, A. J., Oliver, D. P., Washington, K., Benson, J. J., & Jorgensen, L. (2020). Preliminary Results of Caregiver Speaks: A Storytelling Intervention for Bereaved Family Caregivers. *Journal of Loss and Trauma*, 25(5), 438–453. 10.1080/153250 24.2019.170798533335452

Rosenblatt, P. C. (2017). Researching grief: Cultural, relational, and individual possibilities. *Journal of Loss and Trauma*, 22(8), 617–630. 10.1080/15325024.2017.1388347

Ruíz, F. M. D., Fernández, M. I. M., Granero, M. J., Hernández, P. J. M., Correa, C. M., & Fernández, S. C. (2021). Social acceptance of death and its implication for end-of-life care. *Journal of Advanced Nursing*, 77(7), 3132–3141. 10.1111/ jan.1483633755231

Runkle, J. D., Sugg, M. M., Yadav, S., Harden, S., Weiser, J., & Michael, K. (2023). Real-time mental health crisis response in the United States to COVID-19: Insights from a national text-based platform. *Crisis*, 44(1), 29–40. 10.1027/0227-5910/ a00082634674553

Sandhu, T., & Singh, H. (2021). Counselor Burnout during COVID-19: Predictive Role of Cognitive Emotion Regulation. *Indian Journal of Positive Psychology*, 12(3), 258–262.

Scott, S., Sheperis, D., Simmons, R. T., & Rush-Wilson, T. (2016). *Faith as a cultural variable: Implications for counselor training*. Research Gate. https:// www.researchgate.net/publication/309098355_Faith_as_a_Cultural_Variable _Implications_for_Counselor_Training

Selman, L. E., Chao, D., Sowden, R., Marshall, S., Chamberlain, C., & Koffman, J. (2020). Bereavement Support on the Frontline of COVID-19: Recommendations for Hospital Clinicians. *Journal of Pain and Symptom Management*, 60(2), e81–e86. 10.1016/j.jpainsymman.2020.04.02432376262

Sprang, G., Ford, J., Kerig, P., & Bride, B. (2019). Defining secondary traumatic stress and developing targeted assessments and interventions: Lessons learned from research and leading experts. *Traumatology*, 25(2), 72–81. 10.1037/trm0000180

Sutton, G. W., Arnzen, C., & Kelly, H. L. (2016). Christian counseling and psychotherapy: Components of clinician spirituality that predict type of Christian intervention. *Journal of Psychology and Christianity*, 35(3), 204–214.

Tuna, B., & Avci, O. H. (2023). Qualitative analysis of university counselors' online counseling experiences during the covid-19 pandemic. *Current Psychology (New Brunswick, N.J.)*, 42(10), 8489–8503. Advance online publication. 10.1007/s12144-023-04358-x37193098

Updated National Survey Trends in Telehealth Utilization and Modality. (2023). Office of the Assistant Secretary for Planning and Evaluation, U. S. Department of Health and Human Services. https://aspe.hhs.gov/sites/default/files/documents/7d6b4989431f4c70144f209622975116/household-pulse-survey-telehealth-covid-ib.pdf

Valliani, K., & Mughal, F. B. (2022). Human emotions during COVID-19: A lens through Kubler-Ross Grief theory. *Psychological Trauma: Theory, Research, Practice, and Policy*, 14(2), 247–249. 10.1037/tra000106434323565

Voo, T. C., Senguttuvan, M., & Tam, C. C. (2020). Family Presence for Patients and Separated Relatives during COVID-19: Physical, Virtual, and Surrogate. *Journal of Bioethical Inquiry*, 17(4), 767–772. 10.1007/s11673-020-10009-832840835

Waldrop, D. P. (2007). Caregiver Grief in Terminal Illness and Bereavement: A Mixed-Methods Study. *Health & Social Work*, 32(3), 197–206. 10.1093/hsw/32.3.19717896676

Wilson, D. M., Darko, E. M., Kusi-Appiah, E., Roh, S. J., Ramic, A., & Errasti-Ibarrondo, B. (2022). What exactly is "complicated" grief? A scoping research literature review to understand its risk factors and prevalence. *Omega*, 86(2), 471–487. 10.1177/00302228209773053259275

Worden, J. W. (2018). *Grief counseling and grief therapy: A handbook for the mental health practitioner* (5th ed.). Springer. 10.1891/9780826134752

An Overview of the Impact of COVID-19 on Grief

ADDITIONAL READING

Alsan M, Wanamaker M. (2018). Tuskegee and the health of Black men. *Q J Econ., 133*(1), 407-455. 10.1093/qje/qjx029

Burke, C., Hampel, S., Gholson, K., Zhang, P., & Rufkhar, B. (2021). COVID-19 family support team: Providing person and family centered care during the COVID-19 pandemic. *Journal of Social Work in End-of-Life & Palliative Care*, 17(2–3), 158–163. 10.1080/15524256.2021.192212634057887

Corless, I. B. (2014). Transitions: Exploring the Frontier. *Omega*, 70(1), 57–65. 10.2190/OM.70.1.f25351590

Del Río-Lozano, M., García-Calvente, M., Elizalde-Sagardia, B., & Maroto-Navarro, G. (2022). Caregiving and Caregiver Health 1 Year into the COVID-19 Pandemic (CUIDAR-SE Study): A Gender Analysis. *International Journal of Environmental Research and Public Health*, 19(3), 1653. 10.3390/ijerph1903165335162675

Haliwa, I., Wilson, J., Lee, J., & Shook, N. J. (2021). Predictors of Change in Mental Health during the COVID-19 Pandemic. *Journal of Affective Disorders*, 291, 331–337. 10.1016/j.jad.2021.05.04534087628

Heymann, J., & Sprague, A. (2022). Paid Leave and Beyond: The Urgency and Feasibility of Addressing Structural Inequalities Across Race, Gender, and Class. *American Journal of Public Health*, 112(7), 959–961. 10.2105/AJPH.2022.30691135728035

Keating, N. L., Landrum, M. B., Samuel-Ryals, C., Sinaiko, A. D., Wright, A., Brooks, G. A., Bai, B., & Zaslavsky, A. M. (2022). Measuring Racial Inequities In The Quality Of Care Across Oncology Practices In The US. *Health Affairs*, 41(4), 598–16. 10.1377/hlthaff.2021.0159435377762

Mathew, L. E. (2021). Braiding western and eastern cultural rituals in bereavement: An autoethnography of healing the pain of prolonged grief. *British Journal of Guidance & Counselling*, 49(6), 791–803. Advance online publication. 10.1080/03069885.2021.1983158

Schoenbeck, S. L. (2011). Experiences of the Dying. *The Journal of Practical Nursing*, 61(2), 7–9. https://www.proquest.com/scholarly-journals/experiences-dying/docview/927668263/se-223252027

KEY TERMS AND DEFINITIONS

Counselor Burnout: Counselors experienced exhaustion from overwork in supporting others in their mental health but can be prevented or managed through self-care

Counselor Education: A graduate program which offers education in the counseling field of study.

COVID-19: A worldwide pandemic occurring between 2019 and 2021 in which millions of lives were lost globally

Grief: The experience of suffering loss of a loved one and which causes emotional anguish and sadness

Mental Health Professional: A licensed or credentialed counselor, counselor educator, therapist, psychologist, or other professional who supports clients in mental health

Chapter 2
Anticipatory Grief:
The Pain of What's to Come

Amy Maturen
https://orcid.org/0009-0003-9262-1145
Mid America Christian University, USA

ABSTRACT

Anticipatory grief is unique from traditional grief as it involves experiencing a loss prior to the loss actually occurring. This form of grief can be experienced by an individual, family members, or both. This grief is not exclusively due to the loss of another person. Anticipatory grief can include loss of dreams, safety, autonomy, marriages, homes, and many others. During the COVID-19 pandemic, the number of anticipatory losses the world faced all at the same time was monumental. Those effects are still affecting many people today. In this chapter, the theory of anticipatory grief will be explored in detail along with the impacts from COVID-19, therapeutic interventions that can be utilized when working with clients and family members and how those implications impact counselors within the field.

HISTORY

Anticipatory grief (AG) differs from traditional grief in that it is not about the loss of someone or something *after* the fact. Anticipatory grief is about contemplating, planning, and mourning future losses *prior* to the actual loss. This can include loved ones, pets, hopes, dreams, future plans, an individual's health or even one's own mortality. The concept of anticipatory grief was first introduced in 1940 by Erich Lindemann, a German-American psychiatrist (Dekker, 2023; Najafi et al. 2022). During his work in psychiatry, Lindemann became interested in the psychological effects that were present when a patient experienced an amputation or surgical removal

DOI: 10.4018/979-8-3693-1375-6.ch002

Copyright © 2024, IGI Global. Copying or distributing in print or electronic forms without written permission of IGI Global is prohibited.

of organs (Rosenfeld, 2018). Lindemann felt that the patients experienced a "loss" when they were missing a limb or an organ even though they were still alive. This led to studies about how grief worked. Lindemann was a psychiatrist in a hospital in Boston in 1942 when there was a fire at Boston's Cocoanut Grove Nightclub which led to the deadliest nightclub fire in United States history with over 492 deaths. As Lindemann studied the reactions of survivors to the loss of their loved ones, he began to realize that this was similar to a loss of part of the person themselves. Anticipatory grief grew from Lindemann's studies on the survivors of the nightclub fire and Sigmund Freud's psychoanalytic theory where Freud conceptualized grief as an "object" and that an individual needed to be able to detach themselves from that lost "object" in order to move forward (Dekker, 2023).

Building on those concepts, Lindemann began to take an interest in the wives and girlfriends of World War II soldiers and the grief that they experienced while waiting for their husbands or boyfriends to return home from the war (Plant, 2022). The women began actively grieving to prepare for the potential loss and the fear that they would never see their loved one again. An interesting aspect of anticipatory grief that Lindemann discovered was that once that type of grief had been completed, it was not possible to reverse it as that person had already fully processed the grief (Plant, 2022). In the case of wives and girlfriends during World War II, many ended up divorcing their husbands or breaking off the relationship when they returned home due to processing the loss already and not wanting to work through that a second time.

TYPES OF ANTICIPATORY GRIEF

Illness and Age

There are many categories of anticipatory grief. Two of the most common that are considered anticipatory involve grief with a loved one suffering from a chronic or terminal illness and the other is with the elderly, whether that is with medical illness or dementia/Alzheimer's disease (Ghezeljeh et al., 2023; Najafi et al., 2022; Supiano et al., 2022). In the case of chronic or terminal illness, it is not just the loss of life that can be grieved early. There is the potential limitation of one's length of life which previously may not have been considered if the individual is not elderly. Watching the slow decline of the health of a loved one can lead to an extended period of grief which can be very traumatic for the caregiver (Varga & Gallagher, 2020). When there is a chronic illness, there is also the anticipatory grief of the caregiver and the losses within their life, which includes: loss of quality time with their own family, inability to go far from their loved one, loss of social support and activities,

Anticipatory Grief

and perhaps loss of income or career due to caring for a loved one. The individual with the chronic illness may grieve not only the limitation of their quantity of life, but also their quality of life which could include their individual functioning, future with family, security, autonomy, and fears of the unknown (Patinadan et al., 2022). In the cases of dementia, a family member may grieve for the loss of what makes the person who they are as they slowly fade away inside of their body which can be a gradual loss or a more sudden loss. The individual with the illness may also experience moments of decline and then hit a plateau which can give a false sense of hope, only to be followed by another decline and plateau. This cycle can be repeated multiple times increasing the grieving cycle for the family (Dekker, 2023).

Loss of Pet

Loss of a pet is another potential anticipatory grief that can be experienced. Due to the shorter life span of a household pet, individuals often begin anticipating the death of their pet as they recognize changes in their physical abilities such as having difficulty running or jumping, grey hair or even not acting as spry as they had before. Pets today are many times considered a member of the family and not "just an animal." The loss of a pet is also often one of the first losses of life that a child experiences. For some families, they work to anticipate that potential loss by getting another pet prior to the passing of the other so that they can avoid dealing with the direct loss.

Preparatory Grief

Preparatory grief is when an individual is anticipating their own impending death (Varga & Gallagher, 2020). This may occur due to an illness, a history of genetic family health issues, or due to anxiety about the future and the unknown. In addition to facing their own death, an individual can also suffer from anticipatory-vicarious grief where they would be concerned with the harm that their own death would have on loved one's that are left behind. They begin to worry about their futures and anticipate what life without them will be like. Self-mourning also causes individuals to reflect on the fragility of life and how there is so much outside of one's control that life may end at any point (Plant, 2022). However, when an individual does explore preparatory grief or self-mourning, especially in cases where death is not clear due to medical reasons, it can often be seen as narcissistic or as hypochondriasis as it is not considered "natural" to ponder one's death early (Plant, 2022).

Anticipatory Grief

WHAT MAKES ANTICIPATORY GRIEF DIFFERENT

Anticipatory grief differs from traditional grief due to the fact the death or loss is still future oriented. As such, it may diminish the weight that loss will have with others including those in the mental health field. Grief is often seen as a problem focused treatment as it is based on the loss of someone (Rogalla, 2020). With anticipatory grief, it is the anticipation, but with post death loss, it is the reality of the loss of the individual. For many, anticipating the loss of a person, object, dream, future plan, etc. is not seen as a genuine loss but instead as something that one has the choice to move past or that they should not give up hope with, therefore it is not an actual thing to grieve.

Many individuals experience anticipatory grief and cannot understand why they feel the way they do. They often are not even aware that there is a name for it and that it can be something they can seek help for (Walsh, 2022). Due to the fact many do not even realize there is a name for what they are experiencing, it becomes difficult to reach out to them to recommend additional services such as therapy. This creates a gap between the medical and psychological fields when there is no definitive timeline for the loss of an individual. Therefore, a person that is experiencing anticipatory grief may not feel that they need to seek help because they have not actually experienced a loss yet (Rogalla, 2020). To date, anticipatory grief has not been defined well, is not understood completely, nor has there been adequate training available on the subject for the majority of health professionals that may encounter it, other than perhaps hospice personnel (Patinadan et al., 2022). This is a specialization that is rarely acknowledged within the mental health field (Amdurer, 2019).

Anticipatory grief and traditional grief may differ in how it is experienced and the degree of intensity at the time of the loss of the loved one, however, they tend to share the same characteristics and symptoms (Rogalla, 2020). Anticipatory grief is also unique in that it is experienced not only by the family (as in traditional grief), but also by the individual themselves (Patinadan et al., 2022). Anticipating the grief from loss also is not finite like traditional death because it is unknown exactly how long the experience will continue. Unlike traditional grief, it also accelerates with time, whereas traditional grief decreases as time passes. Hopefulness is an aspect that can be present with anticipatory grief as there can be moments of change, which is something that is not possible in traditional grief. Traditional grief, while not having a specific timeline, has a sense of inevitable adjustment to a new normal without a loved one, anticipatory grief can lead to fears of uncertainty of how long it will go on or when things will "normalize". Grief after the loss of a loved one leads to everyone grieving together; however, in anticipatory grief there can often be two losses that are experienced by the family....one during the anticipatory phase and one after the actual loss (Supiano et al., 2022). The problem is that by the time of the

Anticipatory Grief

actual loss, other people may have already become used to that person being gone or they have been expecting the loss so their grief response to the family is less intense leaving the family to feel the loss was not as important to others (Walsh, 2022).

Caregiver Role in Anticipatory Grief

As the majority of anticipatory grief does pertain to chronic illness and the loss of another, it is vital to look at the role that anticipatory grief plays in the life of the caregiver of the individual who is sick. Generally, most caregivers in families tend to be either a spouse, a parent, or an adult child (most often one of the daughters). When the patient is elderly, it often changes the perspective of the caregiver (being a spouse or adult child) as to how they perceive the impending loss. With parents of a small child who has been diagnosed with a chronic illness, the parent may know that the disease is terminal, but they do not give up hope for a miracle one day; however, this can often be different in the case of anticipatory grief for someone in a later stage of life (Najafi et al., 2022). Caregivers for elderly facing the possibility of death may instead see it as a natural aspect of life, hence being more accepting of the loss to come.

Caregiving may include living with the individual, whether that is moving in with them or moving them to your family home, or it can include the loved one living in a nursing home or assisted living facility. As the caregiver expects to continue with their normal functioning (career, family, household chores, etc.) while now adding on the role of caregiver, it can lead to increased fatigue and distress leading to psychological conflicts (Najafi et al., 2022). Depending on the circumstances, caregiving may include placing a loved one in a nursing home for their own safety, however for the caregiver that can lead to increased feelings of sadness, separation anxiety and even guilt.

As a caregiver begins to look at the impending loss of a loved one, they may begin to see each event with their loved one as the potential last time to experience it due to the uncertainty of time (Dekker, 2023). This leads to anticipating the future without their loved one and preparing for the loss.

Common Symptoms of Anticipatory Grief

Symptoms of anticipatory grief can closely mimic traditional grief. There can be a fear of loss, increased depression, isolation, and hopelessness (Holm et al., 2019; Najafi et al., 2022). As the caregiver begins to accept that they will eventually lose their loved one, they begin to process that grief much earlier than traditional grief. Due to the increase of their responsibilities in caring for a loved one, they can also experience isolation as they can no longer leave their loved one for long periods of time leading to cancelled vacations, missing out on children's sporting/school events, inability to go out with friends, or on a date with their significant other. When the loved one has dementia, it adds another layer as there is the fear that you cannot leave them with others due to them not recognizing new caregivers or fear that they may wander off. Most people with dementia prefer to remain at home in a familiar environment, but it creates challenges for the caregiver, which over time may even lead to the caregiver having increased physical health issues (Meichsner & Wilz, 2018). Dementia can also lead to multiple losses as the individual begins to slip away not only physically, but also cognitively, which would lead to a loss of communication with them and ultimately increased frustration for the caregiver. This leads to the caregiver having increased feelings of loneliness and hopelessness. According to Meichsner and Wilz (2018), 71% of caregivers experience pre-death grief with a loved one with dementia.

Symptoms of anticipatory grief can vary from physical (shortness of breath, loss of appetite, decreased appetite and sleep, headaches, extreme fatigue, and body aches and pains), to behavioral changes (crying excessively or not at all, avoiding dealing with the impending loss or completely focused on preparing for the death). Caregivers can also experience cognitive challenges like confusion, difficulty concentrating, and forgetfulness due to increasing expectations to care for their loved one and their own family. This can lead to increased anger and fear as well. Due to the increased mental and physical strain of being a caregiver, another common symptom that can be seen in the caregiver is accelerated aging (Li et al. 2023).

Guilt is an aspect of caregiver burden that often weighs heavy as they have feelings of "missing out on life", a loss of "normalcy", and "wanting the loved one's suffering to end" therefore, feeling they are "wishing the impending death". There is also the guilt that perhaps they did not do enough, or that if they had invested more time their loved one could have lived longer. There is also the possibility that certain aspects, such as resentment from childhood can come to the surface during caregiving and then that will lead to additional guilt (Amdurer, 2019). Guilt is one of the most common emotions experienced by caregivers. Once the loved one passes this guilt can then turn into shame as they have a deep sadness for the loss of their loved one, but also relief that the caretaking is over and that they are no longer suffering. Guilt and shame may also come from planning ahead and making funeral arrangements prior to the individual passing (Khanipour-Kencha et al., 2022). The caregiver may feel they should not be making those arrangements as it is going to increase the chances of it happening sooner.

Anticipatory Grief

Caregiver Burden

Caregiver burden is often experienced after caring for a loved one over a period of time. The changes in the individual's role from spouse or child to caregiver can be intense, overwhelming and frustrating at times. Many caregivers experience increased depressive symptoms from the role and rather than dealing with the feelings, they choose to compartmentalize those emotions to help them function on a daily basis (Meichsner & Wilz, 2018). However, this can build up to an increase in frustration, isolation, and sadness. Feelings of anger and sadness are often seen more in female caregivers than male caregivers and the intense feelings of sadness are more profound in spouses than in adult children.

Caregiver burden can also lead to lack of social support as the individual is unable to keep up with social demands from children's school activities, work obligations, friends or even their normal spiritual/religious practices. Due to the lack of support, caregivers also do not know how to deal with what they are experiencing. They do not know what to call it, they do not have the knowledge of who they can speak to about it, and do not have the time to seek any outside help. Caregivers will often wait until they feel completely overwhelmed and perhaps that it has even taken a toll on their physical health.

Role of Family

Support from a caregiver's family can be a valuable support to the caregiver's well-being. However, this is not always the case in all families. Some families are also hostile and distant, creating an even deeper wedge between the caregiver and their family as they feel forced to choose between their family or the care of their loved one (Li et al., 2023). Family members can assist the caregiver by providing supporting roles such as household duties, financial support, emotional support for the caregiver and childcare to lessen the burden. By having a positive sense of family connectedness and support, the caregiver can feel love, encouragement, trust and support leading to a more positive outcome.

It is also important to remember that not all family members will grieve the same way. If an adolescent is anticipating the loss of a grandparent that perhaps they never knew very well, they will struggle to process the loss in the same manner as the adult child who is now the caregiver (Walsh, 2022). This may lead to feelings of anger and hostility from the caregiver as they are expecting everyone in the family to feel the same level of grief as they are experiencing. The depth of the relationship between the person grieving and the individual with the illness will often determine the level of loss they feel, both in an anticipatory phase and post loss grief (Walsh, 2022)

Anticipatory Grief

Cultural roles within a family may also have an effect on how the grieving process occurs. For some cultures, discussing feelings or death prior to the actual loss is prohibited (Walsh, 2022). When there is an incongruence between family cultures, this may also lead to some frustration between the caregiver and spouse.

Grieving Process With Anticipatory Grief

One of the most widely used versions of the cycles of grief is the Kubler-Ross cycles of grief which contain five stages: denial, anger, bargaining, depression and acceptance (Walsh, 2022). These stages are not sequential and anyone experiencing grief can actually fluctuate throughout the stages multiple times. There has since been an adaptation to Kubler-Ross' original cycles of grief for individuals experiencing grief with chronic illness (Martin, 2015). The seven cycles for chronic illness include: denial, pleading, bargaining and desperation, anger, anxiety and depression, loss of self and confusion, and acceptance. Due to the cycles being very similar, caregivers often experience grief symptoms prior to the actual physical loss of their loved one, which fits the expanded Kubler-Ross chronic illness cycle (Rogalla, 2020).

Even before the loss of a loved one, it is important for the individual to recognize they are still in the process of grieving so that they can begin working on preparing for the eventual loss. Experiencing anticipatory grief does not mean that one is "giving up", but instead, they have the ability to do what needs to be done with their loved one such as: supporting their needs, making sure that their final wishes are carried out, creating final memories with their loved one, and ultimately providing their loved one with the ability to have peace at the end. Providing this care to a loved one is also a way for the caregiver to begin the grieving process by experiencing the loss with their loved one, rather than after the loved one has passed, which creates a continual progression of the relationship and allows it to come full circle (Dekker, 2023).

With anticipatory grief, caregivers may feel that their loss is not necessarily as tragic as others as they have had time to grieve while their loved one was alive hence minimizing the potential support they receive from others. The role of anticipatory grief is not to alter the expressions of grief (Rogalla, 2020), but instead it may be seen as a way to prepare and protect against the sudden feeling of loss (Patinaden et al., 2022). Anticipatory grief has been shown to lessen the stages of denial and depression as the family has a longer period of time to adjust and understand the death prior to the physical loss. When families did not prepare for the loss prior to the grief it instead led to poorer outcomes for the caregiver. While making funeral arrangements prior to one's physical death can feel unnatural, it also allows the family to now feel that arrangements are made with the family member's wishes in mind and alleviates some of the heavy burden post-death to make those arrangements.

Anticipatory Grief

However, this can also lead to uncomfortable conversations with a loved one if the family members do not feel comfortable discussing death. Preparing for one's final wishes is ultimately moving towards the acceptance that death is inevitable (Dekker, 2023).

Support for Grieving

If a loved one is in a hospice setting, there are often additional services provided prior to the individual's death through nurses, pastoral care, funeral arrangements, etc. However, if hospice is not involved, caregivers are often left feeling alone and not knowing where to receive the help they need (Fee et al., 2023). Facing the loss of the caregiver role and their purpose in life can also lead to additional symptoms of emptiness. Speaking with mental health providers can assist the client in gaining knowledge about the subject of anticipatory grief, hence empowering them and decreasing the feelings of helplessness. This in turn will help to make communication clearer with other parties that are involved, can fill the gap that is felt by the caregiver/family, and in the end help with overall grief symptoms.

Depending on the scope of the practice a counselor is working within, the client's spiritual beliefs may also become a vital aspect of processing anticipatory grief as they consider thoughts about heaven, a higher power or what that means for their loved one. By exploring spirituality, it helps the client to find a deeper meaning and a sense of hope (Khanipour-Kenche et al., 2022).

IMPACT OF COVID-19

As of March of 2024, there have been more than 775 million reported cases of COVID-19 and 7 million reported deaths worldwide (World Health Organization, 2024). COVID-19 changed the way most people saw not only the world they lived in, but also the hopes for their future. As restrictions and lockdowns began, fears of what tomorrow entailed were present on everyone's doorstep and presented an overwhelming amount of anticipatory grief (Khanipour-Kencha et al., 2022). The losses that arose from COVID-19 did not only come from the deaths of loved ones, but so much more. As previously mentioned in the chapter, anticipatory-vicarious grief may have been another form of grief experienced during COVID-19 by the majority of the population as they began to experience fears about their own death, regardless of age, and the potential that things may never return to "normal" (Varga & Gallagher, 2020).

Anticipatory Grief

Connection With Anticipatory Grief

Prior to February of 2020, most people went on with their daily lives with expectations of safety and security and dreams for their future (as well as their family members). All that came to a halt as the COVID-19 pandemic quickly spread. During COVID-19, anticipatory grief was experienced by most individuals and often in multiple ways all at once. Even anticipatory grief varied during the pandemic as families lost elderly loved ones from chronic illnesses or dementia, but they felt guilty that their particular form of grief may not be seen as tragic as someone that died from COVID-19 (Scheinfeld et al., 2022). The phenomenon of having so many people experiencing vast amounts of anticipatory grief all at once throughout the world has not been experienced for decades. Due to the overlap of various anticipatory grief, there has been a concern about how all of this has affected the long-term mental health of the world.

Types of Anticipatory Grief Losses During COVID-19

Health Losses During COVID-19

One of the earliest concerns for most families was the fear of contracting COVID-19 with no vaccines or remedies for the disease. As the disease began quickly spreading from person-to-person, individuals and families began taking an inward look into how to protect their immediate family members. For families with loved ones and chronic illnesses, the pandemic reached new fears that due to their compromised immune systems or illnesses they may be more susceptible to death with the disease and may not be able to fight or even survive the disease (Statz et al., 2023). The pandemic created an even earlier experience with anticipatory grief as they began considering that they may die much sooner from something that they originally thought they had years to deal with. This created challenges for seeking ongoing treatment such as chemotherapy, dialysis and even planned surgical interventions (Statz et al., 2023). Now patients were forced to choose between missing lifesaving procedures or interventions or potentially contracting a new disease that could end their life even quicker. There were also shortages in many different medications leading to others grieving the normalcy they had found with maintenance drugs to now feeling out of control. Many physicians switched to telemedicine which left certain populations without access and creating a complete sense of isolation (Khanipour-Kencha et al., 2022). This underserved population were then left struggling to find proper medical care. This increased their fears, anxiety, and anticipatory grief. Mental health needs were met as many counselors switched over to telehealth services, however some populations either did not have access to Wi-Fi

Anticipatory Grief

or the necessary equipment or even may not be technologically literate leaving them to feel even more stressed to utilize the services.

As individuals became more fearful of contracting COVID-19, the fears of being hospitalized increased their grief even more. Hearing stories of individuals being placed on ventilators in ICUs, or even needing a ventilator only to have those in short supply made many people grieve the access to medical services that they always had at their fingertips (Khanipour-Kencha et al., 2022). As stories began to come out about the loss of an individual's autonomy when they were sick or receiving unwanted medical interventions due to the fact family could no longer be present in the hospitals to advocate for loved ones, people began to grieve the loss of their safety and the safety of their loved ones. One fear that many had never really considered prior to COVID-19 was the fear of dying alone. Most people believe they will have family and others around when it is the end of their life. However, with COVID-19, families were not allowed to be present for so long that a staggering number of people only had a phone held up to say goodbye to their loved one, if they were lucky (Statz et al., 2023). This increased anticipatory grief not only for a loved one passing away this way when they entered the hospital, but just becoming sick at the beginning as well. There was an increase in fears of dying without dignity and for individuals with young children, the fear of not having a will or legal guardian if they both passed away. This is a fear for many parents, but this fear became a very real possibility at the beginning of the pandemic for many families. For some, the anticipatory grief became so overwhelming due to the large number of losses all at one time, it led to an increase in suicidal ideation and attempts during COVID-19 (Yan et al., 2023).

Life Losses During COVID-19

The disease quickly spread to the point where the government ordered a federal shutdown which led to restrictions and even more anticipatory grief (Walsh, 2022). Businesses limited access to buying basic necessities such as toilet paper, food, milk, etc. The fears of not having adequate supplies led to hoarding behaviors and the anticipated grief that life may never be the same again. As most businesses closed for the government shutdown, many people lost their jobs and their income leaving them to fear how they would pay for their home, food for their family, etc. Children were not allowed to go to school and were forced to utilize virtual outlets and eventually hybrid models as the disease fluctuated. This led to fears of developmental delays in children, lack of socialization skills, missing important milestones such as graduations, proms, etc. There was a fear of the lack of control which is a basic need for mental health (Statz et al., 2023).

Teachers had to find a new "normal" in life by thinking outside of the box and teaching children (sometimes even very young children) virtually without any interaction. This led to frustrations as teachers grieved the loss of the functionality of their careers and whether they could experience the same joy they had in the past without having children in their classroom. Medical personnel and first responders experienced fears of contracting COVID-19 due to the necessity of their jobs and potentially bringing it home to their families (Statz et al, 2023). They missed out on contact with their children and even attachment with young children during a pivotal point in their development for fears of spreading potential disease. Students who were off to college experiencing their first time away from home, quickly had to return home leaving them feeling like they were unable to complete the transition into early adulthood.

There was also the loss of social support and physical contact leading to feelings of isolation. Loss of physical contact created a sense of grief for many as well. The fears of never being able to touch or hug others again. Fears of not being able to date someone and do something as basic as a first kiss created a feeling of loss for finding a significant other. Families felt the pain of missing out on precious time with aging parents for fear that they might infect them and with the higher risk for the elderly it meant missing out on connections in turn creating an anticipatory grieving process much earlier than they were prepared for (Statz et al., 2023). Many were fearful to leave their houses at all, creating a feeling of agoraphobia due to the fear of contracting COVID-19. Travel was limited and caused grief as many either were forced to stay home and miss flights due to testing positive for COVID-19 or not being able to return home on their flight due to contracting COVID-19 while visiting another city. The focus of safety with everything one did became a source of anticipatory grief. How will society ever return back to normal after this? It led to a loss of community and an increase in grief and sadness for the fear things would never be the same (Statz et al, 2023).

Another form of anticipatory grief during Covid-19 was implications for the future. Plans for weddings, giving birth to children, raising families, spending time with aging parents, etc. suddenly seemed as though it would never happen. This led to feelings of grief and despair. Personal freedoms also became a consideration of anticipatory grief as people feared not being able to be in public without face masks, keeping social distancing from others, and even the freedom to choose what they did with their body due to how it could affect others (Walsh, 2022). Even the ability to grieve was part of anticipatory grief. Families feared that if a loved one did become sick and died that they would not be able to be present with them in their last moments.

Anticipatory Grief

Anticipatory Grief in Outside Facilities

While most people were forced to lock down in their homes or apartments, the elderly community along with those with pre-existing conditions had even larger challenges. Being in a close setting with people that had no choice but to interact with staff who may bring in an infection such as in a hospital setting, an assisted living facility or even a nursing home, the fears were exacerbated.

Nursing Homes

In nursing homes, families were not allowed to visit their family members except through windows or via phone. While this was acceptable for some, many elderly with hearing loss struggled to hear and it became frustrating for them. Family members were frustrated as they were not able to provide the care they would have given their parents and loved ones. This may include basic needs of hygiene or even just the need of human connection. For patients with dementia this could lead to confusion and even anger thinking they were abandoned by family leaving them scared and grieving the loss of their family. The challenge with dementia patients often included the fact that they were unable to use phones to talk to loved ones as they struggled with even remembering loved ones on a daily basis let alone hearing just their voice. Families were left with an even greater feeling of losing their parents before they had passed. If there was a need for medical services from a fall and surgery was required, family members could not be there to assure their loved ones they would be fine and instead it left those elderly patients confused and disoriented and the family members in desperate need of communication with medical personnel. The challenge was that medical personnel were in such shortage and their skills were needed with patients, they often did not have time to be present for family members, leading to anticipatory grief over the loss of control and safety once again. When families had both parents in facilities, one spouse may be unable to visit the other spouse and if one passed, they were unable to see them in the end leaving them to grieve daily as to whether their spouse was safe or not. Another challenge for patients in a nursing home was the use of protective equipment like masks. Not being able to see the medical personnel's faces or see their smiles became confusing and sometimes even frightening, leading to grief over the loss of their safety and the world they knew.

CLINICAL INTERVENTIONS

Clinical interventions are vital in working with anticipatory grief. The aim is to prepare the individual for the changes that are inevitable and to utilize resources to minimize the effects from grief as well as provide them with positive coping skills to maneuver through the process (Najafi et al., 2022). Whether the loved one is in a palliative/hospice setting or whether they have not taken that step, the goal is to minimize the effects of sorrow. To date, most practices focus on the negative symptoms and reactively treating them as dysfunctional (such as substance abuse, depression, etc.) rather than helping to instill resilience and growth in clients (Rogalla, 2020).

Role of Counselor

Counselors often provide the first opportunity for the client to process their loss in a safe and non-judgmental environment (Dubi et al., 2017). The role of the counselor when working with anticipatory grief includes validating the client's feelings of grief and utilizing active listening, and empathy (Walsh, 2022). When working with grief clients, counselors often rush to present solutions or to explain concepts to the client in an effort to suppress their own anxiety (Dubi et al., 2017). Instead, the client is looking for a counselor to listen to them and allow them time to verbalize their fears and process the feelings they are experiencing. By creating a strong therapeutic alliance, the counselor has the opportunity to create trust and eventually they will be able to add interventions to help the client further deal with their losses. Normalize the feelings of grief and let the client take the lead sharing what changes they would like to make and how they would like to process their loss(es).

Theories and Interventions

There is no specific evidence based therapeutic models for grief like there are for other mental health conditions (Walsh, 2022). This is because in reality it is not a pathological condition but instead a way of life and something everyone will experience and there is no way you can avoid it (Dubi et al, 2017). To begin working with a client with anticipatory grief, a life review may be a good place to start to begin exploring inner strengths and fears that are being experienced as the impending loss is considered (Walsh, 2022). When one is inadequately prepared for the loss of another it can increase the level of post-death grief due to regrets in caretaking decisions and not processing the loss with their loved one (Supiano et al., 2022). Working with caregivers, it is important for counselors to not only work with them to face the impending loss, but to also maintain life at their current home with family (Meichsner & Wilz, 2018). This can be done by helping the caregiver to redefine their relationship with their loved one as well as advocating for the family to provide necessary resources that they may be too overwhelmed to begin exploring.

Regardless of the intervention used for anticipatory grief, there are a couple of basic steps to use with clients. To begin, always validate their pre-loss grief and normalize the feelings they may be experiencing (Meichsner & Wilz, 2018). Assist the client in managing and accepting painful emotions and fears of loss along with new ways of approaching the future loss. Finally, explore ways to reframe the situation to a more positive goal-oriented reorganization of their life/roles. Successful interventions or theories should contain a common theme which is to encourage gradual closure of the experience, normalize emotions and feelings of guilt and grief, making necessary changes to create a resiliency and to accept the loss (Patinadan et al., 2022).

Cognitive Behavioral Therapy (CBT)

Cognitive behavioral therapy is one of the most commonly used therapies with anticipatory grief due to challenging cognitive distortions and reframing them to create a more positive, hopeful future (Khanipour-Kencha et al., 2022; Walsh, 2022). CBT is one of the most successful modalities utilized when working with anticipatory grief and dementia caregiver grief (Meichsner & Wilz, 2018). By challenging cognitive distortions the caregiver or family members are experiencing, they can work to reframe cognitions in a more positive mindset while adding in some coping skills to help them self-regulate and address the grief.

Dignity Therapy

Dignity therapy is one that is used with the individual who is experiencing grief as they prepare for their own loss of life. The purpose is to provide the client with a sense of meaning in their life and to feel they are able to close their life with dignity (Khanipour-Kencha et al., 2022; Walsh, 2022). This has been shown to improve the overall quality of the client's life as they can share future hopes as well as discussing past memories (Patinadan et al., 2022). The client has the opportunity to discuss openly how they want to be remembered when they are gone and to discuss what matters most to them.

Often when experiencing anticipatory grief, it is important to remember that there is a difference between the experience of the client and their family, and those differences absolutely must be addressed. This can be done using a family-based dignity intervention that can assist the family and especially the caretaker in respecting their loved ones wishes to pass with dignity (Ghezeljeh et al., 2023). The family therapy when used with cancer patient's families showed there was an improvement in anxiety and depression levels as they were able to focus on the client's spiritual well-being and hope for a "good death". Family members have the opportunity to openly discuss their feelings and concerns about their loved one's future passing as well. This is often completed by sharing old memories through a life review to increase support for one another. Some family members may be uncomfortable discussing their loved one's passing or making arrangements prior to the actual loss and therefore the client will keep those thoughts to themselves leading to an uncomfortable taboo type of feeling between members of the family. However, the client can then be left to feel shame or guilt for wanting to prepare for a dignified ending. Assisting the family and client to address these issues can help bridge that uncomfortable topic in a manner that can help all members alleviate additional stress.

Meaning Reconstruction Theory

The theory of Meaning Reconstruction is a more recent model to explore grief after the Kubler-Ross model (Supiano et al., 2022). This theory can be a beneficial way for the caretaker and their family to begin to process anticipatory grief. There are three parts to this model, beginning with assisting the family facing the loss to come to terms with the loss, followed by exploring potential growth or benefits that they may experience from the loss. This stage can be difficult for the family as they may not see a sense of growth or benefit from loss so being mindful of the wording that the clinician utilizes with this model is extremely important. Some examples of potential growth from anticipatory grief could be they gave their loved one a dignified closure to their life, that they can find ways to feel like they were capable of more than they ever thought (especially if they counted on the individual for help throughout life such as a parent or spouse), or that they had a great deal of strength moving through this potential loss and it will help them to learn to overcome future losses. Finally, they can explore how this loss and experience has reorganized their personal identity, such as taking on a new role or becoming a stronger person than they ever felt possible.

Personal Growth Theory

When life brings challenges and struggles, individuals often get trapped in feelings of helplessness and loss of control. They have a difficult time finding a way to move forward from the situation. In the Personal Growth Theory, the counselor works with the client to take the future loss and gain a stronger control of the situation by minimizing the effects of stress earlier rather than after the stress has become overwhelming (Rogalla 2020). By utilizing positive coping skills, a person can become more resilient in the face of challenges, set more proactive goals, implement a

Anticipatory Grief

more positive outlook on life in general, and ultimately gain a better understanding of themselves. Studies have shown that the use of positive coping skills leading to personal growth along with strong social support in cases of anticipatory grief has a positive outcome for clients (Rogalla, 2022). Clients need to be made aware that personal growth does not have to begin after a loss but instead can begin prior to the loss to make the effects less problematic.

Additional Theories and Interventions

The use of Existential therapy can be utilized with group grief work to explore a sense of meaning (Walsh, 2022). This could be helpful in cases of anticipatory grief where individuals feel hopeless or helpless about their future. Experiential interventions focus on the experiences of the individuals allowing them to explore their mind, body and spirit. This includes utilizing deep breathing and relaxation skills to help one achieve peace. With the mind/body connection, the focus turns to relaxing the body in order to eventually relax the mind.

When a loved one is facing their final days, an intervention that can help not only the client, but the family as well is to use positive memory construction (Supiano et al., 2022). This allows for the family to reminisce about positive memories while the individual is still alive which can be very beneficial to the family, especially when the loved one has had dementia to allow the family to focus not on the cognitive losses but instead on the life the individual has led. This can be very beneficial to both the individual and the caretaker.

Music Therapy

Music therapy can be especially useful when working with dementia clients due the fact that music memories can bring back strong emotions and thoughts. Music remains in an active area of the brain much longer than language and short-term memories (Devere, 2017). The music can often stimulate the patient in a way that nothing else can. They may suddenly mouth the words of a song, move their bodies to the music or even shed a tear as they are reminded of days past. Music therapy regardless of conditions has the power to elicit positive changes to mood, behaviors, and cognitions.

When completing interventions with anticipatory grief clients it is also important to always take into consideration the client's cultural backgrounds and how that affects their grief processing (Walsh, 2022). Not all cultures will feel comfortable managing grief and loss the same way. To be culturally competent, the counselor should always inquire with the family about their traditions and how they deal with grief and loss.

Role of Resilience

Some individuals have the ability to demonstrate resilience in the face of adversity. While this may be seen as a personality characteristic, positive coping skills can be taught to help mitigate adverse effects (Li et al., 2023; Rogalla, 2020). In the area of anticipatory grief, whether it is the loss of a loved one, a situation like COVID-19, a change such as divorce, or even loss of a future event, working through a family reliance framework can assist the entire family on recognizing strengths, learning new ways to cope and grow from the experience and becoming more adaptable in the face of challenges and adversities can help mitigate distress and suffering (Walsh, 2022). It is about reframing negative thoughts and helping a person bounce back from a situation that seemed impossible. This includes reminding them of past experiences where they were successful at navigating through difficult times and grew as an individual.

Psychoeducation

Psychoeducation of grief and its symptoms is usually the main intervention in grief counseling (Dubi et al., 2017). Studies have shown that caregivers are desperately in need of help making decisions and having adequate knowledge to do so (Fee et al., 2023). Instead, most of that available knowledge focuses on what to do after the death of a loved one versus before. Medical professionals often feel uncomfortable discussing these issues as they are concentrating on the patient (Fee et al., 2023). Social workers may provide referrals for services but then caregivers are not really sure what they need, and the services appear more disjointed leading to additional frustration and feelings of being overwhelmed. Providing psychoeducation to clients can help them to feel heard about the process of end-of-life decisions and not being tossed between various resources and then still feeling lost. The client can then discuss what those decisions mean not only for their loved one but also how they feel about it both logically and emotionally.

It is important that the clients are provided psychoeducation regarding the symptoms of grief, the importance of not trying to avoid grief and how it varies from person to person (Dubi et al., 2017). Helping to normalize the process can be a great relief alone to clients. A common way that many attempt to deal with anticipatory grief is to just stay busy so they do not have to deal with it; however, the reality is that then it compounds, potentially leading to them experiencing a much deeper level of sadness once the actual loss is experienced (Dubi et al., 2017).

Anticipatory Grief

Anticipatory grief may include the counselor providing psychoeducation to the client about a variety of needs from medical terminology and scenarios within the healthcare field, programs for children in need, respite care for caregivers, and even end-of-life decisions (Walsh, 2022).

Assessments for Anticipatory Grief

The *Anticipatory Grief Scale (AGS)* was developed by Theut, Jordan, Ross and Duetsch in 1991 to look at the major domains involved with grief and is the most widely utilized assessment for anticipatory grief (Holm et al., 2019). The original wording was designed for the caregiver of the family member however it was later added that wording could be changed in the assessment to meet a more specific context such as palliative care. This scale has shown statistical validity and contains two subscales: one for behavior reactions and one for emotional reactions. It contains 27 items that are completed using a Likert scale measure (Holm et al., 2019).

IMPLICATIONS FOR PRACTITIONERS

Education

Researchers have expressed a need for more curriculum to include grief counseling (Wheat et al., 2022). According to Blueford et al. (2022), a recent study showed that participants in a counseling program only received less than 10 hours of training on grief counseling even though in their fieldwork 98% of them stated that they had worked with at least one client experiencing grief. There is a scarcity of literature available currently on educating counselors in the field in grief therapy and part of this is due to the fact that the Council for Accreditation of Counseling and Related Educational Programs (CACREP) has never included grief counseling education as part of their requirements in masters or Ph.D. level training (Blueford et al., 2022). In the same study, 70 CACREP programs were evaluated, and it was found that less than half of those institutions had a specific course dedicated to grief. An additional study showed that 55% of participants never had any course work regarding grief in their counseling degree program (Wheat et al., 2022). This is concerning due to the fact that grief will eventually affect every single individual and therefore is something that upcoming counselors should feel prepared to handle once they are in the field. While half of the universities did provide those courses, there is a lack of consistency in what is taught and the expectations for outcomes leaving counselors feeling inadequate to work with this population (Blueford et al., 2022). Per the ACA (2014), best ethical practices include exposing students to latest education and research to provide their clients with safe, proven methods of treatment. Without those consistent standards, counselors may be left with a feeling of imposter syndrome when treating clients unless they have any personal experience with grief; however, that can then lead to countertransference with clients and an unethical treatment (Blueford et al., 2022).

Additional Training

Once a counselor has completed the educational aspects of their counseling career, additional training may be necessary to feel properly trained and effective at working with the grief population. As students complete their internship fieldwork experience, both clinical supervisors and counselor educators can assist in this process by having more discussions about grief and how to properly work with this clientele (Blueford et al., 2022). One aspect of this that is important to remember as well is that clinical supervisors must also be able to self-reflect on their level of competency when working with this specific group.

Other available training options include ongoing continuing education credits or certifications to specialize the counselor in working with that specific population. This training is available at in-person training sessions (which may require travel), or there are many that are also available through an online/webinar platform. One barrier for this type of additional training can be the high cost involved for the certification, course work or travel which many counselors feel prevents them from seeking that training (Blueford et al., 2022). The Association for Death Education and Counseling (ADEC) also provides additional specialized training for grief as well.

As most anticipatory grief deals with chronic illness and loss from medical issues it is also important to look at the statistics of individuals facing anticipatory loss just through Alzheimer's and cancer. According to the World Alzheimer's Report (Long et al., 2023), 55 million people had Alzheimer's in 2019 worldwide, but that number is expected to grow to 139 million by 2050. In regard to cancer, according to the American Cancer Society (2024), predicts that in 2024 alone, over 2 million people are expected to be diagnosed with cancer this year and over 611,000 people will die of cancer which is 1,680 people per day. These two statistics alone reflect the need for more work with anticipatory grief and counselor self-efficacy/education when working with grief. Completing more research utilizing resources (proactive) rather than risk factors (reactive), can help to increase individuals' ability to navigate the strain and struggle of anticipatory grief (Rogella, 2020).

Anticipatory Grief

REFERENCES

Amdurer, T. (2019, March). *The caregiving conundrum.* CT Counseling. https://ct .counseling.org

American Cancer Society. (2024). *Cancer Facts and Figures.* ACS. https://www .cancer.org/research/cancer-facts-statistics/all-cancer-facts-figures/2024-cancer -facts-figures.html

American Counseling Association. (2014). *ACA code of ethics.* ACA. https://www .counseling.org/resources/aca-code-of-ethics

Blueford, J. M., Diambra, J. F., & Wheat, L. S. (2022). Counselor preparedness to counsel grieving clients: Insights and implications. *Death Studies*, 46(10), 2413–2423. 10.1080/07481187.2021.195664434308795

Dekker, N. L. (2023). Anticipatory grief in dementia: An ethnographic study of loss and connection. *Culture, Medicine and Psychiatry*, 47(3), 701–721. 10.1007/ s11013-022-09792-335767160

Devere, R. (2017). *Music and dementia: An overview.* Practical Neurology. https:// www.practicalneurology.com

Dubi, M., Powell, P., & Gentry, J.E. (2017). *Trauma, ptsd, grief & loss.* Pesi Publishing & Media.

Fee, A., Hanna, J., & Hasson, F. (2023). Pre-loss grief experiences of adults when someone important to them is at end-of-life: A qualitative systematic review. *Death Studies*, 47(1), 30–44. 10.1080/07481187.2021.199893534751635

Ghezeljeh, T. N., Seyedfatemi, N., Bolhari, J., Kamyari, N., & Rezaei, M. (2023). Effects of family-based dignity intervention and expressive writing on anticipatory grief in family caregivers of patients with cancer: A randomized controlled trial. *BMC Psychiatry*, 23(1), 220. 10.1186/s12888-023-04715-x37005577

Guise, R. (2015). *Study guide for the national marriage and family licensing exam.* Family Solutions Institute.

Holm, M., Alvariza, A., Furst, C. J., Ohlen, J., & Arestedt, K. (2019). Psychometric evaluation of the anticipatory grief scale in a sample of family caregivers in the context of palliative care. *Health and Quality of Life Outcomes*, 17(1), 42. 10.1186/ s12955-019-1110-430837000

Khanipour-Kencha, A., Jackson, A. C., & Bahramnezhad, F. (2022). Anticipatory grief during COVID-19: A commentary. *British Journal of Community Nursing*, 27(3), 114–117. 10.12968/bjcn.2022.27.3.11435274970

Li, C., Tang, N., Yang, L., Zeng, Q., Yu, T., Pu, X., Wang, J., & Zhang, H. (2023). Effect of caregiver burden on anticipatory grief among caregivers of elderly cancer patients: Chain mediation role of family functioning and resilience. *Frontiers in Psychology*, 13, 1020517. 10.3389/fpsyg.2022.102051736704702

Long, S., Benoist, C. & Weidner, W. (2023). *World Alzheimer's report 2023*. Alzheimer's Disease International. World-Alzheimer-Report-2023.pdf (alzint.org)

Martin, J. (2015). *The 7 psychological stages of chronic pain*. Pain News Network. www.painnewsnetwork.org

Meichsner, F., & Wilz, G. (2018). Dementia caregivers' coping with pre-death grief: Effects of a CBT-based intervention. *Aging & Mental Health*, 22(2), 218–225. 10. 1080/13607863.2016.124742827792398

Najafi, K., Farahani, A. S., Rassouli, M., Majd, H. A., & Karami, M. (2022). Emotional upheaval, the essence of anticipatory grief in mothers of children with life threatening illnesses: A qualitative study. *BMC Psychology*, 10(1), 196. 10.1186/s40359-022-00904-735953867

Patinadan, P. V., Tan-Ho, G., Choo, P. Y., & Ho, A. H. Y. (2022). Resolving anticipatory grief and enhancing dignity at the end-of-life: A systematic review of palliative interventions. *Death Studies*, 46(2), 337–350. 10.1080/07481187.2020.172842632079501

Plant, B. (2022). Living posthumously: From anticipatory grief to self-mourning. *Mortality*, 27(1), 38–52. 10.1080/13576275.2020.1810650

Rogalla, K. B. (2020). Anticipatory grief, proactive coping, social support, and growth: Exploring positive experiences of preparing for loss. *Omega*, 81(1), 107–129. 10.1177/0030222818876146129516784

Rosenfeld, E. K. (2018). *The fire that changed the way we think about grief*. The Harvard Crimson.

Scheinfeld, E., Gangi, K., Nelson, E. C., & Sinardi, C. C. (2022). Please scream inside your heart: Compounded loss and coping during the COVID-19 pandemic. *Health Communication*, 37(10), 1316–1328. 10.1080/10410236.2021.188641333586557

Anticipatory Grief

Statz, T. L., Kobayashi, L. C., & Finlay, J. M. (2023). 'Losing the illusion of control and predictability of life': Experiences of grief and loss among ageing US adults during the COVID-19 pandemic. *Ageing and Society*, 43(12), 2821–2844. 10.1017/S0144686X21001872

Supiano, K. P., Luptak, M., Andersen, T., Beynon, C., Lacob, E., & Wong, B. (2022). If we knew then what we know now: The preparedness experience of pre-loss and post-loss dementia caregivers. *Death Studies*, 46(2), 369–380. 10.1080/07481187.2020.173101432093533

Varga, S., & Gallagher, S. (2020). Anticipatory-vicarious grief: The anatomy of a moral emotion. *The Monist*, 103(2), 176–189. 10.1093/monist/onz034

Walsh, K. (2022). *Grief and loss: Theories and skills for the helping professions* (3rd ed.). Waveland Press, Inc.

Wheat, L. S., Matthews, J. J., & Whiting, P. P. (2022). Grief content inclusion in CACREP-accredited counselor education programs. *The Journal of Counselor Preparation and Supervisor*, 15(2). https://digitalcommons.sacredheart.edu/jcps/vol15/iss2/14

World Health Organization (WHO). (2024, March 31). *WHO COVID-19 dashboard*. WHO.

Yan, Y., Hou, J., Li, Q., & Yu, N. X. (2023). Suicide before and during the COVID-19 pandemic: A systematic review with meta-analysis. *International Journal of Environmental Research and Public Health*, 20(4), 3346. 10.3390/ijerph2004334636834037

Zanville, N., Cohen, B., Gray, T. F., Phillips, J., Linder, L., Starkweather, A., Yeager, K. A., & Cooley, M. E. (2021). The oncology nursing society rapid review and research priorities for cancer care in the context of COVID-19. *Oncology Nursing Forum*, 48(2), 131–145. 10.1188/21.ONF.131-14533600397

ADDITIONAL READING

Pratt, T. K. (2019). *Anticipatory grief: The journey of a thousand losses and endless grace*. Living Parables of Central Florida, Inc.

Rando, T. A. (2000). *Clinical dimensions of anticipatory mourning: Theory and practice in working with the dying, their loved ones, and their caregivers* (1st ed.). Research Pr. Publishers.

Wolfelt, A. (2021). *Expected loss: Coping with anticipatory grief (words of hope and healing)*. Companion Press.

KEY TERMS AND DEFINITIONS

Anticipatory Grief Scale (AGS): A 27-item Likert Scale assessment designed to measure caregiver anticipatory grief.

Anticipatory Grief: A form of grief that involves processing the loss of someone or something prior to the actual loss.

Anticipatory-Vicarious Grief: Fearing the loss of one's own life but being concerned about how their death will affect loved one's that are left behind instead.

Caregiver Burden: The complicated feelings that occur when one is caring for another and can include feelings of being overwhelmed, frustrated, angry, guilty, and being torn between everyday activities and the new role as a caretaker for a period of time.

Council for Accreditation of Counseling and Related Educational Programs (CACREP): The accrediting board that maintains a level of expectations for counseling programs at graduate level Universities to maintain a consistent standard of education for the field.

Personal Growth: Accepting challenges and changes in life and finding a way to grow as an individual physically, mentally and/or spiritually which often includes increasing one's resilience.

Post-loss Grief: Grief that occurs once an actual loss has occurred.

Pre-loss Grief: Experiencing the same stages and emotions as traditional grief but this occurs prior to the death of a loved one.

Preparatory Grief: Anticipating one's own death.

Proactive coping: Finding ways to overcome challenges in life by addressing the issues prior to them affecting one in a negative manner.

Resilience: The ability to recover and rise above challenges that occur in life continually bouncing back.

Self-efficacy: An individual's perception of their confidence and competency to complete specific tasks.

Chapter 3
Death Anxiety:
The Denial of Our Impermanence

Aaron Suomala Folkerds
https://orcid.org/0009-0007-5918-2469
Minnesota State University, Moorhead, USA

Diane Coursol
Minnesota State University, Mankato, USA

ABSTRACT

This chapter will help counselors and counselor trainees develop the capacity to understand the concept of death anxiety for themselves and for those they serve. Moreover, this chapter will define death anxiety, discuss the history of death anxiety within the helping professions, and provide guidelines for exploring one's own death anxiety and the death anxiety of clients. This chapter will describe terror management theory (TMT) and how the denial of death and death anxiety lies at the heart of human behavior and cultural affiliation. This chapter introduces cultural humility as a foundation for engaging in conversations about death and a model for clinically applying cultural humility is examined. In addition, creative teaching strategies are offered for engaging students in self-reflective learning about death anxiety. Finally, this chapter will provide a foundation to normalize Barbie's question in the blockbuster movie, "Do you guys ever think of death?" (Gerwig, 2023).

INTRODUCTION

"Do you guys ever think about dying?" This was a question that Barbie asked her friends in the middle of a wild dance party scene in the summer 2023 blockbuster movie, *Barbie*. The loud blaring music suddenly stops at her question and Barbie has an uncomfortable look on her face and everyone is staring at her. Barbie's naming of

DOI: 10.4018/979-8-3693-1375-6.ch003

Copyright © 2024, IGI Global. Copying or distributing in print or electronic forms without written permission of IGI Global is prohibited.

a very present death anxiety that is within all of us was just too painful for all those at the party. Noticing the awkward nature of her question, Barbie quickly works to change the subject by saying, "I'm just dying to dance." The music and dancing quickly resume, and all her friends ignore her original question about dying (Gerwig, 2023). This scene serves as a metaphor for the pervasive denial of death in the US culture. Death is one of those few universals in life, and yet it is so challenging to talk about and to face the reality of our anxiety about death (Becker, 1997; Jong, 2021; Menzies & Menzies, 2021; Ozguc et al., 2024; Solomon et al., 2016). It also begs the question, "Why is it so hard to talk about Death in US Culture?" Perhaps at the heart of this difficulty is that there is pervasive death anxiety that is all around us. But what exactly is death anxiety?

DEFINING DEATH ANXIETY

Humans have been contending with death anxiety since the beginning of time and death has been a constant pariah to manage. One of the key aspects of human experience is that the human creature is the only being on the planet that knows that it will one day die (Becker, 1997; Jong, 2021; Solomon et al., 2004; Solomon et al., 2016). Such knowledge can overwhelm a person and work to create a very present death anxiety. This death anxiety can be overt or covert. Death anxiety is overt when the individual directly faces their mortality and deeply considers it. But such overt death anxiety, as Yalom (2008) has stated is like staring at the sun. A person can only do it for so long without burning their eyes or perhaps in this case, burning their soul.

Covert death anxiety is more insidious in nature and lies at the heart of the human experience and human motivation. It is as though the individual knows subconsciously that they will one day die and are therefore driven to find ways to assuage that anxiety sometimes without even realizing it (Yalom, 2008). Becker (1997) wrote about this type of death anxiety in his book, *The Denial of Death*. He described how each person is engaged on a sort of immortality or hero project in a symbolic effort to live forever (Munley & Johnson, 2003).

Some work to alleviate their death anxiety through an absolute devotion to science and this can be seen through the growing literature on defeating aging and living longer. Others mitigate their death anxiety through getting caught up in trivial things and overstating their importance, through frenetic activity, and in focusing on the petty things in life (Becker, 1997). Today, Becker might even add the extreme devotion to social media to confirm that your own life is better than your neighbors. One study found a positive correlation between social media addiction and death anxiety. This suggests that individuals overuse social media to buffer the threat of

Death Anxiety

death anxiety and other existential concerns, (Kumpasoglu et al., 2020). Another major way people work to alleviate their death anxiety is through centering their attention on possessions and money. People seem to have the misconception that a bigger bank account, a bigger house or a fancier car might in some way stave off the undeniable fact that death will touch all people (Becker, 1997; Gasiorowska et al., 2018; Munley & Johnson, 2003).

The COVID-19 epidemic made the experience of death anxiety very real and powerful with the uncertainty of how Covid-19 would affect the world population. This feeling was especially salient for those at-risk populations like the chronically ill and elderly (Menzies et al. 2020; Menzies & Menzies, 2020). One can hypothesize that death anxiety was at the heart of the strong disagreements among citizens around masking, vaccines, and other curative medicines. Naming and understanding the experience of death anxiety may lie at the heart of helping the nation to heal from the division that came from the Covid-19 epidemic.

The main purpose and goal of this chapter is to define and name the experience of death anxiety and to help the reader to think about dying. Thinking of death and its associated anxiety is extremely challenging and this chapter is designed to give the reader tools for how to do this important work. The chapter will first offer a contextual examination of death anxiety to provide a basic understanding of the experience of death anxiety which includes a foundation in Terror Management Theory. The reader will be introduced to a set of skills to help others explore the concept of death anxiety including cultural humility, a case study, and other creative approaches such as music, literature and art to be used in counseling, supervision, and educational settings.

CONTEXTUAL EXAMINATION OF DEATH ANXIETY

Philosophers have been thinking about death and considering how to assuage death anxiety since modern thought began. Plato in his work *Phaedo*, discussed how philosophy is a sort of training for the dying (Plato, 1975). Death has and continues to play a central role in major philosophy. This is especially true when Kierkegaard (1981; 1983) considered the father of existential philosophy, called death a certain uncertainty and that death will eventually touch all people. Yet one will not know the day, the time or the hour of when death will strike. Schopenhauer another philosopher, described death as finding one's ultimate purpose in life. Life is forever traveling towards death and that is when the individual will experience a final release of one's suffering (Magee, 1997). The philosopher Heidegger stated that to understand what life is, one must contend with the reality of death (Heidegger, 2008).

Death Anxiety

The third force of psychology is humanistic or existential psychology which focuses on the study of the existence of life (Serlin & Criswell, 2014). Yalom (1980) is one of the key leaders of this movement and wrote about Existential Psychology. In his book, *Existential Psychotherapy* he utilizes the term *ultimate concern* to describe those concepts that ultimately concern human existence. The four ultimate concerns that he described are death, freedom, isolation, and meaninglessness. Death is an ultimate concern because it is something with which all people must contend; and many will work hard to deny its existence. Freedom is a concern because human beings must ultimately contend with the fact that they have freedom in life. Having freedom creates anxiety for humans because they do not necessarily know what they will do with such freedom. Isolation refers to the fact that humans are born into the world alone and that they will leave the world alone. It creates anxiety because humans are ultimately alone in this world and must work to connect with others. Lastly, the fourth ultimate concern is meaninglessness, and this ultimately describes that the world lacks any sort of meaning and that we are tasked to bring meaning to the world (Yalom, 1980).

It is interesting to note that the concept of ultimate concern originated from theologian Paul Tillich (1952) who coined the term *ultimate concern*. For Tillich the ultimate concern had to do with God whom he described as the ground of all being. Tillich also discussed the concept of courage and its relationship to death anxiety. He detailed how humans are the only creatures that know that they will one day die and no longer be in existence. In other words, there is a threat of non-being for the individual. Yet despite this threat of non-being the individual continues to live each day despite the knowledge that they know that they will one day die. Tillich affirms that this takes a sort of existential courage to face each day knowing that one day we will die (Tillich, 1952).

It takes courage to face death anxiety, but we cannot necessarily stare at the sun of death each day; yet it still must be faced (Yalom, 2008). Yalom (1980) described the two paths of facing death. The first path is one in which death can work to bring a new sense of quality to one's life. Having an awareness of death in their life such that it gives a new sense of urgency to live life to its fullest. Yalom provided the example of someone living with a terminal illness who can embrace their illness in such a way that it provides a new sense of appreciation in and zest for life. Inversely, the second path is when individuals do not fully embrace their death, they can develop a sense of anxiety and a desire to find ways to repress and suppress their eventual death (Yalom, 1980).

This anxiety can lead to many strategies to deal with that anxiety. It is not uncommon for people to employ strategies of specialness, personal heroism or even narcissism to contend with and suppress the inevitability of death. The notion of specialness lies at a deep level in that while the individual knows rationally that

Death Anxiety

they will one day die, deep down there is sort of denial or sense of being special in that they will not die. Death will come for my neighbor, but it will not come for me is a protective mechanism that can keep people going in the face of death. Our personal belief in being special can help us face the harsh and cruel world. It is this specialness that drives people to work to get ahead in life, to have a better job and a bigger home. There is an irrational belief that if I just accomplish enough, I will not have to face my mortality. Yet no matter how special an individual may be, they will always succumb to death's grip (Yalom, 1980).

This specialness leads to work on one's own personal hero project (Becker, 1997; Yalom, 2008). The hero project works to drive the person to believe in their immortality because of their stellar accomplishments. The concept of narcissism may also play a role in viewing oneself as special and this feeds into assuaging death anxiety. Control is yet another way to feed into the idea of being special. People who enter professions such as the military, medical professions or spiritual professions are often driven by a need to control death. Yalom (1980) speculated that this may be an effort to control death anxiety. Yet, the day will arrive when despite one's best efforts to demonstrate that they are special and set apart from society, they too will die.

Another defense mechanism Yalom (1980) discussed was that of the ultimate rescuer. When the quest for specialness breaks down, many seek out the ultimate rescuer. The ultimate rescuer can be a supernatural being like a God/Higher Power or the rescuer could come in the form of a charismatic person or cause. One example of such a person could be a doctor and it is not uncommon to put a high degree of faith into a doctor when staring death in the face. Eventually these ultimate rescuers will fall apart and will not be able to fully save all others or themselves from death (Yalom, 1980).

How then does a therapist help a client who is staring at the sun of death anxiety? (Yalom, 2008). First, the therapist should normalize and help the client to accept the death anxiety experience. This can be done by helping the client recognize that all people will face death anxiety to a certain extent. It is simply a part of the human condition. This acceptance is a great first step for an individual to work through their death anxiety. It is not the goal of the therapist to completely wipe away death anxiety, but rather to help a client to corral it into a manageable level. Yalom (1980) advocates doing this through helping the client find a greater degree of life satisfaction. It is through the finding of a greater sense of life satisfaction that lowers client levels of death anxiety and provides more meaning in life. The goal then of engaging death anxiety is to help people to transform the reality of their death into new life (Yalom, 1980).

TERROR MANAGEMENT THEORY

There is also an underlying death anxiety that is at play within the culture of the US and there are many symptoms that give evidence to this fact. One symptom of death anxiety is the extreme fear of aging within US culture and how society works to outsource death to hospitals, hospices, and nursing homes. Terminology has changed through the years as well with terms like end-of-life care, palliative care, expiration, and passing. US culture also emphasizes ideas of wealth and beauty to assuage the underlying death anxiety present in society (Applewhite, 2020; Levy, 2022; Wass, 2004).

One of the ways that society has worked to pacify death is through the popular model of grief developed by Kubler-Ross (1970). This model of grief has worked to mitigate the grief experience through five linear steps including, Denial, Anger, Bargaining, Depression and Acceptance. This model was never intended to be a model for grief and Kubler-Ross originally intended it for being a model for those who are living with a terminal illness. Eventually the model was utilized to describe the grief experience because of its ease of use and understanding. Through the years the model has taken off as the quintessential approach to use for those who are grieving and has spread across many disciplines. However, the model does not fully capture how complicated grief really is for those who are experiencing it (Konigsberg, 2011; McCoyd et al. 2023; Sawyer, 2024).

The extreme consumption and desire for wealth are also symptoms of an underlying death anxiety. Researchers have discovered that those with high levels of death anxiety work to assuage that death anxiety through consumption. Buying larger homes, more expensive cars and more expensive clothing are all indicative of those people who have higher levels of death anxiety. In addition, research has demonstrated that consuming material goods can also work to lower levels of death anxiety. Money in some ways is a sort of balm for the existential dread and anxiety that people face. Money represents a way that people can work to buy the freedom from the grip that death takes hold on them. Money means that people can buy access to better healthcare and a life that can ignore death because the individual already possesses so much. In a way money and having possessions represents a sort of immortality or set of blinders for the certain certainty of death. However, money will never buy you immortality (Gasiorowska et al., 2018). Actor Denzel Washington (2019) stated at a commencement address at The University of Pennsylvania, "You will never see a U-Haul behind a hearse." The implication being that you cannot take your possessions with you. Possessions will not buy you immortality. Yet, despite this very present truth, the denial of death is strongly at play within US culture and there remains an underlying death anxiety within society.

Death Anxiety

One of the major theories that works to explore this underlying level of death anxiety in US culture is Terror Management Theory (TMT). TMT was developed by three social psychologists that were deeply influenced by the work of Becker (1997) and his notions on the experience of death anxiety and its subsequent death denial (Solomon et al., 2004; Solomon, et al., 2016). They were also influenced by the existential approach, and wanted to determine if Becker's work could be empirically proven. Their main hypothesis in their studies is that death salience or being reminded about one's death can deeply influence actions towards others. In addition, culture is one of the main ways of assuaging death anxiety. One study examined how Christian and Jewish participants of similar socio-economic levels viewed one another. The control group measured their level of fondness towards the other group of people. The experimental group was first reminded of their death which they referred to as mortality salience (MS) and were then asked to rate their fondness for the other group. The researchers reported that after participants were reminded of their death, they had lower levels of fondness for the other group of people (Greenberg et al., 1990).

There are countless additional studies that have examined other influences such as how one makes political decisions after a MS prompt and how they choose their ideological beliefs (Castano et al., 2011). That is to say that participants in these studies were reminded of their death. Researchers have discovered that MS prompts can contribute to people choosing a more charismatic leader versus one who is more relationship oriented (Cohen et al., 2004). In addition, another study showed that a MS prompt resulted in an increased preference for a candidate with a more charismatic approach within their own party (liberal or conservative). Mortality salience resulted in lower opinion ratings of those that were considered uncharismatic and those who had a different political orientation. In other words, MS prompts the individual to dig in more in terms of political affiliation and to choose those candidates who are more charismatic in nature. Therefore, political decisions when made in the face of remembering our mortality will lead to choosing a more charismatic leader and will increase the dislike of the other party representative. Charismatic leaders are seen to be more confident and to have all the answers that society is looking for. This is appealing in the midst of uncertain times and provides a sort of balm for society. In summary, leaders are raised up to leadership based upon charisma rather than on what might be most needed for society (Kosloff et al., 2009).

Thus, TMT has affirmed that when an individual's system for assuaging death is threatened, they will defend that worldview because it is what they depend on for making sense of the world and for dealing with their death anxiety. Given studies of this nature it would make sense to develop methods of communication that would promote peace and harmony (Pyszczynski et al. (2015); Solomon, et al.

(2016). Cultural humility might be one of those ways of working towards peaceful communication amongst differing groups of people (Tervalon & Garcia, 1998).

CULTURAL HUMILITY

One of the ways that society could work to understand one another and to not feel threatened by another person's culture or understanding of how to assuage death anxiety is through the concept of cultural humility. Cultural humility was originally developed by two family practice doctors, Tervalon and Garcia (1998), as a different way of thinking about multicultural competence. They argued that one simply cannot become an expert in all cultures and in all languages. There are simply too many expressions of culture and there is also a great deal of differences within cultures as well. That is to say, each person experiences their culture in a different way, and it is impossible to fully know how each person experiences their culture.

Cultural humility is less about having knowledge and more about an orientation towards others. Cultural humility is about having a deep reverence for the other and even holding the other up a little higher than oneself. In addition, it is about learning from the other and being open to understanding how the individual experiences their culture. In addition, cultural humility requires engagement in continuous self-reflection and self-critique. This is a never-ending process that must continue. With cultural humility, one is always walking on the path towards competence, but one will never fully arrive. It is all about the process (Tervalon & Garcia, 1998; Singh et al, 2023).

Researchers have also developed a model to operationalize what it looks like to practice cultural humility. The model is called the ORCA model which is a mnemonic that stands for Openness, Respect, Curiosity, and Accountability. Cultural humility requires the individual to practice from a perspective of openness, that is, always practicing an open orientation to the other. In this practice judgement of the other is suspended thereby allowing the individual to embrace the other for who they are. It is so natural for a human to simply judge the other and the O of the ORCA model reminds us to suspend that judgement. Practicing openness leads to a deepened respect for the other and their beliefs. Having a deep respect for the other leads to the development of a curiosity of the other and their background. Lastly, accountability speaks to remembering the importance of creating an environment where there is equality. Accountability reminds us to think of the power differentials between the two people and to work towards equity and understanding (Grauf-Grounds & Rivera, 2020). It is not enough to simply be aware of the differences between people, but to work towards changing the system that one lives in. This speaks to the fifth force of counseling which is a focus on issues of social justice (Ratts, 2009).

Death Anxiety

THE COVERT BECOMING OVERT: A CASE STUDY

For the most part, people can keep their death anxiety under control and work to ensure that the covert does not become overt. Nonetheless, there are times in life when covert death anxiety will become overt because death is always hanging in the balance (Yalom, 2008). The following case study of Anthony and his experience with death anxiety is drawn from the counseling work of one of the chapter authors (A. Suomala Folkerds, personal communication, 2024). Anthony was raised in large midwestern city by two parents as an only child. His mother died when he was only 16 years old from cancer and he remembers the death very well. It was the late 1970s and many in his community told him to be strong and that he will work through the loss of his mother like a man.

His father was devastated by the loss and did not know what to do without his wife. To deal with his wife's death he went inwards and entered a period of deep depression that he never fully managed. Anthony did not know what to do with his absent father and to deal with his grief Anthony doubled his efforts at school. He worked tirelessly to get good grades and excel academically and as a three-sport athlete. Eventually Anthony worked to go to school in California and to get away from his father.

Because of his death anxiety, Anthony never married and dedicated his life to making money. He became a very successful real estate developer and eventually got involved in the technology industry in the Bay Area in California. He would occasionally visit his father once or twice a year and eventually only for a few days at Christmas. One day he received a call from a nurse at a hospital telling him that his father was not doing well and that his father needed him at the hospital. Anthony was so wealthy he was able to book a private plane to fly back to be with his father. However, Anthony was too late, his father died just a few minutes before his arrival to his father's hospital room.

When Anthony arrived in the room, a chaplain was there with whom he started talking to about his father. He told the chaplain his whole life story, about his mother dying, about all the money he made and then there was a long pause and he then said, "I have all the money I could ever want, but I can't buy my father back. I can't buy my way out of death. I have been trying to buy my way out of death my whole life and look what it has gotten me. Absolutely nothing." He then went on to say, "I wish I just had one more minute with my father, I would give up all my money to spend one more minute with my father to tell him that I love him."

Upon returning to California after his father's death and funeral, Anthony sought out professional counseling at the suggestion of the chaplain. It was during these sessions that Anthony was able to further name his death anxiety and the multiple levels of losses that he had experienced throughout his life. These losses were covert in nature because he suppressed and supplanted them with his quest for success.

The counselor facilitated a recognition that he possessed a deep covert death anxiety which he had been battling since the loss of his mother. This of course confirmed the multiple levels of loss that had built up throughout his life. The counselor helped Anthony acquire the skills and tools to face his loss overtly. Anthony then told the counselor that he needed to get his life in order, make up for lost time and continue to explore how his suffering is informing his way of living. This case study demonstrates how confronting death can help to remind us how it is our relationships that are priceless, not one's possessions. Yalom (2008) summed up this idea when he stated, "The physicality of death destroys us, but the idea of death saves us." New life can be found when we confront death. Life is therefore all about confronting death and not shying away from the question, "Do you ever think about death?" The next section will discuss practical ways of engaging and considering death, loss, and grief.

ENGAGING WITH DEATH AND LOSS

Individuals experiencing grief and loss are often challenged to find words to express the level and intensity of their feelings, experiences, and thoughts. Further, when supporting someone in the midst of their grief and loss, finding the words to provide comfort for that person is extremely difficult. Complicating things further, many suffering with loss and grief often feel compelled to mask their feelings, experiences, and thoughts because finding words to express the level of personal suffering seems impossible.

Exacerbating this problem is the fact that many counseling training programs leave graduates ill-equipped to engage openly and confidently with grief and loss (Gamino, 2017; Wass, 2004). It seems that the topic is only briefly addressed in human development courses but the time and depth necessary for deep understanding does not typically occur for counselors in training. In fact, many licensed counselors have indicated that they have pursued training post-graduation to build their skill for working with clients struggling with loss and grief (Suomala Folkerds, 2019; Suomala Folkerds & Coursol, 2023; Kaus, 2022). This suggests that many counseling professionals are ill prepared to help clients if they have not engaged in death education or pursued their work in the journey through grief and loss. This death education also must work to include a multicultural counseling focus due to the wide variety of approaches and understandings of the death experience (Breen et al. 2022; Fowler, 2008).

Death Anxiety

In addition, seminal research has demonstrated that beginning counselors rank situations that deal with death as more uncomfortable (Kirchberg & Neimeyer, 1991; Kirchberg et al., 1998). Jankauskaite et al. (2021) supported this finding as only 18.3% of their sample of university counseling center therapists reported that they had received graduate coursework in death education. In addition, over half of this sample endorsed that they would benefit by further clinical training in grief and bereavement. Furthermore, research suggests that experience and training can help to lower levels of discomfort and the more experience one has, the more comfortable when working with death and loss situations (Blueford et al. 2022;Terry et al., 1996). Thus, the more experience the clinician has with grief and bereavement, the more they are poised to confront their death anxiety.

Jeffreys (2011) has described the importance of what he termed the *exquisite witness*. The *exquisite witness* is a health care, pastoral, or volunteer care provider who enters the sacred space between two human souls—having the deepest respect for the yearning, seeking, and wishful hopes of the other to diminish pain and survive in a new world after a loss. Meaning one must have the capacity to sit with a person in their suffering until their words can be articulated. An *exquisite witness* must address personal loss issues through three dimensions (the heart - emotions), have knowledge about what to expect from grieving people (head dimension-cognitions), and the skills to respond both usefully and reassuringly (hands dimension - behaviors). Without appropriate training and self-awareness these dimensions of helping can be difficult to achieve.

It is important to understand that American culture often intimates that there is a proper timeline and way to grieve because there is such value placed upon getting back to normal. This is demonstrated in polices surrounding bereavement leave whether in business or educational settings. It is important to affirm that there is no one way to properly grieve and everyone has their own unique process and timeline.

Clearly, we need to learn how to talk about death in order to be responsive and effectively support those experiencing death and loss. Thus, counselor educators are called to engage in teaching strategies to help students more deeply engage with topics of change, loss, and grief. One way to achieve a greater understanding of these topics and develop greater self-understanding and skill set is through creative pedagogical approaches.

Counselor educators have engaged in creative approaches to teaching using small group activities, art appreciation, acting theory, photovoice and music (Davis et al., 2020; Gladding, 2020; Hammond & Gantt, 1998; Henderson & Gladding, 1998; Jodry & Reid, 2020; Lenes et al., 2015; Minor et al., 2013; Zeglin, 2019). One common thread through all of these approaches is the goal of enhancing the level of processing within the student to have a more meaningful connection to the material. Such techniques help the student more deeply understanding the content they are studying and to personally relate to course material. In addition, such reflection also helps the student to reflect upon their own use of self in the counseling process. It is critical that counselor trainees have the capacity to more deeply understand course material and how such material relates to their own selves in their practice of counseling (Gladding, 2020; Schwartz, 2019; Wosket, 1999).

This chapter describes three creative strategies including music, literature, and art as a means to encourage students engagement in critical self-reflection with loss and grief material. These creative strategies are based upon the pedagogical philosophy of Freire (2000). Freire eschewed the banking style of education and instead prescribed a model that promoted a critical consciousness encouraging a deeper engagement with course material and how such material is integrated into the students' life. Thus, the importance is placed upon the student to first and foremost think critically. Through critical consciousness and dialogue, the student becomes more conscious of their situation in life and the material they are learning. He referred to this process as conscientization. Thus, the creative approaches provided in this chapter are more concerned with the process of learning rather than overly focusing on content. By focusing on the process of education, the student will gain the necessary content and perhaps learn it even more effectively (Schwartz, 2019).

Relatedly, Schwartz (2019) in her book *Connected Teaching* references relational cultural theory which emphasizes the importance of connection and relationship with students. Schwartz affirmed the importance of relationship in teaching and that by focusing on relationship, students will gain the knowledge and content being taught in the course (Schwartz, 2019). In a profession that has consistently affirmed the value of a positive relationship with clients, it seems critical to affirm the value of relationship with students to elicit their willingness to engage in challenging content and with a self-reflective lens. The overarching goal then is to embed one's teaching in a relational model that can provide a safe learning environment where students are more comfortable to share their own perspective, questions, and ideas. As such students will experience the freedom to engage in deep critical thinking about themselves, the course topic, the profession, their community, and world (Knewstubb, 2016; Karpouza & Emvalotis, 2019; Hobson & Morrison-Saunders, 2013).

Creative strategies speak to Schwartz's recommendations and to students across a range of diverse cultures and backgrounds. Every culture around the world typically has music, literature, and art that represents who they are as a people. And, in many ways these creative products represent a universal language that all people speak. In fact, creative activities can work to unite people across different cultures and backgrounds and help students to connect in deep ways (Gladding, 2020; Henderson & Gladding, 1998; Schwartz, 2019).

Death Anxiety

ENGAGING STUDENTS WITH CREATIVE STRATEGIES

When implementing creative strategies, the instructor plays the role of a facilitator who works to co-construct the dialogue and facilitate self-reflection. The instructor works to promote a non-hierarchical approach within the activities and discussions, recognizing the importance of also participating and engaging with the topic.

When using this approach, it is critical to set up the ground rules of engagement with the creative strategies and the reflective process. Such ground rules include demonstrating respect for each other as each person shares from their own particular background and perspective. It is important to affirm from the outset of the activities that the sharing with one another is done with a spirit of cultural humility, respect, and confidentiality. The instructor plays the role of a facilitator who works to co-construct the dialogue. While working to promote a non-hierarchical approach, it is important for the instructor to also be a participant (Freire, 2000). This also has the added benefit of the instructor modeling what it might look like to engage in critical self-reflection and discussion. The following sections will describe the use of music, literature, and art as strategies to engage meaningfully with loss and grief.

Music

In this activity the student is asked to identify a song that represents or speaks to their personal story related to grief, loss, or change. After choosing a particular piece of music the student will share what their music means to them and how the song or music speaks to their grief and loss story and how it contributes to self-understanding. The instructor facilitates discussion inquiring as to how the lyrics and music may also speak to them and express their story. This activity will help students engage at a deeper level of thinking about loss and grief and will likely increase connections with their peers (Gladding, 2020). Again, it is recommended that the instructor share their own chosen music piece or song to engage in a non-hierarchical dialogue with their students (Cardany, 2018; Freire, 2000; Watkins, 2012).

Literature

For this activity, the authors have found it very helpful to read a children's book aloud to the class with messages about loss, grief or change. The rationale for this approach includes the fact that we all house a child within us and most of us have positive memories of being read to as a child. Additionally, Children's literature tends to be brief and the word choices are generally simplistic but deeply speak to feelings (D. Coursol, personal communication, 2024). After modeling this process, students are then directed to select a poem or excerpt from a piece of literature that is descriptive of their experience with grief, loss, or change. This type of engagement allows the student to experience and discuss issues surrounding grief and loss more deeply. In addition, it helps students begin to personally understand the complicated nature of death and that death is permanent. Thus, communication that is open and honest is paramount. **Art**

In this activity the student is asked to find a piece of art that represents a topic related to loss, grief, or change. The student selects a piece of art that would represent how the art contributes to expressing their personal journey. Again, the student will share with the class how their experience with grief or loss is represented by their chosen art piece. This helps students to engage a deeper level of thinking on the topic and provides a means of connecting with their fellow students. As with the previous strategies it would be beneficial for the instructor to share their own chosen art piece to further engage in a non-hierarchical dialogue with their students (Freire, 2000; Watkins, 2012). Counselors in training must learn to use themselves as instruments to help other people and it is critical therefore to engage in self-exploration; art can help the student to go deeper with their own self-reflection (Gladding, 2020; Hammond & Gantt, 1998; Shukla et al. 2022).

Creative approaches such as music, art, literature, and art can help students to engage more deeply with the content grief and loss. Furthermore, it can facilitate students forming stronger relationships with their instructor, greater self-understanding and increased engagement and understanding of the counseling curriculum (Zeglin et al, 2019). The literature has affirmed that creative approaches provide a more relational bond between the students and the instructor ultimately leading to the student seeing the value of course material on both a personal and professional level (Schwartz, 2019; Quinlan, 2016).

SUMMARY

This chapter has attempted to provide an understanding of death anxiety in American Culture. The historical contributions to death anxiety and its context in the US were also described. TMT was offered evidential information as to how human beings are on a constant mission to avoid the certainty of death. This chapter has worked to normalize the concept of death anxiety and its relationship to grief and loss. The reader was provided with several creative strategies to engage with death and loss to facilitate student engagement and self-reflection around grief and loss. In addition, a case study was provided to help the reader acknowledge the value of unmasking covert death anxiety. The unmasking of covert death anxiety takes courage but will lead to new insights, potentially less regret and new life. The concept of cultural humility was introduced along with creative strategies to help

Death Anxiety

the counselor trainee to name their own death anxiety and subsequently, to serve as an exquisite witness with their clients as they attempt to manage their loss and grief. This work of sitting with others in their suffering was best stated by Thomas Hardy in his Poem Tenebris II, when he stated (p.13), "If a way to the better there be, it exacts a full look at the worst," (Maynard, 1991).

Barbie tried to bring her personal death anxiety to her community of friends, but they initially shut her down. This could be in part because they too had death anxiety but were not ready to face it. The movie was all about a sort of coming together to face the problems of the world. This also leads one to consider that death anxiety should not be dealt with on an individual basis, but rather from a collective perspective (i.e., one's community). It is when the community comes together that we can transform our death anxiety into new life and growth. Finally, the hope of this chapter is to help the reader begin to seek and find answers to Barbie's question, "Do you ever think about death?" (Gerwig, 2023).

DISCUSSION QUESTIONS

1. Do you ever think about death? How does death inform your life and your practice as a counselor?
2. In your own words, how would you define death anxiety?
3. Where have you seen examples of death anxiety both personally and professionally?
4. Can you think of other creative approaches that might help you to explore your experience of death?
5. How has Covid-19 influenced and impacted your experience of death anxiety in the United States and the world?
6. How might you engage in a conversation with a client or supervisee about death anxiety?

REFERENCES

Applewhite, A. (2020). *The chair rocks: A manifesto against ageism.* Celedon Books.

Becker, E. (1997). *The denial of death.* Free Press Paperbacks.

Blueford, J. M., Diambra, J. F., & Wheat, L. S. (2022). Counselor preparedness to counsel grieving clients: Insights and implications. *Death Studies*, 40(10), 2413–2423. 10.1080/07481187.2021.195664434308795

Breen, L. J., Kawashima, D., Joy, K., Cadell, S., Roth, D., Chow, A., & Macdonald, M. E. (2022). Grief literacy: A call to action for compassionate communities. *Death Studies*, 46(2), 425–433. 10.1080/07481187.2020.173978032189580

Cardany, A. B. (2018). Mitigating death anxiety: Identifying music's role in terror management. *Psychology of Music*, 46(1), 3–17. 10.1177/0305735617690600

Castano, E., Leidner, B., Bonacossa, A., Nikkah, J., Perrulli, R., Spencer, B., & Humphrey, N. (2011). Ideology, fear of death and death anxiety. *Political Psychology*, 32(4), 601–621. 10.1111/j.1467-9221.2011.00822.x

Cohen, F., Solomon, S., Maxfield, M., Pyszczynski, T., & Greenberg, J. (2004). Fatal Attraction: The effects of mortality salience on evaluations of charismatic, task oriented, and relationship-oriented leaders. *Psychological Science*, 15(12), 846–851. 10.1111/j.0956-7976.2004.00765.x15563330

Davis, E. S., Norton, A., & Chapman, R. (2020). Counselors'-in-training perceptions of using music for theoretical conceptualization training. *Journal of Creativity in Mental Health*, 15(4), 443–456. 10.1080/15401383.2020.1731041

Fowler, K. L. (2008). The wholeness of things: Infusing diversity and social justice into death education. *Omega*, 57(1), 53–91. 10.2190/OM.57.1.d18507327

Freire, P. (2000). *Pedagogy of the oppressed* (30th anniversary ed.). Continuum.

Gamino, L. A. (2017). ADEC at 40: Second half of life wisdom for the future of death education and counseling. *Death Studies*, 41(3), 188–195. 10.1080/0748118 7.2017.128933128151061

Gasiorowska, A., Zaleskiewicz, T., & Kesebir, P. (2018). Money as existential anxiety buffer: Exposure to money precents mortality reminder from leading to increased death thoughts. *Journal of Experimental Social Psychology*, 79, 394–409. 10.1016/j.jesp.2018.09.004

Gerwig, G. (Director.) (2023). *Barbie* [Film]. Warner Brothers Pictures.

Death Anxiety

Gladding, S. T. (2020). *The creative arts in counseling* (6th ed.). American Counseling Association.

Grauf-Grounds, C., & Rivera, P. M. (2020). The ORCA-stance as a practice beyond cultural humility. In C. Grauf-Grounds, T Schermer Sellers, S. Edwards, H.S. Cheon, D. MacDonald, S. Whitney & P. Rivera. (Eds.). *A practice beyond cultural humility: How clinicians can work more effectively in a diverse world* (pp. 8-25). Routledge.

Greenberg, J., Pyszczynski, T., Solomon, S., Rosenblatt, A., Veeder, M., Kirkland, S., & Lyon, D. (1990). Evidence of terror management II: The effects of mortality salience on reactions to those who threaten or bolster the cultural worldview. *Journal of Personality and Social Psychology*, 58(2), 308–318. 10.1037/0022-3514.58.2.308

Hammond, L. C., & Gantt, L. (1998). Using art in counseling: Ethical considerations. *Journal of Counseling and Development*, 76(3), 271–276. 10.1002/j.1556-6676.1998.tb02542.x

Heidegger, M. (2008). *Being and Time*. Harper Perennial Modern Classics.

Henderson, D. A., & Gladding, S. T. (1998). The creative arts in counseling: A multicultural approach. *The Arts in Psychotherapy*, 25(3), 183–187. 10.1016/S0197-4556(98)00011-2

Hobson, J., & Morrison-Saunders, A. (2013). Reframing teaching relationships: From student-centered to subject centered learning. *Teaching in Higher Education*, 18(7), 773–783. 10.1080/13562517.2013.836095

Jankauskaite, G., O'Brien, K. M., & Yang, N. (2021). Assessing knowledge and predicting grief counseling skills among university counseling center therapists. *The Counseling Psychologist*, 49(3), 458–484. 10.1177/0011000020983525

Jeffreys, S. (2011). *Helping grieving people: When tears are not enough* (2nd ed.). Routledge. 10.4324/9780203856154

Jodry, J., & Reid, M. (2020). Acting theory applied to counseling: Stanislavski continues to contribute to psychic healing. *Journal of Creativity in Mental Health*, 15(2), 223–234. 10.1080/15401383.2019.1683110

Jong, J. (2021). Death anxiety and religion. *Current Opinion in Psychology*, 40, 40–44. 10.1016/j.copsyc.2020.08.00432942111

Karpouza, E., & Emvalotis, A. (2019). Exploring the teacher student relationship in graduate education a constructivist grounded theory. *Teaching in Higher Education*, 24(2), 121–140. 10.1080/13562517.2018.1468319

Kaus, K. J. (2022). *Death Anxiety: A Quantitative Exploration of Professional Counselors Experiences* [Doctoral dissertation, Minnesota State University, Mankato]. Cornerstone: A Collection of Scholarly and Creative Works for Minnesota State University, Mankato. https://cornerstone.lib.mnsu.edu/etds/942/

Kierkegaard, S. (1981). *The concept of anxiety*. Princeton University Press. 10.1515/9781400846979-002

Kierkegaard, S. (1983). *The sickness unto death*. Princeton University Press.

Kirchberg, T. M., & Neimeyer, R. A. (1991). Reactions of beginning counselors to situations involving death and dying. *Death Studies*, 15(6), 603–610. 10.1080/074 81189108252548101115708

Kirchberg, T. M., Neimeyer, R. A., & James, R. K. (1998). Beginning counselors' death concerns and empathic responses to client situations involving death and grief. *Death Studies*, 22(2), 99–120. 10.1080/07481189820162310182421

Knewstubb, B. (2016). The learning-teaching nexus: Modelling the learning-teaching relationship in higher education. *Studies in Higher Education*, 41(3), 525–540. 10.1080/03075079.2014.934802

Konigsberg, R. D. (2011). *The truth about grief: The myth of its five stages and the new science of loss*. Simon & Schuster.

Kosloff, S., Greenberg, J., Weise, D., & Solomon, S. (2009). The effects of mortality salience on political preferences: The roles of charisma and political orientation. *Journal of Experimental Social Psychology*, 46(1), 139–145. 10.1016/j.jesp.2009.09.002

Kubler-Ross, E. (1970). *On death and dying*. Collier Books/Macmillan Publishing Co.

Kumpasoglu, G. B., Eltan, S., Merdan-Yilidiz, E. D., & Batigun, A. D. (2020). Mediating the role of life satisfaction and death anxiety in the relationship between dark triad and social media addiction. *Personality and Individual Differences*, 172, 1–8.

Lenes, E., Swank, J., & Nash, S. (2015). A qualitative exploration of a music experience within a counselor education sexuality course. *Journal of Creativity in Mental Health*, 10(2), 216–231. 10.1080/15401383.2014.983255

Levy, B. (2022). *Breaking the age code: How your beliefs about aging determine how long and how well you live*. William Morrow & Co.

Magee, B. (1997). *The philosophy of Schopenhauer*. Clarendon Press. 10.1093/0198237227.001.0001

Maynard, K. K. (1991). *Thomas Hardy's tragic poetry*. University of Iowa Press.

Death Anxiety

McCoyd, J. L., Goldblatt, H. E., Hennessy, K., & Akincigil, A. (2023). Revising ruling discourses: The griefwork evidence-to-practice gap and the mental health workforce. *Death Studies*, 47(10), 1–10. 10.1080/07481187.2023.217115936695284

Menzies, R. E., & Menzies, R. G. (2020). Death anxiety in the time of COVID-19: Theoretical explanations and clinical implications. *Cognitive Behaviour Therapist*, 13, e19. 10.1017/S1754470X2000021534191938

Menzies, R. E., & Menzies, R. G. (2021). *Mortals: How the fear of death shaped human society*. Allen & Unwin.

Menzies, R. E., Neimeyer, R. A., & Menzies, R. G. (2020). Death anxiety, loss, and grief in the time of COVID-19. *Behaviour Change*, 37(3), 111–115. 10.1017/bec.2020.10

Minor, A. J., Moody, S. J., Tadlock-Marlo, R., Pender, R., & Person, M. (2013). Music as a medium for cohort development. *Journal of Creativity in Mental Health*, 8(4), 381–394. 10.1080/15401383.2013.857928

Munley, P. H., & Johnson, P. D. (2003). Theory and practice: Ernest Becker: A vital resource for counseling psychology. *Counselling Psychology Quarterly*, 16(4), 363–372. 10.1080/09515070310001636779

Ozguc, S., Serin, E. K., & Tanriverdi, D. (2024). Death anxiety associated with coronavirus (COVID-19) disease: A systematic Review and Meta Analysis. *Omega*, 88(3), 823–856. 10.1177/00302228211050503334622711

Plato, . (1975). *Phaedo* (Gallop, D., Trans.). Clarendon Press.

Pyszczynski, T., Solomon, S., & Greenberg, J. (2015). Thirty years of terror management theory: From genesis to revelation. In Olson, J. M., & Zanna, M. P. (Eds.), Vol. 52, pp. 1–70). Advances in Experimental Social Psychology. Academic Press.

Quinlan, K. M. (2016). How emotion matters in four key relationships in teaching and learning in higher education. *College Teaching*, 64(3), 101–111. 10.1080/87567555.2015.1088818

Ratts, M. J. (2009). Social justice counseling: Toward the development of a fifth force among counseling paradigms. *The Journal of Humanistic Counseling, Education and Development*, 48(2), 160–172. 10.1002/j.2161-1939.2009.tb00076.x

Sawyer, J. S. (2024). Grief and bereavement beliefs and their associations with death anxiety and complicated grief in a U.S. college student sample. *Death Studies*, 1–12. Advance online publication. 10.1080/07481187.2024.234993338713539

Schwartz, H. L. (2019). *Connected teaching: Relationship, power and mattering in higher education*. Stylus Publishing.

Serlin, I. A., & Criswell, E. (2014). Humanistic psychology and women: A critical historical perspective. In Schneider, K. J., Fraser Pierson, J., & Bugental, F. T. (Eds.), *The Handbook of Humanistic Psychology: Theory, Research, and Practice* (pp. 27–40). SAGE Publications, Incorporated.

Shukla, A., Choudhari, S. G., Gaidhane, A. M., & Quazi Syed, Z. (2022). Role of Art Therapy in the Promotion of Mental Health: A Critical Review. *Cureus*, 14(8). Advance online publication. 10.7759/cureus.2802636134083

Singh, H., Haghayegh, A. T., Shah, R., Cheung, L., Wijekoon, S., Reel, K., & Sangrar, R. (2023). A qualitative exploration of allied health providers' perspectives on cultural humility in palliative and end-of-life care. *BMC Palliative Care*, 22(92), 1–14. 10.1186/s12904-023-01214-437434238

Solomon, S., Greenberg, J., & Pyszczynski, T. (2004). The cultural animal: Twenty years of terror management theory and research. In Greenberg, J., Pyszczynski & Koole, S. (Eds.), *Handbook of experimental psychology*. (pp. 13-34). Guilford Press.

Solomon, S., Greenberg, J., & Pyszczynski, T. (2016). *The worm at the core: On the role of death in life*. Penguin.

Suomala Folkerds, A. (2019). *Death: A qualitative content analysis of counseling journals, 1986-2016* [Doctoral dissertation, Minnesota State University, Mankato]. Cornerstone: A Collection of Scholarly and Creative Works for Minnesota State University, Mankato. https://cornerstone.lib.mnsu.edu/etds/942/

Suomala Folkerds, A., & Coursol, D. H. (2023). An Examination of Death in Premier Counseling Journals. *The Interactive Journal of Global Leadership and Learning, 2*(3).

Terry, M. L., Bivens, A. J., & Neimeyer, R. A. (1996). Comfort and empathy of experienced counselors in client situations involving death and loss. *Omega*, 32(4), 269–285. 10.2190/WJ89-KCTY-DBWG-8QTX

Tervalon, M. and Murray-García, J. (1998). *Cultural Humility Versus Cultural Competence*.

Tervalon, M., & Murray-García, J. (1998, May). Cultural Humility Versus Cultural Competence: A Critical Distinction in Defining Physician Training Outcomes in Multicultural Education. *Journal of Health Care for the Poor and Underserved*, 9(2), 117–125. 10.1353/hpu.2010.0233

Tillich, P. (1952). *The courage to be*. Yale University Press.

Death Anxiety

Washington, D. (2019). *Fall Forward.* Commencement address at University of Pennsylvania.

Wass, H. (2004). A perspective on the current state of death education. *Death Studies*, 28(4), 289–308. 10.1080/07481180490043231515129687

Watkins, M. (2012). Revolutionary Leadership: From Paulo Freire to the Occupy Movement. Journal for Social Action in Counseling and Psychology. *Journal for Social Action in Counseling and Psychology*, 4(2), 1–22. 10.33043/JSACP.4.2.1-22

Wosket, V. (1999). *The therapeutic use of self: Counselling practice, research, and supervision.* Taylor & Frances/Routledge.

Yalom, I. D. (1980). *Existential Psychotherapy.* Basic Books.

Yalom, I. D. (2008). *Staring at the Sun.* Jossey-Bass.

Zeglin, R. J., Niemela, D. R., Rosenblatt, K., & Hernandez-Garcia, J. (2019). Using photovoice as a counselor education pedagogical tool: A pilot. *Journal of Creativity in Mental Health*, 14(2), 258–268. 10.1080/15401383.2019.1581116

ADDITIONAL READING

Bonanno, G. A. (2019). *The other side of sadness: what the new science of bereavement tells us about life after loss.* Hachette Book Group.

Boss, P. (2022). *The myth of closure: Ambiguous loss in a time of pandemic and change.* W.W. Norton and Co.

Clark, M. H. (2024). Everywhere still: A Book About Loss, Grief, and the Way Love Continues. *Compendium (Newtown, Pa.).*

Hansen, W. (2002). *The next place.* Waldman House Press.

Hooyman, N., Kramer, B., & Sanders, S. (2021). *Living through loss: Interventions across the lifespan.* Columbia University Press.

Viorst, J. (1998). *Necessary losses: The loves, illusions, dependencies, and impossible expectations that all of us have to give up in order to grow.* Simon and Schuster.

Chapter 4
Grief on Pause:
Understanding the Concept of Grief Avoidance Behaviors

Tobi Yvette Russell

Central Michigan University, USA

ABSTRACT

This chapter reviews the experience of grief that focuses on avoidance. Avoidance can be adaptive in certain situations, including in some cultural practices. However, at other times, avoidance can be maladaptive for the griever. When avoidance is maladaptive for the griever, both physical and emotional concerns can cause long-term difficulties for the grieving process. The purpose of this chapter is to provide the reader with an understanding of grief avoidance behavior. The chapter will describe the common patterns that are seen in grief avoidance behavior, types of experiences leading to grief avoidance behavior, the physical and emotional outcomes of grief avoidance behavior, various assessment tools for grief avoidance behavior and evidence-based treatment for prolonged grief disorders. Dr. Wolfelt created a framework of common patterns of grief avoidance that included: the postponer, the displacer, the replacer, the minimizer, and the somaticizer.

INTRODUCTION

Grief is one of the most universal experiences that human beings have in their lives. For many, the grief experience is accompanied by sadness, loneliness, and despair. Others express anger, numbness, confusion and/or guilt (Ang, 2023). People can also report positive feelings such as happiness, contentment, and acceptance of the loss as well. However, one significant component of grief can also be grief-related avoidance or what this author calls grief on pause. When one avoids, it is typically to

DOI: 10.4018/979-8-3693-1375-6.ch004

Copyright © 2024, IGI Global. Copying or distributing in print or electronic forms without written permission of IGI Global is prohibited.

Grief on Pause

escape distressing emotions, to escape emotionally intense situations, or to manage the impact of the loss (Meichenbaum & Myers, 2016).

Avoidance can be an adaptive way for some to deal with grief. Some grievers struggle to detach from thinking about the loss and the thoughts are in the form of rumination. Rumination in bereavement is defined as a "conscious, recurrent, repetitive, and self-focused thinking process that revolves around the death, the deceased person, and the feelings associated to the bereavement experience" (Tang, 2022). Rumination in bereavement is seen through three different lenses: as a way to cognitively process the loss, as a way to avoid coping with the loss, or as a way to confront coping with the loss. Cognitively processing the loss is seen as an adaptive form of grieving that promotes growth. Avoiding coping with the loss is when the griever is not able to deal with the emotional pain in reality and removes themselves from the grieving process. Confronting the coping process occurs when the grieving individual solely focuses on the negative emotions of grief (Tang, 2022). When an individual ruminates to confront the coping, the behavior was seen as making the emotions worse instead of making them better. In fact, severe ruminators became so avoidant of reality that they were not aware of stimuli (Eisma et al., 2021).

While ruminating about grief work is counterproductive, suppression of grief also does not help individuals cope over time (Eisma, Lang & Boelen, 2020). In fact, there are studies that indicate deliberate grief avoidance was a precursor to poor adjustment to loss (Eisma, Lang & Boelen, 2020). Avoidance is seen as a symptom that maintains maladaptive grief reactions.

Grief is not the only concern that people try to avoid. For example, phobias are behaviors that individuals also try to avoid in an effort to feel better. However, what has been learned over time is that to gain relief from a phobia, individuals need to approach, not avoid the feared object. Avoiding the object may help in the short-term, but long-term deliberate avoidance maintains the fear.

In 2020, the COVID-19 pandemic posed a global concern that had wide-reaching implications due to the contagiousness and severity of respiratory disease. Due to these and other factors, physical distancing measures and lockdowns were put in place to protect individuals prior to access to a vaccine. Several research studies found increases in psychological concerns including higher levels of anxiety and stress. In one international study, that looked at 1408 individuals living in Italy and ranging in age from 18 to 88 years old, researchers set out to explore the role of anxiety, coping strategies and defense mechanisms as they related to the COVID-19 pandemic (Gori et al., 2021).

Participants completed four different measures including the Ten-Item Perceived Stress Scale (PSS-10), the State-Trait Anxiety Inventory-Form X3 (STAI-X3), the Coping Orientation to Problems Experienced-New Italian Version (COPE-NVI) and the Forty Item Defence Style Questionnaire (DSQ-40). The study found that avoid-

Grief on Pause

ance as a coping strategy was linked to higher perceived stress levels. Ultimately, short-term avoidance may relieve negative feelings for a short period of time, but it did not alleviate long-term psychological distress (Gori et al, 2021).

In another study that surveyed 3075 American and Canadian adults, worry, self-protection, and avoidance were explored. These adults aged 18 to 94 years old, completed 16 different surveys related to COVID-19 stress responses. It was determined that worry about the severity of COVID-19 was central to the development of COVID Stress Syndrome. COVID Stress Syndrome is comprised of five interconnected factors: Fear of contracting COVID-19 through contaminated objects or breathing contaminated air; worry about financial and social impact of COVID-19, fear that individuals outside of one's own country of origin are spreading COVID-19, symptoms of traumatic stress, and compulsive checking in addition to seeking reassurance from others (Taylor et al., 2020). Worry was found to be related to many forms of avoidance such as avoidance of the symptoms of COVID-19, avoidance of socioeconomic impact and even avoidance of the belief that COVID-19 was dangerous (i.e. minimizing the seriousness of COVID-19) (Taylor et al., 2020).

Brennan wrote in Psychology Today (Sussex Publishers, 2020) that the mental health concerns as they relate to COVID-19 were developing into an avalanche of psychological turmoil. A study that included 6854 adults from the United States and Canada, with an average age of 49.8 years old utilized the Covid Stress Syndrome scales developed by Taylor et al., 2020. Correlations between anxiety, depression and other demographics with Covid Stress Syndrome were analyzed. About half of the sample self-isolated for an average of 10 days. Participants that scored higher on the Covid Stress Syndrome scales, reported more distress during their self-isolation (Sussex Publishers, 2020).

This chapter will describe the common patterns that are seen in grief avoidance behavior, types of experiences leading to grief avoidance behavior, the physical and emotional outcomes of grief avoidance behavior, various assessment tools for grief avoidance behavior and evidence-based treatment for prolonged grief disorders.

BACKGROUND ON GRIEF AND GRIEF TREATMENT

In the United States, somewhere around 10 million individuals experience grief every year. In 2016 alone, more than 2.7 million people living in the United States died and because of their passing, left between 1-5 family members and/or friends impacted by their loss (Iglewicz et. al., 2019). A population-based study found that 96% of all adults have had the feeling of grief after the death of loved one a minimum of one time but with a median number of five times in one's life (Wilson et al., 2020). In addition, the prevalence of individuals struggling with grief symptoms

Grief on Pause

has increased as a result of the COVID-19 pandemic although the exact number is not yet known (Prigerson, Shear & Reynolds, 2022).

In 2020, prior to the pandemic, a literature review was completed looking at articles on the topics of prolonged grief, complicated grief, traumatic grief, complex grief, persistent grief, or complicated bereavement. There were 11 research studies reviewed (3 from the United States, 1 each from Italy, the Netherlands, Spain, Denmark, South Korea, Germany and Sweden) and 1 multi-country study from Canada, Australia, the United Kingdom and the United States. All of these studies focused on adults and there were 551 participants. There were a variety of grief symptoms identified in these studies, however the most commonly identified was that of grief avoidance coping strategies (Wilson et al., 2020).

While there were considerations made regarding the process of some of the 11 studies, the notable finding that was highlighted was the number of individuals that were impacted by prolonged or persistent grief (Wilson et al., 2020). Nearly one-third to one-half of the participants were suffering from prolonged or persistent grief, which highlighted the ongoing need for assessment, identification and treatment of grief (Wilson et al., 2020).

COMMON PATTERNS OF GRIEF AVOIDANCE BEHAVIOR

Coping strategies are behaviors that someone does to deal with or attempt to deal with problems and/or difficulties that arise. Coping is typically not linear. More often than not, individuals may take steps forward only to take steps back or to stay stagnant (Mansoori et al, 2023). This is true of coping with loss. The feelings that an individual experiences often times has an impact on the coping strategies they choose to use (Mansoori et al., 2023). Further, some have suggested that there are specific problem-focused or emotion-focused coping strategies. This idea was ultimately developed into an assessment tool known as the Ways of Coping Questionnaire (Folkman & Lazarus, 1988; 1980). The Ways of Coping Questionnaire detailed eight types of problem or emotion-focused strategies that include: confrontive coping, distancing, self-controlling, escape-avoidance, seeking social support, planful problem-solving, accepting responsibility, and positive reappraisal. These strategies will be discussed later in conjunction with various types of avoidance patterns (Mansoori et al, 2023).

Dr. Alan Wolfelt, a leading death educator, believed that there a number of ways that individuals retreat from grief expression. Some will move back and forth between several of the patterns described below and some will remain static within one pattern. The level of impact that the avoidance has on the individual is largely based on the personal characteristics and societal influences of that person. The consequences of the avoidance are dependent upon the degree of the avoidance, however prolonged avoidance will lead to a loss of self as we "deaden our feelings" (Mosse, 2024).

Avoidance can create a stressful experience when it is combined with stress and emotional responses. However, avoidance for the purpose of protection of self, or other family members can be constructive. It can be useful in the first days after a loss when trying to manage affairs. Also, vacillating between addressing their loss and seeking respite from it can be an adaptive response (Wilson et al., 2020). Examples of maladaptive uses of avoidance could be emotional dysregulation, refraining from thinking about the person who died or places that they went, or use of substances to numb the feelings (Iglewicz et al., 2019).

Every individual has their own grief journey and within that journey each person who avoids as a coping strategy, has their own pattern of avoiding. The following sections will cover some of the avoidance patterns that may be seen during the grief experience.

The Postponer

The postponer is the individual who wants to put off their grief until another time (Wolfelt, 2021). Delay, delay, delay is the theme for this person. The belief is that the longer the grief expression is delayed, the better it will be, and that maybe over time it will eventually just go away. Unfortunately, this is not the case, as all the feelings that have been building up over time will be released, but just not in the way the individual wants them to. This unhealthy explosion of feelings then makes the person feel less able to manage their grief.

Similarly, the Ways of Coping Questionnaire (WCQ) discussed patterns of distancing and self-controlling where the individual avoids reminders of the loss. Others have described patterns of emotional suppression which included denial or refusing to accept the reality of the loss, minimizing the intensity of the loss, avoiding triggers, or numbing to avoid feeling the pain of the loss (APA, 2020).

The Displacer

The displacer is the individual who takes their grief and "moves" it elsewhere. Projection is the theme for this person. The belief is shifting grief away from the internal source and onto an external source, such as work, family, or other relationships is a less emotionally threatening situation. However, what tends to happen is that the person becomes increasingly more isolated and frustrated with life. The cycle of irritation at the smallest of events can lead to depression.

Grief on Pause

The concept of escape-avoidance from the WCQ also talked about the individual who needs to focus their attention elsewhere in order to deal with the feelings they are having. The escape is a turning away from the grief and a turning towards another activity (Brown, Bond & Topa, 2019). Displacement, distraction, or overcompensation can all be behaviors that suppress grief with something less painful (APA, 2020).

The Replacer

The replacer is the individual who takes all of the emotions they had for the person who has died and reinvests those feelings into a brand-new relationship. Move on is the theme for this person. Most often, this is done in a subconscious manner without understanding that their behavior is blocking the work of grief. This can also happen with an individual who takes all of their emotion and puts it into their job or school, resulting in overworking. The belief is that the person tries to avoid the pain of the loss by not allowing time to experience the grief.

Seeking social support (Wolfelt, 2021) can be one way that the replacer creates new relationships. This can be adaptive as long as the individual is processing the grief while engaging in social support. Substance abuse can be another way that someone "replaces" the emotions they are feeling and puts all of that feeling into a substance like alcohol or other drugs (APA, 2020).

The Minimizer

The minimizer is the individual who does not acknowledge the level of their feelings and uses rationalizations to explain their grief. Everything is okay is the theme for this person. From the outside, it may appear that the person is doing well based on what society may expect. However, internally the person is struggling as they valiantly try to convince themselves that they are getting back to their baseline. The belief is similar to other patterns as the minimizer wants to get back to their normal routine to avoid the feelings. Thinking through is valued more than feeling through.

Intellectualizing can suppress the emotional space and allow the griever to stay in a more cognitive space. Projection can be another way that someone can take the feelings they are experiencing and try to explain away any grief feelings (APA, 2020). Planful problem-solving can be another way to present to the outside world that they are getting through the grief and moving on (Wolfelt, 2021).

The Somaticizer

The somaticizer is the individual whose feelings of grief are seen through physical symptoms. Sickness/illness is the theme for this person. Vague somatic complaints are reported and for some, can become a preoccupation which then delays the grief work. The individual worries that people will not stay around with them if they are emotionally struggling, but if they are "physically struggling", they will be taken care of and comforted. This comfort is ultimately the need that they are trying to satisfy.

This pattern does not apply to those individuals who are actually experiencing physical illness during the grieving process. It should not be assumed that someone reporting physical symptoms must be somaticizing their grief. A general physical examination with a physician is the recommended way to determine if there are indeed physical symptoms that need to be treated.

Confrontive coping can occasionally happen as a result of somatization. It is described as an aggressive way of altering a situation. Risk-taking and anger can also be components of confrontive coping (Wolfelt, 2021).

As stated earlier, all patterns of the grief journey are not maladaptive. Accepting responsibility of processing the experience of grief and positive reappraisal or creating positive meaning through personal growth are both examples of adaptive ways of grieving. The positive reappraisal pattern is most often connected to religious perspectives of grief (i.e., they have gone home to be with God or it's all part of God's plan) (Magin et al., 2021).

EXPERIENCES LEADING TO GRIEF BEHAVIOR

Grief that does not appear to be effective in the healing process for individuals has been termed in many ways. Words such as absent, pathological, complicated, abnormal or conflicted are just some examples. While the vast majority of individuals experience intense emotion directly after a loss and then feel symptoms subside after a few months, there are some that become frozen in their grief state and this experience persists for years. This description does not include individuals who miss the person whom has died, but they continue to participate in daily functioning. However, what are the situations that may lead up to a person having difficulties in their grieving process?

The COVID-19 experience impacted how individuals moved through the grieving process. A common response to grief is to reach out to others in one's support system, however during the pandemic lockdowns, physical in-person connection was impossible. The social isolation inherent during COVID-19 did not allow people to grieve in a traditional way. For example, funeral services were not held in person in

Grief on Pause

most cases and some families made the choice to stream funeral services online so that others could be present virtually. Still others utilized communication through phone calls, emails, or letters. However, the grieving process was still isolating (Selman, 2020).

During the pandemic, approximately 6.6 million individuals died as a result of COVID-19 related symptoms and still more individuals died during that period of time, but for other reasons. One article reviewed 28 different studies that had been completed throughout the world regarding the coping reactions to grief during the pandemic. The overview showed that there was an impact on an individual level (affecting people being able to say goodbye, social support systems); through social distancing measures (inability to care for a loved one at their time of death, having to be physically distant from others so inability to hug or be close); and on a cultural level (inability to have a sense of community, inability to carry out cultural practices or rituals) (van Schaik et al., 2022).

Mansoori et al. (2023) identified characteristics through a study done with 20 participants living in Iran and had lost someone due to COVID-19. The average age of the participants was 39.5 years old, and they had reported grieving for at least 10 weeks. A semi-structured interview asking general questions including "What is your relationship with the deceased", "Can you explain to me how your life was after losing your loved one?" and "How do you balance family and work duties?" Patterns were identified through the participant responses. Underlying factors affecting mourning addressed responses relating to not having control over outcomes in life and death, acceptance and dealing with grief in a positive and logical way as well as the belief in religion as a foundation in healing (Mansoori et al., 2023). The public reaction to grief addressed responses relating to not feeling like others understood their grief, not having physical connection due to COVID-19 and so there was lack of understanding and receiving dismissive or curiosity responses by others (Mansoori et al, 2023). The special position and role of the deceased addressed responses related to the emotional connection to the deceased, the economic connection to the deceased and the overall presence of the deceased in their life (Mansoori et al., 2023). The nature and development of grief were responses related to the stages of grief including anger (Mansoori et al., 2023). Blaming oneself for the illness and deceased included responses of anger and sadness regarding not being with the deceased at the end of their life and feeling guilty for not being able to do anything to help the deceased (Mansoori et al., 2023). Last, confronting and managing grief addressed responses that discussed the griever changing their patterns of thinking and behavior towards people to match what the deceased did prior to passing away. Examples were behaviors such as good manners, kindness, enjoying life, and being together (Mansoori et al., 2023).

These next sections are patterns that this author proposes as evolutions from the patterns described above (postponer, displacer, replacer, minimizer, somaticizer) as well as the patterns described in the previous paragraph (underlying factors affecting mourning, the public reaction to grief, the special position and role of the deceased, the nature and development of grief, blaming oneself for the illness and death of the deceased, and confronting and managing grief).

The High Achiever Griever

The "high achiever" griever is the individual who focuses on keeping everything looking like it is going smoothly (Mansoori et al., 2023, vanSchaik et al., 2022, Wolfelt, 2021). Whether at work, school, in relationships, in family, or even in volunteer activities, the individual spends a great deal of time pretending that everything is the same as before the loss. The difference between "the replacer", discussed in the previous section, and the "high achiever" griever is that there is more of a conscious effort to make everything look effortless in their life. Typically, individuals who struggle with asking for help in a variety of situations may be more susceptible to this experience of grief avoidance.

In an interview with author Laurel Braitman, she shared that she became a grief counselor for bereaved children. Through that experience, she stated that she learned that achievement or overachievement was an effort to "control the uncontrollable". Dr. Braitman described these behaviors as a trauma response. Ultimately, she explained that she realized that it was an unhealthy coping mechanism she was receiving positive reinforcement and that the better she did, the more accolades and praise that she received. Over time, the losses caught up to her and the coping skill stopped working for her (Braitman, 2023).

The Caregiver Griever

The caregiver griever is the individual that is currently taking care of someone else either in their family or as part of their profession (Mansoori et al., 2023, vanSchaik et al., 2022, Wolfelt, 2021). The term "sandwich generation" was created by social workers Dorothy Miller and Elaine Brody in the 1980s (Page, 2023). Members of the "sandwich generation" who are taking care of children and elderly parents or those just in charge of taking care of a parent/parents can fall into this experience. Other examples may be emergency room physicians or other helping professionals such as nurses, counselors, or first responders. The focus becomes helping the other person process their grief and to put their own grief responses on hold.

Grief on Pause

The average age of a caregiver in the United States is approximately 48 years old. There has not been enough research done on the caregiving experience of emerging adults. Informal and family caregivers are typically unpaid and the majority of them are female, making up 66% of the caregiving population (Horowitz, 2022). While some studies have shown the positive effects of caregiving, such as mastery, increase in emotional closeness with the family member and sense of purpose, the majority of the literature has found negative effects. The impact appears to be both on the family member and the caregiver. Examples of the negative effects are physical demands, cost, mental health risks and exhaustion (Horowitz, 2022).

Researchers have indicated that caregiving itself can determine the trajectory of grief. For example, when caregivers described their experience as positive, they tended to report less mental health symptoms, better quality of life, increased social activity and decreased use of medications. Conversely, when caregivers identified their experience as negative, they reported guilt, depression, and increased stress (Page, 2023).

The Traumatic Event Griever

Some grief occurs after a trauma such as a house fire, car accident, mass shooting, natural disaster, as well as COVID-19. When a trauma occurs, the individual experiences the symptoms of Posttraumatic Stress Disorder in addition to the grief process.

The first study to look at prolonged grief disorder (PGD), posttraumatic stress disorder (PTSD), and depression in a sample of individuals who had been exposed to trauma and engaged in treatment was able to look specifically at the relationships between the symptoms of PGD, PTSD and depression (Djelantik et al., 2019). There were 458 participants with an average age of 49.1. Results suggested that excluding symptoms of PGD would omit a large part of the picture that would help to create better treatment options for individuals experiencing traumatic grief. Results showed that symptoms of PGD, PTSD, and depression tended to show up in clusters. The clusters were identified as symptom level: 'avoidance of reminders of the loss' and 'avoidance of the traumatic event' tended to be strongly connected when the loss was the triggering event for trauma (Djelantik et al., 2019). The second cluster was at the syndrome level, when symptoms that normally would be part of one diagnosis were seen as a part of multiple diagnoses. For example, "loss of interest" typically seen in depression, was often presented with "difficulty concentrating" and "irritability" typically seen in PTSD (Djelantik et al., 2019). Last, there appeared to be a connection between distinct, but conceptually related reactions such as "feeling distant from others" (PTSD), "feelings of worthlessness" (depression), and "confusion about one's role in life" and "difficulty trusting others" (PGD). Therefore, treatment interventions that focus on identity disruptions and finding purpose after the loss of a loved one have been shown to be effective (Djelantik et al., 2019).

In this particular study, violent loss and the loss of a partner or child yielded more PGD symptoms than depression or PTSD symptoms. Violent loss was most strongly associated with difficulty accepting the loss, a continued sense of shock, bitterness, and yearning. This connection further identifies the relationship between PGD, PTSD, and depression. PGD symptoms preceded higher PTSD symptoms over a period of time for grieving adults (Djelantik et al., 2019). In addition, the loss of a partner or child was most strongly related to difficulty moving on with life and that life has no meaning. The findings from this study highlight the need for clinicians working with clients experiencing trauma to also assess for bereavement and PGD symptoms in order to obtain the most thorough clinical presentation possible (Djelantik et al., 2019).

No matter whether the trauma was natural or human-caused, traumatic grief can be compounded by anger, anxiety, loss of safety/security and sadness. Traumatic grief often lasts much longer and individuals struggle to get back to their normal activities of living (SAMHSA, 2017). One study in Israel looked at eighty-four staff members at schools (teachers, counselors, psychologists and principals) where there was a student suicide within the past five years. The study set out to determine where there were differences in symptoms of traumatic grief among the four categories of staff members. The results concluded that the staff members who had less coping and crisis training, and more administrative responsibilities showed more symptoms of trauma and complicated grief (Tiech Fire et al, 2022).

The Cultural Expectations Griever

As indicated at the beginning of this chapter, grief is a universal experience. However, not everyone grieves in the same way. Western cultures tend to grieve individually and people talk about their grief in an individual manner. This is not an exhaustive list of cultural grief practices, but the following are examples of how grief can look depending on one's culture.

In Hindu families, grief is collective and relatives come together in a 13-day ritual. In Native American culture, death is felt by everyone in the tribe. The Buddhist culture and the Chinese culture also process grief collectively as a family (Wilson, 2023).

Mourning is a brief process and crying is not encouraged in the Indonesian culture. Egyptian culture on the other hand sees tearful grieving after seven years as a normal practice. In Western cultures, any intense grieving beyond a year is diagnosed as prolonged grief disorder (Wilson, 2023).

Grief on Pause

This experience depends on the cultural practice of the individual. However, some individuals may find themselves wanting to experience their grief in a way that is contrary to the grief practice of their culture. This becomes a challenge for the individual to be at odds with their own feelings and may cause confusion for them regarding whether they should do what their culture tells them or follow what they feel (Wilson, 2023).

The "Abracadabra" Griever

The "Abracadabra" griever wants the grief to go away immediately. If the individual had a magic wand, they would use it to send the grief to some unknown place. They may speak of wanting to "fix" it, as they would fix a problem. The desire comes from a place of wanting to avoid the pain. The individual may engage in searching for quick resolutions such as substance use, medications or holistic practices to get rid of the pain without having to process the emotion. (Mansoori et al., 2023, vanSchaik et al., 2022, Wolfelt, 2021).

The more the person tries to make the grief go away, the more the symptoms are experienced, which leads to trying even harder to make the grief go away. The reason that it is difficult for individuals to "just get over it" has to do with neuroscience and attachment. For example, the process of grief has been described as a form of learning. The neural encoding that happens during the building of a relationship forms the foundation for separation distress (O'Connor & Seeley, 2022). The learning that develops over time in the course of a relationship is manifested in the attachment bond one has with their loved one. Not only will rumination about the loss prevent the process of grief and acknowledgment that the person is gone, but avoidance prevents the person from learning that the loss is part of their reality. Unfortunately, at this time all of the functional and structural neuroimaging studies about grief are of a point in time, rather than the trajectory in which grief actually develops (O'Connor & Seeley, 2022).

OUTCOMES OF GRIEF AVOIDANCE BEHAVIOR

The next two sections highlight the ways that grief can impact the body as well as how grief can manifest through feelings. Grief can be shown through physical means and emotional means. Responses are not going to look the same in every individual. These descriptions are not exhaustive, but rather they give some of the more common expressions of grief as reported by clients.

Physical

As discussed in the previous sections, in addition to the emotional experience of grief avoidance, there are physical responses in the body. When individuals engage in deliberate grief avoidance, it can cause fatigue, the immune system can weaken, and inflammation in the body can increase. Individuals can have changes in appetite, experience headaches and pains in the body, shortness of breath, chest pain, sleep disturbance, and dry mouth/dehydration. If the individual already has physical health concerns, grief avoidance can prolong those other health ailments (Mundell, 2024).

Emotional

For the emotional component of grief avoidance, it is important to remember that even though feelings may not be expressed outwardly, the feelings may still be there. A griever may have feelings that they are disconnected from. The person may also become irritable when thinking about the loss and therefore, they avoid thinking about the loss. Individuals who are grieving report sadness, shock, numbness, difficulty making decisions, guilt, emptiness, anxiety, and sometimes thoughts of harming oneself to be with the deceased individual. Another part of the emotional component of avoidance is the experience of denial. Denial is often referred to as the first stage of grief based on Elisabeth Kubler-Ross' work. Some grievers stay stuck in the denial stage after a loss and therefore stay in grief avoidance (Mayo Clinic, 2022).

ASSESSMENT OF GRIEF AVOIDANCE BEHAVIOR

We have discussed so far that there are a variety of grief-avoidance behaviors. There are even different ways that people grieve based on one's culture. There are ways that people grieve based on how the loss occurred. It is difficult to determine just based on observation. But how does a clinician determine whether or not their client is experiencing a healthy grief trajectory? There are several assessment tools that are helpful in identifying if the avoidance is maladaptive. (Szuhany et al., 2021). First, determine if the client meets criteria for prolonged grief disorder.

The loss of a loved one had to have occurred at least a year prior for adults, and at least 6 months prior for children and adolescents. In addition, the griever must have experienced at least three of the symptoms below nearly every day for at least the previous month prior to the diagnosis.

Symptoms of prolonged grief disorder (APA, 2022) include:

Grief on Pause

- Identity disruption (such as feeling as though part of oneself has died).
- Marked sense of disbelief about the death.
- Avoidance of reminders that the person is dead.
- Intense emotional pain (such as anger, bitterness, sorrow) related to the death.
- Difficulty with reintegration (such as problems engaging with friends, pursuing interests, planning for the future).
- Emotional numbness (absence or marked reduction of emotional experience).
- Feeling that life is meaningless.
- Intense loneliness (feeling alone or detached from others).

In addition, the person's bereavement lasts longer than might be expected based on social, cultural, or religious norms (Wilson, 2023).

Yearning is a gateway feature of prolonged grief disorder and may be key in triggering other grief-related symptoms, such as preoccupation with the deceased and feeling life is meaningless after the loss (Szuhany et al., 2021). An estimated 7%-10% of bereaved adults will report persistent symptoms of prolonged grief disorder (Szuhany et al., 2021).

After determining if the client meets criteria for prolonged grief disorder, the clinician can use any of the following assessment tools listed to understand where the griever is on the spectrum of grief-avoidance behavior.

Grief-Related Avoidance Questionnaire (GRAQ)

Counselors need to be able to assess avoidance in individuals who may be at risk for prolonged grief due to avoidance or avoidance-related behaviors. In addition, this tool assists clinicians in tracking treatment outcomes. The Grief-Related Avoidance Questionnaire (GRAQ) was created by Shear et al. in 2007 with the goal of examining predictors of avoidance. There were 128 participants, mostly women (103), all adults that had experienced bereavement for at least 6 months. There were no other significant mental health conditions. The causes of death of the loved one were varied and included homicide/accident/suicide (35%) with the remainder by natural causes. The individual that had died was a spouse (29%), a parent (28%), a child (27%), or a close friend or relative (16%). The median time since the death was a little over 2 1/2 years, with a range of 6 months to 36 years. (Szhuany et al., 2021)

The Grief-Related Avoidance Questionnaire (GRAQ) is a 15-item, self-report questionnaire that assesses avoidance behaviors of bereaved individuals. There is a scale of 0 to 4 (Never, Rarely, Sometimes, Often, Always). The internal consistency and validity for this instrument were found to be high (Szuhany et al., 2021). There are three distinct themes to this assessment: avoidance of places and things that remind the griever of the loss, avoidance of activities that remind the griever of how the person died and avoidance of situations that remind the griever of physical sickness or death and that trigger grief-related emotions (i.e. funerals, going to visit someone in the hospital) (Szuhany et al., 2021).

Brief Grief Questionnaire (BGQ)

The Brief Grief Questionnaire (BGQ) is a five-item scale that was originally developed for a study of individuals who were struggling following the 9–11 terrorist attacks in New York. The questionnaire was developed by Kathleen Shear and Susan Essock (Szuhany et al., 2021). The participants included 149 individuals that primarily were female (103). There was a fairly varied ethnic distribution (84 Caucasian, 26 African-American, 29 Hispanic). The participants ranged in age from 20 to 86 years old. There were good levels of internal consistency and validity to this assessment (Szuhany et al., 2021).

The BGQ is known to be the first survey to screen for disaster-related prolonged grief. The five questions were on the topics of trouble accepting the death, interference of grief in their life, distressing images or thoughts of the death, avoidance of anything related to the person who died and feeling distant from others (Szuhany et al., 2021).

The BGQ asks grievers to rate their difficulty accepting the loss/death, how much grief is interfering in their life, how intense the grief thoughts are, how much does the griever avoid reminders of the loss/death, and how disconnected is the individual from other supports. The rating scale is from 0 to 2 (0=not at all, 1=somewhat, 2=a lot) (Szuhany et al., 2021).

Structured Clinical Interview for Complicated Grief (SCI-CG)

The Structured Clinical Interview for Complicated Grief (SCI-CG) was developed by Eric Bui and several other researchers in 2015. There were 281 participants in a multi-state clinical trial sponsored by National Institute of Mental Health (NIMH) where the majority of individuals were female (219) with a mean age of 52.4 years. Individuals had to have had someone die at least 6 months prior, a score ≥ 30 on the Inventory of Complicated Grief and a primary symptom of complicated grief. The ethnic distribution was Caucasian (226), Hispanic (33), African American (32), and other (22). There were no other mental health conditions. The range of time since the death was an average of 2.2 years (Szuhany et al., 2021, Bui et al., 2015).

At the time, a structured clinical assessment of complicated grief was needed. There is a high degree of bias involved with self-report instruments and structured clinician-administered instruments can make clinical judgments (Szuhaney et al., 2021, Bui et al., 2015).

Grief on Pause

The SCI-CG is a structured clinical interview that includes questions covering 31 different symptoms of grief. There is a screening section of the interview that asks about the nature of the death, the relationship to the person who has died and how long it has been since the death. The rating scale is from 1 to 3 (1 = *"Not present"*, 2 = *"Unsure or equivocal"*, 3 = *"Present"*) over the prior month (Szuhany et al., 2021, Bui et al., 2015).

Typical Beliefs Questionnaire (TBQ)

The Typical Beliefs Questionnaire (TBQ) was created to have an assessment that was specific to maladaptive cognitions related to complicated grief. Some of the assessments listed in this section mention cognitions briefly or have emotions only, but the TBQ is focused solely on thoughts. This assessment can be utilized diagnostically, as a treatment plan tool, and to track treatment outcomes (Skritskaya et al., 2017).

There were 394 adults as part of this multi-state study with a mean age of 53 years old. There were no other significant mental health conditions, the presenting symptom however was complicated grief as evidenced by scoring more than 30 on the Inventory of Complicated Grief (ICG). 308 participants were females and 324 were Caucasian, with the remainder being Hispanic, African-American and other. There was strong internal consistency, test-retest reliability and validity (Skritskaya et al., 2017).

The Typical Beliefs Questionnaire (TBQ) is a 25-item, self-report assessment of how individuals with prolonged grief symptoms are currently thinking about the death. There are five themes: conflict regarding the death, globally negative thoughts, thoughts of dependency on the person, the belief that not grieving is not honoring the person, and rumination about grief. The rating scale is from 0 to 4 (0= not at all to 4 (very strongly) (Szuhany et al., 2021).

Inventory of Complicated Grief (ICG)

The Inventory of Complicated Grief (ICG) was given to 97 widowed elders who were part of a program designed to study sleep and physiological changes in major depression and bereavement. 70 of those were contacted about being a part of the pilot for the ICG. There were 51 females with an average age of 66.9 years and 67 of the participants were Caucasian. The reliability and validity were both high for this assessment (Szuhany et al., 2021, Prigerson et al., 1995).

The scale was a 4-point Likert scale that asked respondents to report the frequency (0 = never; 1 = rarely; 2 = sometimes; 3 = often; 4 = always) for which they currently experienced each of the emotional, cognitive, and behavioral states as part of their grief (Szuhany et al., 2021, Prigerson et al., 1995).

Themes in the assessment are preoccupation with thoughts of the deceased, anger about the death, distrust and detachment from others as a result of the death, pain in the same areas of the body as experienced by the deceased, avoidance of reminders of the deceased, feeling that life is empty without the deceased, auditory and visual hallucinations of the loved one, survivor guilt, loneliness, feeling bitter about the death, and being envious of others who have not lost someone close (Szuhany et al., 2021, Prigerson et al., 1995).

Loss Summary (LOSS SUM)

The Loss Summary asks the griever to make a list of close friends and relatives that they have lost and rate how difficult losing the person was. The rating scale is from 0 to 4 (0= not at all to 4 (severe). This screening tool was created through The Center for Prolonged Grief and gives an overview of all of the relationships and all of the losses that may need to be discussed (The Center for Prolonged Grief, 2023).

Difficult Times Questionnaire (DTQ)

The Difficult Times Questionnaire is an assessment was created at The Center for Prolonged Grief and asks the griever to rate specific calendar dates and how difficult these dates are. Examples of calendar dates would be things like the anniversary of the death, the deceased's birthday, wedding anniversaries, holidays, or other significant occasions. This is helpful for clinicians to help prepare for which dates or times of year are going to be more difficult for the griever (The Center for Prolonged Grief, 2023).

Grief Support Inventory (GSI)

The Grief Support Inventory, from The Center for Prolonged Grief is a 2-item questionnaire that asks patients to list people in their life who have been supportive since the loss and people who have been actively unsupportive. Giving this to a patient helps her consider if there are supportive people, even if she is not feeling very close to them. It also allows the patient to see that we know people can be unsupportive. This can feel very validating (The Center for Prolonged Grief, 2023).

Grief on Pause

EVIDENCE-BASED TREATMENT FOR PROLONGED GRIEF DISORDERS

While most individuals will go through their grief process without any need for counseling, some will meet the criteria for prolonged grief disorder. There have been several evidence-based interventions developed that can help to reduce or eliminate symptoms that are impacting overall functioning.

In the following sections, some of the most widely used evidence-based treatments for prolonged grief disorder are discussed. This list is not exhaustive but highlights the wide variety of ways that grief symptoms can be managed clinically.

Complicated Grief Treatment (CGT)

Complicated Grief Treatment (CGT) is a 16-session, manualized intervention. CGT has been shown in several randomized clinical trials to be efficacious. The approach is a combination of attachment theory, cognitive-behavioral therapy (CBT), as well as other approaches that allow the griever to naturally process their grief in an authentic way. The underlying belief of CGT is that grieving is an event that is universal (Alioto et al., 2020).

Adaptation is facilitated through the dual process model of grief which includes loss and restoration. The dual process model of grief is a theory developed by Margaret Stroebe and Henk Schut in the mid-1990s that suggests that people cope with grief by going back and forth between two modes of processing: loss-oriented and restoration-oriented. Loss-oriented processing involves a focus on the deceased and the emotional responses to grief, while restoration-oriented processing is often when people are trying to distract themselves from the loss and participating in new roles and new activities (Szuhany et al., 2021). Loss and restoration are seen as innate responses (Alioto et al., 2020). Loss explores a change in relationship with the deceased along with an acceptance of the death. Restoration allows the client to feel competent in a world without the deceased and being able to work on achieving goals without the deceased being present in their life (Szuhany et al., 2021).

CGT covers seven core themes including 1) educating clients on the concept of acceptance of grief, 2) exploring ways to manage emotional pain and tracking symptoms, 3) helping the client to be future-focused, 4) developing new relationships with others, 5) allowing the client to narrate the story of the death, 6) understanding new ways of adjusting to external reminders, and 7) having new engagement with the memories of the person who has died (Szuhany et al., 2021). CGT is effective in group formats as well as individual (Alioto et al., 2020).

CBT

Cognitive-Behavioral Therapy (CBT) is an approach whose theoretical underpinnings are that one's thoughts influence feelings and one's feelings influence behavior. Grief-specific techniques are used to encourage clients in acceptance of the loss, to change unhelpful grief-related appraisals, and challenge any avoidance behavior that supports ineffective grief responses (Alioto et al, 2020).

There are four core components to grief-related CBT that include 1) didactic information about the difference between normal and prolonged grief responses, 2) exposure to the most emotionally difficult parts of the loss, 3) cognitive restructuring of the loss and 4) behavioral activation modified for grief, to help patients re-engage in previously meaningful activities.4 CBT for grief can be utilized in group and individual settings over the course of 12 sessions (Alioto et al, 2020).

One specific CBT for grief program is Healthy Experiences After Loss, which is an online intervention that helps clients to re-engage with self-care and social connections. This program has been seen as positive for clients experiencing grief as well as depression, anxiety and/or posttraumatic stress disorder (Szuhany et al., 2021). Another benefit of CBT is that it can help clients with comorbid symptoms. For example, grievers may struggle with getting enough sleep after a loss. CBT for insomnia (CBT-I) is designed to help clients with sleep hygiene and improving their insomnia symptoms (Szuhany et al., 2021).

Support Groups

Grief support groups are described as being helpful the closer in time attendance at the groups were to the death. Overall, support groups are useful because disconnection and lack of social support is a risk factor to developing prolonged grief disorder (Szuhany et al., 2021). More research is needed to determine if there is any difference between in-person support groups and online support groups (i.e. social media groups).

Psychotherapy

The most traditional form of individual grief treatment is grief-focused psychotherapy. The foundation of the therapy sessions are to help the client to achieve specific tasks. Rando and Pearlman et al. created tasks called the "R" processes in 2014. Rando believed that complicated mourning happens when one of the six R processes of mourning is distorted. (Frazer Consultants, 2020).

The "R" processes (Frazer Consultants, 2020) are as follows:
1. Recognize the loss

Grief on Pause

2. React to the separation
3. Recollect and reexperience the deceased and the relationship
4. Relinquish the old attachments to the deceased and the old assumptive world
5. Readjust to move adaptively into the new world
6. Reinvest in life

Another framework used in grief-related treatment was created in 2002 by Robert Neimeyer that includes the griever creating a narrative of the loss, holding on to the memories, emotions and distressing feelings and learning to cope with them, change the relationship with the deceased rather than eliminating it, and formulating new life goals (Harris, 2020).

HOLISTIC PRACTICES

There are many holistic practices that could be used with clients depending on what the client is open to using as part of their healing process. The practices listed below are categories of approaches that would need to be tailored to the individual client.

Dance/Movement Therapy

Dance/movement therapy is defined as a therapeutic use of movement based on the principle of emotions and motion being interconnected (Brooke & Miraglia, 2015). Dance/movement therapy goes back centuries and is connected to individual and community healing rituals associated with many indigenous cultures (Fracasso et al., 2020). Dance/movement therapy has become a specialization within the counseling field. This approach was recently applied to clients experiencing grief as a valid therapeutic approach because of the benefits of motion on healing (Brooke & Miraglia, 2015). However, movement and dance have historically been used to create a healing or therapeutic effect for clients. Expressive movement therapies and creative expression art forms were reintroduced as a valid therapeutic modality in the 1940s around the time that humanistic psychology was blossoming. The physicality of the movement was having an impact on clients by elevating their mood (Fracasso et al., 2020).

One study looked at a group held in a private practice in Poland consisting of six women aged 32-39. All of the women had experienced perinatal loss. The group met for about four months and the sessions were two hours in length. There was a movement warm-up at the beginning to increase body awareness, then separation from the group to have individual time, then verbal sharing by members about their experience with movement. The group then would use group themes to embody an improvised movement. An example of this might be that the group moved like a glass of water or like the ocean whereby the group traveled together across the sea. A movement coding sheet was filled out by the therapists. The ending of the group was determined by the group and then they could share what they chose to share (Fracasso et al., 2020, Brooke & Miraglia, 2015).

A number of participants shared that some of their somatic symptoms had abated (stiff neck, feeling of separation from body and head, not wanting to touch their abdomen, or breathing problems. There were many participants who reported not having anxiety anymore and depressive states were minimal. Participants who experienced yet another loss during the group however, expressed feelings of inadequacy and either no change or a decrease in energy. Changes were maintained six months after the termination of group and therefore this modality was seen as an effective approach for women experiencing grief as a result of perinatal loss (Brooke & Miraglia, 2015).

Drama Therapy

Drama therapy introduces improvisation, role-play, theater games, and mask and puppet work. Clients do not need to be well-versed in acting or to be extroverted to gain the benefits of this approach. Drama therapy emerged around 1979 in the United States. Other countries including England, the Netherlands, Israel, Japan, India, Taiwan, and Hong Kong are utilizing drama therapy as a therapeutic tool (Fracasso et al., 2020). One specific form of drama therapy is known as the Playback Theatre, which was founded by Jonathan Fox and Jo Salas in 1975. Playback Theatre was affiliated with the original Playback Theatre in New York and the group has performed in over 60 countries around the world (Brooke & Miraglia, 2015).

The purpose of Playback Theatre is to offer a way to create a community among the actors and audience. It is set up as an improvisational theater made up of citizens, not necessarily individuals who have experience in acting. One example of how this holistic approach was used was a performance having to do with family members and veterans of World War II and the Vietnam War. Fear and grief were themes of the stories that were shared. One woman raised her hand to tell her story, so the conductor (or director) invited her to come to the stage and sit in the teller's chair. This is known as the interview phase. She shared her story and then the conductor encourages the young woman to choose someone from the audience to play her, her mother and grandfather in the story. This begins the enactment phase. Music is played and then falls to silence before the actors chosen from the audience begin to enact the story. Through the performance, the individual can witness their loss, find hope and/or gain resilience. The goal is for the individual or teller to begin to reframe their story (Fracasso et al., 2020, Brooke & Miraglia, 2015).

Grief on Pause

The use of drama is helpful for the processing of grief. Psychodrama, commonly known as a therapeutic approach developed by J.L. Moreno was created to assist individuals to process their thoughts and feelings. As individuals we use stories as a way to heal our emotional health but also to cement our place in the world. Many individuals report being helped by telling their story and allowing it to impact others in the audience, then audience members can reflect and heal from their own stories (Fracasso et al., 2020, Brooke & Miraglia, 2015).

Music Therapy

Music Therapy is often used to address emotional and mental health. Songs and the lyrics to songs can be a healing tool for many dealing with grief. In cultures around the world, drums, rattles, and chanting have been used as part of healing ceremonies. The Greek culture viewed music as a way to cure emotional dysregulation. Plato used to provide clients with homework to listen to music in order to change their mood. Aristotle saw music as the vehicle to letting go of painful emotions (Fracasso et al., 2020).

The pandemic posed challenges to delivery of behavioral health therapy and the use of telehealth significantly increased as a method to provide services safely. Telehealth would take a great deal of creativity on the part of the practitioner if the results were going to be positive. Music therapy was one of those ways. In one article, three different case studies were done with pediatric clients using music therapy. (Goicoechea & Lahue, 2021). One of those case studies, a 15- and 17-year-old who were siblings of a 16-year-old female, who had passed away from leukemia in June 2020 showed how music therapy was used. The 16-year-old had worked with the music therapy team prior to her passing. The mother of the siblings reached out requesting virtual music therapy sessions using legacy songwriting. In normal times, music therapy was something that would have been conducted face-to-face (Goicoechea & Lahue, 2021). The siblings verbalized wanting to learn how to play guitar as a coping skill and a way to continue their relationship with their sister who had played music herself before her death. Despite challenges of teaching guitar with internet lag, technology difficulties, and poor audio quality, the music therapist was able to think outside of the box. The music therapist made videos and sent them so that the siblings could watch them outside of session. They used screen-sharing videos and played music during sessions. The brothers were even referred to resources and materials to practice on their own outside of session. The use of music as a way to connect to their sister has helped them to move towards engagement in the legacy songwriting, combining emotional expression with the guitar skills resulting in a songwriting experience to honor their relationship with their sister (Goicoechea & Lahue, 2021).

Art Therapy

Art therapy can often be a very powerful communication tool because of the symbolism and creative nonverbal expression of feeling. Grievers can utilize art as a way to confront choices they are making, identify their personal values, and express cognitive, tactile, and emotional meaning (Fracasso et al., 2020).

Expressive arts therapies are known to be effective in areas such as grief and loss because they allow the griever to process their relationship with the deceased in nonverbal ways that circumvent some of the social and cultural barriers. One approach that works very well is called the Mandala Assessment Research Instrument or MARI. The MARI works with all stages of grief and looks at deeper components of the grief process. Clients draw mandalas and select cards with symbols on them along with colors. Cards and colors are connected to a circular grid that corresponds to developmental stages. In one case, a client was invited to look at the symbol cards and choose six that they felt drawn to and one card that they were least drawn to. Afterwards, the client matched the color cards with each of the seven symbols. The client is then asked to think of an issue in their life and then two of the cards that connect most closely to the issue. The client is invited to draw two separate mandalas and to fill in colors in the four sections of the mandala design. In consultation with the MARI-trained clinician, the mandalas were evaluated in conjunction with the symbol cards and colors. In this case, it was determined that the client was more motivated intrinsically than extrinsically (Brooke & Miraglia, 2015).

As with all forms of art therapy, the MARI focuses on the client's deepest feelings that they have not been able to express verbally. The difference between art therapy from more traditional verbal forms of therapy is the freedom and creativity viewpoint. Art therapists for grievers do not focus on diagnosis or a treatment model. The focus is rather to assist clients in having a safe space to achieve personal growth and working towards self-direction without the loved one in their lives (Fracasso et al., 2020).

Emotional Freedom Techniques (EFT)

Emotional Freedom Techniques (EFT) is a treatment approach that is easy for practitioners and non-practitioners to learn. It has been utilized for many issues including anxiety, depression, chronic pain, and trauma but also has been used for grief. One of the positives of EFT is that the effects are felt immediately and last for a long time. Developed by Gary Craig and Adrienne Fowlie in 1995, it is typically used as an adjunct to therapy, so the clinician will develop rapport with the client, complete an intake, assess risk for suicide, and rule out dissociative symptoms (Flint, Lammers & Mitnick, 2014).

Grief on Pause

EFT is often called "tapping" because the individual uses two fingers to tap on the seven meridians of the body while stating a positive cognitive acceptance statement out loud. The intervention itself is brief and is a combination of exposure, somatic stimulation, and cognitive approaches. The basic steps include forming a positive affirmation connected to a reminder phase that is easy for the client to remember the issue, a measurement of the emotional intensity on a scale of 0 to 10, repeating the affirmation, tapping on the meridians/acupressure points, process the feelings of healing, and then repeating the aforementioned steps until the client rates themselves at a 0 (Flint, Lammers & Mitnick, 2014).

EFT has been widely studied in over 10 countries throughout the world and over 100 journal articles. These studies have shown that EFT allows individuals to minimize emotional distress that is triggered by memories or other situations that bring up painful emotions for the griever (Fracasso et al., 2020).

Massage Therapy

Massage therapy has been used for thousands of years in many countries including such as China, Australia, India and ancient Greece. During the early 20th century, massage therapy became part of standard health care in North America. The confusion about massage therapy is often the fact that there are over 200 different bodywork massage techniques that are called massage (Fracasso et al., 2020).

It is important to recognize that each of these massage types vary in the emotional and physical effects, the training and education required to practice and when it should and should not be used. Therefore, individuals choosing to use this in practice must be knowledgeable about possible outcomes. Some of the more commonly used massage therapy practices are Reiki energy healing, Rolfing, and classic Swedish massage (Fracasso et al., 2020).

Soft tissue massage is one type of massage that uses gentle but firm movements of the skin. These movements activate receptors on the skin that release oxytocin, the hormone known for feelings of well-being and relaxation. The mental health impact after stillbirth for women is considerable. The grief process often causes feelings of loss of control, feelings of isolation, exhaustion, anxiety, depression and fatigue among other reactions (Fogarty, 2022). Based on research on massage during pregnancy, Swedish massage including these specific massage strokes: longitudinal gliding, transverse gliding, digital ischemic pressure, transverse frictions, and transverse gliding. Massage from the cervical spine to the lumbar area including the shoulders was utilized. To begin, the therapist utilized light-pressure Swedish massage to relax the client and to warm the muscles. There were also sessions, depending on the purpose of the massage, where deeper work in the shoulders, gluteal area, and lower back area was applied. The role of massage in one particular case discussed in the article by Fogarty (2022), was to relieve symptoms, reduce pain, improve mood state and reduce muscle tightness (Fogarty, 2022). After the massage sessions, the client provided written feedback stating that she experienced less shoulder stiffness and sciatica, she was better able to manage her anxiety and depression and she was able to utilize strategies to manage her emotions. In addition, the client reported benefits of massage therapy as having continuity of care after a pregnancy loss, being listened to, having a break from grieving, having a safe place to experience her grief and feeling safe (Fogarty, 2022).

Massage can be a source of support during a time of grieving. Grief often triggers feelings of intense stress and massage allowed the griever to reintegrate into their lives through an increase in meaning, purpose, feeling whole and taking a moment to breathe.

Yoga Nidra

Yoga Nidra (or dynamic sleep) is a form of yoga that includes both guided relaxation and meditative inquiry. Individuals are asked to take in and acknowledge what is at the "root of their suffering" (Fracasso et al., 2020). Clinicians must be trained in Yoga Nidra to use it with clients. The practice can be used individually but is often used in groups.

For grievers, Yoga Nidra can be helpful in that it helps to recreate a feeling of being whole again and emotionally connected. Not only is Yoga Nidra effective with grief, it is also helpful with anxiety, depression, sleep disorders, addictions, posttraumatic stress disorder, sexual abuse. Yoga Nidra has been utilized as well with physical health concerns such as hypertension, diabetes, multiple sclerosis, pain management and cancer (Fracasso et al., 2020).

Yoga Nidra allows individuals to stay awake and aware while experiencing different levels of consciousness. Individuals practicing Yoga Nidra go through four distinct stages. The first stage is diaphragmatic breathing, next is systematic relaxation of the entire body, then visualization and last resting between sleeping and wakefulness. The meditative state of Yoga Nidra provides the individual with four states of consciousness: waking, dreaming, deep sleep and a state known as Turiya, also referred to as union. Research indicates that the practice of Yoga Nidra promotes theta brainwave states known for deep healing. Delta brain waves are present when we in deep sleep and also promotes healing. Through clear steps of grounding, feeling supported, observation, focus, deepening awareness and returning to present (Stanley, 2020).

Grief is often helped by support. When individuals receive support, it is then that they can experience rest. The place of rest allows the griever a break from the pain, and to experience grief fully while remaining in a calm state (Stanley, 2020).

Grief on Pause

Going through the stages of yoga nidra can provide that healing that could be needed desperately for a grieving individual.

Mindfulness

Mindfulness, also known as Vipassana meditation, is an ancient meditative technique developed in India. The practice was created from using traditional Buddhist meditation practices. Mindfulness calls for an individual to connect to "the awareness that emerges through paying attention on purpose, in the present moment, and non-judgmentally to the unfolding of experience moment by moment" (Fracasso et al., 2020, p. 222).

Buddha described that mindfulness meditation can end suffering. However, this can be incredibly difficult for an individual who is at the early stages of their grief but can be very helpful for someone as they have moved through their grief journey. The skill that clients can learn from mindfulness is the ability to observe their environment without judgment. There is a self-empowerment component that encourages responding rather than reacting (Fracasso et al., 2020).

The mindfulness perspective states that when we as individuals are not mindful, we are prisoners of the senses. This creates an opening for us to judge our thoughts, perceptions, feelings and desires that leads to further mental and emotional anguish. Memory is yet another mental event that trigger reactions that are not based in the reality of the present moment (Fracasso et al., 2020).

Continuing states of awareness can be achieved through mindfulness meditation. This takes regular practice and is not achieved in one sitting. However, once the habit is formed, it can help the griever choose the actions they are going to engage or not engage in and feel more in control of their lives (Fracasso et al., 2020).

FUTURE DIRECTIONS

Grief is a natural response to the impact of grief. However, grief avoidance is not a universal response and is an area that needs to be studied more significantly. For example, more awareness of how the COVID-19 pandemic impacted the likelihood of grief avoidance because of the overwhelming and sudden deaths of millions. During this time of physical distancing, it was perhaps easier for individuals to avoid because of the inability to connect with others. An increased prevalence of prolonged grief may be a long-term concern in need of further study (Alioto et al., 2020) (Szuhany et al., 2021).

One component of grief response has been discussed in writings from physicians and the helplessness felt during the pandemic. The emotional upheaval was difficult for frontline workers due to the inability to do anything other than witness their patients' pain and grief (Salisbury, 2021). Further research on understanding any patterns of grief avoidance because of their experiences from the pandemic would be an area for counselors to understand more about. In part, this is important because counselors were part of the frontline work that happened during this time.

Further research on the impact on families during COVID-19 is another space to explore. Due to the millions of people who died during the pandemic, the overwhelming nature of the grief experience was difficult to process. Due to the isolation and loss of physical contact, individuals were forced to grieve in different ways than they may have been used to grieving. Their sense of normalcy was shattered in an instant (Walsh, 2020). Understanding patterns of grief avoidance in the family members who lost someone during the pandemic, as well as in the family system. The patterns that a family member may have developed during this time, could be passed on to future generations and therefore, researching this population is important.

Last, understanding how social media influences how individuals grieve is a future source of research. Due to the increase of mental health discussions on social media, exploring the impact of how posts or online support groups are helping or hurting the grieving process. Asking questions such as Does the Internet create isolation or connection is just one area in grief work that is just at the surface of research. How individuals orient themselves in networks online to process their grief is a future direction for more study. Brubaker, Hayes, & Mazmanian (2019) have started this process by identifying five orientations to grief online. Reinforcing, supporting, transferring, objecting, and isolating are not prescriptive or exhaustive descriptions of how individuals online behave but they can begin to help us understand patterns.

For example, reinforcing is when individuals turn to those online to deepen their relationship with the deceased. Supporting is when individuals become immersed in providing care to family or close friends even when they do not know the deceased person. However, transferring is when the individual feels obligated to provide support to family or friends of the deceased. They connect with others through their relationship with the deceased. Objecting is actively rejecting how others are expressing their grief online. Isolating is when the individual chooses not to engage with the online grieving networks but rather wants to grieve privately (Brubaker, Hayes & Mazmanian, 2019). With the expansion of social media, future counselors could understand more about the patterns of how grievers engage or avoid and the impact on their reaction to the loss.

Grief on Pause

SUMMARY

Grief is an important part of the human experience as it honors the person who has died. Individuals have different perspectives on the concept of death, usually based on how death was talked about in their own families growing up. If there were open discussions and acceptance of feelings, the grief process would not be seen as something to avoid. However, if discussions are not open or an emphasis on "moving on" or "getting over it" is the theme, then avoidance of grief becomes a part of the grieving process. Continued awareness and practice of evidence-based treatments for prolonged grief disorder will assist individuals who are on pause with their grief.

DISCUSSION QUESTIONS

1. In what ways can avoidance patterns during grief impact long-term mental health, and what therapeutic approaches are effective in addressing these patterns?
2. How can contemporary models of grief (e.g., the Dual Process Model, the Five Stages of Grief) be integrated into clinical practice to support individuals experiencing loss? How can holistic practices be integrated into clinical practice to support individuals experiencing loss?
3. How do cultural differences influence the expression and management of grief, and what are some culturally sensitive approaches to supporting individuals in grief?
4. What role do social support systems play in the grief process, and how can clinicians facilitate effective support networks for those experiencing grief?
5. How do different types of loss (e.g., loss of a spouse, child, parent, friend) impact the grieving process, and what unique challenges do they present? Compare and contrast the grieving experiences associated with different types of significant losses. Discuss the specific emotional, psychological, and social challenges that each type of loss might entail.

REFERENCES

Alioto, A. G., Chadwell, M., Baran-Prall, J., Canelo, R., Casillas-Carmona, A. D. S., Gotham, H., Kurtz, L., Rivera, K., Wenger, P. J., & Wolf-Prusan, L. (2020). *Grief, Loss, and Bereavement Fact Sheet #5: Evidence-Based Treatments for Grief.* MHTTC Network. https://mhttcnetwork.org/sites/mhttc/files/2020-09/Fact%20Sheet%205%20EBT%20for%20Grief%2009082020_0.pdf

American Psychiatric Association. (2022). *Diagnostic and Statistical Manual of Mental Disorders, Fifth Edition, Text Revision (DSM-5-TR).* American Psychiatric Association Publishing. https://www.psychiatry.org/psychiatrists/practice/dsm

American Psychological Association. (n.d.). *Grief: Coping with the loss of your loved one.* American Psychological Association. https://www.apa.org/topics/families/grief

Ang, C. S. (2023). Life Will Never be the Same: Experiences of Grief and Loss among Older Adults. *Current Psychology (New Brunswick, N.J.),* 42(15), 12975–12987. 10.1007/s12144-021-02595-6

Braitman, L. (2023). *"What Looks Like Bravery" explains how achievement can't protect us from grief. interview.* NPR.

Brooke, S. L., & Miraglia, D. A. (2015). *Using the creative therapies to cope with grief and loss.* Charles C. Thomas Publisher, LTD.

Brown, L. J., Bond, M. J., & Topa, G. (2019). The pragmatic derivation and validation of measures of adaptive and maladaptive coping styles. *Cogent Psychology,* 6(1), 1568070. 10.1080/23311908.2019.1568070

Brubaker, J. R., Hayes, G. R., & Mazmanian, M. (2019). Orienting to networked grief. *Proceedings of the ACM on Human-Computer Interaction, 3*(CSCW), (pp. 1–19). ACM. 10.1145/3359129

Bui, E., Mauro, C., Robinaugh, D. J., Skritskaya, N. A., Wang, Y., Gribbin, C., Ghesquiere, A., Horenstein, A., Duan, N., Reynolds, C., Zisook, S., Simon, N. M., & Shear, M. K. (2015). The Structured Clinical Interview For Complicated Grief: Reliability, Validity, and Exploratory Factor Analysis. *Depression and Anxiety,* 32(7), 485–492. 10.1002/da.2238526061724

Djelantik, A. A., Robinaugh, D. J., Kleber, R. J., Smid, G. E., & Boelen, P. A. (2019). Symptomatology following loss and trauma: Latent class and network analyses of prolonged grief disorder, posttraumatic stress disorder, and depression in a treatment-seeking trauma-exposed sample. *Depression and Anxiety,* 37(1), 26–34. 10.1002/da.2288030724427

Eisma, M. C., de Lang, T. A., & Boelen, P. A. (2020). How thinking hurts: Rumination, worry, and avoidance processes in adjustment to bereavement. *Clinical Psychology &amp. Psychotherapy (Chicago, Ill.)*, 27(4), 548–558. 10.1002/cpp.244032969670

Eisma, M. C., Franzen, M., Paauw, M., Bleeker, A., & aan het Rot, M. (2021). Rumination, worry and negative and positive affect in prolonged grief: A daily diary study. *Clinical Psychology &amp. Psychotherapy (Chicago, Ill.)*, 29(1), 299–312. 10.1002/cpp.263534170063

Flint, G. A., Lammers, W., & Mitnick, D. G. (2014). Emotional freedom techniques. *Journal of Aggression, Maltreatment &amp. Journal of Aggression, Maltreatment & Trauma*, 12(1–2), 125–150. 10.1300/J146v12n01_07

Folkman, S., & Lazarus, R. S. (1980). An analysis of coping in a middle-aged community sample. *Journal of Health and Social Behavior*, 21(3), 219. 10.2307/21366177410799

Folkman, S., & Lazarus, R. S. (1988). The relationship between coping and emotion: Implications for theory and research. *Social Science &amp. Medicine*, 26(3), 309–317. 10.1016/0277-9536(88)90395-43279520

Fracasso, C. L., Krippner, S., & Friedman, H. L. (2020). *Holistic Treatment in Mental Health: A Handbook of Practitioners' Perspectives*. McFarland.

Frazer Consultants. (2020, August 17). *Grief theories series: Rando's six R process of mourning*. Frazer Consultants. https://web.frazerconsultants.com/grief-theories -series-randos-six-r-process-of-mourning/

Goicoechea, T., & Lahue, K. (2021). Case studies in pediatric music therapy during COVID-19. *Music Therapy Perspectives*, 39(2), 126–132. 10.1093/mtp/miab009

Gori, A., Topino, E., & Caretti, V. (2021). The impact of Covid-19 Lockdown on perceived stress: The role of Defence Mechanisms and coping strategies. *Journal of Contingencies and Crisis Management*, 30(4), 379–390. 10.1111/1468-5973.12380

Horowitz, J. M. (2022, April 14). *More than half of Americans in their 40s are "sandwiched" between an aging parent and their own children*. Pew Research Center. https://www.pewresearch.org/short-reads/2022/04/08/more-than-half-of-americans -in-their-40s-are-sandwiched-between-an-aging-parent-and-their-own-children/

Iglewicz, A., Shear, M. K., Reynolds, C. F.III, Simon, N., Lebowitz, B., & Zisook, S. (2019). Complicated grief therapy for clinicians: An evidence-based protocol for Mental Health Practice. *Depression and Anxiety*, 37(1), 90–98. 10.1002/ da.2296531622522

Magin, Z. E., David, A. B., Carney, L. M., Park, C. L., Gutierrez, I. A., & George, L. S. (2021). Belief in god and psychological distress: Is it the belief or certainty of the belief? *Religions*, 12(9), 757. 10.3390/rel12090757

Mansoori, J., Khodabakhshi-Koolaee, A., Falsafinejad, M. R., & Kashani Vahid, L. (2023). Bereavement for a loved person: A look at the opinions and process of coping with grief in the covid-19 ERA. *Practice in Clinical Psychology*, 11(3), 223–238. 10.32598/jpcp.11.3.746.4

Mayo Foundation for Medical Education and Research. (2022, December 13). *Complicated grief.* Mayo Clinic. https://www.mayoclinic.org/diseases-conditions/complicated-grief/symptoms-causes/syc-20360374

Meichenbaum, D., & Myers, J. (2016). Checklist of Strategies for Coping with Grief. In R.A. Neimeyer (Ed.). *Techniques of grief therapy (Vol. 2): Assessment and interventions*. Routledge

Mosse, E. (2024). *Grieving and Ritualizing Marriage Death: The Garden as Outer World Companion and Inner World Landscape* [Dissertation].

Mundell, E. (2024). *Grief affects the body, not just the mind.* Healthday. https://www.healthday.com/a-to-z-health/mental-health/grief-affects-the-body-not-just-the-mind

O'Connor, M.-F., & Seeley, S. H. (2022). Grieving as a form of learning: Insights from neuroscience applied to grief and loss. *Current Opinion in Psychology*, 43, 317–322. 10.1016/j.copsyc.2021.08.01934520954

Page, D. (2023, July 31). *What is The sandwich generation? experts explain this unique type of caregiving.* Care.com. https://www.care.com/c/what-is-the-sandwich-generation/

Prigerson, H. G., Maciejewski, P. K., Reynolds, C. F.III, Bierhals, A. J., Newsom, J. T., Fasiczka, A., Frank, E., Doman, J., & Miller, M. (1995). Inventory of complicated grief: A scale to measure maladaptive symptoms of loss. *Psychiatry Research*, 59(1–2), 65–79. 10.1016/0165-1781(95)02757-28771222

Prigerson, H. G., Shear, M. K., & Reynolds, C. F.III. (2022). Prolonged grief disorder diagnostic criteria—Helping those with maladaptive grief responses. *JAMA Psychiatry*, 79(4), 277. 10.1001/jamapsychiatry.2021.420135107569

Salisbury, H. (2021). Helen Salisbury: Dealing with covid trauma and grief. *BMJ (Clinical Research Ed.)*, n649. 10.1136/bmj.n64933687946

Grief on Pause

Selman, L. S. R. F. (2020, April 17). How coronavirus has transformed the grieving process. *The Conversation.*https://theconversation.com/how-coronavirus-has-transformed-the-grieving-process-136368

Skritskaya, N. A., Mauro, C., Olonoff, M., Qiu, X., Duncan, S., Wang, Y., Duan, N., Lebowitz, B., Reynolds, C. F.III, Simon, N. M., Zisook, S., & Shear, M. K. (2017). Measuring maladaptive cognitions in complicated grief: Introducing the typical beliefs questionnaire. *The American Journal of Geriatric Psychiatry*, 25(5), 541–550. 10.1016/j.jagp.2016.09.00327793576

Stanley, T. (2020). Yoga nidra for releasing grief. *Yoga Journal*, (317), 44–45.

Substance Abuse and Mental Health Services Administration. Department of Health & Human Services, Tips for Survivors: Coping with grief after a disaster or traumatic event (2017). Rockville, Md.

Sussex Publishers. (2020). Covid Stress Syndrome: What it is and why it matters. *Psychology Today.* https://www.psychologytoday.com/au/blog/experimentations/202007/covid-stress-syndrome-what-it-is-and-why-it-matters

Szuhany, K. L., Malgaroli, M., Miron, C. D., & Simon, N. M. (2021). Prolonged Grief Disorder: Course, Diagnosis, Assessment, and Treatment. *Focus - American Psychiatric Publishing*, 19(2), 161–172. 10.1176/appi.focus.2020005234690579

Tang, S., & Chow, A. Y. M. (2021). *Rumination in Bereavement.* Springer International Publishing. https://doi-org.huary.kl.oakland.edu/10.1007/978-3-030-22009-9_1027

Taylor, S., Landry, C. A., Paluszek, M. M., Rachor, G. S., & Asmundson, G. J. G. (2020). Worry, avoidance, and coping during the COVID-19 pandemic: A comprehensive network analysis. *Journal of Anxiety Disorders*, 76, 102327. 10.1016/j.janxdis.2020.10232733137601

The Center for Prolonged Grief. (n.d.). *Overview.* Center for Prolonged Grief. https://prolongedgrief.columbia.edu

Tiech Fire, N., Gvion, Y., Alkalay, S., & Zalsman, G. (2022). The "Forgotten grievers": The impact of pupil suicide on post-trauma and grief symptoms in school staff. *International Journal of Environmental Research and Public Health*, 19(19), 12160. 10.3390/ijerph191912160 36231464

van Schaik, T., Brouwer, M. A., Knibbe, N. E., Knibbe, H. J., & Teunissen, S. C. (2022). The effect of the COVID-19 pandemic on grief experiences of bereaved relatives: An overview review. *Omega*, 003022282211438. 10.1177/0030222822114386136453639

Grief on Pause

Walsh, F. (2020). Loss and resilience in the time of Covid-19: Meaning making, hope, and transcendence. *Family Process*, 59(3), 898–911. 10.1111/famp.1258832678915

Wilson, D. M., Darko, E. M., Kusi-Appiah, E., Roh, S. J., Ramic, A., & Errasti-Ibarrondo, B. (2020). What exactly is "complicated" grief? A scoping research literature review to understand its risk factors and prevalence. *Omega*, 86(2), 471–487. 10.1177/00302228209773053259275

Wilson, J.F. (2023). Death and dying: How different cultures deal with grief and mourning. *The Conversation.*https: theconversation.com/death-and-dying-how-different-cultures-deal-with-grief-and-mourning-197299

Wolfelt, A. (2021). *Nature heals: Reconciling your grief through engaging with the natural world.* Companion Press.

ADDITIONAL READING

Boelen, P. A., Smid, G. E., & Lenferink, L. I. M. (2019). Prolonged Grief Disorder in DSM-5 and ICD-11: Clinical Utility and Validation of Severity and Impairment Thresholds. *Psychological Medicine*, 49(3), 470–478.31779729

Djelantik, A. A. A. M. J., Smid, G. E., Kleber, R. J., & Boelen, P. A. (2020). Symptoms of Prolonged Grief, Post-Traumatic Stress, and Depression in Recently Bereaved People: Symptom Profiles, Comorbidity, and Correlates. *Journal of Affective Disorders*, 274, 1122–1129.

Eisma, M. C., & Stroebe, M. S. (2021). Rumination Following Bereavement: An Overview. *Bereavement Care*, 40(2), 60–67.

Neimeyer, R. (2018). *Grief and Bereavement in Contemporary Society: Bridging Research and Practice.*

Lenferink, L. I. M., Wessel, I., & Boelen, P. A. (2019). Exploring the Relationships Between Forms of Rumination and Symptoms of Prolonged Grief, Posttraumatic Stress, and Depression in Bereaved Individuals: A Cross-Lagged Longitudinal Study. *Clinical Psychology & Psychotherapy*, 26(4), 560–570.

Smid, G. E., Groen, S., de la Rie, S. M., Kooper, A. W. M., Boelen, P. A., & Boelen, P. A. (2020). Toward Cultural Assessment of Grief and Grieving: A Mixed-Method Study. *PLoS One*, 15(4), e0230094.

O'Connor, M. (2022). *The Grieving Brain: The Surprising Science of How We Learn from Love and Loss.* Harper One.

Grief on Pause

KEY TERMS AND DEFINITIONS

Dual Process Model: Dual process model is a model used for coping with grief. The two processes are loss-oriented stressors and restoration-oriented stressors. Loss-oriented stressors relate to any thoughts, emotions or behaviors that bring up strong emotions about the loss. Restoration-oriented stressors relate to any thoughts or behaviors that bring relief from intense feelings.

Grief Avoidance: Grief avoidance is any behavior that is used to escape thoughts, or feelings that are too painful for the griever to experience.

Holistic Practices: Holistic practices are forms of therapy that utilize both traditional and nontraditional treatments to assist the grieving individual without the use of medication.

Prolonged Grief Disorder (PGD): Prolonged grief disorder is a condition that involves intense and chronic symptoms of grief after the loss of a loved one.

Rumination: Rumination is the repetition of thoughts that are focused on the griever's distress. Grievers can try to use rumination as a way to resolve the problem, however, rumination does not remove the intense thoughts and feelings experienced.

Chapter 5
When a Balm Aggravates Pain:
The Wrong Words to the Bereaved in Grief and Trauma Counselling

Onijuni Olatomide
https://orcid.org/0009-0001-0973-6968
Obafemi Awolowo University, Ile-Ife, Nigeria

ABSTRACT

The death of a beloved person usually traumatises the bereaved, causing grief. Remarkably, social supports—family members, friends, religious faithful, clergies, neighbours, and sympathisers—give available support, rich in physical, social, and psychological contents. Words are normally used to convey their support during their visits to the bereaved. However, contrary to expectation that their words would heal the bereaved, such words could eventually aggravate their grief condition. Not only could such words emanate from outside of the bereaved—they could also issue from the bereaved, but producing the same lethality. This chapter provides some of those aggravating words such as "This is a catastrophe," "Again?" "Just forget about it," "I know exactly how you feel," and "you should have ...," etc. It similarly offers systematic steps on how rehabilitative counsellors could assist social support and the bereaved to acknowledge the dangers inherent in such words, and how to recast them for desirable therapeutic effect.

DOI: 10.4018/979-8-3693-1375-6.ch005

Copyright © 2024, IGI Global. Copying or distributing in print or electronic forms without written permission of IGI Global is prohibited.

When a Balm Aggravates Pain

INTRODUCTION

There is likely no living person who has surpassed the age of six, in the view of this writer, who has not experienced loss of a dear one, although the frequency, incidents leading to the loss, experience of attendant grief and trauma, coping and rehabilitative assistance provided and received during the phase may vary. The death could be that of a child, classmate, father, friend, mother, neighbour, sibling, extended family member, or workmate, to list a few. Whoever the deceased is to the bereaved, the loss of a beloved person remains one of life's highly stressful events (Rajic et al., 2023). Thus, one of the prominent ways people react to the loss of loved ones is to grieve. According to Asgari et al. (2023), and Skalski et al. (2022), grief is individual's natural reaction to a loss or absence of a dear person or object considered valuable to the bereaved, or after encountering disasters and traumatic events.

During bereavement, Worden (2018) established that the bereaved passes through four stages of grief corresponding to tasks. These are bereaved person's acceptance of the reality of the loss, their experiencing of the pains attached to the grief, adjusting to new environment, and building of new relationship. Across ages and cultures, network of supports ranging from family members, friends, neighbours, workmates, clergies, classmates, etc., come around to comfort, console, and demonstrate how much they cared for the bereaved in their moment of grief (Aoun et al., 2018; Bottomley, Burke, & Neimeyer, 2017). Either in one-on-one visits or in groups, one invaluable tool possessed and used by the people to convey their care and sympathy to the bereaved is words.

Words spoken at such bereavement visits are meant to strengthen, motivate, encourage, sustain, transform, and restore equilibrium (or peace of mind) of the bereaved. However, either because the utterers are overwhelmed by the occurrence, or imagine the pains the bereaved must have undergone, their words are often not well thought-out, censored, or evaluated for desirable therapeutic effect. The reason is that such words usually offer the direct opposite of their intentions. Thus, they end up weakening, demoralising, discouraging, deflating, transfixing and befuddling the receiver. Therefore, while the statements are intentionally meant to enhance the rehabilitation process of the bereaved, they inadvertently undermine their healing process. In that connection, Rajic et al. (2023) asserted that despite the good intentions of social supports during bereavement, they sometimes say some words or do certain things perceived by the bereaved as either unhelpful or even harmful.

Exploring the nature of the messages offered by social supports to bereaved individuals, Rajic et al. (2023) classified them into two, namely good and supportive messages, and unhelpful or harmful messages. On the one hand, good comments about the deceased, good comments about the bereaved, discussing memories of the deceased, expressing good aspects of the loss, expressing meeting the deceased after death, physical presence with the bereaved, provision of physical help, religious support, showing concerns for the bereaved well-being, and talking about feelings of the bereaved are supportive and therapeutic. On the other hand, the scholars identified interference in the bereaved life, minimising pains or inventing cheerful mood, offering advice, striving to heal up the healing process, undesirable practical assistance, unpleasant remarks, unwanted discussion about the deceased, and total identification with the bereaved emotion, exemplified by "I completely understand you" as unhelpful or in fact harmful. Indeed, one of the messages classified as unhelpful is focused on accelerating the bereaved healing process. Yet, grief is neither a problem nor illness meant to be cured or fixed; it is a natural process to be navigated as the bereaved goes through a normative and natural human experience that calls for facilitation instead of elimination (Ogunleye, 2021). Thus, rehabilitation from grief requires time, attention, and corrective gestures (Gross, 2015).

Specifically, Rajic et al. (2023) found that statements such as "Don't cry, tears won't bring him back", "Prayers will certainly help you", "Don't worry so much about it", are defective as coping strategies during bereavement. Therapeutically, these words are not merely unhelpful, as they not only leave the bereaved unhelped, but they are rather aggravating. Given that they are merely unhelpful, they would leave the receiver without soothing their pains, but considering that the words potentially take their grief to a higher level, the words are irritating

Experientially, and from literature, such as Ellis (2001) as cited in Tanhan (2014), unpleasant words are not limited to those coming from social supports alone, but a measure of them do emanate from the bereaved, either vocally or sub-vocally, with either of them carrying the same lethal effects on their target. It must be emphasised and admitted, however, that aggravating words made by social supports are not made with predetermined intention to hurt the receiver, nor the ones said by the bereaved themselves, rather, the utterers lack a deeper understanding, adequate assessment and judgement of the therapeutic implications of their statements, thus complicating the grieving process and its attendant rehabilitation.

MANAGING AGGRAVATING WORDS DURING GRIEF REACTIONS

Social support is a crucial factor that greatly influences bereavement outcomes (Aoun et al. 2018). Social support encompasses spoken and non-verbal communication between providers and recipients which reduces doubts about the given situation, oneself, and other people, and serves to facilitate perception of being in control of one's life situations (Albrecht & Adelman, 1987, as cited in Aoun et al., 2018). In this contribution, the providers of social support are termed social sup-

When a Balm Aggravates Pain

ports. Relatedly, both Bottomley et al. (2017) and Aoun et al. (2018) individually submitted that social supports which include friends, co-workers, family members, classmates, neighbours, religious faithful, and clergies are partakers of the healing process of bereaved persons. These social supports serve as buffer against the negative weight of grieving, as well as serving as additional resource to the bereaved efforts at rehabilitation (Bottomley et al., 2017). Realising that each of these persons could inadvertently offer aggravating words to the bereaved, counsellors have a professional responsibility to tutor and educate the social supports on the damaging effects of such words on the psyche of the bereaved, including how such words could be modified for meaningful therapeutic results. Similarly, noting that such aggravating words are not limited to social supports alone, since they could emanate from the bereaved themselves, the rehabilitative counsellor also has a professional duty to the bereaved on how to manage such words for accelerated desirable therapeutic outcome. Following are exploration of such aggravating words or statements.

This is a Catastrophe

Across all cultures, humans have learned to sympathise with people who are grieving, consequent upon occurrence of any unfavourable situation - whether man-made or natural, such as the COCID-19 pandemic. Notably, Tang and Xiang (2021) posited that the coronavirus pandemic is similar to a natural disaster that resulted in huge rise in Prolonged Grief Disorder (PGD) among the bereaved all over the world. In their eagerness to demonstrate their care and love toward grieving people, they make some utterances and statements meant to alleviate the pains experienced by the bereaved, but which could turn out to aggravate their discomfort. One of such statements is: "This is a catastrophe!" The statement can be likened to be a two-way dagger. Whenever this is said to the bereaved, they are cued to perceive the situation that befalls them as unprecedented in human history, such as loss of loved ones during the COVID-19 pandemic. Losing a beloved person to death is one of the most stressful life events (Rajic et al., 2023), and linking such death to a pandemic such as the COVID-19 can be more devastating. For, during the coronavirus pandemic, bereaved peoples' grieving situation and grief procedures were disrupted (Wallace et al., 2020), bereaved people usually require social supports to accelerate their healing process without which complicated grief could develop, leading to severe psychological stress (Bath, 2009, as cited in Rajic et al., 2023), but their participation was halted by social distancing controls and isolation (Eisma & Tamminga, 2020), and aggravated by shifting collective family grief to individual grief, shifting burial sites, as well as separation of family members from burial and post-burial rites (Asgari et al., 2023; Mitima-Verloop et al., 2022). Similarly, should the bereaved also initiate this untoward perception of the occurrence, they react to the loss as irrecoverable. Ellis (2001), as referenced in Tanhan (2014) listed this as one of the irrational and destructive beliefs that could hamper effective growth and functioning among humans.

Not minding the source of the statement – whether from within the bereaved, sympathisers, or from other social supports, it has potential for demoralising the bereaved, reduce their coping ingenuity and creativity, or completely destroy their creative coping. When this results, their resilience may have been deflated. Yet, Zalli (2024) described resilience as an essential element in functional adaptation to loss such as bereavement. According to Zalli, individuals who successfully deploy their resilience while going through bereavement often build emotional strength, adaptive coping mechanisms, as well as a feeling of growth following any traumatic experience. Stated differently, this is the bereaved person's ability to remain relatively stable in a life-enhancing way while navigating difficulties in their life trajectories.

Again?

Some unpleasant occurrences befall some people in quick succession. For instance, an individual who previously lost a car to a road crash wherein they came out unhurt may lose a sick child to death shortly thereafter. Similarly, the death of a sibling may follow that of a spouse for an individual. In each of these cases, on the one hand, the bereaved may ask rhetorically: "Again?" It could be also be: "Why me, again?". At some other time, on the other hand, they could also utter it questioningly in the presence of trusted sympathisers, or social supports. Often times too, social supports and sympathisers, or ask: "Again?" or "You, again?" To the bereaved, it could be uttered to report the weight of additional grief the second occurrence has brought on them, and perhaps crave for more sympathy, but it could add up to making them believe that nature and externalities are cruel to them, which may cripple self-initiatives toward rehabilitation. Even though the utterance is intended to pacify the trauma of the bereaved, they may end up doing more damage than good. In such statement, the bereaved cognitively recollects and adds the pains of earlier unpleasant occurrence to the one at hand, and likely reacts to double loss instead of the one at hand. Notably, every occurrence of a loss in whatever form is unpleasant, and when such loses follow in succession, the effects can be traumatic, but every misfortune should be treated on its own merit, rather than conjoining them to mean serial mishaps.

In all, such statement is injurious, as they enhance externalisation of events in one's life trajectories, which could greatly undermine ingenuity, creativity, and initiatives to creatively deploy resources to navigate unpleasant situation. Interestingly, while Zeigler-Hill and Shackelford (2020) found that internal locus of control people who demonstrate convictions of being in control of their life and their situations reported

When a Balm Aggravates Pain

enhanced psychological wellness, perseverance, and higher satisfaction with life, including conscientiousness, internal locus of control and self-control individuals have been reported by Botha and Dahmann (2023) to exhibit healthier lifestyle and enhanced physical and mental wellness. Thus, on the one hand, "I feel sorry for you on this happening" could be healing to the bereaved when said by sympathisers than 'Again?'. On the other hand, the bereaved would feel self-involved and self-helpful by saying "This is discouraging, but I can manage it well".

Just Forget About it

Students in Crisis Intervention Counselling class were asked to recount any emotional hazard they had encountered in their previous past, which almost resulted in, or actually led to crisis, and how they managed it. One of the students narrated how she was devastated when she lost her highly treasured mother following a one-day-sickness. Narrating how she was inconsolably mournful for weeks, she recalled that the statement: "Just Forget about It" wounded her so much that anytime it was uttered, she would look at the face of the utterer and cry the more, and finally mark the utterer as one of her avowed enemies. Additionally, when she was asked to reveal what was injurious in the advisory statement, she said she interpreted it to being exhorted to forget her late mother with all the good she meant to her, and stop further tribute. The unprofitability of such statement is strengthened in Rajic et al. (2018) who established that "Don't worry so much about it" as lacking in healing when said to the bereaved by social supports. Similarly, Oh et al. (2021) classified messages offered people in crisis into low person-centred, moderately person-centred, and high person-centred. An example of the low person-centred is "You need to move on with life". Such message is believed to refuse to acknowledge an individual's emotion and declare how they ought to think, behave, and feel.

Therapeutically, when asked how the statement could have been recast for measurable healing effect, she said: "You can't forget it, but don't overdo your crying so you do not injure yourself", or "It is unforgettable, but just take it as it has happened". Thus, it can be inferred that therapeutically, the grieving person could reassure themselves, or offer the assurance that their loss is huge, but it is desirable to move on with life. Building on this, Ogunleye (2021) averred that a statement such as: "What will it look like when you are remembering (the deceased or incident) but also moving forward?" would be clinical than exhorting the bereaved to forget about their grief.

You Will Have Another ...

In the same Crisis Intervention Counselling class (mentioned earlier), in which students were asked to recount any emotional hazard they had experienced in time past, which almost led to crisis, or actually resulted in crisis, and how they walked through it, another student also narrated how he felt when he lost his mother at the time he was writing his Senior Secondary School Certificate Examination. He recounted that he grieved uncontrollably for weeks, and that the resulting consequences negatively contributed to his poor performance in the examination. In his own case, the statements that infuriated him most were: "Act like a man", and "You will have another mother". He said the statements enraged and injured him intensely such that he felt like slapping everyone who uttered such statements. Interestingly, when asked what was injurious to him in the statements, he narrated that the deceased cared for him as a male child; he wondered why anyone would encourage him to mourn her as a female. He concluded that he knew he could not have another mother, and that even if his late mother was a twin, her twin sister must be another children's mother, not his own mother. In literature such as Oh et al. (2021), a message typified by "You need to move on with life " is categorised as being low person-centred, because the receiver's emotions are not acknowledged by the sender while prescribing how the recipient should behave, feel, and think. Critically examined, therefore, if the statement that urged someone in crisis to move on with their life is preposterous and lacking in healing, the one that prescribes how a bereaved ought to mourn is also anti-healing.

Furthermore, when asked how he would have preferred the utterers reword the statements in order to remove their inherent injuries, and heal his grief, he said: "The loss of your mother is obviously very painful to you, but bear it with manly strength", and "Be hopeful that someone else will help you in place of your mother wherever you need her" respectively would have been useful. It does appear therefore, that any statement that assures bereaved individuals of exact replacement of their loss may be impishly injurious to their recovery, and should be avoided for their total wellness.

You Should Have ...

One of the emotional reactions to loss, especially during bereavement, is feelings of guilt by the bereaved (Asgari et al., 2023; World Health Organisation, 2018). Human beings usually look back at the antecedents preceding an untoward occurrence, and strive to identify a point in the series of events where they think there was something they ought to have done but failed to do, which in its entirety or in conjunction with other faults, led to the present undesirable incident. When a be-

When a Balm Aggravates Pain

reaved person perceives such personal failure to act decisively and appropriately at one point or the other, resulting in the loss, they may utter the statement: "I should have ...", but when it comes from any of the social supports, it is usually in the form of: "You should have ...". The statements should be avoided by the bereaved person, as well as social supports. For, instead of ameliorating the agonies and pains of the bereavement, they could aggravate it, making the bereaved seem carefree, unsupportive, culpable, and irresponsible. The loss of a loved one in itself can be demoralising, and the added feelings of being culpable in the loss can be overbearingly traumatic. Additionally, given that such statement as "You should have ..." is silently disapproving of the bereaved person's choice of action while confining them to another one valued by the sympathiser, it still falls under Oh et al. (2021) low person-focused message, having refused to acknowledge the receiver's emotions, yet declaring how they should feel, think, and behave.

To therapeutically facilitate healing, on the one hand, social supports could recast the statement thus: "You tried all you could to avert it, but human beings are not perfect". On the other hand, the bereaved could reassuringly tell themselves: "I tried everything I could do to prevent it, but I am fallible as a human". Each of these provides commendation and reassurances instead of subtle indictment and condemnation.

I Know Exactly How You Feel

During many graphic outpouring of emotions relating to antecedents preceding sudden death, or such death coming after a protracted sickness of a beloved one, the bereaved may narrate their feelings in words or using catharsis. Catharsis describes the discharge of strong emotions or acting out of earlier experience of grief without having to relive it in the present; it is also called dramatic relief (Seligman & Reichenberg, 2015). Responding to this emotive narration, the listener in their zeal and zest to display oneness with the bereaved may say: "I know exactly how you feel". This statement could be highly offensive to the receiver even though the utterer never meant to hurt the feelings of the bereaved. Recalling that factors influencing grief reactions are many and may not be totally comprehensible to anyone per time, it would be wrong to assume that any social support or sympathiser can feel exactly what the bereaved feels. For death of a child for instance, the bereaved person could be terribly grieved seeing the deceased as a friend and not just a child. The age of the deceased, the cause of the death, and the circumstances leading to the death could greatly influence the extent of grieving for the bereaved. Given this, whoever is sharing the bereaved grief on account of a dead child is not equally feeling for them on account of losing a friend. This fact that no sympathiser can feel exactly the way a bereaved feels is established in Asgari et al. (2023) where one of

119

the respondents during COVID-19 pandemic reported that the death of her marriageable daughter was not just the loss of the deceased, but equally a loss of future aspirations of getting the deceased married, and getting grandchildren from her. In this case, for instance, a sympathiser may not feel beyond the loss of a grown-up daughter to coronavirus pandemic, as the loss of the attached future aspirations, being unregistered, would be unsearchable to them.

And especially where culture is involved, the death of a child could be more traumatising from one culture to the other. Among the Yoruba particularly, parents are expected to be survived by their children, and not the other way round. Additionally, among the same ethnic group, the death of a child whose corpse could be found by the bereaved for burial would be less grieving than one whose corpse they could not possess for burial - may be because the child drowned, or died in kidnapper's enclave. Furthermore, whereas the loss of an aged person who died in their sleep in their home is borne with less grief because it is believed that the deceased died while resting on their palm as pillow, the loss of another aged person (even older that the first) who died outside of their home in culturally detestable circumstances (ghastly motor accident, gun shot, or drowning) would engender heightened grief for the bereaved. Therefore, any sympathiser who would qualify to feel exactly what the bereaved whose aged deceased died in undesirable circumstances should be able to have understanding of the culture of the bereaved.

How undesirable the statement: "I know exactly how you feel" could be is established in a similar statement: "I completely understand you" described by Rajic et al. (2023) as a useless or potentially harmful message that social supports could say to bereaved individuals. For therapeutic effect, however, the statement could be: "No one can possibly understand exactly how you feel – so, you are the best comforter to yourself".

What You are Experiencing is Not So Bad as …

This statement is usually made before a bereaved to compare two (seemingly) unpalatable situations, in which either the person uttering the statement had gone through, or knew someone who had experienced it in time past. It is established that an individual who has had similar traumatic experience being undergone by a given bereaved can be invited to share their experiences with the bereaved whose grief is acute, prolonged or abnormal (Aoun et al. 2018). Among the Yoruba, the statement is often made to reassure a bereaved person that their present loss is not as terrible as one encountered by another bereaved who had two such experiences previously. For instance, if the bereaved lost his child during labour, it could be said to console the husband so as not to grieve excessively, reminding him that someone else had lost both spouse and the child before now. Again, if a parent lost

When a Balm Aggravates Pain

their child to drowning but the corpse was recovered, they could be reminded of another parent who never recovered the corpse of their child. Thus, to the bereaved who never wanted any of the tragic occurrences, the statement could be infuriating. In addition, the death of an adult child whom the parents have come to depend on would be more damaging than an adult child without such status but who looked up to their parents for survival.

By and large, considering that no two individuals grief exactly the same way, it can be inferred that grieving is personal to each individual grieving (Gross, 2015), and the grieving process may differ from one bereaved to another, and their coping usually may hinge on application of environmental, cultural, psychological, and religious factors which are not same for all persons, and across climes.

I Cannot Bear This!

Among those actions and activities described by Rajic et al. (2023) to be therapeutically healthful are discussing memories of the deceased, and saying pleasant things about the deceased both by sympathisers and bereaved persons. It is therefore desirable and in fact profiting for any bereaved to engage in cognitive evaluation of the value and worth of the deceased for proper placement, and to pay deserving tribute to the life and time the deceased shared with the bereaved. But whenever this could lead the bereaved to making a statement as: "I cannot bear this" (or I cannot live without him/her), the outcome may be undesirable. It is close to expecting that life must go the exact way the bereaved had pre-planned it, that it must not be difficult and at no time frustrating. This is what Ellis (2001) as cited in Tanhan (2014) described as low tolerance, whereby a person draws an illogical conclusion that an undesirable event is awful, unbearable, and unmanageable. Of note, irrational beliefs are extreme statements that potentially lead to negative emotions and difficulties in coping with difficult life experiences. Furthermore, Alvarenga et al. (2021) asserted that one of the elements required by bereaved persons to successfully work through their grief and trauma is hope. The scholar noted on the one hand, that while the bereaved hope enlarges when they can (hopefully) visualise the possibilities of living beyond their on-going grief to a rewarding future, their hope wanes when they become discouraged, on the other hand. Notably, one of the hope killers is such statement. Rather than: "I cannot bear this" (or I cannot live without her/him), the better, useful and therapeutically helpful statement could be: "It will certainly be difficult to bear your absence, but I shall live on to keep your memory alive".

Do Not Do Anything For Now!

At the outset of some bereaved persons starting to engage in some therapeutic physical and productive activities such as gardening, laundering, taking a walk outside of the house, cooking, etc., social supports around them used to advise them not to do anything yet, believing that they might be careless in doing some of the activities. In an activity such as gardening, for instance, it is believed it could result in self-injury arising from worry-induced absent-mindedness. Besides, in an activity such as laundering, it is believed the bereaved would not be able to wash clean. Some things could be inherently wrong with the advisory statement that the bereaved should not do anything yet. To start off, it could be that the bereaved decision to commence any of such physical exercises is hinged on rehabilitative counsellor's therapeutic guidance. Besides, it is unhealthy to discourage any bereaved to return to functionality after normal exhibition of grief reactions consequent upon loss of their loved one. Finally, the advice fails to indicate for how long the bereaved might still wait before engaging in such therapeutic exercise. Interestingly, Seligman and Reichenberg (2015) submitted that clients have some roles to play in their adjustment, coping, and rehabilitation, and one of these is full participation in their treatment plans, in order to facilitate their recovery. Additionally, physical activities positively accelerate mental health for all people, being able to block anxiety and depression (McMahon et al. 2017), and for bereaved individuals particularly, Williams et al. (2023) established that physical activities is therapeutic, promotes confidence, consolidates emotional outlet, facilitates self-discovery, as well as offers opportunity for expanded social support.

Instead of obstructing physical engagements for the bereaved, they should be encouraged by asking them if they require assistance to do the same task, or are careful enough to do them; social supports could also monitor how well they do what they chose to do, in order to ascertain if there is no lethality in the activities they engage in.

Do Not Vicariously Narrate the Occurrence for the Bereaved

In clinical practice, one of the rehabilitative processes that enhances recovery from grieving is allowing the bereaved to narrate the antecedents to the occurrence, dramatize their grief and pains, anxieties, and hopelessness, among other feelings, using catharsis. More often than not, when a bereaved individual commences to narrate their ordeals in the presence of others, some zealous social supports thought it wise to assist the bereaved do their narration, either because such social support felt the bereaved person had done it a couple of times, or they observed a pause by the bereaved person mid-way into their narration. Additionally, it could be that the

When a Balm Aggravates Pain

social support who usurped the bereaved narrative role did not like their perceived accompanying distress, and therefore assumed it would not help their healing. Yet, such narration could be very useful to accelerating the bereaved recovery. Given this, it could be seen as preposterous to the social support who usurped the narrative role of the bereaved. The intention of any sympathiser to assist bereaved people narrate their loss could be counterproductive, no matter how good their intention may seem facially. It could be seen as assisting the bereaved to postpone their grieving. And given this, Asgari et al. (2023) reasoned that if grieving is not done timely, it is a lump in the throat of the bereaved, leading to enhanced grieving and extension of its duration; and the grief may still resurface in other situations and in different forms, which may predict some psychological problems.

According to Ogunleye (2021), one of the practices that facilitate desirable change in a bereaved person is (for counselling professionals) to allow them to do their homework without intruding on their silence, or not leading clients to say what they think and feel, but rather encourage them to explore, identify, and own their feelings and thoughts and express them by themselves. Therefore, on the one hand, rehabilitative counsellors should encouragingly facilitate the bereaved narration of their experience by themselves, using their own thoughts and feelings expressed in words and actions, while discouraging social supports from vicariously narrating their agonies for them, on the other hand.

CONCLUSION

Having exhaustively explored the objectives of this contribution, the conclusion can be drawn that no human being can successfully escape the loss of dear ones in a lifetime, and one of the ways to react to such loss is through grieving. Similarly, sympathisers and a network of social support people including clergies, religious faithful, classmates, neighbours, friends, and family members of the bereaved assign themselves the social responsibility of condolences visits with a view to comforting and consoling them and facilitate their healing process. Furthermore, because of the ignorance of some of the social supports, and their failure to critically analyse the therapeutic outcome of the words they say to the bereaved, or such words that the bereaved individuals utter to themselves, words that are supposed to serve as balm to their pains subsequently become aggravating, worsening their grief reactions. In addition, rehabilitative counsellors have a dual role both to bereaved individuals and social supports to inform, educate, and enlighten them on the lethality of such aggravating words, and how they could be modified for positive therapeutic effect. For the counsellors to be able to perform these roles professionally and adequately, grief and trauma education counselling must be essentially part of the curricular of counsellor-training institutions, and student-counsellors must be adequately trained in this. It is only after this that rehabilitative counsellors can become proficient in the techniques of healing bereaved people in order to enhance their return to pre-grief functionality, thus contributing to their overall wellness.

Discussion Questions

1. Differentiate between grief and bereavement.
2. Identify, and explain the stages involved in bereavement process, according to Worden (2018).
3. Identify any four distinctive groups of people that constitute social supports to the bereaved in a given culture, and explain their roles in the healing process of the bereaved individual.
4. What makes a word aggravating to the bereaved in grief and trauma counselling? Explain any four aggravating words said the bereaved persons, and recast each of the words for therapeutic effect.
5. Contrast what social supports meant to achieve with aggravating words, and what such words might bring upon the bereaved ultimately.

REFERENCES

Alvarenga, W. A., deMontigny, F., Zeghiche, S., Verdom, C., & Castanheira, L. (2021). Experience of hope: An exploratory research with bereaved mothers following perinatal death. *Women and Birth; Journal of the Australian College of Midwives*, 34(4), e426–e434. 10.1016/j.wombi.2020.08.01132950437

Aoun, S. M., Breen, L. J., White, I., Rumbold, B., & Kellehear, A. (2018). What sources of bereavement support are perceived helpful by bereaved people and why? Empirical evidence for the compassionate communities approach. *Palliative Medicine*, 32(8), 1378–1388. 10.1177/026921631877499529754514

Asgari, M., Ghasemzadeh, M., Alimohamadi, A., Sakhael, S., Killikelly, C., & Nikfar, E. (2023). Investigation into grief experiences of the bereaved during the covid-19 pandemic. *Omega*, 0(0), 1–20. 10.1177/00302228231173075371 84963

Botha, F., & Dahmann, S. C. (2023). Locus of control, self-control, and health outcomes. *SSM - Population Health*, 25, 101566. 10.1016/j.ssmph.2023.10156638077246

Bottomley, , Burke, L. A., & Neimeyer, R. A. (2017). Domains of social support that predict bereavement distress following homicide loss. *Omega*, 75(1), 3–25. 10.1177/0030222815612282 28395645

Bottomley, J. S., Burke, L. A., & Neimeyer, R. A. (2017). Domains of social support that predict bereavement distress following homicile loss. *Omega*, 75(1), 3–25. 10.1177/0030222815612282 28395645

Eisma, M. C., & Tamminga, A. (2020). Grief before and during the COVID-19 pandemic: Multiple group comparisons. *Journal of Pain and Symptom Management*, 60(6). https://doi.org/10.1016/j.jpainsymma.2020.10.004

Gross, R. (2015). *The nature and experience of grief. In understanding grief: An introduction* (1st ed.). Routledge. 10.4324/9781315727936

McMahon, E. M., Corcoran, P., O'Regan, G., Keely, H., Cannon, M., Carli, V., Wasserman, C., Hadlaczky, G., Sarchiapone, M., Apter, A., Balazs, J., Balint, M., Bobes, J., Brunner, R., Cozman, D., Haring, C., Iosue, M., Kaess, M., Kahn, J. P., & Wasserman, D. (2017). Physical activity in European adolescents and associations with anxiety, depression and well-beign. *European Child & Adolescent Psychiatry*, 26(1), 111–122. 10.1007/s00787-016-0875-927277894

Ogunleye, T. (2021). Effective grief management: The role of the professional counsellor. In T. D. O. Adewuyi, B. K. Odu., & K. Olagunju (Eds.), *Topical issues in socio-personal guidance and counselling* (68-74). Brightways Publishers.

Oh, S. K., Yoo, K. H., & Owlett, J. (2021). Focusing on the "public" in public relations: The importance of person-centred messages (PCMs) in crisis communication on Twitter. *Journal of International Crisis and Risk Communication Research*, 4(1), 93–128. 10.30658/jicrcr.4.1.4

Rajic, I., Genc, A., & Batic-Ocovaj, S. (2023). Relationships between bereavement support strategies and empathy dimensions. *Primenjena Psihologia*, 16(2), 229–267. 10.19090/pp.v16i2.2449

Seligman, L., & Reichenberg, L. W. (2015). *Theories of counselling and psychotherapy; Systems, strategies, and skills* (4th ed.). Pearson.

Skalski, S., Konaszewski, K., Dobrakowski, P., Surzykiewics, J., & Lee, S. A. (2022). Pandemic grief in Poland: Adaptation of a measure and its relationship with social support and resilience. *Current Psychology (New Brunswick, N.J.)*, 41(10), 7393–7401. 10.1007/s12144-021-01731-633935472

Tang, S., & Ziang, Z. (2021). Who suffered most after deaths due to COVID-19? Prevalence and correlates of prolonged grief disorder in COVID-19 related bereaved adults. *Globalization and Health*, 17(1), 1–9. 10.1186/s12992-021-00669-533573673

Tanhan, F. (2014). An analysis of factors affecting teachers' irrational beliefs. *Educational Sciences: Theory & Practice*, 14(2), 465–470. 10.12738/estp.2014.2.1724

Wallace, C. L., Wladkowski, S. P., Gibaon, A., & White, P. (2020). Grief during the COVID-19 pandemic: Considerations for palliative care providers. *Journal of Pain and Symptom Management, 60*(1), Article e70-e76. 10.1016/j.jpainsymman.2020.04.012

Williams, J., Howett, N., & Shorter, G. W. (2023). What roles does physical activity play following the death of a young person? A qualitative investigation. *BMC Public Health*, 23(1), 210. 10.1186/s12889-022-14542-636721110

Worden, J. W. (2018). *Grief counselling and grief therapy: A handbook for mental health practitioner*. Springer. 10.1891/9780826134752

World Health Organisation (2018). *International classification of diseases for mortality and morbidity statistics* (11th Revision). WHO.

Zalli, E. (2024). Grief and resilience: Finding strength and growth through the grieving process. *Norwegian Journal of Development of the International Science*, 128, 48–55. 10.5281/zenodo.10817324

Zeigler-Hill, V., & Shackelford, T. K. (2020). *Encyclopedia of personality and individual differences*. Springer. 10.1007/978-3-319-24612-3

When a Balm Aggravates Pain

KEY TERMS AND DEFINITIONS

Aggravating Words: These are words said by social supports to the bereaved, or uttered by the bereaved, meant to assuage the pains of loss, but which worsen the bereaved pains.

Bereaved: An individual who has lost a dear person.

Catharsis: A situation which encourages a bereaved person to dramatise or act out their grief without having to relive the grief in the present.

Crisis Intervention Counselling Class: A class in which crisis intervention course took place among students and their teacher.

Grief: A condition of intense unhappiness experienced by someone following the death of their beloved.

Rehabilitation: The process of assisting the bereaved person to overcome their grieving condition and return to normal life.

Rehabilitative Counsellor: A trained professional counsellor who is skilled in using grief and trauma counselling to assist the bereaved return to pre-bereavement functionality.

Social Supports: The network of people such as friends, members of family, neighbours, classmates, clergies of the bereaved who actively participate in the bereaved recovery.

Sympathisers: These are the people who visit the bereaved at their convenience, without the zeal and zest to facilitate the healing process of the bereaved.

Therapeutic Effect: This is the outcome or consequence that the professional intervention of rehabilitative counsellors or social supports could have on the recovery on the bereaved.

Yoruba: The ethnic group who live in the six Southwestern states of Nigeria, comprising Oyo, Osun, Ondo, Ogun, Lagos, and Ekiti; the people also speak Yoruba as their language.

Chapter 6
Children Grieve Too:
Offering School–Based Bereavement Support Groups

Kailey Bradley
Refuge Counseling, LLC, USA

Emily Horton
https://orcid.org/0000-0002-7084-4853
University of Houston-Clear Lake, USA

ABSTRACT

Children represent an often-forgotten group of mourners. Helping professionals must be cautious about making assumptions regarding the inherent resilience of children. Moreover, helping professionals need to avoid minimizing the deleterious effects of grief on young clients. Grief impacts all children differently. Because children's grief often manifests differently than adults' grief, bereaved children can go underassessed and undertreated. Grief support groups in local school settings can be an efficacious way of supporting bereaved youth. The facilitative nature of peer support can promote healing through elements of universality and shared experiences. Due to their developmental level, students may benefit from knowing a fellow student has navigated something similar. In this chapter, the authors detail a grief support group model for mental health professionals tending to the unique mental health needs of bereaved youth.

DOI: 10.4018/979-8-3693-1375-6.ch006

Copyright © 2024, IGI Global. Copying or distributing in print or electronic forms without written permission of IGI Global is prohibited.

Children Grieve Too

INTRODUCTION

Over 7.3% of children experience the death of a parent or sibling by the age of 18 (Burns et al., 2020). According to the Judith Ann Griese (JAG) institute, one in twelve U.S. children will experience the death of a parent or sibling by age 18. If there are 24 children in a kindergarten class, two of them will lose a parent or sibling by the time they turn 18 (Burns et al., 2020). Importantly, the bulk of the statistics only emphasize children who experience parent or sibling loss, not accounting for the grief experiences of children navigating other types of loss. The COVID-19 pandemic has brought increased attention to the impact of childhood bereavement. More than one million COVID-19 deaths in the United States include parents, grandparents, and other caregivers for children (Treglia et al., 2023). BIPOC children were more than twice as likely as White children to experience caregiver loss (Centers for Disease Control and Prevention, 2021).

The support group model provided in this chapter will highlight the benefits of offering support groups for grieving children within a school setting for school counselors, school-based counselors, and counselors who collaborate with local school districts. We provide practical and applicable strategies for helping professionals working with grieving individuals in earlier stages of development. The group curriculum will highlight the unique challenges and symptoms of younger elementary aged children and older elementary aged children. An intervention will be provided that is applicable to each age group. This chapter is unique in that it provides concrete suggestions and although research has been done on childhood bereavement support groups, this book chapter sought to provide applicable and accessible strategies for mental health professionals. Consequently, this chapter seeks to bridge the gap between research and clinical practice.

UNIQUE CHALLENGES FACED BY CHILDHOOD AND ADOLESCENT GRIEVERS

The loss of a loved one, especially a parent or other caregiver, is a significant moment in a child's life. Although many bereaved children exhibit resiliency, children who experience bereavement are at higher for mental health diagnoses like depression, anxiety, alcohol and substance abuse disorders, and suicidality if they are not provided with adequate support and early intervention (Linder et al., 2024; Treglia, 2023). Children from marginalized communities are at higher risk for poor outcomes including post-traumatic stress symptoms, stress and anxiety, and a lack of access to mental health support (Treglia et al., 2023).

Children face unique challenges and a wide range of emotions when they experience grief (Lytje & Dyregrov, 2023). The group model proposed in this chapter will provide strategies for elementary aged children, with an intervention relevant to younger elementary school students (grades kindergarten through second grade) and older elementary school children (third grade through sixth grade). Children are confronted with a wide range of emotions such as anger, guilt, sadness, and anxiety (Lytje Dyregrov, 2023). Additionally, grieving children may encounter somatic symptoms, such as sleep disturbances, an increase in infections, confusion, and difficulty focusing. Children may also experience cognitive distortions such as feeling a sense of responsibility for caregivers' deaths (i.e., that they somehow caused the death (Treglia et al., 2023). Grieving may face an increased awareness of mortality, such as talking frequently about death, having a lot of questions about what comes after death, and a fear of death or sickness (Assadi, 2023).

The mental health challenges unique to bereaved children necessitate creative and engaging interventions on the part of professionals working with them. Children grieve developmentally; they encounter different symptoms and experiences based on how old they are. A developmental perspective on grief means that the needs of children based on their ages are different, and thus interventions should be tailored to fit those needs. For example, a young child in younger grades (kindergarten through second grade) may not grasp the permanency of death, whereas older elementary school aged children do. Consequently, supporting grieving children necessitates an awareness of where the individual is developmentally (Alvis et al., 2023; Treglia et al., 2023).

SUPPORTING GRIEVING CHILDREN

Accessing mental health support is integral for grieving children. Many options exist for supporting childhood grievers including child-focused individual counseling, family counseling, and grief camps, and all of which have been shown to be effective (Alvis, et al., 2023). Nevertheless, the completion of treatment is not consistent due to a wide range of barriers including transportation, insurance coverage, and caregiver grief (Linder et al., 2024). School-based support groups are an additional option for supporting grieving children. Support groups can facilitate opportunities for verbal processing, creative interventions, and peer support (Linder et al., 2024).

Given the barriers to supporting childhood mental health, school-based support groups have been found to be effective in decreasing mental health symptoms for bereaved youth (Treglia et al., 2023). School-based groups can provide space for peer support among students who already know one another and can support one another during the school day (Linder et al., 2024). Moreover, school-based men-

Children Grieve Too

tal health groups have been shown to be effective in treating traumatic stress and complicated grief (Alvis et al., 2023). While existing literature denotes the impact of school-based support groups for bereaved children, gaps in understanding and implementation remain. Despite recognizing the impact of school-based support groups, the literature on the nuances of the support group's delivery and curricula remains scant. Thus, this book chapter attempts to begin filling the gap in the literature for helping professionals who recognize the impact of school-based bereavement groups with an appropriate curriculum tied to the unique mental health needs of youth navigating loss.

CURRICULUM

We designed the school-based support group curriculum to target common themes that arise among bereaved children. Although the terminology of support group tends to be associated with a group that is open-process and has no curriculum, we believe that curriculum within a six-week childhood bereavement group can add structure and that children experiencing loss need structure embedded within the support group due to their unique needs (Linder et al., 2024). The curriculum is evidence based and this will be reflected in the description of each intervention.

Each week will highlight a particular theme that arises in grief. The following themes will be included: (1) introduction/ground rules of the group, (2) emotions: what does my grief feel like, (3) relationships, why don't my friends get it, (4) physical impact of grief, what grief feels like in my body, (5) spiritual impact of grief, I have a lot of questions, and lastly (6) wrap up/what I will be taking with me from my grief. According to Coenen (2024), grief affects all areas of our lives, including the cognitive, emotional, physical, and spiritual domains. Thus, this group curriculum will focus on each domain by providing a brief description of the domain, and an activity that can be done within the group that can help grieving students process the loss in helpful ways.

The group curriculum is designed for younger elementary aged (grades kindergarten through second grade) students and older aged elementary aged students (grades third grade through sixth grade). Each theme will be described with attention to how the theme manifests in both younger elementary students and older elementary students. Additionally, there will be an intervention provided for younger elementary aged students and an intervention provided for older elementary aged students. This was done to make the group curriculum accessible and inclusive of elementary aged students.

Week One: Introductions, Ground Rules

During the first week, facilitators will address group guidelines and go over the format of the group. Wolfelt (2021) opined that offering a closed, structured group helps instill safety within the group. A closed group, where participants are not able to come and go from the group, will be used for this group. The ground rules will set the tone for the remaining 6 weeks of the group. Sample group rules include (1) respect for each participant's grief response (2) avoid advice giving and focus more on listening to one another (3) participation is voluntary, but it will help instill safety if group members engage within the activities each week (4) kindness and compassion will guide each week.

Group facilitators can ask participants to add items to this list of sample ground rules and ask participants what they would need to feel safe within the group. One theme within the sample ground rules is establishing safety. A children's book which presents specific ways to create safety including active listening, not giving advice, and being respectful of differences in how we might process hard things will be used as a template for group members to consider safety within this group. The interventions used in this first week of group are evidenced based, as Hanauer et. al, (2024) posited that providing opportunities for sharing memories is effective and helpful for childhood grievers in group settings.

Weekly Activity

During the first week, group members will be given a chance to share the name of their person of their loved one who died and a favorite memory they have of them if they are comfortable. In this group, sample questions that can be used to help participants begin to talk about memories include: (1) what was your person's favorite holiday, (2) share about a trip you took with your loved one, (3) talk about your person's laugh, (4) what type of music, movies, or TV did your person enjoy, (4) what is a recipe your loved one like to make?

The questions above may not developmentally appropriate for younger elementary aged children; thus, the following activity is proposed for younger children to better fit their developmental needs. Younger children could take a piece of construction paper and simply draw a favorite memory they have with their loved ones.

Week Two: Emotional Impact/Psychological Impact of Grief

Identifying the wide-ranging, and often conflicting emotions can be challenging in grief for both children and adults (Lytje & Dyregrov, 2023). This week's theme is experienced differently between younger and older elementary aged students.

Children Grieve Too

For example, older elementary aged students may be able to verbally identify the emotions they are experiencing; whereas younger elementary aged students may struggle to identify the emotions they are experiencing (Treglia et. al, 2023).

The importance of attending to emotions of grieving children is evidenced by research done by (Hanauer et al., 2024) whose metanalysis of various interventions used to help grieving children process. This research identified that in general psychosocial interventions reduce grief symptoms, with the acknowledgement that further empirical studies would strengthen and reinforce the importance and efficacy of psycho-social interventions for grieving children. Thus, the interventions for this week focus on emotional processing with an intervention provided for younger elementary aged students and older elementary aged students.

Weekly Activity

This week, group participants will play a game that the authors are labeling "emotion freeze tag." This game was selected as it reflects the developmental stage of younger children, who may have difficulty processing feelings. Moreover, this game involves movement and encourages participants ways to not get stuck in the feeling. For students who cannot read yet, feeling faces or feeling pillows can be used instead of words on paper. First, participants will notice that the facilitator has brought a large bowl with slips of paper on it. On each sheet of paper, a feeling word is written. A few sample feelings that facilitators might want to include are sadness, anger, frustration, confusion, anxiety, and fear. The facilitator will play music and when the music stops, the last group member to freeze selects one of the slips of paper from the bowl and will share a time where they have felt the emotion written on the sheet of paper. For example, a participant may select sadness and share that sometimes it makes them sad that some of their friends do not understand how hard grief is.

Older elementary aged students will engage in an emotion collage this week. These students will use old magazines to cut up words, images, and colors that they associate with the emotions they are experiencing in their grief. We feel that this activity resonates with adolescent grievers as it allows them to creatively express and engage with themselves, and others in the group.

Week Three: Social Impact of Grief

Children and adolescent grievers may experience feelings of isolation because they may feel that peers who have not encountered loss do not understand what they are going through. Support from peers who have also encountered loss can help grieving children as feelings of isolation can be common and developmentally children may not feel that they are the ones who have encountered significant loss and thus may worry that there is something wrong with them or that they did something wrong (Joy et. al., 2024). For younger elementary aged grievers, isolation may look clinginess or out of the norm tearfulness or even behavior regression like bedwetting (Treglia et al., 2023). For older elementary aged grievers, isolation may manifest as acting out (getting into fights), withdrawing from extracurricular activities and a decline in grades (Joy et al., 2024; Treglia et al., 2023).

According to (Hanauer et. al, 2024) grief support groups have been found to be efficacious in reducing feelings of social isolation as they are a place for students to process feelings and a way to brainstorm how to interact and engage in social situations during and after loss. This week's interventions leverage the benefits of social interaction in groups by allowing students to brainstorm together ways to process frustration and anxiety during social interactions.

Weekly Activity

This week in the group, the facilitator will share the following scenario that might be relatable to group participants. This scenario can be written out on a flash card and reads as follows: "Your best friend is complaining about their mom saying, 'She's so annoying, I hate her. You struggle to know how to respond because your mom died, and you would give anything to feel annoyed at her." After the scenario is read aloud, group members will take roughly five minutes to write out on a scrap sheet of paper to reflect on the following: (1) how would you respond if this were you in this scenario, (2) has this happened to you before, (3) how have you responded in the past, and (4) do you wish you had reacted differently? These questions may be abstract for younger elementary aged participants but are resonant for older grievers.

For younger elementary aged grievers, facilitators can have cards examples of how grief makes us feel. For example, a card might include a scenario stating, "I'm sad and mad that my daddy can't come to the school's daddy-daughter breakfast." Then, the group facilitator can ask "Have you ever felt like this?" This can engender conversation in ways that younger kids can relate to with a practical example that helps them identify their feelings associated with loss.

Week Four: Physical Impact of Grief

Grief can impact our body in numerous ways including, but not limited to, immune dysfunction, such as increased infections, brain fog, concentration problems, disturbed sleep, and restlessness (Cook et al., 2005, Kaplow et al., 2006). Moreover, according to Brown (2021), processing grief through activities that use the body, such as, walking, deep breathing, stretching, yoga, and dance aids individuals in

Children Grieve Too

processing cumulative grief. Thus, this activity will seek to help participants identify how their bodies grieve. The physical impact of grief manifests in both younger and older elementary aged grievers but like many of the week's themes, older grievers may be able to identify or associate their physical discomfort with grief which may be more challenging for younger grievers (Brown, 2021).

Weekly Activity

This week's activity will invite members to participate in a conversation about how their bodies have responded to the loss. A book associated with the many ways our bodies send messages if we listen will be provided to facilitate conversation on the theme. Children will be given a chance to practice listening to their bodies by taking one minute to identify what their body feels like exactly at that moment. The children could consider the following: Are you (1) tired, (2) hungry, (3) anxious, (4) bored, (5) hot or cold, (6) something else? Next, the group facilitator will invite participants to share. For example, one group member might say that they realized that their stomach was growling, and they were hungry and that they did not realize that until taking the time to listen. The group facilitator can then ask members to reflect on the following question: has it been easy or hard to listen to your body since your loss.

Older elementary aged students will jot down on a piece of paper the ways in their bodies respond to stress (via journaling). They will respond to the following prompt, "I know I am feeling upset when my body feels….".

Week Five: Spiritual Impact of Grief

Children who are grieving have a lot of questions including: is it my fault, why did this happen, is my person coming back, were they mad at me, where did they go, and using spirituality as a coping strategy can be beneficial to grieving children. One study found that children who used spiritual coping (but not necessarily religious coping) encountered greater personal growth after their loss (Hidalgo et al., 2022). This week's theme, spirituality is one that is consistent with both younger and older grievers; but may be particularly prominent in adolescent grievers who are already wrestling with existential and meaning-making questions (Hidalgo et al., 2022).

Weekly Activity

This week group members will read a book about the afterlife that is not specific to any religious or spiritual tradition. After reading the book, you can invite a discussion between group members based on the following questions: (1) What rituals

Children Grieve Too

did your family engage in, (2) did your family attend a funeral, and if so, what was that like, (3) did you have questions when you attended the funeral or even what a funeral was? Group facilitators should be careful to not assume any spiritual or religious affiliation of their group members and work to balance different belief systems within the group. These questions are relevant for younger elementary aged grievers, and an adapted activity for older elementary aged grievers is depicted below.

Older elementary aged grievers may have more existential questions and may desire a space to grapple with questions such as, why do bad things happen to good people? Group facilitators can encourage these questions by having participants anonymously write down big spiritual questions and put them in a box and the group leader read them off and talk about them. The group leader can also put in some common ones like the question, "Why do bad things happen to good people?"

Week Six: Wrap Up/Moving Forward with Our Grief

Group members may be sad to see the group end, so enough time must be dedicated to verbalizing the feelings of the group ending. Children who have encountered a loss are familiar with how difficult transitions can be and may feel anxiety about the transition of a group ending (Hooyman et al., 2021). Thus, having space for group members to transition from the group with hope, purpose, and meaning is vitally important.

Weekly Activity

This last week the participants will make a collage that depicts words, images, and insights that will take with them from the group. Facilitators can provide group members with old magazines and construction paper for the collage activity. In this activity, a participant might locate an image that shows sunshine that reminds her she is not alone in her loss which is something that they learned during the group.

Collage-making might be developmentally inappropriate for a younger elementary student so group facilitators might consider alternatives that align with the student needs. Specifically, facilitators can have members engage in a handprint painting with all individuals involved in the group as a takeaway reminder that they are not alone.

ETHICAL CONSIDERATIONS AND PRAGMATIC CHALLENGES

Group facilitators should be aware of several ethical and pragmatic considerations as they develop a grief support group within school settings. Pragmatic challenges can be addressed through a conversation with local schools in which the group

Children Grieve Too

will take place; consider the following questions as part of an initial meeting with school personnel: (1) where will the group be held, (2) are school counselors/school personnel acting as co-facilitators in the group or will they be available during the group, (3) what is the procedure for participant needs that go beyond the scope of the goals of the group. The school-based support groups can be facilitated by school counselors or others who collaborate with local school districts. For example, a local hospice organization or non-profit bereavement center can offer groups within a school setting.

School counselors can consider the following when implementing this group, starting with what to name the group. Grieving kids may feel like outliers if the group is identified as a "Grief Group." School counselors could consider naming the group "Coping with Transitions Group" to help alleviate any sense of isolation or feeling odd or weird for experiencing grief. Another practical consideration for school counselors is navigating how to locate students who may benefit from the group. One way to do this is to email school personnel (teachers and administrators) with a flyer with information about the group and asking them if they have any students in their class who might be interested in the group. School counselors can then contact students' guardians to obtain permission for their child to attend the group.

One important ethical consideration within a group is establishing its goals and purposes. This support group within school settings can be labeled a support group with aligned goals of offering support to grieving children. Secondly, it is an important ethical consideration to consider when to refer a child to more intensive mental health services. Wolfelt (2019) identified the importance of pre-screening potential group members and referring to individual counseling if the loss was particularly traumatic, if the student is currently struggling with suicidal ideation, and if the loss was very recent. The parameters of this support group should also include parameters on how long ago the loss was; for example, a relatively recent loss is different than a loss that occurred 2-3 years ago. For this support group, the recommendation would be that the loss occurred between 6 months and 2 years ago.

Additional ethical considerations in the development and implementation about this group should align with the American School Counseling Code of Ethics and facilitators should ensure that group is mindful about ethical mandates about confidentiality, respect for diversity/culture, selection of books, research-based interventions, competence in practice, and spirituality (American School Counselor Association, 2022). This manuscript concludes with discussion questions for counseling students that are compiled to help in ethical development of grief support groups for children.

CONCLUSION

Grieving children face a wide range of challenges, and need to be supported in creative and innovative ways that engender resiliency. This book chapter illuminates how to implement a childhood bereavement support group within schools. A curriculum was developed and described to highlight six important themes that grieving children may engage with during their loss. Lastly, some challenges and ethical considerations were considered.

DISCUSSION QUESTIONS

We propose that discussion questions could be used in a counselor education classroom to solidify learning of the content of this chapter. These questions include: (1) what barriers do you envision could occur in implementing a grief support group in a school setting (2) what solutions do you propose in reducing these barriers (3) what interventions do you feel most confident in using and which do you feel anxious about (4) what general challenges that childhood grievers encounter do you think would be addressed by this grief group curriculum?

Children Grieve Too

REFERENCES

Alvis, L., Zhang, N., Sandler, I. N., & Kaplow, J. B. (2023). Developmental manifestations of grief in children and adolescents: Caregivers as key grief facilitators. *Journal of Child & Adolescent Trauma*, 16(2), 447–457. https://doi-org.proxy.library.ohio.edu/10.1007/s40653-021-00435-0. 10.1007/s40653-021-00435-035106114

American School Counseling Association. (2022). *2022 ASCA code of ethics*. ASCA. https://www.schoolcounselor.org/About-School-Counseling/Ethical-Responsibilities/ASCA-Ethical-Standards-for-School-Counselors-(1)

Assadi, F. (2023). Understanding the Childhood Grief: What Should We Tell the Children? *International Journal of Preventive Medicine*, 14(1), 1–3. https://doi-org.proxy.library.ohio.edu/10.4103/ijpvm.ijpvm_371_22. 10.4103/ijpvm.ijpvm_371_2237855003

Brown, J. C. (2021). *An epidemic of violence. Fatal violence against transgender and gender non-conforming people in the United States in 2020*. Human Rights Campaign. https://reports.hrc.org/an-epidemic-of-violence-fatal-violence-against-transgender-and-gender-non-confirming-people-in-the-united-states-in-2020?_ga=2.185816937.1993557673.1707439958-2145036884.1707439958

Burns, M., Griese, B., King, S., & Talmi, A. (2020). Childhood bereavement: Understanding prevalence and related adversity in the United States. *The American Journal of Orthopsychiatry*, 90(4), 391–405. 10.1037/ort000044231999137

Centers for Disease Control and Prevention. (2021). *Distribution of COVID-19 deaths and populations, by jurisdiction, age, and race and Hispanic origin*. CDC. https://data.cdc.gov/NCHS/Distribution-of-COVID-19-Deathsand-Populations-by/jwta-jxbg.

Coenen, C. (2024). *Seasons of grief*. Jessica Kingsley Publishers.

Cook, A., Spinazzola, J., Ford, J., Lanktree, C., Blaustein, M., Cloitre, M., & Van der Kolk, B. (2005). Complex trauma. *Psychiatric Annals*, 35(5), 390–398. https://sites.northwestern.edu/cans/files/2022/08/Complex-trauma-in-children.pdf. 10.3928/00485713-20050501-05

Doerrfeld, C. (2018). *The rabbit listened*. Scallywag Press.

Garcia, G. (2019). *Listening to my body: A guide to helping kids understand the connection between their sensations (what the heck are those?) and feelings so that they can get better at figuring out what they need*. Skinned Knee Publishing.

JAG Institute. (2023). *Annual report indicating increased rate of childhood bereavement*. JAG Institute.

Hanauer, C., Telaar, B., Rosner, R., & Doering, B. K. (2024). The efficacy of psychosocial interventions for grief symptoms in bereaved children and adolescents: A systematic review and meta-analysis. *Journal of Affective Disorders, 350*, 164–173. https://doi-org.proxy.library.ohio.edu/10.1016/j.jad.2024.01.063

Hanson, W. (2002). *The next place*. Walden House Press.

Hidalgo, I. (2021). Spiritual coping and its effects on children's grief, personal growth, and mental health 2-24 months after the death of a parent, grandparent, or sibling. *Journal of Pediatric Healthcare, 36*(2), 212. .10.1016/j.pedhc.2021.07.003

Hooyman, N. R., Kramer, B. J., & Sanders, S. (2021). *Living through loss: Interventions Across the Life Span*. Columbia University Press.

Hussain, S. (2023). *Hamza attends a funeral*. Kube Publishing.

JAG Institute. (2023). *Annual report indicating increased rate of childhood bereavement*. JAG Institute. *https://www.prweb.com/releases/jag-institute-releases-annual -report-indicating- increased-rate-of-childhood-bereavement-876461466.html*

Joy, C., Staniland, L., Mazzucchelli, T. G., Skinner, S., Cuddeford, L., & Breen, L. J. (2024). What bereaved children want to Know About Death and Grief. *Journal of Child & Family Studies, 33*(1), 327–337. 10.1007/s10826-023-02694-x

Kaplow, J. B., Saxe, G. N., Putnam, F. W., Pynoos, R. S., & Lieberman, A. F. (2006). The long– term consequences of early childhood trauma: A case study and discussion. *Psychiatry*, 69(4), 362–375. 10.1521/psyc.2006.69.4.36217326730

Linder, L., Lunardini, M., & Zimmerman, H. (2024). Supporting Childhood Bereavement Through School-Based Grief Group. *Omega*, 89(2), 741–758. https:// doi-org.proxy.library.ohio.edu/10.1177/00302228221082756. 10.1177/00302228 22108275635357962

Rolls, L., & Payne, S. A. (2007). Children and young people's experience of UK childhood bereavement services. *Mortality*, 12(3), 281–303. 10.1080/13576270701430585

Treglia, D., Cutuli, J. J., Arasteh, K., & Bridgeland, J. (2023). Parental and other caregiver loss due to COVID-19 in the United States: Prevalence by race, state, relationship, and child age. *Journal of Community Health*, 48(3), 390–397. 10.1007/ s10900-022-01160-x36515763

Wolfelt, A. (2021). *The understanding your grief support group guide: Starting and leading a bereavement support group*. Companion Press.

Children Grieve Too

KEY TERMS AND DEFINITIONS

Younger Elementary Aged Students: In this manuscript, this refers to children in grades kindergarten through second grade.

Older Elementary Aged Students: In this manuscript, this refers to children in grades third grade through sixth grade.

APPENDIX I

Table 1. Grief group curriculum

Week Theme	Intervention (Younger Elementary Aged Children)	Intervention (Older Elementary Aged Children)	Suggested Readings
Week One: Ground Rules Interventions	Use a piece of construction paper and simply draw a favorite memory of loved ones.	During the first week, group members will be given a chance to share the name of their person of their loved one who died and a favorite memory they have of them if they are comfortable. In this group, sample questions that can be used to help participants begin to talk about memories include: (1) what was your person's favorite holiday, (2) share about a trip you took with your loved one, (3) talk about your person's laugh, (4) what type of music, movies, or TV did your person enjoy, (4) what is a recipe your loved one like to make?	The Rabbit Listened (Doerfeld,(2018)
Week Two: Emotional Impact/ Psychological Impact of Grief	This week, group participants will play a game that the authors are labeling "emotion freeze tag." For students who cannot read yet, feeling faces or feeling pillows can be used instead of words on paper.	Complete an emotion collage. These students will use old magazines to cut up words, images, and colors that they associate with the emotions they are experiencing in their grief.	

continued on following page

Children Grieve Too

Table 1. Continued

Week Theme	Intervention (Younger Elementary Aged Children)	Intervention (Older Elementary Aged Children)	Suggested Readings
Week Three: Social Impact of Grief	Facilitators can have cards examples of how grief makes us feel. For example, a card might include a scenario stating, "I'm sad and mad that my daddy can't come to the school's daddy-daughter breakfast." Then, the group facilitator can ask "Have you ever felt like this?" This can engender conversation in ways that younger kids can relate to with a practical example that helps them identify their feelings associated with loss.	This week in the group, the facilitator will share the following scenario that might be relatable to group participants. This scenario can be written out on a flash card and reads as follows: "Your best friend is complaining about their mom saying, 'She's so annoying, I hate her. You struggle to know how to respond because your mom died, and you would give anything to feel annoyed at her." After the scenario is read aloud, group members will take roughly five minutes to write out on a scrap sheet of paper to reflect on the following: (1) how would you respond if this were you in this scenario, (2) has this happened to you before, (3) how have you responded in the past, and (4) do you wish you had reacted differently? These questions may be abstract for younger participants but are resonant for older grievers.	

continued on following page

Children Grieve Too

Table 1. Continued

Week Theme	Intervention (Younger Elementary Aged Children)	Intervention (Older Elementary Aged Children)	Suggested Readings
Week Four: Physical Impact of Grief	Participants will read a book, which depicts the many ways our bodies send messages to us if we listen. Children will be given a chance to practice listening to their bodies by taking one minute to identify what their body feels like exactly at that moment. The children could consider the following: Are you (1) tired, (2) hungry, (3) anxious, (4) bored, (5) hot or cold, (6) something else? Next, the group facilitator will invite participants to share.	jot down on a piece of paper the ways in their bodies respond to stress (via journaling). They will respond to the following prompt, "I know I am feeling upset when my body feels…."	Listening to Your Body (Garcia, 2019).
Week Five: Spiritual Impact of Grief	This week group members will read book about what comes after death that is not specific to any religious or spiritual tradition. After reading the book, you can invite a discussion between group members based on the following questions: (1) What rituals did your family engage in, (2) did your family attend a funeral, and if so, what was that like, (3) did you have questions when you attended the funeral or even what a funeral was?	Group facilitators can encourage existential questions by having participants anonymously write down big spiritual questions and put them in a box and the group leader read them off and talk about them. The group leader can also put in some common ones like the question, "Why do bad things happen to good people?"	Hanson, W. (2002). *The next place.* Hussain, S. (2023). *Hamza attends a funeral.*

continued on following page

Children Grieve Too

Table 1. Continued

Week Theme	Intervention (Younger Elementary Aged Children)	Intervention (Older Elementary Aged Children)	Suggested Readings
Week Six: Wrap Up/ Moving Forward	Handprint painting	This last week the participants will make a collage that depicts words, images, and insights that will take with them from the group. Facilitators can provide group members with old magazines and construction paper for the collage activity. In this activity, a participant might locate an image that shows sunshine that reminds her she is not alone in her loss which is something that they learned during the group.	

Chapter 7
Assisting Teachers With Grieving Students:
Strategies for School Counselors

Kimberly Tharpe
Azusa Pacific University, USA

ABSTRACT

The educational setting has provided students with supports in the event of emotional struggles such as grief. Teachers are often the first individual a student seeks for support and some understanding. This chapter involves dividing the content into logical, structured sections that guide educators and counselors through understanding the role of the school, school counselors and teachers when effectively assisting grieving students. Issues of grief associated with the impact of COVID and the school will be addressed. A brief theoretical background examining relational developmental systems (RDS) metatheory as a conceptual framework will be discussed understanding the outcomes of school relationship and connectivity. Additionally, specific strategies for school counselors will be provided, to utilize when assisting teachers with grieving students.

INTRODUCTION TO UNDERSTANDING GRIEF IN THE EDUCATION SETTING

Experiencing the death of a loved one or caregiver is one of the most distressing and commonly reported traumas experienced by school-aged youth (Alvis et al., 2022; Linder et al., 2022). Data from 2015 shows that approximately 140 minors worldwide experienced parental death (Alvis et al., 2022). Estimates indicated that over 6% of school-aged children in the U.S. would experience parental death before

DOI: 10.4018/979-8-3693-1375-6.ch007

Copyright © 2024, IGI Global. Copying or distributing in print or electronic forms without written permission of IGI Global is prohibited.

Assisting Teachers With Grieving Students

the age of 18 (Alvis et al., 2022). These statistics rose during COVID-19 (Tempski et al., 2020). Some racial minorities, such as Black and Hispanic students, experience grief at a higher rate than White students. The issue of bereavement for school-aged children is essential because grief, and especially unaddressed grief, is associated with an array of mental and behavioral health issues that can compromise learning and educational outcomes, including but not limited to depression, maladaptive social behaviors, developmental impairment, suicidal ideation, poor academic outcomes, and posttraumatic stress symptoms (Alvis et al., 2022). Therefore, understanding grief, identifying grief-related symptoms, and supporting students through the grieving process are critical skills for educators. Educators, including teachers and school counselors, serve a crucial role in cultivating a supportive and empathetic learning environment for students who are grieving the loss of a caregiver or loved one so that students can thrive emotionally, socially, and academically.

Grief is a multifaceted experience encompassing psychological, emotional, and cultural domains. This chapter offers aspiring school counselors an empirical exploration of the role of schools and supporting teachers with strategies for working with grieving students. Key concepts related to grief in the context of education, and a description of the theoretical underpinnings of the relational developmental systems meta theory and its practical applications to strategies school counselors can leverage. An exploration of the multidimensionality of grief, including psychological, emotional, and cultural components will also be presented. The chapter concludes by discussing practical strategies and tips for school counselors based on three case studies as well as a discussion of the impacts of COVID-19 on grief in the context of education.

Understanding Grief

Each young person's reaction to grief is different, depending upon a variety of factors, such as ongoing developmental processes, disposition, and cultural context. Because children and adolescents depend significantly on adults in their immediate environment for support in navigating the grieving process of a parent or adult caregiver, teachers, and school counselors serve a critical role in supporting students through this process and mitigating the potential development of long-term maladaptive mental, emotional, or behavioral consequences (Alvis et al., 2022). According to the American Psychological Association, grief is described as the experience of emotional pain, discomfort, or anguish after a loss. This discomfort may be characterized by feelings of separation anxiety, psychological distress, using the restroom on themselves, apprehension toward future events, and sometimes, a sense of confusion (APA, 2022). Addressing grief in an educational setting requires acute sensitivity and understanding of the potential psychological and emotional symptoms students may be experiencing, as well as the cultural and contextual factors that could influence individual students' experiences of the grieving process and the manifestations of grief-related behaviors in the classroom (Lawrence, 2019). Often, educators lack sufficient training in the psychology of grieving and how to properly support students through the grieving process (Greiner et al., 2022). By better understanding and normalizing grief, teachers and counselors can play a crucial role in helping students recognize and accept their feelings and find healthy outlets of expression while grieving. Also, by recognizing that expressions of grief can take various forms depending on a student's sociocultural background, educators can play a key role in minimizing potential stigmatization otherwise associated with grief.

Role of Schools in Supporting Grieving Students

Young children and adolescents are navigating formative developmental years. The adults in a young person's life can significantly influence a young person's development through modeling, exemplary behavior, and providing support. Considering that students spend a significant percentage of waking hours in school settings, schools, and school staff have a responsibility to cultivate a supportive social and learning environment for students who are experiencing the challenging emotional and psychological symptoms of grief. Educators have the opportunity to leverage school environments as a context within which to provide routine and normalcy, social support systems, educational adaptations, and grief counseling services to bereaved students. Research conclusions indicate that consistency, routine, and supportive social environments are some of the most critically impactful factors in supporting youths' healthy advancement through the grieving process and the minimization of prolonged, adverse outcomes (Chronister et al., 2021; Lawrence, 2019; Levkovich & Elyoseph, 2021; Price et al., 2021). With the support and collaboration of sensitive leadership, school counselors, teachers and individuals supporting, the educational environment can foster supports that promote transparent and honest communication, trust between students and teachers, and a sense of connection—all of which are found to support grieving youths' psychological health adaptively (Chronister et al., 2021; Lawrence, 2019; Levkovich & Elyoseph, 2021). However, most teachers evaluated and surveyed feel helpless or overwhelmed when attempting to assist grieving students and seek help from faculty and staff (Hay et al., 2022; Levkovich & Elyoseph, 2021), thus pointing to the need for increased grief awareness and strategic intervention at district and institution levels. DeMuth et al. (2020) found that teachers surveyed desired a more structured bereavement assistance plan that would guide them in helping students, which supports the notion that schools and educational leaders have an important role to play in supporting grieving students.

Key Concepts

The following key concepts are fundamental to understanding childhood and adolescent grief in the context of classrooms and education settings.

Individualized Grief

The experience of grief is individual and unique to each student. Although theories concerning the grief process provide frameworks that can be used to explain and generalize the various psychological and emotional phases one may experience, such experiences are unique to the personal, cultural, and contextual background of each individual, influencing that individual's unique expressions, coping mechanisms, and needs (Kaplow et al., 2023).

Academic Grief Triggers

Certain factors inherent in a school's environment, such as the nature of pure relationships, academic pressure or stress, cultural components, or relationships with teachers and faculty, may amplify or trigger grief experiences and subsequent reactions in students. Recognizing these potential triggers can help school counselors provide students with more targeted and proactive support (Alvis et al., 2022).

Developmental Grief Dynamics

An individual's experience of the grieving process and corresponding symptoms or manifestations of grief vary depending upon the psychological developmental stage. Therefore, educators need to recognize age-related manifestations of grief and develop age-appropriate interventions that address the specific grief-related needs of students according to their developmental level (Kaplow et al., 2023).

Impact of Grief on Academic Outcomes

Recent empirical literature includes discussions pointing to significant adverse impacts of grief on academic outcomes for elementary, secondary, and Higher Education students (Price et al., 2021; Varga et al., 2021). For example, grief can affect social interaction and, thus, student learning. Because learning is significantly influenced by social interaction through processes such as scaffolding and peer support, some grief-related symptoms, such as social isolation and withdrawal, can negatively impact learning. Moreover, grief can impair students' concentration, minimize motivation, result in attendance issues, and increase the risk of bullying, which can lead grieving students to retreat into isolation. One recent study includes findings showing that approximately 10% of students using counseling services used off-campus professional counselors, while only 8% used campus center counseling services. Even fewer students used face-to-face, in-school support groups, suggesting that students may fear stigmatization and bullying from peers if seen using in-school counseling services (Varga et al., 2021). These findings highlight the importance of destigmatizing grief among teachers and students so that students face fewer social barriers in navigating the grieving process and, ultimately, potentially fewer academic detriments. If left unaddressed, grief can have significant long-term implications, such as exacerbated and potentially clinical depression, anxiety, and posttraumatic stress disorders, or can lead to prolonged grief disorder (PGD) (Alvis et al., 2022). Consequently, grief can negatively impact social relationships later in life and continuing education or career prospects due to compromising one's mental health. Specifically, researchers of a recent study found that among medical graduate students surveyed, over half experienced a loss within one month of being surveyed. Nearly 25% of students indicated that they would use institutional grief support resources if those resources were available (Price et al., 2021), which points to the opportunity educational facilities face in supporting grieving students through the continuation of their academic careers. The remaining 75% who would not use institutional grief support resources (Price et al., 2021) did not clarify why, but this statistic points to the potential influence of a fear of stigmatization in deferring students from seeking institutional support (Alvis et al., 2022).

ADDRESSING THE IMPACT OF COVID-19

A discussion of the grieving process in the education context would not be complete without mention of the significant impact the COVID-19 pandemic had on students across the globe. Not only were students, families, and educators faced with the stress of uncertainty and major transitions accompanying the pandemic, but students, educators, and families also experienced the compounded stress of the death of loved ones due to the pandemic (Tempski et al., 2020). The pandemic-associated losses give insight to educators concerning how school programs may be better adapted to support students through similar crises in the future and cultivate greater levels of resilience for all.

Unique Grief Challenges

The grief-related challenges associated with the pandemic were unique primarily because of their compounded nature. Pandemic-related grief experienced by educators and students alike was experienced alongside job loss, transitions to remote learning, and the uncertainty of global economic and public health scenarios (Tempski et al., 2020). All these factors significantly exacerbated students' stress levels, on top of the normal developmental stress of adolescence and school-age transitions students experience. Research indicates that the challenges students faced during the pandemic intersected all levels of students' social, emotional, and psychological functioning, involving educational, cognitive, relational, and logistic challenges. Students were forced to abruptly assume new routines, adapt to at-home learning environments, and learn to use new technologies, all while navigating loss, grief, and the uncertainty ahead (Karaman et al., 2021). The enormous challenges faced by students during the pandemic point to the need for educators to pay particularly close attention to the effect of compounded stress on students' academic outcomes and develop effective intervention strategies that prioritize grief education and counseling in future school settings (Castrellón et al., 2021).

Practical Application

Counselors can take an active role in encouraging grief education and practical interventions by continuing to encourage and engage in grief-related research and discussions with colleagues, board members, principals, and education associations. Additionally, Pincus et al. (2020) assert that school counselors have historically been under-recognized concerning their support for students and suggest that school administrators ought to prioritize the role of school counselors in supporting students' mental health, including through the grieving process. Also, expanding leave of absence policies to include greater inclusivity toward grieving students is recommended (Liew & Servaty-Seib, 2019; Sunde, 2021). For instance, the Grief Absence Policy for Students (GAPS) allows students to take a brief leave of absence for the death of an immediate family member as a granted bereavement leave. This policy was tested in various U.S. schools and found to be correlated with improvements in mental health measures (Liew & Servaty-Seib, 2019). Critics suggested the program would encourage abuse of the policy, but no significant associations were found with increased non-grief-associated absenteeism or significantly declined academic outcomes.

Practical Tips

- Review the school's current grief absence policies with board members and administrators. Work to expand the grief absence policy in alignment with cultural frameworks of students most served by the school. This may include drafting new preliminary absence policies, qualifications and requirements. It will also include collecting cultural data about students, and losses experienced by students through demographic census data as well as teacher observations and potential discussions with students and families.
- Work with administrators and board members to ensure COVID Safety protocols are in place, and comply with current regulatory guidelines.

THEORETICAL UNDERPINNINGS: RELATIONAL DEVELOPMENTAL SYSTEMS (RDS) METATHEORY

The relational developmental systems (RDS) metatheory (Wang et al., 2016) is valuable and appropriate in contextualizing and understanding the grieving process students may experience and how that process interfaces with the role the education environments, academic outcomes, teachers, faculty members and school counselors serve in supporting students. The RDS metatheory specifically addresses the positive connectivity between students and their school environment. As an interdisciplinary framework explaining human development through the lenses of psychology, systems theory, and neuroscience; the media theory posits that human development cannot be understood solely in isolation but is best explained and understood by accounting for complex, multifaceted social and environmental factors (Wang et al., 2016). In the context of grief and education, the theory can be used to explain that a student's progression and development through the grief process is not a solitary journey but requires the active, positive support and engagement of peers and adults (Hay et al., 2022). Moreover, the RDS has been applied in education settings to explain how educational staff, such as teachers, can support students' thriving by better understanding the psychological and developmentally influenced experiences of students and adapting classroom, instructional, and social interventions accordingly (Dick & Mueller, 2018). The RDS metatheory was initially inspired by the ecological systems theory, which underscores the impact of multiple contexts on an individual's psychological and behavioral development (Wang et al., 2016).

Assisting Teachers With Grieving Students

One of the primary guiding assumptions of the RDS meta theory is the assumption of contextual embeddedness, meaning that human development cannot be understood in isolation, but rather, that development is the result of multiple interacting cultural and societal influences. In the context of grief, this assumption can be used to explain that a student's development and behavior through the grief process cannot be generally predicted but will depend on that student-specific experience and cultural context (Wang et al., 2016). The RDS media theory also ensures that relational dynamics are central and fundamental to human development, implying a bidirectional impact between social environments and an individual. The concept of relational dynamics is useful to apply and understand how school counselors can better serve the needs of bereaved students by engaging in a supportive, bidirectional relationship with them. This relationship, characterized by mentorship, can provide stress reduction strategies to students, trust, care, and understanding, as well as psycho-counseling services (Wang et al., 2016). Additionally, the RDS metatheory is an interdisciplinary approach that involves a comprehensive and holistic understanding of how social relational dynamics influence psychological and behavioral development.

The RDS metatheory emphasizes relational dynamics, an application of the theory's assumptions to the context of assisting grieving students points to the importance of fostering connective, trusting relationships between students, teachers, faculty members and counselors. The development of trusting relationships, through the lens of the RDS metatheory, can be leveraged to foster emotional resilience for students navigating the grief process. As students feel more supported through healthy, trusting, and supportive relationships with peers and mentors, they may experience a greater sense of belonging, which offsets feelings of loneliness or isolation resulting from grief. In this way, a sense of belonging, relatedness, and support offers students a psychological coping mechanism, thereby bolstering their resilience. Practically, the development of resilience through trusting relationships may take the form of increased student engagement in classroom activities or socially oriented group projects rather than solitary behavior or isolation.

The implementation of the evidence based, multi-tiered, mental wellness, school-based curriculum known as social-emotional learning (SEL) programs (CASEL, 2003) provides skills for social and self awareness, emotional regulation, relationship management, decision making and coping skills (CASEL, 2003). SEL may be used to foster and encourage students' engagement with peers, teachers, and faculty members to incentivize and develop trusting relationships. However, teachers and staff must be pre-informed of and educated about the grief process so that teachers and school counselors can lead students to feel supported rather than feeling stigmatized or misunderstood due to their grief (Hay et al., 2022; Wang et al., 2016). Hence, the use of trauma-informed training and practices can be useful

153

for school teachers and counselors. By recognizing the influence of adverse experiences on childhood development, the RDS meta theory specifically informs and supports trauma-informed practices in schools. Because trauma is relational by nature, educators need to build resilience-fostering strategies through trauma-sensitive and trauma-informed instruction, relational dynamics, and classroom environments that prioritize psychological safety. For example, psychological safety can be fostered using positive versus negative reinforcements, inviting students to share their feelings and experiences without repercussions openly, and teaching other students that ownership and acceptance of feelings are healthy. Rather than shaming students for feeling or behaving a certain way, educators may seek to explore the root causes of students' behavior and invite students to share their feelings and experiences so that they feel heard, understood, and supported (Hay et al., 2022). By applying the RDS meta theory to practical classroom implementations and approaches to student counseling, school counselors can assist teachers in lessen the impact that grief has on students learning and academic outcomes.

Applying the RDS Metatheory: Practical Strategies for School Counselors

Considering the important role connectivity and relational interactions play in fostering resilience for grieving students, highlighted by the RDS metatheory, several practical strategies arise that school counselors can use to apply concepts of the RDS in classroom settings. First, school counselors may prioritize building strong, trusting relationships with students. Skills such as active listening, demonstrating empathy, sharing, and sharing in open communication can help students feel heard, valued, and understood while modeling practical communication skills and encouraging students to open up about their feelings and experiences rather than socially withdrawing (Hay et al., 2022).

Second, school counselors may work to integrate relational components into social-emotional learning programs. Social-emotional learning programs leverage social interaction, emotional awareness, and education as foundational tools facilitating behavioral development and content learning acquisition. As students learn skills such as emotional regulation, recognizing their feelings, finding healthy outlets for expressing their feelings, and interacting with peers in healthy ways, it is thought that students are more able to learn effectively through social interaction, observe modeled skills, and acquire information. Thus, by incorporating exercises such as positive communication skills, active listening, positive pure interactions, and conflict resolution tactics, the relational components of the RDS metatheory can be integrated into practical classroom activities and group work activities with teachers and peers, that foster social and emotional learning and development (Hay

Assisting Teachers With Grieving Students

et al., 2022). School counselors can assist teachers by integrating a specific program inclusive of RDS components that would suit the developmental level of the students as well as the classroom environment.

Finally, building and encouraging a supportive school and extracurricular community is imperative to supporting grieving students and represents a fundamental way in which the interrelation components highlighted through the RDS metatheory can be leveraged and practically applied. For example, as school counselors work collaboratively with teachers, other faculty and staff to establish grief training and education programs, peer support groups, and parental education programs, such communities can begin to be established. Furthermore, school counselors may work one-on-one with teachers to educate both grieving and non-grieving students about the signs and symptoms associated with grief, to dismantle existing stigma, and to create more supportive communities.

Practical Tips

* Keep a calming environment: Open window shades, allow natural light into the classroom, avoid excess clutter, and minimize disruptive background sounds.
* Practice active listening. Use eye contact when students speak, and allow students to finish their questions or comments fully, before interrupting.
* For distraught students: Use 'feeling' questions. Ask students, first, how they feel. Allow them to answer without passing judgement.

Summary

The first section of this chapter provided an overview of grief in the context of education, understanding grief, and the role school counselors play in facilitating students and navigating the grieving process. This section also described the main components of the relational developmental systems metatheory, which emphasizes the interdisciplinary and interconnected nature of multiple factors influencing individual development, in this case, the development of students during the grieving process. The theory emphasizes the role relationships play in fostering emotional resilience and highlights the importance of trusting relationships between school counselors, teachers, faculty and students, which can be used to support students in thriving, socially and academically, despite experiencing grief. The next section explores the multidimensional nature of grief, including psychological, emotional, and cultural components.

155

GRIEF'S MULTIDIMENSIONALITY

Grief is inherently a multidimensional experience characterized by a complex interplay of social, cultural, cognitive, and emotional factors. Due to the multidimensional nature of grief and the fact that the experience of grief is unique to each individual, symptoms are associated with responses to grief very individually (Alvis et al., 2022). For instance, some students may experience more difficulty with memory or concentration in the classroom, while others may experience little academic interruption but feel socially withdrawn. Cultural differences can also contribute to how students cope with grief, seek support, or express their feelings following bereavement. Herein, the psychological, emotional, and cultural dimensions of grief are explored, along with practical strategies counselors can use to recognize signs of grief and support students psychologically and emotionally with cultural sensitivity.

Psychological Dimensions

The psychological dimensions of grief relate to the way an individual interprets grief, experiences his grief emotionally, responds to, and copes with grief. Grief can cause intense emotional responses in individuals, depending upon an individual's affect, pre-existing psychological condition, and existing resilience, resources, or scope of coping skills. In the case of youth, it is not uncommon for grieving students to experience significant anger, guilt, anxiety, or sadness. These emotions may fluctuate and be experienced simultaneously, cyclically, or in varying orders. Furthermore, the range and array of intense emotions likely to be experienced during the grieving process can disrupt optimal cognitive function, thereby inhibiting academic performance. Grief triggers, and the initial experience of grief altogether can cause a student's limbic brain region to activate more frequently and significantly, which can detract from and disrupt the rational, logical thought patterns otherwise present in the prefrontal cortex (Hay et al., 2022). Distraction from prefrontal cortex activity and activation of limbic brain regions can inhibit tasks such as memorization, test taking, recital, critical thinking, and problem-solving skills (Morell-Velasco et al., 2020). Hence, when identifying students facing challenges with such cognitive-based skills, school counselors ought to consider potential root causes and work to support students in regaining prefrontal cortex function and executive function through support and sensory-based and somatic activities (Braude & Dwarika, 2020). Hay et al. (2022) assert that activating the senses through routine exercises such as breathing, tapping, or other somatic activities can aid students in cultivating emotional regulation and psychological balance.

Assisting Teachers With Grieving Students

School counselors can assist teachers in understanding some of the psychological dimensions that students may encounter and provide support and sensory-based and somatic activities that students might address in the classroom, such as box breathing exercises.

Other psychological dimensions and manifestations of grief include social isolation and hyperactivity. Some students may socially withdraw due to intense feelings of grief, which may compromise their relationships with peers and school leaders. Addressing signs of social isolation and students through kind, considerate curiosity, and support, rather than negative reinforcement or punitive repercussions, is important to fostering psychological safety that will allow students to open up about their experience and begin to establish trusting relationships as well as resilience skills (Braude & Dwarika, 2020). Moreover, Braude and Dwarika (2020) described that some students respond to grief through hyperactivity and may develop symptoms or signs of attention deficit hyperactivity disorder. Thus, educators ought to avoid misdiagnosing such signs or symptoms and recognize that hyperactivity may be a behavioral coping mechanism for the emotional intensity experienced during the grieving process. School counselors are key in assisting teachers in understanding manifestations of grief and providing some psychological safety for students in the classroom.

School Counselor Strategies

School counselors may use strategies to address the psychological signs and symptoms of grief, such as intense emotional responses, decreased problem-solving and critical-thinking capacities, social isolation, and hyperactivity, including careful observation, routine check-ins with students, open communication, and collaboration. By being aware of such signs and symptoms and regularly observing students who exhibit these symptoms, counselors can become aware of students potentially requiring support. Counselors may also regularly communicate with teachers and schedule routine check-ins with students in need (Wango & Gwiyo, 2021). Routine check-ins may include fostering a safe and supportive environment for students to open up about their experience, as well as offering suggestions and strategies for resilience and coping skills, such as somatic breathing techniques, tapping, or journaling feelings (Hay et al., 2022). Collaborations with parents, teachers and third parties are also critical. Counselors can work with teachers to communicate about the signs and symptoms of grief so that teachers can effectively refer students to counseling rather than practice or rely upon negative reinforcement strategies. Counselors may also work to develop community outreach education programs with external counseling services or developmental education facilities so that caretakers of bereaved students can learn to support children more successfully at home (Dyregrov et al., 2020).

In today's digital age, leveraging technology to disseminate information through email or social platforms, in alignment with school regulations, can be particularly helpful in overcoming the logistic and time-constrained barriers many caretakers and school faculty face (Beaunoyer et al., 2020).

Practical Tips:

- Observe: During each class, observe students who exhibit any distressful behavioral patterns, such as reclusion, interrupting, distractibility, or stress.
- Check in: Use 'feeling' questions to ask these students how they feel, allowing time for response, and validating their feelings with statements such as, "I can see you feel____. What do you feel you need right now?" Allow the student to fully respond. Make a suggestion based on what is possible for the student, even if their full needcannot be met, such as, "I'd like to share an exercise with you that might help you feel better right now." Then, move on to breathing.
- Breathing exercises. Lead the distressed student through a four, two, six count breathing exercise. Encourage them to breath into their abdomen/belly, in for four counts, holding for two, and exhaling for six.

Emotional Dimensions

Just as the psychological dimensions of grief, emotional dimensions of grief include and may be characterized by an array of fluctuating feelings, such as profound sadness, anxiety, anger, anguish, guilt, and regret. Traditionally, the grief cycle is characterized by a procession through sequential emotions of denial, anger, bargaining, depression, and acceptance (Kubler-Ross, 1969). However, more recent research continues to show that these emotions may not be experienced in the same way or in sequential order but that individual experiences vary. Just as explained by the RDS metatheory, Ratcliffe and Byrne (2021) describe how human emotional regulation and development are influenced by social and interpersonal dynamics such that the course of grief one experiences depends on the thoughts and subsequent emotions and activities one engages in, in addition to one's cultural upbringing and environment.

Grief in students commonly manifests as a pervasive, deep sense of sadness and expressed melancholy. When under-supported and unaddressed, grief can lead to prolonged grief disorder (PGD) (Lund, 2020). Lund (2020) suggests that the degree

Assisting Teachers With Grieving Students

to which many students experience the profundity of emotions associated with grief is because of surrounding Westernized societal constructs that largely marginalize and stigmatize the grief experience. Therefore, by allowing students safe spaces to express their feelings and emotions, school counselors can assist with de-stigmatization and alleviate the otherwise damaging consequences of restrained or withheld expressions of the natural grief process bereaved students experience (Brinkmann, 2020). Guilt and regret are also common emotions experienced by bereaved students as they may grapple with thoughts and feelings concerning what they could have done differently to prevent their loss hypothetically. Recent research findings indicate that when mentors or leaders such as teachers are encouraged to openly express these thoughts and feelings in school environments, children's perceived feelings of fear, shame, or guilt lessen over time (Duncan, 2020).

School Counselor Strategies

Counselors can apply several strategies to assist students in navigating the challenging and intense emotional journey of grief. First, it is essential counselors learn to recognize changes in student behavior that may be indicative of the emotional dimension of grief. These behavioral changes may include increased irritability, social withdrawal, decreased concentration, hyperactivity, or a sudden decrease in activity (Dyregrov et al., 2020; Hay et al., 2022; Lund, 2020). When interacting with bereaved students, it is essential for school counselors to provide a safe, confidential, and calm environment. This includes a private setting, protected from outside noise or visibility to other students, so that participating, bereaved students feel safe to express themselves (Kennedy et al., 2020). Additionally, counselors need to practice active listening so that students confiding in counselors feel psychologically safe and heard (Lipp & O'Brien, 2020). School counselors can assist teachers in navigating students with grief by simply showing teachers the stratiegies of active listening. Often teachers are the first person to hear the student upon arriving to school, it is important for teachers to understand how to use active listening stratiegies and respond with empathy. Additionally, seek the professional assistance of the school counselor to further navigate the students emotional grief.

School counselors may use expressive writing, art, and positive physical activities to aid students in processing these emotions. Writing and artistic expression, along with developing social support networks, are positively and significantly correlated with the development of resilience, adaptive coping, and social thriving among various college students studied (Lipp & O'Brien, 2020). Students may be prompted to keep a journal in which they free-write their thoughts and feelings for a set time every day. This activity can be modeled and practiced during counseling sessions. Additionally, school counselors may provide students with colored pens, pencils, and paper, which they may use to freely scribble colors associated with their emotions as a way to explore, express, and accept their internal experiences as normalized. Finally, somatic exercises such as tapping on acupressure points while speaking or saying feelings and emotional triggers, breathing deeply and slowly while raising the hands, or tapping opposite shoulders with arms crossed over the chest can aid students in regaining a sense of temporal presence and connection with the physical body, rather than preoccupation with fear or negative emotions (Hay et al., 2022). As apart of the students trusting relationships, teachers can utilize some of the activities in the classroom as a means to support students. In the event that a classroom of students are grieving, creative art activities can provide a sense of unity among peers.

One recent study found that when properly supported, the provision of active listening, adaptive coping strategies such as free writing or artistic expression, and social support networks were associated with increased experiences of personal growth among international, mostly European, college students (Tureluren et al., 2022), which suggests that with sufficient support, the experience of grief can foster resilience, emotional and character development in students, rather than resulting in long term, maladaptive trauma responses.

Practical Tips

- Whole class teaching: Schedule a meeting with teachers to discuss in-class strategies for educating classrooms about grief. Encourage teachers to set aside 10-15 minutes each quarter, during class time, to discuss with students, that it is ok to feel grief, how grief may feel, and how they can support their peers during times of grief.
- Use words or statements when connecting with students that can be helpful and emotionally supportive, such as: "It's ok that you feel that." "Tell me about how you feel."

Cultural Dimensions and Diverse Student Experiences

Despite the social dynamics and factors influencing the psychological and emotional dimensions of grief, these two dimensions previously discussed are commonly conceptualized as dimensions of grief characterizing an individual's internal experience. Cultural dimensions of grief describe the external environmental, familial, racial, ethnic, and cultural influences on an individual's experience of grief. Culture is understood as a shared set of values, beliefs, and practices. Therefore, familial, ancestral, and societal values, beliefs, and behaviors, which are learned, can influence how one perceives and understands loss, associates meaning with loss, and navigates the resulting emotions (Silverman et al., 2020). Additionally, according to Garcia (2021), thoughts and the meaning attached to experiences are the primary instigators of emotions. Therefore, an individual's cultural upbringing and background play an important role in the way one psychologically and emotionally experiences grief and the intensity of grief (Silverman et al., 2020). For instance, societal norms, rituals, and roles influence the mourning process. In many Western societies, loss is recognized through mournful funeral ceremonies (Wojtkowiak et al., 2021). However, in some indigenous cultures, such as the Paraguayan Chaco of South America, song and wailing rituals are practiced, accompanying the grieving and mourning process (Árnason, 2007). In indigenous Paraguayan culture, the feelings associated with grief are recognized as acceptable, neither good nor bad, and are provided an outlet of expression to avoid emotional 'buildup' otherwise viewed as socially, psychologically, and physically dangerous and detrimental. Hence, song, dance, and wailing ceremonies are fundamental to maintaining individual health and social order for the Paraguayan Chaco (Árnason, 2007). Many collectivist cultures, such as South and Central American cultures, prioritize the provision of community support for those grieving to lessen the potential damaging influence of social isolation and withdrawal (Árnason, 2007). Moreover, beliefs concerning the afterlife, which vary culturally, can influence the degree of comfort one feels during the grieving process (Blueford et al., 2021).

School counselors can assist teachers with cultural sensitivity and understanding the psychological and emotional dimensions of the students grief.

The findings of Blueford et al. (2021) indicate that a lack of culturally sensitive grief training and support exists in today's school settings and among school counselors. Thus, actions and strategies counselors can assume to increase culturally sensitive approaches to supporting grieving students include but are likely not limited to enrolling in cultural competence training, working to implement inclusive support groups and cultural competence training for teachers, other staff and families, and acquiring knowledge about specific student demographics and cultural backgrounds the school serves so that grief coping strategies can be developed in a way that is supportive to and respective of students' specific cultural backgrounds. For instance, if cultural competence training is not presently offered as a component of institution-based, ongoing professional development for counselors; school counselors may seek third-party accreditation and training. Furthermore, school counselors can advocate for the implementation of cultural competence training at their respective institutions during staff meetings;inclusive of teachers and staff, feedback sharing, or review sessions. By formally researching a school's student body demographics and informally observing students visiting counselors' offices and occupying student bodies, counselors can begin to gain an understanding of students' potential cultural backgrounds. However, during the process of observation, it is important counselors maintain and practice reflexivity, the process of noting and becoming aware of potential personal biases, to avoid making assumptions about students' cultural backgrounds or beliefs, and to maintain curious, open inquiry, and seek information about specific cultures, practices, and beliefs. Finally, counselors may ask students, during one-on-one sessions, if they are open to sharing information and experience about their cultural experience, background, or family. As part of this inquiry, a counselor may ask a student what they were taught about loss, dying, or grief without judgment or expectation (Meagher, 2001). Doing so can aid the counselor in better understanding a student's context and assumptions about loss so that supportive coping strategies specific to those beliefs can be developed.

Researchers' recent findings support the implementation of cultural competence training and inquiry by school counselors concerning students' cultural backgrounds. For example, Tan and Andriessen (2021) show that providing formal grief support for bereaved students informed through the lens of cultural competence was positively associated with increased self-reported personal growth among students surveyed. Moreover, an 8-week, in-school grief program involving 296 children used adaptive coping strategies such as journaling, individual counselor sessions, and guidance provided with cultural sensitivity (Linder et al., 2022). Post-intervention results indicated significant improvements in students' emotional regulation skills (Linder et al., 2022).

Practical Tips

- Devote time each year or quarter to some type of cultural competence professional development training for teachers and staff members.
- Notice what cultures are most-served by your corresponding school.
- Keep a journal: In what ways do these cultures perceive or navigate grief? Does your school have provisions in place to assist this? (i.e. time off for grieving students, appropriate grief language). If not, schedule a meeting with the school leaders to discuss how the school may become more culturally-sensitive to grieving students.

Summary

The experience of grief is multidimensional, encompassing psychological, emotional, and cultural domains, each of which interface with a student's personal background, disposition, and social dynamics. Grief may be experienced through intense emotions such as sadness, anger, and guilt. Each experience of these emotions, their progression, intensity, and interrelatedness are unique to each student. Counselors can recognize grief through behavioral changes such as withdrawal, hyperactivity, or melancholy. Engaging teachers and staff in cultural competence training and learning about students' cultural backgrounds can aid in fostering a supportive, culturally inclusive environment in which students feel safer to express their feelings to counselors without fear of stigmatization, discrimination, or marginalization. Pro-social and positive activities such as establishing connections with supportive peer groups, journaling or drawing feelings, and engaging in political, physical activity can aid students in developing resilient, positive coping mechanisms.

PRACTICAL IMPLEMENTATION AND CASE EXAMPLES

Existing case studies provide examples of how counselors may exercise practical implementations for assisting teachers in navigating students through simple grief processes in the education settings. Practical implementations demonstrated through the following case studies include the use of positive expressive activity to support culturally diverse students through the grieving process, using educational outreach to support students through the process of loss, and leveraging mindfulness techniques to bolster students' emotional regulation capacities through the experience of grief. Each of the following subsections includes a discussion of a particular case study, followed by practical applications.

Case Study One: Culture Change, Grief, and Drawing Expression

The process of international migration can entail grief and loss, both in the form of the loss of loved ones due to death and the loss of cultural identity. Researchers conducting a recent qualitative case study explored the impact of drawing and creative expression exercises on an Egyptian immigrant girl's experience of bereavement and loss, both resulting from loss due to death and loss of perceived cultural identity. The case study involved an implementation through which the 11-year-old Egyptian girl immigrating to the United States was facilitated through free flow, expressive drawing, and painting exercises (Beauregard, 2020). During each weekly session, the participant was encouraged to express her feelings and emotions concerning loss, grief, and cultural identity. Through the process, the girl began to develop and relate to a new sense of personal autonomy and cultural identity. The researchers of the case study concluded that the exercises helped the girl navigate the transition between cultures, as well as better understand her relationship to loss and death (Beauregard, 2020). In this way, the case study findings illustrated that not only does the right creative expression aid in bereavement related to the death of a loved one or caregiver but also concerning cultural bereavement. This case study is particularly useful to consider in the context of increasingly culturally diverse classrooms, where students may not only be navigating the loss of a caretaker, but concurrently navigating complex emotions related to experiences of cultural transition, discrimination, stereotyping from peers, or marginalization. Although, teachers will not guide students through intense and deeply rooted bereavement, the utilization of art and creativity can assist students in creative expression of bereavement and grief. Drawing, painting, and free-flow creative expression are safe, non-threatening outlets through which students may explore and gain awareness of their internal emotional experience, thereby developing more adaptive, positive emotional regulation techniques.

Application

Beauregard's (2020) case study illustrates the potential power of creative exercises in helping culturally diverse students navigate experiences of grief, loss, and transition. An application of the case study findings suggests that school counselors may incorporate drawing and creative expression sessions into counseling sessions targeting bereaved students. Drawing and creative expression may be particularly useful for culturally diverse students, who may be navigating the compounded stress of cultural transition in addition to the loss of caretakers. Based on the methodology used in Beauregard's (2020) case study, school counselors may adopt the following suggested steps as a potential intervention to aid culturally diverse, bereaved students. First, a supportive, private, calm, and quiet environment must be created, within which counseling and creative exploration sessions can be conducted. It is important for students to feel safe in the presence of a counselor and protected from potential observation or stigmatization by other students. After establishing an initial supportive relationship and report with a bereaved student, a school counselor may describe the potential benefit and intention of free-flow drawing and painting. This benefit includes allowing a student to express or explore their emotions non-threateningly through texture, shape, color, and visualization. It is essential that the school counselor explain to the student that there is no right or wrong way to express themselves. The objective of drawing is not to create a realistic or representative image but rather to

Assisting Teachers With Grieving Students

allow the student space for self-reflection and felt experience. After the explanation, the counselor may provide the student with markers, crayons, colored pencils, paints, or other creative materials. It is recommended that calming music be played while the student is allowed the chance to feel and express. Prompts may be used, such as encouraging the student to choose a color that represents their emotions or to define and express their emotions through simple shapes or lines (Beauregard, 2020). After a 20- to 30-minute drawing or painting session, the counselor may ask the student to share or reflect on any insights or experiences they had.

Practical Tips:

- Keep drawing supplies in your office. Offer it as a simple exercise for students during visits. Breifly explain to each student how expression with color can help calm the nervous system and that there is not correct or incorrect way to express.
- Ask the student if they'd like calming, instrumental music while they draw, and adjust the room accordingly.
- Next, prompt the student with, "I encourage you to ask yourself how you feel right now, and then try to draw that feeling. It might be a color, or a certain texture you choose. It doesn't have to make sense. Simply feel and draw." Then, allow the student 10 minutes or so, without watching them directly, so they feel a sense of privacy, to draw. This is a great time to work on another task while they draw, such as reading.

Case Study Two: Supporting Students Through the Process of Loss

The second case study described herein explored the impact of a grief education program on higher education nursing students' experiences with grief and loss (Byrne, 2020). The education program is intended to help nursing students feel more comfortable about caring for dying patients while also feeling more confident to navigate personal experiences of the loss of caregivers successfully. Although the case study evaluated young adults rather than children or all adolescents, the case study nonetheless provides important insight concerning the value of education programs in assisting students in navigating the grief process, which can be applied to personal or professional settings. The education program involved an end-of-life simulation through which students participated in a simulated experience of loss. Education was provided to students before and following the simulation concerning how to actively engage in active listening, emotional regulation, and presence. Skills taught included body language, eye contact, breathing, and emotional awareness. Following the intervention, most participants reported an increased sense of knowing what to say during an experience of loss, how to offer comfort, and an increased sense of individual presence. Students also reported that this experience helped them feel more comfortable navigating personal experiences of grief and loss with resilience (Byrne, 2020). Byrne's (2020) Case study illustrates the importance of grief education for those facilitating the grieving process, such as school counselors, as well as students experiencing grief. The implementation used in Byrne's (2020) study, since targeting young adults, may be particularly useful among older youth, such as secondary school and higher education students. Teaching adolescents and young adults emotional regulation skills may foster resilience through grief, contributing to their personal, academic, and professional lives.

Application

An application of Bryne's (2020) case study methodology to modern school counseling settings in which counselors are supporting bereaved adolescents may include a structured, emotional regulation curriculum targeting grieving students. This curriculum may be offered as an extracurricular, classroom activity led by the school counselor and teacher, group class, or through individual counseling sessions. In either event, curriculum content may include addressing stress and positive coping mechanisms with stress, educating students concerning the process of reflexivity or becoming aware of one's own emotions, and third, providing emotional regulation tactics and skills to students. The curriculum also may include time and space for students to practice these emotional regulation skills in a safe setting. The first component of the curriculum, which might include addressing stress and providing positive coping mechanisms for stress, would include awareness and education concerning the signs and symptoms of stress, such as emotional outbursts, social withdrawal, overwhelm, reactivity, or even physical symptoms such as fatigue. Adaptive stress coping mechanisms taught may include cognitive behavioral therapy techniques such as pleasant activity scheduling, journaling, regular exercise, and spending time cultivating positive social relationships. The second component, awareness and reflexivity, will include psychoeducation, aiding adolescents and young adults in becoming aware of their emotions and the potential influence of those emotions on behaviors. Psychoeducation curriculum content may be adapted from various positive psychology publications informed by internal family systems frameworks and the RDS metatheory. Practical emotional regulation tactics and techniques taught to students may be like those used to address the psychological and emotional dimensions of grief. These include somatic exercises such as tapping,

Assisting Teachers With Grieving Students

positive physical activities, and regulated breathing. Additionally, journaling one's thoughts and feelings can foster a sense of self-awareness that helps students to become reflexive and aware of their feelings, and therefore, choose corresponding behaviors that involve healthy outlets of expression, such as drawing, exercise, or writing, rather than externalizing and projecting their feelings of grief or sadness onto others.

Practical Tips

- Work with teachers to educate teachers about how 10-15 minutes every few class periods, devoted to active listening and emotional intelligence training an improve class dynamics and student performance.
- Provide teachers with helpful instructional strategies such as demonstrating active listening, discussing the importance of open body language while listening, with students, and the use of questions and affirmative statements following listening such as, "I'm hearing you express____," or, "It seems as if you are feeling____. Is that correct?"

Case Study Three: Cultivating Mindfulness as Resilience

The final case study discussed involves the use of a program called BREATHE, which school counselors can use to teach mindfulness practices to high school students navigating grief and loss (Schussler et al., 2020). School counselors can also assist teachers in facilitating breathing mindfulness practices and techniques in class settings to help in creating a calming environment. In the particular case study discussed herein, the researchers sought to understand how the program impacted high school students' experiences of stress and well-being following an experience of grief or loss. Surveys and interviews were used to evaluate student experiences across two different schools. The results indicated statistically significant, positive outcomes as a result of using the BREATHE program. Moreover, the researchers found that the program was easy to incorporate into students' lives, making it logistically feasible for students, teachers, school counselors and educators to implement. Positive outcomes included improvements in students' emotional regulation skills, improvements in mindful breathing, which supports physiological health through the process of emotional distress and grief, and self-reported improvements in positive social interactions as a result of the intervention (Schussler et al., 2020). The case study findings suggest that counselors may implement the BREATHE program as

Assisting Teachers With Grieving Students

a way to help support students' psychological, physical, and social health, all of which support optimized academic outcomes.

Application

Based on Schussler et al.'s (2020) methodology, a school counselor's role in applying the BREATHE program in a secondary school setting may involve facilitating mindfulness practices for group and or individual settings involving bereaved students. Schussler et al. (2020) recommend first implementing the program within individual one-on-one counselor sessions with students to test students' receptivity to the practice being taught. Students' receptivity towards mindfulness practices may vary depending on their cultural background and the context of student demographics within a particular school setting. Additionally, implementing the practices one-on-one first can help foster a sense of shared understanding of mindfulness practices among students and a sense of psychological safety. Practices may include, but are not limited to, self-reflection, internal reflection or meditation, and mindful breathing. Because the term 'meditation' is associated with various spiritual and philosophical traditions, it is recommended that school counselors use the term internal reflection, which simply refers to quiet time provided to students, within which they may work to pay particular focus and attention to their internal emotional experience, their breath, and the physical sensations in their bodies, rather than externalizing their emotional experience. This practice of internal reflection and awareness is found to foster improved emotional awareness, maturity, and thus regulation (Schussler et al., 2020). Mindful breathing encompasses the use of steady, slow, gentle breaths as a way to help students somatically regulate their emotional experience and move from limbic system activity associated with dominant feelings of fear, shame, and guilt into prefrontal cortex activity associated with rational thought and logical decision making (Schussler et al., 2020). Mindful breathing can be practiced by prompting students to place one hand on their diaphragm, or abdominal region, to fuel the expanse and contraction of each breath. A counselor can then lead students through the process of breathing to four-count inhalations, two-count holds, and six-count exhalations. Students should be encouraged to practice breathing into their abdominal region rather than inflating the chest since the former stimulates parasympathetic nervous system activity that is calming and regulating, and chest breathing stimulates the sympathetic nervous system and corresponding physiological stress responses (Schussler et al., 2020).

Assisting Teachers With Grieving Students

Practical Tips

- Encourage students to pause and become aware of how they are feeling. This strategy can be used during counseling sessions, 1:1, or in groups.
- During each pause, lead students through a four, two, six count breath.
- Add additional skills during each five minute awareness pause break, such as tapping, which can be done by guiding students to gently tap on their chest, forehead, top of the head, and cheek bones, using their index and middle finger, while slowly breathing or humming, to calm the nervous system and turn attention inward toward their feelings, for improved emotional regulation.

Summary

The case studies described in this section explored various ways in which school counselors can assist bereaved students through the grieving process. The first case study illustrated the usefulness of free-flow creative drawing exercises in fostering elementary students' psychological and emotional health through the process of loss. The second case study demonstrated the importance of educating adolescents and young adults about loss and grief so that students are more equipped with resilient skills and effective coping strategies. Finally, the third case study showed how mindfulness practices, such as self-reflection and mindful breathing, can assist secondary school students in developing emotional regulation skills Despite the intense emotions associated with grief.

SUMMARY

Grief is a complex experience characterized by social, emotional, psychological, and cultural dimensions that can influence a bereaved student's academic experience, progress, and success. Bereaved youth are undergoing pivotal developmental stages, immediate adults in their lives can have a profound influence on whether these students navigate and cope adaptively or maladaptively with the loss of a caregiver or loved one. Thus, school counselors and educators at large serve an important role in cultivating inclusive, safe environments for grieving students and effectively supporting students through the grieving process. This chapter reviewed the psychological, emotional, and cultural domains of grief, showing that the provision of effective support for grieving students entails a multifaceted approach, including grief education, collaboration with families, colleagues, and students, cultural competence training, and the application of coping-skills and strategies through counseling sessions. The literature reviewed in this chapter also demonstrated the need for increased cultural competence training among educators, as cultural background, including one's beliefs, values, and shared behaviors, influence one's experience of grief. Practical strategies that may be used to assist students through the grieving process were adaptively demonstrated through three reviewed case studies and included creative expression, grief education, and mindfulness practices. Finally, the compounded stress and loss experienced during the COVID-19 pandemic highlighted the importance of placing greater emphasis on grief education and support in today's schools.

DISCUSSION QUESTIONS

1. Understanding that mental and behavioral health issues can compromise learning and educational outcomes, what would be the school counselors role in cultivating a supportive and empathetic learning environment for students who are grieving?
2. During the shutdown of COVID-19, many families experienced emotional pain based on the loss of family and friends, producing post-traumatic stress symptoms. What role should school counselors play in providing tier 2 services for emotional and behavorial supports for students?
3. Traditionally, grief counseling has been serviced by agencies outside of the school setting. As a school counselor, how can you assist teachers in helping students process grief, while maintaining confidentiality and integrity of the students grieving process.
4. Examine the Relational Developmental Systems (RDS) Metatheory as a conceptual framework to understand outcomes of school relationships and connectivity. In doing so, which strategies would you utilize to assist in school wide processing of grief? Discuss a scenario related to the death of a teacher, student or prominent role model within the school.
5. Discuss the loss of a loved one that affected yourself or a friend between the ages of early childhood and adolescence. How did this loss shape or alter your worldview of grief? Reflect on school supports provided to assist during the grieving time. If supports were not provided, which interventions should have been in place as support?

REFERENCES

Alvis, L., Zhang, N., Sandler, I. N., & Kaplow, J. B. (2022). Developmental manifestations of grief in children and adolescents: Caregivers as key grief facilitators. *Journal of Child & Adolescent Trauma*, 16(2), 447–457. 10.1007/s40653-021-00435-035106114

APA. (2022). *Grief*. APA. https://www.apa.org/topics/grief

Árnason, A. (2007). "Fall apart and put yourself together again": The anthropology of death and bereavement counselling in Britain. *Mortality*, 12(1), 48–65. 10.1080/13576270601088335

Beaunoyer, E., Hiracheta Torres, L., Maessen, L., & Guitton, M. J. (2020). Grieving in the Digital Era: Mapping online support for grief and bereavement. *Patient Education and Counseling*, 103(12), 2515–2524. 10.1016/j.pec.2020.06.01332591255

Beauregard, C. (2020). Being in between Exploring cultural bereavement and identity expression through drawing. *Journal of Creativity in Mental Health*, 15(3), 292–310. 10.1080/15401383.2019.1702131

Blueford, J. M., Diambra, J. F., & Wheat, L. S. (2021). Counselor preparedness to counsel grieving clients: Insights and implications. *Death Studies*, 46(10), 2413–2423. 10.1080/07481187.2021.195664434308795

Braude, S., & Dwarika, V. (2020). Teachers' experiences of supporting learners with attention-deficit hyperactivity disorder: Lessons for professional development of teachers. *South African Journal of Childhood Education*, 10(1). 10.4102/sajce.v10i1.843

Brinkmann, S. (2020). Learning to grieve: A preliminary analysis. *Culture and Psychology*, 26(3), 469–483. 10.1177/1354067X19877918

Byrne, D., Overbaugh, K., Czekanski, K., Wilby, M., Blumenfeld, S., & Laske, R. A. (2020). Assessing undergraduate nursing students' attitudes toward the dying in an end-of-life simulation using an ACE.S unfolding case study. *Journal of Hospice and Palliative Nursing : JHPN : the Official Journal of the Hospice and Palliative Nurses Association*, 22(2), E11–E12. 10.1097/NJH.00000000000062631977535

Castrellón, L. E., Fernández, É., Reyna Rivarola, A. R., & López, G. R. (2021). Centering loss and grief: Positioning schools as sites of collective healing in the era of COVID-19. *Frontiers in Education*, 6, 636993. Advance online publication. 10.3389/feduc.2021.636993

Chronister, J., Castruita Rios, Y., & Rumrill, S. (2021). Crisis and trauma counseling and intervention. *Certified Rehabilitation Counselor Examination Preparation.* 10.1891/9780826158253.0005

Collaborative for Academic, Social, and Emotional Learning (CASEL). (2003). Safe and sound: *An educational leader's guide to edidence based social and emotional learning programs.* Chicago, IL: CASEL.

DeMuth, M., Taggi-Pinto, A., Miller, E. G., & Alderfer, M. A. (2020). Bereavement accommodations in the classroom: Experiences and opinions of school staff. *The Journal of School Health*, 90(3), 165–171. 10.1111/josh.1287031957037

Dick, A. S., & Mueller, U. (2018). *Advancing developmental science: Philosophy, theory, and method.* Psychology Press.

Duncan, D. A. (2020). Death and dying: A systematic review into approaches used to support bereaved children. *Review of Education*, 8(2), 452–479. 10.1002/rev3.3193

Dyregrov, A., Dyregrov, K., & Lytje, M. (2020). Loss in the family – A reflection on how schools can support their students. *Bereavement Care*, 39(3), 95–101. 10.1080/02682621.2020.1828722

Garcia, R. B. (2021). Using grief support groups to support bereaved students. *Supporting Bereaved Students at School*, 115-129. 10.1093/med:psych/9780190606893.003.0009

Greiner, C. M., Park, J., & Goldstein, S. E. (2022). Teacher trainees' experiences with and beliefs about responding to students' challenging life events. *Teaching and Teacher Education*, 111, 103603. 10.1016/j.tate.2021.103603

Hay, A., Howell, J. A., Rudaizky, D., & Breen, L. J. (2022). Experiences and support needs of bereaved students in higher education. *Omega*, 003022282210965. 10.11 77/00302228221096565535549940

Kaplow, J. B., Layne, C. M., Pynoos, R. S., & Saltzman, W. (2023). *Multidimensional grief therapy: A flexible approach to assessing and supporting bereaved youth.* Cambridge University Press. 10.1017/9781316422359

Karaman, M. A., Eşici, H., Tomar, İ. H., & Aliyev, R. (2021). COVID-19: Are school counseling services ready? Students' psychological symptoms, school counselors' views, and solutions. *Frontiers in Psychology*, 12, 647740. 10.3389/fpsyg.2021.64774033868121

Assisting Teachers With Grieving Students

Kennedy, C. J., Gardner, F., & Farrelly, C. (2020). Death, dying and bereavement: Considering compassion and empowerment. *Pastoral Care in Education*, 38(2), 138–155. 10.1080/02643944.2020.1725905

Lawrence, S. T. (2019). *The grieving child in the classroom: A guide for school-based professionals*. Routledge. 10.4324/9780429055515

Levkovich, I., & Elyoseph, Z. (2021). "I don't know what to say": Teachers' perspectives on supporting bereaved students after the death of a parent. *Omega*, 86(3), 945–965. 10.1177/00302228219936243358258

Liew, C. H., & Servaty-Seib, H. L. (2019). College students' feedback on a student bereavement leave policy. *Journal of Student Affairs Research and Practice*, 57(1), 55–68. 10.1080/19496591.2019.1614940

Linder, L., Lunardini, M., & Zimmerman, H. (2022). Supporting childhood bereavement through school-based grief group. *Omega*, 003022282210827. 10.1177/00302228221082756353357962

Lipp, N., & O'Brien, K. M. (2020). Bereaved college students: Social support, coping style, continuing bonds, and social media use as predictors of complicated grief and posttraumatic growth. *Omega*, 85(1), 178–203. 10.1177/003022282094195232664785

Lund, P. C. (2020). Deconstructing grief: A sociological analysis of prolonged grief disorder. *Social Theory & Health*, 19(2), 186–200. 10.1057/s41285-020-00135-z

Meagher, D. K. (2001). School based grief crisis management programs. *What Will We Do? Preparing a School Community to Cope with Crises, 2nd Edition.* 10.2190/WW2C3

Morell-Velasco, C., Fernández-Alcántara, M., Hueso-Montoro, C., & Montoya-Juárez, R. (2020). Teachers' perception of grief in primary and secondary school students in Spain: Children's responses and elements which facilitate or hinder the grieving process. *Journal of Pediatric Nursing*, 51, e100–e107. 10.1016/j.pedn.2019.12.01631928803

Pincus, R., Hannor-Walker, T., Wright, L., & Justice, J. (2020). COVID-19's effect on students: How school counselors rise to the rescue. *NASSP Bulletin*, 104(4), 241–256. 10.1177/0192636520975866

Price, M. J., Wachsmuth, L. P., Ferguson, K. A., Robbins-Welty, G. A., Riordan, P. A., Pieper, C. F., & Galanos, A. (2021). Grief in medical students: The short and long-term impacts on health and well-being. *The American Journal of Hospice & Palliative Care*, 39(2), 196–204. 10.1177/10499091211011722339910376

Ratcliffe, M., & Byrne, E. A. (2021). The interpersonal and social dimensions of emotion regulation in grief. *Cultural, Existential and Phenomenological Dimensions of Grief Experience*, (pp. 84-98). Taylor & Francis. 10.4324/9781003099420-8

Schussler, D. L., Oh, Y., Mahfouz, J., Levitan, J., Frank, J. L., Broderick, P. C., Mitra, J. L., Berrena, E., Kohler, K., & Greenberg, M. T. (2020). Stress and well-being: A systematic case study of adolescents' experiences in a mindfulness-based program. *Journal of Child and Family Studies*, 30(2), 431–446. 10.1007/s10826-020-01864-5

Silverman, G. S., Baroiller, A., & Hemer, S. R. (2020). Culture and grief: Ethnographic perspectives on ritual, relationships and remembering. *Death Studies*, 45(1), 1–8. 10.1080/07481187.2020.185188533272138

Sunde, A. (2021). When Schools Go Dark, School Counselors Shine: School Counseling during a Global Pandemic. Brief. *ERIC*, 1-15. https://eric.ed.gov/?id =ED613589

Tan, J., & Andriessen, K. (2021). The experiences of grief and personal growth in University students: A qualitative study. *International Journal of Environmental Research and Public Health*, 18(4), 1899. 10.3390/ijerph1804189933669340

Tempski, P., Danila, A. H., Arantes-Costa, F. M., Siqueira, M. A., Torsani, M. B., & Martins, M. A. (2020). The COVID-19 pandemic: Time for medical teachers and students to overcome grief. *Clinics (São Paulo)*, 75, e2206. 10.6061/clinics/2020/ e220632756822

Tempski, P., Danila, A. H., Arantes-Costa, F. M., Siqueira, M. A., Torsani, M. B., & Martins, M. A. (2020). The COVID-19 pandemic: Time for medical teachers and students to overcome grief. *Clinics (São Paulo)*, 75, e2206. 10.6061/clinics/2020/ e220632756822

Tureluren, E., Claes, L., & Andriessen, K. (2022). Help-seeking behavior in bereaved university and college students: Associations with grief, mental health distress, and personal growth. *Frontiers in Psychology*, 13, 963839. 10.3389/ fpsyg.2022.96383935992443

Varga, M. A., Lanier, B., Biber, D., & Stewart, B. (2021). Holistic grief effects, mental health, and counseling support in bereaved college students. *The College Student Affairs Journal*, 39(1), 1–13. 10.1353/csj.2021.0000

Wang, J., Batanova, M., Ferris, K. A., & Lerner, R. M. (2016). Character development within the relational developmental systems Metatheory: A view of the issues. *Research in Human Development*, 13(2), 91–96. 10.1080/15427609.2016.1165932

Wango, G., & Gwiyo, L. M. (2021). When death strikes early as often will: How counsellors and schools can support grieving pupils and students. *Improving Schools*, 26(1), 39–53. 10.1177/1365480221996847

Wojtkowiak, J., Lind, J., & Smid, G. E. (2021). Ritual in therapy for prolonged grief: A scoping review of ritual elements in evidence-informed grief interventions. *Frontiers in Psychiatry*, 11, 623835. 10.3389/fpsyt.2020.62383533613334

Chapter 8
Advancing the Wellbeing of Bereaved People Toward Effective Rehabilitation

Onijuni Olatomide
https://orcid.org/0009-0001-0973-6968
Obafemi Awolowo University, Ile-Ife, Nigeria

ABSTRACT

Among the inevitable traumatic hazards that people encounter is death of a loved one. A notable reaction to such loss is grief. Individuals in grief could develop a crisis and suddenly start to function with diminished capacity. While some individuals navigate their grieving phase with minimal damage and return to functionality, others lack the requisite resources to manage the phase, leading them to crisis. This latter group needs counsellors to assist them navigate the phase and return to pre-crisis functionality. This chapter provides two-way effective grief and trauma counselling therapies. To social supports, it provides empathic listening, tolerating awkward responses from the bereaved, and observing a task that needs to be done and do it vicariously, etc. To the bereaved, it offers cognitive restructuring, self-monitoring of thoughts and recording, increasing help-seeking behaviours, Premack principle, time out, self-compassion, bibliotherapy, and reinforcement, among other therapies, to manage grief and trauma during bereavement.

DOI: 10.4018/979-8-3693-1375-6.ch008

Copyright © 2024, IGI Global. Copying or distributing in print or electronic forms without written permission of IGI Global is prohibited.

INTRODUCTION

Emotional hazard describes any situation that brings about unexpected upset within the social forces in which an individual lives, in which the individual is capable of navigating with insignificant amount of stress. These emotional hazards could be brought by natural events such as war, earthquake, maturational challenges, sudden death of a loved one, flooding, tornado, plane crash, inferno, etc., or man-induced such as divorce, terrorism, kidnapping, armed robbery, rape, gun shooting, building collapse, to list a few, each of which could adversely affect just a person or affect entire community (James, 2017; Roberts, 2015). For some other individuals, however, working through the same emotional hazard disorganises and immobilises them, such that they experience acute and protracted disturbance called crisis, consequent of the emotional hazard (Roberts, 2015).

One of the notable reactions to emotional hazards linked to loss of a beloved person is grief. Grief has been defined by Asgari et al. (2023) as an inevitable experience of individuals' response to the death of a beloved person, while Skalski et al. (2022) described grief to be emotionally a painful and natural response to loss by individuals, with manifestations such as aggression, anxiety, and depression, denial, loss of control, extreme sadness, and shock (Gross, 2015; Williams et al., 2023). Interestingly, a number of factors such as culture and personal definition of the position of the deceased to the bereaved could influence the seriousness of the grief being experienced. Admitting the huge negative impacts of what unresolved grief could bring upon the behavioural, physical, emotional, mental, career, and psychological wellness and the health of the people in grief, it is imperative to commence adequate preparation of counsellors in grief and trauma counselling education during their training in order to adequately equip them to help people successfully work through grieving phases occasioned by bereavement. Notably, counsellors have a dual role in such task – to social supports who partner with them on the rehabilitation drives of the bereaved, and to the bereaved persons themselves.

This contribution, therefore, presents grief and trauma intervention counselling as encompassing systematic provision of information, education, and therapies by rehabilitation counsellors (that is, a counsellor who is proficient in application of therapies to help people return to normal life after encountering traumatic experiences) both to social supports – neighbours, friends, family members, clergies, who assist in the rehabilitation of the bereaved, as well as to the bereaved themselves, in order to accelerate the healing of individuals in grief and trauma to successfully work through and subsequently return to pre-bereavement functionality. In literature, such as Sallnow and Paul (2015), and Aoun et al. (2018), social supports are synonymously identified as informal sources of support, and they are reported as the most frequently used forms of the social supports.

Advancing the Wellbeing of Bereaved People Toward Rehabilitation

Of note, the coronavirus pandemic could be said to bring an undesirable twist to bereavement process known to bereaved people on the one hand, and to social supports, including rehabilitative counsellors on the other hand. For an illustration, Bath (2009) as cited in Rajic et al. (2023) posited that being an inherent component of the bereavement process, most bereaved individuals require adequate social support, of which its absence can potentially result in the development of complicated grief and become a significant predictor of severe psychological distress, but social supports were hampered from playing their accustomed role during the phase. Consequently, peoples established grieving condition and grief processes were scuttled (Wallace et al. 2020), as social distancing restrictions reduced the positive impacts of social supports, collective family grief was shifted to individual family member's grief, and family members became non-involved in funeral and after-funeral rites (Asgari et al., 2023; Joseph et al., 2021; Mitima-Verloop et al. 2020). Recalling that the social distancing restrictions also hindered one-on-one encounter between rehabilitative counsellors and bereaved people, compelling them to use the online medium to reach out to bereaved individuals, as well as plan and coordinate the inputs of other social supports, it can be concluded that the pandemic negatively impacted counselling interventions for bereaved people.

MANAGING GRIEF REACTIONS

During bereavement, family members, co-workers, religious faithful, neighbours, classmates, and friends usually visit the bereaved person, either on individual basis, or in groups, so as to offer social support, so as to enhance the process of healing the bereaved (Ogunleye, 2021; Bottomley et al., 2017). Rehabilitative counsellors' role in this situation is twofold. The twofold role has made it compulsory for them to coordinate the efforts of other social supports so that their efforts would not unintentionally undermine the professional inputs of rehabilitative counsellors. Therefore, while rehabilitative counsellors provide direct intervention to grieving persons, they also educate other social supports on how to clean-up their efforts to remove the likely lethality in their approach and contributions. Given this, the roles of rehabilitative counsellors to the bereaved are firstly discussed, followed by their roles to other social supports.

Advancing the Wellbeing of Bereaved People Toward Rehabilitation

Assessment of the Degree of Grief Prior to Rehabilitative Intervention

Assessment can be described as continuous process of evaluating the grieving client's situational bereavement and its impacts on their total well-being. This enables the rehabilitative counsellor to ascertain the severity of grieving prior to rehabilitative intervention, explore the bereaved individual's current emotional, behavioural, physical, and cognitive states, the types and nature of available personal resources within the bereaved, existing informal and formal resources, decision on the requisite intervention to use, including the determination of the effectiveness of the rehabilitative counsellor's intervention, with a view to assisting the rehabilitative counsellor decide the appropriate juncture for termination of intervention. This need for pre-intervention assessment is established as the first step in Roberts' seven stage of crisis intervention model (Roberts, 2015; Roberts & Yeager, 2015).

Assessment is so crucial that it may assist the rehabilitative counsellor to decide whether to refer the bereaved person at the outset if they exhibit psychopathology. Assessment instruments that could be used include observation, interview, self-report from the bereaved, reports from significant others around them, plus rehabilitative counsellor's-constructed, and standardised scales. Additionally, the rehabilitative counsellor needs to ascertain what factors are motivating or exacerbating the grief reactions. Notably, grief reactions can be influenced by the nature of the death. For instance, during the COVID-19 pandemic, families who lost beloved ones experienced severe psychological disturbance arising from stay-at-home restrictions, shifting familial grieving to individualistic one, altered funeral site, non-participation of family members in funerals and post-funeral rites, and absence or reduced social support (Asgari et al., 2023; Mitima-Verloop et al., 2022). Furthermore, the existing structure and stability prior to the loss and after the loss, relationship between the bereaved and the deceased, to list a few, could influence the severity of grieving. In the case of loss of a child, Worden (2018) asserted that such death could be a very difficult loss to a family, as the death may impinge upon the family' equilibrium and sometimes resulting into pathological reactions. Even in such case, is it at post-menopausal? Is it at widowhood? Is it consequent upon a protracted illness or a sudden death? There could additionally be a cultural factor to grieving.

Culturally speaking, among the Youruba in Nigeria (the Youruba predominantly live in Southwestern States of Ekiti, Lagos, Ogun, Ondo, Osun, and Oyo), death is categorised into either bad, good, death of the young, and of the aged. While the good one describes death at ripe old age, the bad explains death tied to anti-wickedness divinities such as iron, thunder, and smallpox, to die young, as well as dying without a surviving child (Joseph et al., 2021), and there are different salutations used to greet the bereaved in different death circumstances. For instance, the death of a child would cause deeper and lasting grief than that of a spouse because the child is not expected to die ahead of the parents. So, it is a dreaded occurrence for parents to lose their children to death, for they would prefer that the death struck them, leaving their children. Being not a natural order, such death could figuratively be perceived as loss of all futuristic hopes: career, dreams, son-in-law, daughter-in-law, heir, to list a few – on the deceased. Similarly, among the same ethnic group, losing both wife and the child during labour can cause an incontrollable grief to the husband, but such grief could be inconsequential if only the child was lost while the mother lived. The consolation is in a common proverb: "If the water is spilled while the calabash remains unbroken, there is less need to mourn". (The spilled water being the child while the calabash is the mother, who would bear other children if alive). In addition, the loss of a loved one whose corpse could not be found for burial would engender devastating grief reactions than the death of a loved one whose corpse can be found for burial. For, the ethnic group belief that: The death of a child whose corpse is found for burial is much preferred to the bereaved parents whose child cannot be found for burial.

With specific reference to the coronavirus pandemic, in one of the reactions to grief occasioned by loss of a child to the pandemic, the loss of a marriageable girl was described as a disruption of future vision of seeing the deceased getting married and getting grandchildren from her (Asgari et al., 2023).

Encourage the Bereaved Person to Grieve Rather Than Repress it

Both Skalski et al. (2022) and Asgari et al. (2023) acknowledged that grieving is an emotionally a painful and natural reaction to loss of a loved one. The grieving process differs from one person to another, and coping styles revolve around application of cultural, environmental, psychological, and religious resources (Ogunleye, 2021). The scholar further elucidated that grieving is personal and individualistic, as every grieving person grieves like themselves and not like other people – which reflect their likes, dislikes, worldview, and uniqueness. Thus, Ogunleye submitted that it is more helpful and respectful to concentrate on the idiosyncratic nature of a person's grief and their unique way of adjusting to loss.

But grieving is usually not encouraged, or less tolerated by sympathisers and some people in the network of social supports. The discouragement or non-toleration could be due to the people's misconception about the grieving processes, underestimation of events leading to the grief, or due to cultural expectations. Among the Youruba, for instance, sympathisers usually encourage bereaved persons to be determined not to weep, to be man enough to block grief, or to be a woman like man (men being expected to bear grief with equanimity), but this is unhealthy in grief management. For, bereaved individuals should be allowed to cry, if they so wish, as crying releases stress and emotional pain (Newhouse, 2021).

Encourage Bereaved Person's Discussion of Their Loss With Significant Others

Following the death of a beloved one, most bereaved individuals are usually filled with lots of stories relating to the loss to share with sympathisers and social supports, even though few others may become taciturn. For those who would voluntarily wish to share their grief and pains, however, they may choose to do that for various reasons. Experientially, there is relief in talking about one's agonies in the presence of sympathisers, which may attract more sympathy and support. In addition, a bereaved individual who is unsettled by guilt feelings may need to validate their innocence by sharing their roles in the antecedents leading to the loss. Moreover, given that the process of grieving is person-specific, and encouraging individual's unique way of grieving as beneficial and respectful (Ogunleye, 2021), it could be their therapeutic approach to quick return to wellness.

Oftentimes, however, bereaved individuals are advised to quit discussing anything relating to the deceased, with a view to assisting them to accelerated recovery from their grieving. This technique of managing grief could be counter-productive, because both Thomassen et al. (2022), and Jacob et al. (2022) separately submitted that keeping hurtful feelings to oneself, keeping away from the source of stress, including avoiding people during traumatic experiences are avoidance coping strategies which are maladaptive in nature. That means, deliberately obstructing positive change in the present circumstance, and similarly preventing effective management of future traumatic situations. On the contrary, however, among those comments and actions identified by Rajic et al. (2023) as healthful and therapeutic to bereaved individuals are pleasant comments about the deceased, as well as discussing memories of the deceased by social supports and the bereaved themselves.

Time Out

Time out is a behaviour modification strategy wherein an individual who is exhibiting excess and disruptive behaviour in a particular environment is taken out temporarily from the environment reinforcing the undesirable behaviour, to a new environment where the behaviour could be extinguished due to absence of reinforcement (Akinade, 2021; Ohuakanwa, 2015). This is one of the ways of modifying the grieving person's environment. In many cases of bereavement, social supports (individually and in groups) thronged the home of bereaved individuals in large numbers each day for several weeks. The number of visitors or sympathisers may be a function of the bereaved person's work, social, religious, and communal status, or the communal, religious, work, or social standing of the deceased. The bereaved requires proper nourishment, healthful exercise, adequate rest, and sleep in order to successfully navigate the grieving phase. However, given that sympathisers and social supports visit in large numbers, some of the recovery exercises required by the bereaved for enhanced rehabilitation from grief (such as uninterrupted sleep, rest, physical exercises, and eating) may be disruptively unattainable.

At such instance, the bereaved should be informed to conviction that sympathisers and social supports intrusion is encouraging but deleterious in obstructing observance of some recovery exercises. The bereaved person should be educated on the dangers inherent in non-observance of recovery enhancers and should be persuaded to time out. In carrying this out, the bereaved one is taken out of the unsupportive environment for a period of time short and long enough for observed improvement in their recovery, and then later returned to the former environment.

Deal With Grief-Enhancing Memorabilia

This strategy is another method of modifying the grieving person's environment to enhance recovery. One of the souvenirs that could enhance the bereaved one's continuous emotional attachment to their departed people is presence of physical memorabilia (clothing, perfumes, photographs, shoes, and other personal effects). Each of these could elongate the bereaved person's undesirable emotional attachment to the deceased so long they serve as reminders to pre-existing bond between the deceased and the bereaved. Among the symptoms of complicated or dysfunctional grief identified by Skalski et al. (2022) are preoccupation with the memories of the deceased, as well as avoiding all reminders of the deceased. Because people are dissimilar in their reactions to grief, however, memorabilia and other souvenirs could be permitted to stay with the bereaved for as long as the grieving person is adjusting desirably, but in situations where the presence of these objects hinder effective rehabilitation of the bereaved, it is suggested that rehabilitative counsellors have a duty to remove the objects and keep them away from the presence of the bereaved one for some reasonable period of time, good enough for observable improvement of the grieving person's adjustment. Thus, rehabilitation counsellors need to explore available souvenirs and memorabilia relating to the deceased that elongate emotional attachment of the bereaved to the deceased, thereby obstructing effective rehabilitative process.

Pay Requisite Attention to the Grieving Person's Physical Health

Without exaggeration, grief and traumatic reactions that come in the wake of bereavement can have a great toll on bereaved person's physical, behavioural, psychological, emotional health (Asgari et al. 2023; World Health Organisation [WHO], 2018), and productivity such that the individual in grief could be excessively tired and innervated if the unpleasant condition persists for long. And should this be, complete demobilisation may ensue. For instance, the grieving individual may experience anorexia, insomnia, and transit to depression (WHO, 2018). In attempting to prevent either of these, however, the bereaved must be motivated to counteract anorexia by eating nutritious food - no matter how uninviting and uninteresting it could be. Similarly, the grieving person must be persuaded to have adequate rest. To accomplish this, however, where there are large numbers of social supports and sympathisers coming to commiserate and assist the bereaved, it is suggested that the rehabilitative counsellor should inform the teeming social supports to respect the rest periods of the bereaved person so that their rest periods are held sacrosanct and not unnecessarily interrupted. According to Akinboye et al. (2016), individuals passing through stressful life situations must prioritise their health in order to return to wellness and happiness.

Engage the Bereaved Person in Healthful Physical Exercises

Conceding that grieving could make the bereaved individuals become lethargic, thereby finding any form of exercise very uninteresting and burdensome, one of the ways to break the bonding to grieving is returning to the bereaved person's pre-grief physical exercises or introducing some new physical exercises in response to the need of the time. Such physical exercises could be laundry, taking a walk out of the house, albeit not in a busy traffic way, cleaning the home surroundings, gardening, singing, and dancing. Such physical exercises have been found to propel the release of endorphins – certain chemical substances from the brain, which assists people who are physically and emotionally weak to feel better (Akinboye et al., 2016; Olatomide, 2021).

Generally, McMahon et al. (2017) found physical activity to positively impact mental health, being antidote to anxiety and depression, and with specific reference to the bereaved, Williams et al. (2023) established that physical activity is therapeutic (blocking preoccupation, and helps thoughts clarity), enhances confidence (by offering inner strength to overcome), strengthens emotional outlet (through diffusion of anger and frustration, including activation of pleasure), invites self-discovery (by becoming a new person, and establishes positive routine), offers opportunity for social support (through friendship, including giving and receiving), as well as improves health and wellness (by assisting to overcome poor health, and provides fitness).

Apply Premack Principle to Prompt the Bereaved to Functionality

A person's degree of productivity wanes drastically during grieving, but the grieving person needs to be assisted to gradually return to pre-bereavement functionality. One of the rehabilitation methods readily applicable to prompt the bereaved to achieve this is Premack principle. This is a practice whereby an activity that an individual is more likely to engage in is used to reinforce any behaviour (or performance of an activity) that the same individual is unlikely to perform (Ohuakanwa, 2015; Watson & Tharp, 2014). The bereaved may still be lethargic, or discouragingly slow at returning to levels of functionality prior to the bereavement, despite the rehabilitative counsellor's initial intervention. Given this, Premack principle could be used.

In the application, a careful observation of what the person who is bereaved enjoys doing (such as receiving sympathisers) would be permitted only after they have taken their baths and dress properly (hygiene). The grieving person could be permitted to take a walk outside of the home before they take their bath and dress nicely. What is important, it needs to be stressed, is for the rehabilitative counsellor to observe what the bereaved person enjoyed doing during the phase and pair it with what they abhor, but arranging the events in a way that engagement in the latter would be permitted only when the former had taken place. This principle has been used to increase making telephone calls, exercise time, checking daily mails, honest statements, eating, as well reduce smoking (Watson & Tharp, 2014). The present writer had applied it on some students – both secondary and tertiary, to up their study time.

Strengthen Help-Seeking Behaviour of the Grieving Person

Chandrasekara (2016) defined psychological help-seeking as every attempt to ask for assistance for mental health challenges from either professional counsellors or informally from friends and family members. For the purpose of this contribution, however, help-seeking behaviour is the tendency of the bereaved individual to ask for assistance from social supports around them in order to meet a need. During grieving phases, the personal hygiene, environmental hygiene, and daily routine of grieving individuals usually suffer automatic disruption and neglect. This can be complicated in situations where there are too many visiting sympathisers and social supports whose presence unintentionally dirtied the environment. At such juncture, a number of tasks could be waiting for attention. These may range from laundering, preparing meals, washing plates and utensils, taking school children to school and bringing them back, etc. The rehabilitative counsellor should tutor the bereaved to speak up about their areas of need for help in the house chores, accept willing help from others, and should equally be encouraged to express their preference for a helper in doing certain task. For instance, a bereaved wife may prefer that a named "friend" does the laundering of the beddings wherein her spouse died, because of some sensitive facts she might not want "outsiders" to know about the deceased. For, many deceased persons who died at home usually messed up their bedding in their last minutes of departure. The counsellor should also tutor other helpers to initiate vicarious help, based on their personal observation, and initiative.

Reduce the Bereaved Person's Guilt Feelings Through Self-Compassion

A feeling of guilt is one of the emotional reactions exhibited by bereaved persons during their loss of loved ones (Asgari et al., 2023; James, 2017; Roberts & Yeager, 2015). Self-compassion describes supportiveness given to oneself during encounter with suffering or pain, be it consequent upon one's personal errors or from external life situations. It is a profitable way of approaching distressful thoughts and emotions which positively result in physical and emotional wellness (Neff, 2023). In it, the rehabilitative counsellor educates the bereaved to be emotionally present at their difficult phase and extinguish illogical self-criticism and self-judgement, to be aligned with other people during the phase rather than isolating; and should not be overwhelmed by their grief. The bereaved needs to be trained by rehabilitative counsellors to perceive that losing a loved one is neither a curse nor a catastrophe, even when such loss may follow in quick succession.

Admittedly, bereaved people during the coronavirus pandemic era might be tempted to perceive their loss as catastrophic because patients usually died in hospitals without the likelihood of any meaningful exchange of words with their relatives prior to their death, or having to bid them farewell, be it physically or using online platforms (Skalski et al., 2022), reduction of social support consequent upon social distancing restrictions and isolation (Eisma & Tamminga, 2020), or due to disruption of established grieving condition and processes, shifting family grieving to individual grieving, and non-involvement of family members in funeral and post-funeral rites (Asgari et al., 2023; Joseph et al., (2021;Mitima-Verloop et al., 2022), but they should be assisted to admit that whatever occurs to a person and which has a name has happened to people earlier in history, and thus not unprecedented. Additionally, it means that many of the victims of such incidents had navigated it, and come out strong, and moved on with life.

Advancing the Wellbeing of Bereaved People Toward Rehabilitation

Therapeutically, the rehabilitative counsellor should assist the grieving person who is brooding with guilt feelings to acknowledge that they have done the best they could do to avert the incident which eventually took place, and to further accept that human beings have limitations, and are not perfectly infallible. Every belief that all our (human) undertakings must be perfectly error-free is a maladaptive belief (Goldfried, 1979, as listed in Watson & Tharp, 2014), which usually results in stress and unhappiness in life (Akinboye et al., 2016). Thus, it must be avoided for happiness to be enthroned.

Cognitive Restructuring

Cognitive restructuring is a general term used to describe the strategies employed to reduce or terminate undesirable and maladaptive thoughts and change such to adaptive and desirable ones. The main objective of this approach is to identify established styles of thinking that are backed by unwavering belief in illogical assumptions and change them directly (Akinade, 2021; Mueser et al., 2015; Nwosu et al., 2022)). In most cases when an individual loses a significant other, they are overwhelmed by guilt feelings, arising from thoughts of omission or commission that must have resulted in the death. At the inception of grieving, culpability thoughts could be tolerable, but when such thoughts become prolonged, exaggerated, or overshadowing, it could lead to maladjustment which is counterproductive, and could do more damage to the wellness of the bereaved.

In one encounter of the writer with a woman who could not be comforted after losing her husband, she reported that the guilt that engulfed her was that she had agreed to travel with her spouse to his workplace for a weekend while she would return on Monday following the weekend. A quarrel had ensued in the morning of Friday, forcing her to refuse to travel with her spouse. The spouse left home, with the quarrel unresolved. He subsequently had a head-on collision with another vehicle before getting to his destination. He was rushed to a nearby hospital by passers-by where he was confirmed dead on arrival. The bereaved confided in the present writer as to why she was not being consoled. She submitted that if she had travelled with the deceased, despite the disagreement, the deceased would have been less preoccupied with the lingering quarrel; he would have been at peace with himself while driving; if she was with him while driving, she would have cautioned him if he was reckless in his driving; if she had travelled with him, the death would have been averted, and the "loads" of two persons (children's responsibility) would not become hers alone. She finally expressed that she felt guilty that she had pushed her spouse to untimely death, and felt she should not continue to live.

Advancing the Wellbeing of Bereaved People Toward Rehabilitation

Applying cognitive restructuring, the writer assisted the bereaved to itemise all the convictions that are reinforcing the guilt feelings, and further assisted her to reconstruct the direct opposite of her thoughts. For instance, she was helped to reason that if she had travelled with her spouse, with the unresolved disagreement, the deceased may have been more preoccupied with the facts of the quarrel, seeing her by his side, as seeing her may cue constant reminders of the quarrel; her dead spouse may not have been at peace with himself in the course of driving, especially if she was with her spouse while driving, she may not have cautioned him if he was reckless in his driving if she was experiencing blame-shifting, adding that even if she cautioned his reckless driving, he could become more infuriated, and saw her caution as indictment; if both of them had travelled together, both of them may have died in the accident, if it was inevitable, and consequently, the one person left to carry the "loads" of two persons (children's responsibility) may also have died, leaving the children as orphans. So, it is reasonable to acknowledge that humans are not infallible, and should be prepared to overlook their errors. The bereaved woman was finally encouraged to imagine that if the deceased was asked his judgement on her feelings of guilt for being responsible for his death while she stayed behind to live, he could have expressed happiness that he did not drive his spouse to untimely death, having wisely refused to journey with him, and therefore rejoiced that she could continue to live. After she was tutored on how to reflect upon this in her quiet time, she reported improved rejection of guilt feelings after two weeks.

Additionally, cognitive restructuring has been established to produce enhanced emotional adjustment in divorcees treated with the approach than the control group (Nwosu et al., 2022), and higher improvement in Post-Traumatic Stress Disorder symptoms and functioning among people with severe mental illhealth exposed to the treatment than those exposed to brief treatment (Mueser et al., 2015).

Prepare the Bereaved to Anticipate and Tolerate Awkward Responses From Others

Often time, sympathisers and social supports ask questions and demand some explanations from the grieving individual on the antecedents to the loss. Some of these could be shocking, naïve, and hurtful to the bereaved. Notably, some of these people may make such inquisitions out of their state of shock, befuddlement, and disbelief, without any intention to hurt or embarrass the bereaved. For an illustration, a 6-year-old boy had a pet dog nurtured from puppy bought him by his mother. The boy and the dog were always found together around the neighbourhood, except whenever the boy was going to school when it would be chased away from following him. The dog bit the boy one day, without the parents' knowledge until his body swelled up, starting from his right hand – before he told his parents that he was bitten by his dog when they were playing together. The swelling continued the second day, compelling the parents to rush him to hospital where he died after about two hours on admission. Following the boy's death, sympathisers came in large numbers to assuage the bereaved pains. However, in quick succession, one of the sympathisers asked the grieving mother: who bought the dog for the boy; where the parents were when the dog bite the deceased; why the parents refused to kill the dog when it became "digbolugi", that is, became rabid; and why none of the parents could notice that the deceased was injured before he owned up to being bitten by his dog. The bereaved struggled to respond but she was advised to maintain her equanimity by ignoring the sympathiser. Interestingly, such questions and insinuations from sympathisers are many and varied, depending on the antecedents to the loss.

Consequently, being ignorant that sympathisers and social supports could come with such questions and demands, the anguish of ignorance of how to respond to such unexpected inquisitions may aggravate the pains of the bereaved, and should they retort in the resultant mindset, their response could be sarcastic or hurtful to the questioners. This may compel them to withdraw intended supports. Given this situation, there could be two undesirable consequences. One is that the bereaved may result to isolation (an avoidance strategy) in order to shield themselves from like social supports, or withdrawal of supports by social supports, which could lead to neglect of the bereaved at such critical time of need.

Therefore, rehabilitative counsellors have a duty to educate the bereaved to expect awkward and rhetorical questions from social supports and sympathisers and be taught to tolerate such embarrassing questions from the questioners with equanimity. Similarly, bereaved persons must be educated to forgive and overlook both imagined and real errors from social supports. According to Akinboye et al. (2016), learning to forgive others and overlooking one's errors heals from stress, and facilitate happiness in life.

Teach the Bereaved Assertive Skill

Being taught to tolerate unreasonable questions and statements from sympathisers may not work well for all bereaved people because of individual differences, as some might want to respond to such unpalatable questions and statements either to show they are not stupid, careless, or irresponsible. Should they be allowed to respond in a riposte, however, their response may ultimately injure and damage the feelings of the sympathiser, who in turn could feel terribly offended. To reduce the possibility of animosity between the bereaved individuals who need to respond to sympathisers' embarrassing questions and comments, and sympathisers who may have asked their perceived unpalatable questions without the slightest intention to hurt the bereaved, rehabilitative counsellors may need to teach bereaved people assertive skills.

Assertive technique is a way of managing anxiety or fear that obstructs individuals from speaking up, expressing their anger, and demand for their rights, without violating the other person(s) (Martha-Rose, 2015; Nystul, 2019; Watson & Tharp, 2014). Assertiveness skill is useful to individuals who find it difficult to express their feelings constructively, or who find it difficult to rise up for their rights (Nystul, 2014), reduces anxiety, stress, and depression among high school students (Eslami et al., 2016), produces significant effect in improving assertive behaviour (Saradha et al., 2020), weakens aggressiveness, submissiveness, and stress among students, while increasing their assertiveness, self-esteem, and psychological wellbeing, ultimately enhancing their academic attainment (Parray & Kumar, 2022), reduces bullying behaviour among secondary school students (Ekwelundu, 2022), as well as promotes self-esteem, and prevent mental health of students (Golshiri et al., 2023).

Thus, an assertively therapeutic response of the bereaved to awkward and embarrassing questions and comments from a given sympathiser could be: "I know you do not mean to hurt me in your questions/statements/comments, but it hurts me, as it makes me feel careless, not proactive enough, culpable, and irresponsible. It would help me better if you stop them".

Apply Bibliotherapy in Managing the Grief of the Bereaved

Aside the rehabilitative counsellor's one-on-one application of intervention, there are about two other prominent ways they could connect bereaved persons to other resources that are equally helpful. One of such is inviting a person who has had a similar encounter that a grieving person is navigating (and had managed it successfully) to share their experience with the bereaved (Aoun et al., 2018). Another one is bibliotherapy. This is a strategy whereby clients are encouraged to read books and other literary works that pertain to their problem so as to facilitate the attainment of a given counselling outcomes (Nystul, 2019; Olatomide, 2019). In that connection, the rehabilitation counsellor can recommend works on grief management phenomena under diverse titles such as rehabilitation counselling, grief management, coping with the death of a loved person, crisis management, coping with disasters, both man-made and natural, etc. In addition, biographies and autobiographies of persons who have traversed exact traumatic phases and experiences of life as well as those similar to it and were able to manage them successfully could be studied. Furthermore, to the spiritually inclined, reading of religious books such as the Holy Bible and the Holy Quran can be of help at such critical periods.

Teach Self-Monitoring, and Recording of Unpleasant Emotional Phases During Grieving

In this technique, a client is encouraged to carefully observe their (especially negative) emotional state and record them for analysis and therapeutic intervention (Akinade, 2021; Olatomide, 2019). In carrying this out, the rehabilitative counsellor educates the grieving client to have a jotter, (that is, a small book that can be used to write notes in) ruled and dated (for instance, from Monday through to Sunday) on a weekly basis, for about three to four weeks. For each of the days, there could be Morning, Afternoon, and Evening (rows or columns). The client is instructed to have a pen permanently attached to the jotter to facilitate easy writing whenever there is need to do so. Thus, for the bereaved, anytime the grief reaction becomes domineering, the grieving person takes their pen and continues to jot down their thoughts, without censuring them. Therapeutically, the data garnered, using this medium can prove very useful for both the grieving client, as well as the rehabilitative counsellor. To the former, it could assist to direct attention to "prompts" that serve as harbingers of unhealthy emotional state; it could help the grieving client to reduce, and systematically terminate unhealthy emotional state. To the latter, it could assist to ascertain the cues to the deleterious emotional state of the bereaved, time of the day, the frequency, as well as use the data to determine the appropriate blocks in their intervention.

Scientifically and behaviourally, it has been established that behaviour usually reacts to itself when it is being observed, either by self, or others. This is termed reactivity in Psychology (Watson & Tharp, 2014). Toward the last quarter of year 2023, a client who was uncontrollably grieved consequent upon losing two twin pregnancies within two years was referred to the present writer. The client was taught self-observation, monitoring, and recording of grieving episodes. Interestingly, she reported that the therapy was highly effective, in terminating her brooding within three-and-half weeks without additional intervention.

Disapprove Alcohol and Drug Use for the Bereaved

For most grieving individuals, the temptation to engage in alcohol and drug use may be high (Drabwell et al., 2020), especially for those who might have had history of drug use and addiction previously. It is essentially profitable to educate the grieving person that whatever relief they acquire through any of these (alcohol consumption and drug use) will be temporary in the short run, as it can be likened to taking a route away from reality, which may be counterproductive in the long run. While the rehabilitative counsellor strives to explore the grieving person's past medical history from the client themselves, and from significant others around

Advancing the Wellbeing of Bereaved People Toward Rehabilitation

them, with particular reference to drug use and alcoholism, it is imperative for the rehabilitative counsellor to educate the client on the overall dangers of alcoholism and use of drugs to work through the phase. Relatedly, both Akinboye et al. (2016), including Drabwell et al. (2020) strongly advised against the use of drugs, alcohol, or smoking of cigarettes and tobacco when facing stressful situations such as bereavement in life, as their relief does not guarantee lasting happiness. If need be, notwithstanding, either of alcohol or drug may be taken but strictly on doctor's recommendation.

Reinforce Positive Improvements Exhibited by the Bereaved

Positive improvements in the behaviour of the bereaved must be publicly acknowledged by the rehabilitative counsellor, and thereafter ask for more positive changes. Reinforcement is a technique of behaviour modification applicable in all behaviour challenges, whether such behaviour is desirable, which needs to be increased, or undesirable, which requires to be weakened (Ohuakanwa, 2015; Watson & Tharp, 2014). Whatever is used to achieve reinforcement is labelled a reinforcer. Thus, a reinforcer could be something tangibly physical (such as food, perfume, necklace, shoe, etc) or verbal (such as Great! Good work! among others). In this case, the verbal one is strongly recommended because it appears to be relatively cheap, comparatively timely, and may not become monotonous. Therefore, expressions such as: "Great work! You have advanced your hygiene", "Good efforts – you have improved upon your diet!" "This is nice – you are picking up gradually on your productivity", are good examples of such verbal reinforcements, after which the rehabilitative counsellor may add: "It is my wish that you continue to build upon what you have achieved".

Simple as this looks, the good in it can be tremendous. Studies have shown that when reinforcement is built into progress made in behaviour modification efforts, it strengthens prior achievement, and potentially produces more desirable change in clients (Watson & Tharp, 2014). Additionally, Carkhuff (2019) argued that a number of helping programmes have been unsuccessful due to inability to attach appropriate reinforcements. This further underscores the indispensability of application of reinforcers in therapies directed at returning bereaved persons to pre-bereavement well-being.

Measure Recovery Rate Before Termination of Intervention

Clinically, any typical grief and trauma intervention counselling must commence with an assessment of what happened during the loss, how it happened, as well as the bereaved physical, behavioural, emotional, and cognitive reactions to the grief.

191

Notably, the rehabilitative counsellor, using their clinical observation of the rate of healing of the bereaved, combined with self-reports of the client, and reports from important others as social supports them around, must be able to use all these to ascertain the rate of recovery of the bereaved with a view to terminating the intervention. The pointer to recovery includes the bereaved returning to pre-grieving period of good sleep, healthful diet, improved personal and environmental hygiene, regained mindfulness, improved social relationship with others, and engagement in productive activities, etc. Recalling that the rehabilitative counsellor conducted pre-intervention assessment of the bereaved person's disturbed state at the outset of intervention, it would be necessary to re-administer the same instrument to validate and strengthen the counsellor's observation, self-reports of the grieving client, and the reports of other important others, following which termination of intervention may follow.

Soon as the inevitability of termination of intervention is ascertained, the rehabilitative counsellor informs the recuperating client and prepares them psychologically for this inevitability (that is, termination of intervention). The rehabilitative counsellor also informs other network of supports who have collaborated with them on the journey to the bereaved recovery. Finally, follow-up modality will be explained to the recuperating client who requires to know that relapse could occur, and how to manage it without losing what had been gained. This is in tandem with Roberts' 7-stage model of crisis intervention where follow-up plan and agreement are featured at the last stage of the model (Roberts, 2015; Roberts & Yeager, 2015).

REHABILITATIVE COUNSELLORS' DUTIES TO OTHER HELPERS

Empathic Listening

Listening is a communicative skill which assists the hearer(s) to leave the speaker better off than they were previously; thus, it calls for being silent, rather than cutting-in to obstruct the flow of the speaker (Uwaoma & Nkwam-Uwaoma, 2015). The bereaved needs someone who can listen empathically to their narration, and not someone who interrupts their narration. To this effect, rehabilitative counsellors need to tutor social supports that the bereaved needs facilitative listening from everyone involved in their rehabilitation, rather than unnecessary questioning or interruptions of their outpouring of emotions, no matter how unreasonable such outpouring may sound. It must be acknowledged that no sympathiser or social supports could bear the brunt like the bereaved do. Such facilitative listening is advantageous to both parties. To the bereaved, it is therapeutic, as it helps them to perceive social supports around them as emotionally involved and partaking in their pains, while it assists rehabilitative counsellors, and social supports to understand both the verbal and non-verbal messages in the actions and inactions of the grieving person.

However, where any social supports feel constrained to pry into circumstances surrounding the loss, they should be educated to ask if the bereaved would be willing to entertain probing questions on the antecedents leading to the loss. And if they do not want to talk about it, their decision should be respected – may be until when they are in the right frame of mind to do so. Attig (2010) submitted that rehabilitative counsellors (and social supports) should put on the role of a witness, meaning that, they should be able to patiently observe, hear, listen, and understand the narratives of grief and trauma of the bereaved, while MacArthur et al. (2022) similarly emphasised that emphatic listening is crucial to bereavement affinities, described as the several ways, both physical and intangible, through which bereaved individuals attach themselves to social supports after the death of a family member. For this to be attained, there is need for emphatic (facilitative) listening.

Prepare Social Supports to Anticipate, and Tolerate Awkward Responses from the Bereaved

Rehabilitative counsellors have a professional responsibility to educate social supports to be ready to receive unfavourable responses to some probing questions from the bereaved. As sympathisers and social supports are prone to ask a number of questions and rhetorics that the bereaved may consider awkward and embarrassing to them, the bereaved could exhibit a number of reactions to such questions, such as keeping mute, or offer just a nod where verbal response is expected. Sometimes, they could refuse to acknowledge sympathetic greetings, or reject an initiated help without giving reasons, to list a few.

While exploring the place of trust and intimacy in behaviour modification with reference to the role of behavioural communication, Uwaoma and Nkwam-Uwaoma (2015) addressed this essential under helper's tolerance. The scholars submitted that helpers should understand that the client's present problematic condition could propel them to become harsh, irrational, emotional, and erratic, thereby provoking their helpers. The helpers should therefore endeavour to demonstrate understanding by seeing the client as someone whose problem is affecting their emotions without which they would not have reacted that way.

Educate Social Supports to Observe an Area of Need, and Meet It

Rehabilitative counsellors should train social supports to take an initiative to be observant enough to discern an area of need and vicariously assist the bereaved to meet the need. Such areas of need could be assisting them to prepare meals, tidying the house, doing laundry, catering for children in case of loss of a spouse, taking children to school and picking them from school (Ogunleye, 2021), or processing release of corpse for burial from morgue or hospital, etc. They need to be assisted unasked because during grieving, the bereaved person usually encounters disruption of daily routine; they usually suffer inertia, and may experience indecision. All these experiences call for people around them to take initiatives and help them out of many lingering tasks. Interestingly, this fact of assisting bereaved people to do some lingering tasks by available social supports is reinforced by the works of Bottomley et al. (2017), including that of Aoun et al. (2018) which individually established that being pleased with practical assistance that is timely following loss of a beloved person predicted accelerated recovery, and equally helps to shield the damaging effects of stress on the bereaved, having reduced situational demands on them.

Encourage Social Supports to Make Physical Contacts With the Bereaved

Aoun et al. (2018) acknowledged social support services as a crucial factor that influences bereavement consequences. Thus, contacts with the bereaved is a form of social support in itself. It ranges from making oneself physically available, through video calls, chats, and short messaging system (sms). Both Asgari et al. (2023) and Rajic et al. (2023) separately contended that neighbours, friends, religious faithful, co-workers, to list a few, pay condolence visits to bereft individuals in order to sympathize and offer them support. Similarly, Rajic et al. (2023) revealed being physically present with the bereaved, and offering physical assistance as supportive and therapeutic to the bereaved.

It does appear, however, that the bereaved person's preference, plus what is attainable for social supports seem to make it difficult to recommend a particular one. Experientially, this writer was a part of a team of sympathisers sent by a primary school authority to visit a widow who had lost her spouse to a sudden death. While there, a relation of the deceased came, and the visiting team welcomed him. This writer, being the youngest member of the condolence team volunteered his seat for the new visitor because available seats were occupied. The bereaved was outraged, insisting that the man should not be offered any seat because he was not wanted. After a brief surprise by all, including the embarrassed man, the bereaved narrated that the man came on the day of the loss, and had been calling ever since, adding that she stopped picking calls from him when she realised that a countless telephone calls from him would not equal one personal visit to assuage her grief.

She concluded her narration using a popular Yoruba adage: "Eniyan boni lara j'aso lo", meaning "People's physical presence provides succour than clothing" at such traumatic phase of life. Thus, the two approaches (personal visits plus any one of the other methods) should be used complementarily as much as practicable. Among the Youruba, for instance, experientially, supportive activities during bereavement include caring for the children, food preparation, household chores, praying, and spending time with the bereaved individuals. Spending time with the bereaved would be unattainable without personal visits.

Taking Care of the Health of the Bereaved

Bereaved individuals require proper nourishment, adequate sleep, healthful exercise, and adequate rest, in order to successfully navigate the grieving phase. To be able to cope with stress in life and workplace so as to return to productive living, Akinboye et al. (2016) recommended pleasurable engagements, rest, sleep, and physical exercises. If these requisites are grossly inadequate or denied, physical and mental exhaustion may ensue, which may lead to system breakdown, sickness, depression, or death in the extreme. In addition, regular medical examination may be required during the phase, and thereafter. To this end, the rehabilitative counsellor has a duty to educate social supports on the health-related areas of need of the bereaved, as well as assign roles they could play in enhancing the health of the bereaved.

According to Eisma and Tamminga (2020), reduced perception of social support by bereaved individuals was pervasive during COVID-19 pandemic due to social distancing restrictions and isolation, thus making group physical activities less attractive. Minding this shortcoming in group physical activities, Olatomide (2021) found physical activities such as trekking, farming or gardening, laundry, sweeping the compound, searching for firewood, washing family car instead of patronising carwash, volunteering work in places of worship, cleaning cobwebs around the house, knitting, and supervising home chores done by children were healthful physical activities to retirees during the phase, while Adegboro et al. (2020) similarly established physical activities such as brisk walk, jogging, running on treadmill, stretching activities, and running within the compound were adequate to buffer the undesirable impacts of stay-at-home restrictions on the physiological health of people.

CONCLUSION

From the in-depth exposition of the focus of this contribution, it can be concluded that emotional hazards is inevitable in the life trajectory of every living person, and one of the constituents of emotional hazards is loss of a beloved person. Similarly, while some people can sail through the test of emotional hazards devoid of external help, many others fail such test and transit into crisis. One of the human reactions to loss of a loved person is to grieve. Furthermore, because the cost of being enmeshed in crisis following bereavement is humongous to the bereaved, family members, and the society, counsellors require mastery of effective skills and therapies that can be used to assist people in grief to navigate the phase in order to return to pre-bereavement productivity. In addition, the roles ascribed to rehabilitative counsellors is twofold – to the bereaved themselves, and to social supports who are partners-in-progress with rehabilitative counsellors to assist in the restoration of grieving individuals to wellness. Unarguably, the link to counsellors' proficiency in grief and trauma education counselling lies in institutions saddled with the responsibility of training counsellors. Therefore, the onus is on counsellor training institutions to modify their training curriculum to include grief and trauma counselling education to adequately equip rehabilitative counsellors on the skills and techniques of healing bereaved individuals so as to facilitate their return to pre-bereavement functionality, thereby advancing their total wellbeing.

Discussion Questions

1. Differentiate between emotional hazard, grief, and bereavement.
2. Explain the concept social support, and list any four (4) components of social supports.
3. Who is a rehabilitative counsellor? Trace the twofold role of rehabilitative counsellors, and provide an outline of any five (5) therapies available for use by rehabilitative counsellors in the rehabilitation of bereaved individuals.
4. Itemise, and briefly explain any five (5) ways in which coronavirus pandemic brought undesirable twist to bereavement processes across the world.
5. Why do you think rehabilitative counsellors ought to coordinate the input of other social supports for the benefit of the bereaved? Identify any four (4) indirect interventions offered the bereaved by rehabilitative counsellors through other social supports

REFERENCES

Adegboro, J. S., Fadero, E. O., Momoh, D. M., & Adedugbe, B. O. (2020). Mitigating the adverse effects of lockdown during COVID-19 pandemic with home-based physical activities. *Educational Thought*, 10(1), 67–73.

Akinade, E. A. (2021). *Modern behaviour modification: Principles and practice.* Brightways Publishers.

Akinboye, J. O., Akinboye, D. O., & Adeyemo, D. A. (2016). Coping with stress in life and workplace. Stirling-Horden Publishers (Nig.) Ltd.

Aoun, S. M., Breen, L. J., White, I., Rumbold, B., & Kellehear, A. (2018). What sources of bereavement support are perceived helpful by bereaved people and why? Empirical evidence for the compassionate communities approach. *Palliative Medicine*, 32(8), 1378–1388. 10.1177/0269216318774995297545 14

Asgari, M., Ghasemzadeh, M., Alimohamadi, A., Sakhael, S., Killikelly, C., & Nikfar, E. (2023). Investigation into grief experiences of the bereaved during the covid-19 pandemic. *Omega*, 0(0), 1–20. 10.1177/003022282311730753718 4963

Attig, T. (2010). *How we grief: Relearning the world* (Revd. Ed.). Oxford University Press.

Bottomley, J. S., Burke, L. A., & Neimeyer, R. A. (2017). Domains of social support that predict bereavement distress following homicile loss. *Omega*, 75(1), 3–25. 10 .1177/003022281561228228395645

Carkhuff, R. R. (2019). *The art of helping in the 21st century* (10th ed.). Human Resource Development Press, Inc.

Chandrasekara, W. S. (2016). Help-seeking attitudes and willingness to seek psychological help: Application of the theory of planned behaviour. *International Journal of Management. Accounting and Economics*, 3(4), 232–245.

Drabwell, L., Eng, J., Stevenson, F., King, M., Osborn, D., & Pitman, A. (2020). Perceptions of the use of alcohol and drugs after sudden bereavement by unnatural causes: Analysis of online qualitative data. *International Journal of Environmental Research and Public Health*, 17(3), 677. 10.3390/ijerph1703067731972984

Eisma, M. C., & Tamminga, A. (2020). Grief before and during the COVID-19 pandemic: Multiple group comparisons. *Journal of Pain and Symptom Management, 60*(6). https://doi.org/10.1016/j.jpainsymma.2020.10.004

Ekwelundu, C. A. (2022). Effect of assertiveness training technique on bullying behaviour of secondary school students in Anambra State, Nigeria. *European Journal of Soil Science*, 7(2), 118–131. 10.46827/ejsss.v7i2.1230

Eslami, A. A., Rabiei, L., Afzali, S. M., Hamidizadeh, S., & Masoudi, R. (2016). The effectiveness of assertiveness training on the levels of stress, anxiety, and depression of high school students. *Iranian Red Crescent Medical Journal*, 18(1), e21096. 10.5812/ircmj.2109626889390

Golshiri, P., Mostofi, A., & Rouzbahani, S. (2023). The effect of problem-solving and assertiveness training on self-esteem and mental health of female adolescents: A randomized clinical trial. *BMC Psychology*, 11(1), 106. 10.1186/s40359-023-01154-x37032337

Jacob, G., Faber, S. C., Faber, N., Barlett, A., Quimet, A. J., & Williams, M. T. (2022). A systematic review of Black People coping with racism: Approaches, analysis, and empowerment. *Perspectives on Psychological Science*, 7(5), 482–495. 10.1177/17456916221100050936006823

James, R. (2017). *Crisis intervention strategies* (8th ed.). Centage Learning.

Joseph, A. O., Fagbamila, O. D., & Joseph, A. A. (2021). COVID-19 pandemic preventive guidelines and protocols: How does this affect the Yoruba funeral rites in Nigeria? *International Journal of Modern Anthropology*, 2(16), 570–585. 10.4314/ijma.v2i16.3

MacArthur, N. D., Kirby, E., & Mowll, J. (2022). Bereavement affinities: A qualitative study of lived experiences of grief and loss. *Death Studies*, 47(7), 836–846. 10.1080/07481187.2022.213504436327234

McMahon, E. M., Corcoran, P., O'Regan, G., Keely, H., Cannon, M., Carli, V., Wasserman, C., Hadlaczky, G., Sarchiapone, M., Apter, A., Balazs, J., Balint, M., Bobes, J., Brunner, R., Cozman, D., Haring, C., Iosue, M., Kaess, M., Kahn, J. P., & Wasserman, D. (2017). Physical activity in European adolescents and associations with anxiety, depression and well-beign. *European Child & Adolescent Psychiatry*, 26(1), 111–122. 10.1007/s00787-016-0875-927277894

Mitima-Verloop, H. B., Mooren, T., Kritikou, M. E., & Boelen, P. A. (2022). Restricted mourning: Impact of the COVID-19 pandemic on funeral services, grief rituals, and prolonged grief symptoms. *Frontiers in Psychiatry*, 13(0), 878818. 10.3389/fpsyt.2022.87881835711586

Mueser, K. T., Gottlieb, J. D., Xie, H., Lu, W., Yanos, P. T., Rosenberg, S. D., Silverstein, S. M., Duva, S. M., Minsky, S., Wolfe, R. S., & McHugo, G. J. (2015). Evaluation of cognitive restructuring for post-traumatic stress disorder on people with severe mental illness. *The British Journal of Psychiatry*, 206(6), 501–508. 10.1192/bjp.bp.114.14792625858178

Neff, K. D. (2023). Self-compassion: Theory, method, research, and intervention. *Annual Review of Psychology*, 74(1), 193–218. 10.1146/annure v-psych-032420-03104735961039

Newhouse, L. (2021, March 1). Is crying good for you? *Harvard Medical School Blog*. https://www.health.harvard.edu/blog/is-crying-good-for-you-2021030122020

Nwosu, N., Enajedu, E. E., Itobore, U. A., & Ncheke, D. C. (2022). Effect of cognitive restructuring intervention on emotional adjustment of sample divorcees in Nsukka Education Zone of Enugu State, Nigeria. *International Journal of Education, Learning and Development*, 10(8), 18–26. 10.37745/ijeld.2013vo10n8pp1826

Nystul, M. S. (2019). *Introduction to counselling: An art and science perspective* (6th ed.). Cognella Academic Publishing.

Ogunleye, T. (2021). Effective grief management: The role of the professional counsellor. In T. D. O. Adewuyi, B. K. Odu., & K. Olagunju (Eds.), *Topical issues in socio-personal guidance and counselling* (68-74). Brightways Publishers.

Ohuakanwa, C. E. (2015). Operant conditioning techniques in behaviour modification. In Uwaoma, N. C., & Chima, I. M. (Eds.), *Behaviour modification: Modern principles and practices* (pp. 124–146). Gabtony Prints Ltd.

Olatomide, O. O. (2019). Counselling for social reformation in Nigeria: The place of traditional moral values as viewed by Obafemi Awolowo University students. In A. Mburza & Emenike, E. H. (Eds.), *Critical considerations on social transformation and national healing for professional practicing counsellors in Nigeria* (pp. 1-14). Counselling Association of Nigeria (CASSON).

Olatomide, O. O. (2021). Socio-physiological adjustment strategies of retirees during the Coronavirus pandemic in Ondo State, Nigeria. *Rivers State Journal of Professional Counselling*, 1(1), 101–117.

Parray, W. M., & Kumar, S. (2022). The effect of assertiveness training on behaviour, self-esteem, stress, academic achievement and psychological wellbeing of students: A quasi-experimental study. *Industrial Research/Development*, 2(2), 83–90. 10.11648/j.r.d.20220302.13

Rajic, I., Genc, A., & Batic-Ocovaj, S. (2023). Relationships between bereavement support strategies and empathy dimensions. *Primenjena Psihologia*, 16(2), 229–267. 10.19090/pp.v16i2.2449

Roberts, A. R. (2015). Building the past and present to the future of crisis intervention and crisis management. In Roberts, A. R. (Ed.), *Crisis intervention handbook: Assessment, treatment and research* (pp. 3–34). Oxford University Press.

Roberts, A. R., & Yeager, K. R. (2015). Lethality assessment and crisis intervention with persons presenting with suicidal ideation. In Roberts, A. R. (Ed.), *Crisis intervention handbook: Assessment, treatment and research* (pp. 35–63). Oxford University Press.

Sallnow, L., & Paul, S. (2015). Understanding community engagement in end-of-life care: Developing conceptual clarity. *Critical Public Health*, 25(2), 231–238. 10.1080/09581596.2014.909582

Saradha, I., Sasikala, T., & Rathinasabapathy, B. (2020). A study to evaluate the effectiveness of Assertiveness Training Programme (Atp) to impart assertive behaviour among adolescents. *Journal of Positive School Psychology*, 6(6), 5054–5061.

Skalski, S., Konaszewski, K., Dobrakowski, P., Surzykiewics, J., & Lee, S. A. (2022). Pandemic grief in Poland: Adaptation of a measure and its relationship with social support and resilience. *Current Psychology (New Brunswick, N.J.)*, 41(10), 7393–7401. 10.1007/s12144-021-01731-633935472

Thomassen, A. G., Johnsen, B. H., Hystad, S. W., & Johnsen, G. E. (2022). Avoidance coping mediates the effect of hardiness on mental distress symptoms for both male and female subjects. *Scandinavian Journal of Psychology*, 63(1), 39–45. 10.1111/sjop.1278234676897

Uwaoma, N. C., & Nkwam-Uwaoma, A. O. (2015). Trust and intimacy in behaviour modification: The role of behavioural communication. In Uwaoma, N. C., & Chima, I. M. (Eds.), *Behaviour modification: Modern principles and practices* (pp. 207–217). Gabtony Prints Ltd.

Wallace, C. L., Wladkowski, S. P., Gibaon, A., & White, P. (2020). Grief during the COVID-19 pandemic: Considerations for palliative care providers. *Journal of Pain and Symptom Management, 60*(1). 10.1016/j.jpainsymman.2020.04.012

Watson, D. L., & Tharp, R. G. (2014). *Self-directed behaviour: Self-modification for personal adjustment* (10th ed.). Centage Learning.

Williams, J., Howett, N., & Shorter, G. W. (2023). What roles does physical activity play following the death of a young person? A qualitative investigation. *BMC Public Health*, 23(1), 210. 10.1186/s12889-022-14542-636721110

Worden, J. W. (2018). *Grief counselling and grief therapy: A handbook for the mental health practitioner*. Springer. 10.1891/9780826134752

World Health Organisation (2018). *International classification of diseases for mortality and morbidity statistics (11th Revision)*. WHO.

KEY TERMS AND DEFINITIONS

Crisis: This is a higher degree of disturbance that someone who has encountered a traumatic occurrence falls into, where professional help is required to assist the person recover.

Emotional Hazards: These are unpleasant occurrences brought by nature or human actions whose negative effects lead to disturbed state for the recipient.

Follow-Up: This occurs when the rehabilitative counsellor continues to reach out to a rehabilitated bereaved person to help them maintain their recovery, and assist them manage relapse.

Grief: The situation of high degree of sadness that a bereaved person experiences after the death of their beloved one; it is synonymous with bereavement.

Intervention: This is the entire rehabilitative counsellor's professional strategies to assuage the grieving condition of the bereaved.

Rehabilitative Counsellor: This is the professional counsellor who is proficient in application of therapies in assisting bereaved person recover from bereavement and return to pre-bereavement productivity.

Reinforcer: This involves presentable gifts or verbal praises offered bereaved person by rehabilitative counsellor to acknowledge improvements in the recovery process of the bereaved person.

Relapse: This occurs when the healing already achieved by the rehabilitated bereaved person is lost due to fresh outbreak of grief.

Social Supports: These are people such as family members, friends, classmates, workmates, religious faithful, and neighbours who work with rehabilitative counsellor to enhance recovery of the bereaved person.

Sympathisers: These are people who pay occasional visits to the bereaved person mainly to commiserate with them rather than offer recovery assistance.

Youruba: These are the ethnic group of people who occupy the six Southwestern states of Ekiti, Lagos, Ogun, Ondo, Osun, and Oyo in Nigeria; their main language is Yoruba.

Chapter 9
Role of a Caregiver:
Emotional Tolls of Caregiving

Diana McCullough
https://orcid.org/0000-0002-7471-0043
Greater Vision Counseling and Consulting, PLLC, USA

ABSTRACT

The role of a caregiver is a noble and often selfless one, encompassing a wide range of professionals, from counselors and social workers to healthcare providers. Caregivers are at the forefront of offering support, compassion, and assistance to individuals navigating grief and loss. However, it is imperative for counselor educators to recognize that caregiving, while rewarding, also imposes a substantial emotional toll on those who provide this essential support. This chapter aims to explore the profound emotional toll that grief can take on caregivers, shedding light on the emotional turbulence, the self-care challenges they encounter, and the significance of seeking support and supervision. Although not a course taught in higher education or as case studies in the classrooms, students should be able to navigate complex situations that are not so cut-and-dry.

EMOTIONAL TOLLS OF CAREGIVING

The role of a caregiver is a noble and often selfless one, encompassing a wide range of family members and professionals, from counselors and social workers to healthcare providers. According to Figley and Roop (2009) "compassionate caregiving requires the act of attending" (p.4). It is by embodying the principles of attending; caregivers create a nurturing and supportive environment that enhances the overall well-being of those they serve. Caregiver burden was originally coined in 1986 by Zarit et al., which was defined as "the extent to which caregivers perceived their

DOI: 10.4018/979-8-3693-1375-6.ch009

Copyright © 2024, IGI Global. Copying or distributing in print or electronic forms without written permission of IGI Global is prohibited.

Role of a Caregiver

emotional or physical health, social life, and financial status as suffering as a result of caring for their relative" (Stevens et al. 2024, p. 2). Caregiver burden was also identified as one's financial strain, responsibility conflict, and lack of social activities, as well the strain of an individual who cares for the chronically ill, disabled, or elderly (Liu et al. 2020).

Caregivers will be defined as care given by a family member rather than a professional (Schulz & Sherwood, 2018). Caregivers are at the forefront of offering support, compassion, and assistance to individuals navigating; while rewarding also imposes a substantial emotional toll on those who provide this essential support. As the population ages, there is a growing need for the aging population to be supported and care is a basic human need. It is often family members that are the primary source of care for the aging population, as opposed to professional services, which would end up costing the family hundreds of dollars (Arno et al., 1999; Schulz & Sherwood, 2018). Due to the American family dynamic changing over the years, approximately 62% of married couples raising children have more than one job, if we were incorporate chronic healthcare needs of children into the mix, caregivers must attempt to balance personal and work demands, which in turn those caregivers experience greater levels of burden (Stevens et al. 2024).

This chapter will aim to explore the profound emotional toll that grief can take on caregivers, shedding light on the emotional turbulence, the self-care challenges they encounter, and the significance of seeking support and supervision as a professional entering the field. There has been an abundance of literature reviews that has shown that caregiving takes an emotional, physical, mental, and financial burden on the family; often seen has hidden burdens (Blair & Perry, 2017; Keefe, 2011; Sinha, 2013). The burden and stress associated with caregiving are known to negatively affect the physical, emotional, social, and financial health of caregivers (Lilly et al., 2012). The caregiving burden is significantly influenced by a range of factors, including the care recipient's dependency on daily activities, prolonged caregiving hours, caregivers' lower educational levels, strained relationships between the caregiver and the elderly, cohabitation with the care recipient, social isolation, financial stress, and the lack of alternatives to caregiving (Marinho et al. 2022).

In the United States, the projected number of individuals aged 65 and older are expected to reach 83.7 million by 2050 (Ortman, 2014; Thorson et al., 2019). With this rise in the aging population, comes consequences and economic changes surrounding home life and healthcare (Hayutin et al. 2010; Thorson et al., 2019). With the increase of the aging population, healthcare demands have shifted from within a hospital to community and family, with family members being the key to long-term delivery for loved ones (Liu et al. 2020). Family caregiving often goes unnoticed among public policy discussions (Gibson & Houser, 2007). Caregivers are classified as either formal or informal, formal caregiver have been through formal training and are paid for their services to the family; informal caregivers are typically family members or friends usually without training and payment performing this role (Marinho et al. 2022). While caregiver is not uncommon in the nursing field, it has lacked a clear-cut definition and is associated with negative terms such as stress and problem (Liu et al. 2020). Some sitters have included family and others are often trained volunteers (Carr, 2013). Hiring caregivers versus an informal caregiver for a loved one involves distinguishing roles that, on the surface, might seem similar but fundamentally differ in qualifications, responsibilities, and goals. Studies have shown that family members are crucial in delivering long-term care for older adults as they assume the role without question (Marinho et al. 2022). Understanding these differences is crucial for relatives seeking the proper level of support for their loved ones and is not always an easy decision to make. Informal caregivers cover an estimated 70% to 95% of the care provided by aiding with bathing, cooking, and managing finances (Dang et al. 2024). When the caregivers are young adults, they often face difficulties in fulfilling personal, social, and professional goals due to their responsibilities of caring for their loved ones (Dang et al. 2024). The nature of caregiving differs substantially between children and adults, and there is an estimate of 28.5% of the U.S. adult population providing unpaid adult care to an adult relative in 2009 (National Research Council, 2010). Caring for a family member with a serious disability or chronic illness can lead to distress or depressive symptoms among the family caretaker (Ngamasana et al. 2024). Caregiving has been seen to having relatives quitting their job, altering their work schedules, as well as compete with work-life balances (Stevens et al. 2024).

Although not a course taught in higher education or as case studies in the classroom, students should be able to navigate complex situations that are not so cut and dry. In the time of grief, caregivers often bear witness to the raw, intense emotions experienced by individuals grappling with grief and loss. They become conduits for their clients' pain, sadness, anger, and confusion. This emotional intensity can have a profound impact on caregivers, who may experience a range of their own emotions, all to be included within this chapter in depth. It has been shown in literature that 70% of the 2.4 million deaths in the United States are a result of some type of chronic condition such as heart disease, stroke, respiratory type illnesses (Schulz et al. 2009).

Compassion Fatigue

Compassion fatigue (CF) was once considered an occupational stress that affected caregivers such as nurses, clergy, clergy, and social workers (Lombardo & Eyre, 2011; Blair & Perry, 2017, p.15), and now rehabilitation counselors and professionals in education settings, especially since COVID times. Compassion fatigue,

Role of a Caregiver

often described as the cost of caring, is an emotional and physical burden borne by those in caregiving roles, leading to a state of tension and preoccupation with the suffering of those being cared for. It manifests as a gradual lessening of compassion over time, akin to the dwindling of physical strength, but in the emotional realm. Although there has not been a consistent definition for CF in literature, there was one proposed in 2006 by Figley who referred to it as "the cost of caring," and had defined it as "the deep emotional, and spiritual exhaustion that can result from working day to day in an intense caregiving environment" as cited by Stoewen (2019, p.1004). Compassion fatigue was later defined as the "natural stress caused by the strong desire to help a valued person and alleviate the pain suffered after undergoing trauma (Orbay et al., 2022, p. 729). Caregivers may find themselves emotionally drained as they absorb the suffering and pain of those they are caring for, it could be seen as the mental occupation that comes with constantly attending to the emotional and physical pains of the one, they love. Compassion fatigue can lead to emotional exhaustion and burnout, as literature suggests compassion fatigue (CF) has become a major concern amongst caregivers (Blair & Perry, 2017). The root of compassion fatigue lies in the empathetic engagement caregivers maintain with those they care for. Constant exposure to suffering, coupled with the desire to help, can lead to an emotional residue that accumulates, eventually overwhelming the caregiver's own capacity for emotional processing. This can result in symptoms similar to those of burnout, including emotional exhaustion, reduced feelings of empathy or sympathy, irritability, and difficulty in making decisions. In a study published in the Journal of Aging and Mental Health (2018), it stated that 59.5% of caregivers experience burnout or CF, while another study in the Journal of Adult Development, claimed that family caregivers are more susceptible to CF than formal caregivers due to the overall lack of systemic support they receive (2019). As time is spent with the caregiver and patient daily, and the care increases, so does the burden. CF is just another risk factor to be experienced due to empathy.

Literature review by Klimecki and Singer (2011) has suggested that CF could possibly be understood as empathic distress fatigue, meaning that one's personal distress is positively associated with secondary traumatic stress (Stoewen, 2019). However, research has shown a series of psychological effects of CF, such as impairments in functioning, lost resources, and points of resiliency (Dwyer et al. 2021). What we have sensed thus far amongst caregivers is that the emotional demands of caregiving can be overwhelming. Caregivers may find themselves immersed in the struggles and challenges of their clients or relatives, often absorbing the emotional weight of traumatic experiences. This constant exposure can result in a gradual erosion of the caregiver's emotional resilience, leading to feelings of helplessness and frustration. When an individual works day in and day out caring for a loved one, it

Role of a Caregiver

has the ability to take an emotional toll on someone, especially when empathy and compassion are displayed (Figley & Roop, 2006; Dwyer et al. 2021).

Grief and Loss

After caregiving for a loved one, an individual may experience a number of psychiatric symptoms that could impair important functioning in someone's life, and apparently Schultz et al., (2009) claimed that about 20% of bereaved caregivers have this experience that could range from depression and even complicated grief. Grief and loss are inevitable aspects of caregiving, and caregivers often find themselves supporting individuals through these challenging experiences throughout their lifetime. Providing caregivers with a deep understanding of the dynamics of grief, the various stages individuals go through, and effective support strategies is essential. Additionally, caregivers should be encouraged to acknowledge and manage their own emotional responses when dealing with clients experiencing grief and loss. Caregivers, including counselors and social workers, often find themselves in the challenging position of supporting individuals through the intricate journey of grief and loss. The caregiver's role goes beyond providing practical assistance; it involves navigating the complex emotional landscape that accompanies these experiences. Witnessing the intense emotions, such as sadness, anger, and confusion, in those they are caring for can evoke a profound empathetic response in caregivers.

As caregivers immerse themselves in the grief and loss experiences of their clients, they may share in the emotional weight of the journey. Empathy, while a cornerstone of effective caregiving, can also expose caregivers to their own emotional vulnerability. In a survey conducted by the University of California, one's very own empathy during caregiving could lead to burnout and emotional distress (2021). Professionals and caregivers may often resonate with the pain of those they support, experiencing a range of emotions themselves, including sadness, helplessness, and sometimes even a sense of personal loss (Schulz et al. 2009). Moreover, caregivers may grapple with the inherent challenges of providing support while accompanying professional boundaries. Balancing empathy with the need for objectivity and keeping a supportive presence without becoming overly emotionally entangled is an intricate dance that caregivers must master. The emotional toll of seeing the profound impact of loss on their clients can leave caregivers introspective, questioning their own ability to provide comfort and solace. Individuals who experience loss need to work through that loss to detach emotionally from the deceased (Wladkowski et al. 2020). The ultimate goal of grief work is for one to begin acknowledging the absence of their person who passed without suppressing feelings (Wladkowski et al. 2020). Grief work refers to the active and intentional process individuals undertake to cope with and navigate the complex emotions associated with loss. This multifac-

206

Role of a Caregiver

eted endeavor involves acknowledging and expressing the range of emotions tied to grief, including sadness, anger, and acceptance. It is a deeply personal journey that varies for each individual, requiring self-reflection, resilience, and often external support from friends, family, or mental health professionals. Engaging in grief work is crucial for healing and adapting to life without the presence of what or whom has been lost, fostering a sense of closure, and facilitating the eventual emergence of a new normal.

In this context, it becomes imperative for caregivers to engage in ongoing self-reflection. Understanding their emotional responses, recognizing potential triggers, and acknowledging the limitations of their role are essential aspects of this process. By doing so, caregivers can not only enhance their ability to provide effective support but also safeguard their own emotional well-being.

Vicarious Trauma

Vicarious trauma (VT) is a phenomenon that significantly impacts caregivers, including counselors, psychologists, and social workers, as they engage in their work of supporting individuals who have experienced trauma. Vicarious trauma is an "occupational hazard for those in helping professions" (Ravi et al. 2021). It is a form of indirect trauma that occurs when caregivers are consistently exposed to the emotional pain and suffering of those they are helping. This exposure can lead to the caregivers themselves experiencing symptoms similar to post-traumatic stress disorder (PTSD), despite not directly experiencing the traumatic event.

Caregivers, due to their empathetic nature and deep engagement with their clients, may absorb the emotional and psychological burdens of the trauma narratives they encounter. Over time, this constant secondary exposure often called VT can have a profound impact on their own mental and emotional well-being (Ravi et al. 2021). Vicarious trauma is the transformative effect of working with clients and having prolonged exposure, therapists' inevitability change (Leung, 2023). The introduction to vicarious trauma involves understanding its nuanced nature, recognizing the potential signs and symptoms, and acknowledging the importance of self-care and support systems for caregivers. It underscores the need for a proactive and preventative approach to mitigate the risk of vicarious trauma, emphasizing the significance of regular supervision, peer support, and self-awareness in maintaining the mental health and resilience of those in caregiving roles.

In exploring vicarious trauma, caregivers can gain insights into the potential challenges they may face, allowing them to implement strategies to protect their emotional well-being and sustain their ability to provide compassionate care over the long term. The introduction sets the stage for a deeper exploration of the causes, effects, and coping mechanisms associated with vicarious trauma in the caregiving context. Vicarious trauma can result tremendously in a change of worldview and disturb an individual's [sense of safety] as they internalize their emotional experiences (Ravi et al. 2021). Understanding vicarious trauma is essential for caregivers as they navigate the emotionally charged terrain of supporting individuals who have experienced trauma. The constant exposure to the emotional pain and suffering of their clients can take a toll on caregivers, leading to symptoms akin to post-traumatic stress disorder. As we understand the challenges caregivers face, it becomes clear that vicarious trauma is not an isolated concern but is interconnected with the broader spectrum of emotions that caregivers grapple with daily, including frustration and a sense of powerlessness. The emotional toll of vicarious trauma lays the foundation for exploring how caregivers cope with the complexities of their roles, acknowledging the need for strategies that address not only the immediate symptoms but also the underlying feelings of frustration and powerlessness inherent in their caregiving journey.

Frustration and Powerlessness

Frustration and powerlessness are two emotional facets that often accompany the compassionate caregiver's journey. While caregiving, where the desire to alleviate suffering meets the inherent challenges of the human condition, caregivers may find themselves grappling with a sense of frustration when faced with barriers to providing optimal support due to family dysfunction (Ngamasana et al. 2024). Whether hindered by systemic constraints, limited resources, or the unpredictable nature of certain situations, caregivers may confront a reality that deviates from their envisioned impact. This frustration is intertwined with a sense of powerlessness, as caregivers navigate circumstances beyond their control. The intersection of frustration and powerlessness becomes a poignant aspect of the caregiving narrative, prompting a deeper exploration of coping mechanisms, resilience, and strategies to reconcile the emotional complexities inherent in providing care to others.

THE IMPORTANCE OF SEEKING SUPPORT AND SUPERVISION

Caregivers, including counselors and social workers should not bear the emotional burdens of their clients in isolation. Seeking support and supervision is a vital part of their well-being and effectiveness. The unexpected loss of a loved one or client can leave many unanswered questions for those surviving, as humans are emotional beings and prone to experiencing grief and loss (Harrichand & Herlihy,2019). As professionals, we undoubtedly will meet moments that challenge us, both personally and professionally; however, it is those moments that we face grief and loss that im-

Role of a Caregiver

pact us the most we are least prepared to handle. This is when seeking the help of a peer group might be recommended; peer groups are counselors who are experienced in personal circumstances of loss and grief (in this instance) and can help process their thoughts and feelings to best help proceed (Harrichand & Herlihy, 2019).

Supervision

Furthermore, caregivers should be encouraged to seek supervision and peer support specifically tailored to addressing the challenges associated with grief and loss. Counseling supervision is a professional and collaborative process in which a more experienced and qualified counselor provides guidance, support, and oversight to a less experienced counselor or a group of counselors. It may also be seen as an intervention process between a senior and junior member of the counseling profession (McKinney & Britton, 2021; Bernard & Goodyear, 2014). Discussing difficult cases and sharing experiences within a supportive professional network can provide a valuable outlet for caregivers to process their emotions, gain insights, and refine their approach to providing empathetic care. In essence, supporting individuals through grief and loss is a multifaceted task that requires caregivers to navigate their own emotional responses while maintaining a steadfast and compassionate presence for those in need. Acknowledging the emotional intricacies of this journey empowers caregivers to provide more nuanced and empathetic support, fostering a sense of connection and understanding between the caregiver and the grieving individual.

The ACA Code of Ethics can help counselors guide their practice when they encounter difficult times, especially during grief and loss. By looking at Section C.2.d. "Monitor Effectiveness," this section informs counselors to take reasonable steps to seek out peer supervision to evaluate their efficacy as counselors (ACA, Code of Ethics, p. 8).

CHALLENGES IN SELF-CARE

Navigating the demanding terrain of caregiving introduces a unique set of challenges, with time constraints and the emotional weight of guilt and self-sacrifice standing as formidable adversaries to the crucial practice of self-care, all which promotes emotional health (Stilos & Wynnychuk, 2021). Caregivers, including counselors and social workers, often find themselves immersed in the needs of those they support, leaving limited time and energy for their personal well-being. The pressing nature of caregiving responsibilities can create a time crunch, making it

Role of a Caregiver

challenging for caregivers to carve out moments for self-care. Self–care is referred to as the "activities that individuals, families, and society, carry out to promote health, prevent disease, reduce health problems, and restore health" (Lima et al., 2023, p. 2). Additionally, the profound sense of duty and compassion that propels caregivers can paradoxically lead to feelings of guilt when considering their own needs or the perceived self-sacrifice involved in prioritizing their own personal well-being. It is vitally important that counselors honor their own needs and find appropriate self-care and supportive places to actively grieve and seek out supervision, consultations or personal therapy in a time of need. In the _ACA Code of Ethics_, counselors guide themselves to also engage in proper practices that includes self-care, wellness activities, personal counseling, peer support, supervision, and consultation. By taking part in these activities, we can acknowledge that we are human beings and have limits and are able to model to our clients what being committed to a journey of healing has to offer.

Per the _ACA Code of Ethics_ Standards C.2.g and F.5.b, it is the responsibility of students and supervisors, and supervisees to monitor their well-being, whether it be their physical, mental, and emotional well-being to avoid any signs of impairment as grief and loss are ubiquitous human experiences. Counselors and all professionals should allow for time to process death by engaging in activities to do such that and should not feel pressured to provide services to others.

While there are so many personal and professional barriers in place, we cannot rely solely on our organizations to ensure our own well-being. As professionals, we must be attentive to our own families, personal and professional self, and our communities, holistically. We have noted the profound empathy needed to navigate grief and loss to the potential toll of vicarious trauma and the persistent challenges of time constraints and guilt in self-care, the narrative has unveiled the profound depth of the caregiving experience. In contemplating the essence of compassionate caregiving, we recognize that attending to others necessitates a deliberate and empathetic engagement. The journey, however, is not without its hurdles. Frustration and powerlessness appear as poignant emotions, linked with the passionate commitment to making a positive impact. Moreover, the pivotal importance of self-care has been underscored, acknowledging the delicate dance between dedicating oneself to the well-being of others and preserving one's own mental and emotional health. As caregivers embark on this demanding but profoundly rewarding journey, it is crucial to continually revisit the principles of active listening, empathy, cultural competence, and holistic care. These principles form the bedrock of compassionate caregiving, fostering a connection that transcends the immediate challenges.

Role of a Caregiver

DISCUSSION QUESTIONS

1. How does the concept of compassion fatigue manifest in the caregiving profession, and what strategies can caregivers employ to mitigate its impact on their well-being?
2. Reflecting on grief and loss, how can caregivers effectively support individuals experiencing grief while managing their own emotional responses to the process?
3. Discuss the importance of seeking support and supervision for caregivers, particularly in light of the emotional challenges faced at work?
4. Explore the concept of self-care for caregivers, considering the barriers posed by time constraints and feelings of guilt and self-sacrifice? What strategies can caregivers implement to prioritize their own well-being?
5. Reflect on the role of active listening and empathy in compassionate caregiving. How do these qualities enhance the caregiver's ability to connect with and support those in their care?
6. What are some potential signs and symptoms of burnout in caregivers, and how can they differentiate between burnout and other emotional challenges such as compassion fatigue or vicarious trauma?
7. In light of the content covered in the textbook, discuss the ethical considerations and responsibilities that caregivers must uphold in their professional practice.

REFERENCES

American Counseling Association. (2014). *2014 ACA code of ethics*. ACA. https://www.counseling.org/docs/default-source/default-document-library/2014-code-of-ethics-finaladdress.pdf

Arno, P. S., Levine, C., & Memmott, M. M. (1999). The economic value of informal caregiving. *Health Affairs (Project Hope)*, 18(2), 182–188. 10.1377/hlthaff.18.2.18210091447

Blair, M., & Perry, B. (2017). Family caregiving and compassion fatigue: A literature review. Perspectives. *The Journal of Gerontological Nursing Association*, 38(2), 14–19.

Dang, S., Looijmans, A., Lamura, G., & Hagedoorn, M. (2024). Perceived life balance among young adult students: A comparison between caregivers and non-caregivers. *BMC Psychology*, 12(1), 1–12. 10.1186/s40359-023-01500-z38185676

Dwyer, M. L., Alt, M., Brooks, J. V., Katz, H., & Poje, A. B. (2021). Burnout and Compassion Satisfaction: Survey Findings of Healthcare Employee Wellness During COVID-19 Pandemic using ProQOL. *Kansas Journal of Medicine*, 14, 121–127. 10.17161/kjm.vol141517134084270

Gibson, M. J., & Houser, A. (2007). Valuing the invaluable: A new look at the economic value of family caregiving. *Issue Brief (Public Policy Institute (American Association of Retired Persons))*, (IB82), 1–12.17612038

Harrichand, J., & Herlihy, B. (2019). Grief and loss: When the professional becomes personal. *Counseling Today*.

Leung, T., Schmidt, F., & Mushquash, C. (2023). A persona history of trauma and experience of secondary traumatic stress, vicarious trauma, and burnout in mental health workers: A systematic literature review. [Supplemental]. *Psychological Trauma: Theory, Research, Practice, and Policy*, 15(Suppl 2), S213–S221. 10.1037/tra000127735511539

Lima, T. M. F., Costa, A. F. D., Lopes, M. C. B. T., Campanharo, C. R. V., Batista, R. E. A., Fernandes, H., & Okuno, M. F. P. (2023). Factors related to burden and self-care for hypertension in family caregivers. *Cogitare Enfermagem, 28.*https://doi.org/10.1590/ce.v28i0.92871

Liu, Z., Heffernan, C., & Tan, J. (2020). Caregiver burden: A concept analysis. *International Journal of Nursing Sciences*, 7(4), 438–445. 10.1016/j.ijnss.2020.07.01233195757

Role of a Caregiver

Lynch, S. H., Shuster, G., & Lobo, M. L. (2018). The family caregiver experience - examining the positive and negative aspects of compassion satisfaction and compassion fatigue as caregiving outcomes. *Aging & Mental Health*, 22(11), 1424–1431. 10.1080/13607863.2017.136434428812375

Marinho, J. D. S., Batista, I. B., Nobre, R. A. D. S., Guimarães, M. S. A., Dos Santos-Orlandi, A. A., Brito, T. R. P., Pagotto, V., Saidel, M. G. B., Fusco, S. F. B., Maia, F. O. M., Corona, L. P., & Nunes, D. P. (2022). Burden, satisfaction caregiving, and family relations in informal caregivers of older adults. *Frontiers in Medicine*, 9, 1059467. 10.3389/fmed.2022.105946736619643

McKinney, R., & Britton, P. J. (2021). Coming alongside supervisees: Introducing the skillset of companioning to counselor supervision. *Journal of Counselor Practice*, 12(1), 23–46. 10.22229/com1212021

Morais, F. L. T., Fachini da Costa, A., Barbosa, T. L. M. C., Vancini, C. C. R., Assayag, B. R. E., Fernandes, H., & Pinto Okuno, M. F. (2023). Factors related to burden and self-care for hypertension in family caregivers. *Cogitagre Enfermagem*, 28, 1-12. https://doi.org/10.1590/ce.v28i.0.92871

National Research Council (US) Committee on the Role of Human Factors in Home Health Care. (2010). *The Role of Human Factors in Home Health Care: Workshop Summary*. Washington (DC): National Academies Press (US). https://www.ncbi .nlm.nih.gov/books/NBK210048/

Ngamasana, E. L., Zarwell, M., Eberly, L., & Gunn, L. H. (2024). Difference in the physical and mental health of informal caregivers pre- and post-COVID-19 National Emergency Declaration in the United States. *SSM - Population Health*, 25, 101609. 10.1016/j.ssmph.2024.10160938313872

Orbay, I., Baydur, H., & Ucan, G. (2022). Compassion Fatigue in Informal Caregivers of Children with Cancer; a Section from Turkey. *Social Work in Public Health*, 37(8), 729–743. 10.1080/19371918.2022.208583735658822

Ravi, A., Gorelick, J., & Pal, H. (2021). Identifying and Addressing Vicarious Trauma. *American Family Physician*, 103(9), 570–572.33929175

Schulz, R., Hebert, R., & Boerner, K. (2008). Bereavement after caregiving. *Geriatrics*, 63(1), 20–22.18257616

Schulz, R., & Sherwood, P. R. (2008). Physical and mental health effects of family caregiving. *The American Journal of Nursing*, 108(9, Suppl), 23–27. 10.1097/01. NAJ.0000336406.45248.4c18797217

Stevens, E. K., Aziz, S., Wuensch, K. L., & Walcott, C. (2024). Caregivers of children with special healthcare needs: A quantitative examination of work-family culture, caregiver burden, and work-life balance. *Journal of Child and Family Studies*, 33(5), 1365–1377. 10.1007/s10826-024-02822-1

Stilos, K. K., & Wynnychuk, L. (2021). Self-care is a must for health care providers caring for the dying. *Canadian oncology nursing journal Revue canadienne de nursing oncologique, 31*(2), 239–241.

Thorson-Olesen, S. J., Meinertz, N., & Eckert, S. (2019). Caring for Aging Populations: Examining Compassion Fatigue and Satisfaction. *Journal of Adult Development*, 26(3), 232–240. 10.1007/s10804-018-9315-z

Wladkowski, S. P., Wallace, C. L., & Gibson, A. (2002). Theoretical Exploration of Live Discharge from Hospice for Caregivers of Adults with Dementia. *Journal of Social Work in End-of-Life & Palliative Care*, 16(2), 133–150. 10.1080/155242 56.2020.174535132223695

Chapter 10
Planning and Support Systems After the Loss of a Loved One

Joetta Harlow Kelly
Campbellsville University, USA

ABSTRACT

Loss and subsequent grief are hard. Picking up the pieces after a death while trying to plan a funeral and take care of other responsibilities can leave people feeling a myriad of emotions. Making sure family members of all ages are cared for while dealing with their feelings is difficult on a regular day, but it is even more complicated amid a pandemic. The author of this chapter shares their insights and suggestions, having been through this themselves. Different cultures, ethnicities, religions, socioeconomic status, and developmental factors must also be addressed. COVID-19 affected people in all these areas and placed restrictions on regular practices that may be felt for years. Suggestions for moving on after this scenario are listed to help those affected. Included are suggestions for teachers and counselors to process their feelings and help their students and clients grieve and heal.

INTRODUCTION

Although there is no set timetable for going through all the emotions of grief, they can be long and varied, experienced separately or several at once, and there are both good and bad ways of dealing with each one. Individuals may feel one or multiple combinations of emotions, and they must seek help from either a physician or counselor/psychologist in order to help them deal with and process their grief. Counselors need to help determine if their environment, personality traits, or even

DOI: 10.4018/979-8-3693-1375-6.ch010

Copyright © 2024, IGI Global. Copying or distributing in print or electronic forms without written permission of IGI Global is prohibited.

Planning and Support Systems After the Loss of a Loved One

chemical makeup are contributing to the situation and help implement ways to treat clients in the best way for them individually. It is not a one-size-fits-all solution for grief; not all clients can be treated equally.

RELATIONSHIPS AND GRIEF

When one loses a loved one, there are different feelings and responsibilities, depending on the relationship with the loved one. Sometimes, a spouse, parent, sibling, or child has specific things they must do. These all include the grieving process but also could include planning a funeral, what they need to do from a legal standpoint, or even just what to do with their loved one's belongings. (Russ et al., 2022)

Loss of a Child

When a child dies, it can be world changing, as this is not the order in which things naturally happen. Parents expect that they will die before their children. So many things change immediately, but there is also a sense of losing what could have been. The hopes and dreams the parent had for the child or that the child had hoped for themselves are gone. Parents who lose children are not only depressed but seemingly more prone to illness, maybe even earlier death. They also wrestle with not being able to protect their children, so guilt many times will make grieving even harder or longer. Siblings miss their deceased sibling and often feel guilty that they survived. Parents may also blame each other and cannot keep their marriage intact. "A stable, secure environment in which both parents nurture each other as they go from one stage of mourning to the next, while also helping their surviving children to express and cope with their feelings, seems likely to foster the best outcome" (Jackson-Cherry & Erford, 2017, p 134).

Loss of a Parent

Several factors make a difference in how a child grieves for the loss of their parent. Age seems to be what makes the most significant difference, especially if the child is noticeably young (Jackson-Cherry & Erford, 2017). Counselors will need to primarily look at the developmental aspects when they are helping these young clients. Teen girls losing their moms can have a more challenging time, and children of all ages may be especially protective of the remaining parent after the loss. Additional issues can occur if both parents are lost, such as who to live with, where they will live, and financial concerns. Studies that assessed children and

Planning and Support Systems After the Loss of a Loved One

caregivers receiving intervention showed more favorable outcomes, especially in group and family-guided sessions. (Bergman et al., 2017)

Losing a parent as an adult can also be a traumatic event with possible negative outcomes. Those people that have been looked to for wisdom and guidance their entire lives are no longer able to give it to them. The sense of loss can be overwhelming and sometimes bring along with it some actual health issues. Weight loss or gain, being confused when making decisions and changes in sleep, blood pressure, heart rates and immune functioning are also possible (Shear, et.al., 2013)

Loss of a Sibling

Like in losing a parent, age also makes a substantial difference, mainly if they are very young, and counselors need to take that into account during their therapy. It is also challenging when they are close in age as they are not only their sibling but also their primary playmate. As mentioned above, they may also feel guilty because they have survived. How the parents deal with the loss and treat the surviving child makes a tremendous difference. In a study by Charles and Charles (2006), they discuss how important it is that families are taught coping skills to deal with this loss, and if they do not, issues can continue to be passed down for generations.

Sibling grief is often misunderstood, and it has been very much overlooked in the literature on bereavement. Common emotions siblings may feel when losing a brother or sister include (Hibbert, 2018):

- Guilt
- Abandonment
- Loss of innocence
- Fallout from the family
- Somatic symptoms
- Fear
- Anxiety

It is also essential for us as counselors to realize that not only younger siblings have trouble dealing with the loss; adult siblings also feel similar emotions but typically have age on their side when trying to understand and process their feelings.

Loss of a Spouse

Losing a spouse is life-changing. The person you have chosen to spend your life with is suddenly not in your life anymore. Even daily routine is different, and it can seem surreal. Social aspects change because some couples feel uncomfortable hanging out with just one remaining spouse, or one may feel threatened in the relationship (Esme, 2023). While there were two couples, there is now one couple and a single. For example, while the wife who still has her husband loves her friend and feels sorry for her because of her loss, she may see her now as a threat to her own secure relationship. The finances and other responsibilities of the household are now on the one remaining spouse. Age also makes a difference here because it is harder to start over when they are older, and they may be unable to find meaning in the loss. The counselor needs to explore all these aspects with the surviving spouse and help them go forward and find meaning and purpose in their life (Jackson-Cherry & Erford, 2017).

RESPONSES TO THE LOSS

Grief can and will happen to everyone at some point in their life. However, sociocultural factors, such as cultural or ethnic identity and religious beliefs, can and will even shape expressions of grief (Silverman, Baroiller & Hemer, 2021). As counselors, it is our job to help our clients understand the ways these factors translate into their experience and guide them in effective coping strategies through these different responses.

Manner/Circumstances of Death

The United States began looking at the manner of death in 1910. A box was added on the Standard Certificate of Death by the U.S. government at this time and thus became a required statistic. It is determined by the doctor or coroner and is at times used for legal purposes and can also be changed if there is new or conflicting evidence (Cooper, 2021). How a loved one passes can also factor into how an individual process the loss. The types of death could be natural, accidental, suicidal, homicidal, or even having an undetermined cause. While no loss is easy, if the circumstances surrounding the event are unpleasant - then dealing with their grief can be combined with a variety of other emotions. Losing a loved one who has been dealing with a chronic illness or condition can sometimes be more accessible to process because their death was expected, and their loved ones slowly came to terms with the loss. Sudden and unexpected deaths, like a car accident, suicide, or homicide, usually are more challenging to process because the shock and rapidness of emotions that a loved one is hit with in the aftermath can be overwhelming (Admin, 2022). Preventable deaths are also challenging to deal with because the mixture of guilt and grief that individuals face can be even more complex to process.

Planning and Support Systems After the Loss of a Loved One

Stigmatized deaths like suicide or overdose introduce a sense of embarrassment and shame to the loved ones because social support from outside friends and family is usually less sufficient. Finding the right tools to help clients in these situations is essential, and introducing them to support groups that deal with their specific needs can be a great tool. There are support groups for family members and friends who have lost someone to suicide, homicide, or even alcohol/drug abuse, which can be an excellent way for your client to gain perspective and peace following a loss.

Cultural, Ethnic, and Religious Factors

Everyone feels grief and sadness regardless of culture affiliation. There are several factors that influence how individuals try to make sense of their loss (Wilson, n.d.):

Collective grief is common. Hindu families have an elaborate 13-day ritual, Native Americans feel that all in their tribe are family so they should grieve together. Those believing in Buddhism in Tibet have a 49-day morning period. In China they make collective decisions which sometimes don't even include the dying person.

Grieving times vary by culture. A brief mourning period with no tears is preferred in Bali, Indonesia while tears even after many years is normal in Egypt.

People want to visit the body of the deceased. Italians have a temporary refrigerated coffin delivered to the home of the family so people can bring flowers, while on the Yorkshire coast the women of the village generally arrange for friends and family to come pay their respects.

Some people look for signs from above to explain why. In the UK they think white feathers are a message from their loved one, while in the sub-Saharan in Africa and even the United States they believe the loved one's spirits may appear in dreams.

Sending on the Spirit is important. In New Zealand and in other religions elsewhere, they have specific rites in order to send off the Spirit that give the loved ones peace of mind in knowing that they honored the deceased.

It is essential when dealing with grief that individuals and families are provided the ability to conduct their own traditional funeral and burial rites, which offer comfort and help them feel they can express themselves in a psychologically appropriate way as they deal with their own loss-related emotions. In addition, this helps them have a starting point for their recovery and social cohesion (Kastenbaum, 2004). As counselors, it is essential to learn what the client believes about life after death and how his/her culture honors their loved ones (American Counseling Association, 2014). Numerous ethnicities in the United States have various traditions, so understanding what our clients believe and how to help them best through this process is crucial. We do not want to assume based on our own experiences and asking them is a great way to build trust and respect between yourself and the client.

Socio-Economic Variables

Variables of grief can also affect the individual and include income, education, employment, community safety, and social support (Kumar, 2021). The issue of paying for medical treatments for family members who passed or for funeral and burial fees can be a tremendous amount of stress if one's financial situation is not the best. Historically, those low-income families who often do not have higher levels of Education struggle with paying for these services, and it can become an increased burden on those already struggling with grief. As counselors, it is beneficial to research local organizations that can aid in financial support if you have a client dealing with this issue.

The Federal Emergency Management Agency (FEMA) offered funeral assistance to those who passed from COVID-19 and paid for expenses like funeral service, cremation, transportation, burial plots, headstones and clergy (COVID-19 Funeral Assistance, 2024).

Developmental Considerations

Before age 2 or 3, young children know when something is different, or someone is missing. Children up to age seven do not always understand that death is permanent and cannot always understand completely the causes and the lengths of people's lives (Jackson-Cherry, et. al., 2017). They may ask when they are coming back or about a person's body after they die. They also do not understand all the burial rituals, like caskets being placed in the ground.

Children up to age 12 are interested more in the details of death and understand on a fundamental level how the body stops working at death (Jackson-Cherry, et. al., 2017). They can know better about the aging process but only sometimes understand why it is not just someone old who dies. They often believe in an afterlife and are curious if they have been taught about it.

When children reach adolescence, they understand death as a natural process and talk about it with their family and friends but do not think as much about it happening to them because they are young and will live forever (Jackson-Cherry, et. al., 2017).

Once more, we look at the effects of COVID-19 when addressing the developmental aspects of grief at different ages. So much of what they experience will have a life-long impact, especially if a loved one is lost. Many circumstances were different during this time; parents were at home with their children due to school closures and parents working remotely. Not knowing what to say about what they were experiencing was difficult for many. An article discussing this issue suggested using Bronfenbrenner's theory and how the child and ecological systems can prove helpful to some when dealing with COVID-19-related grief. These systems include:

Microsystem - home environment, parental anxiety, grief reaction & education

Mesosystem - poor conversation, teacher communication, family values, parenting styles

Macrosystem – irresponsible journalism, cultural beliefs, conspiracy theories, funeral practices

Ecosystem – isolation, contact restrictions, economic shutdown, limited out-of-home leisure time, limited access to healthcare, income loss

Chronosystem – pandemic, travel ban, changing policies, individual characteristics

All these systems and the characteristics within them can make dealing with the loss of a loved one more difficult for children at different developmental milestones. Considering these items as counselors is essential when trying to help children best process their grief and even the period spent in isolation due to the COVID-19 pandemic itself (Chachar et al., 2021).

Helping Children as They Grieve

The following are a list of suggestions for counselors in helping children through the grief process:

Be authentic- they will watch you to see how you grieve. If you show them it is okay to be sad, cry, and talk about the person you have lost, they will follow you.

Let them grieve as they are capable of – Let them be kids. They may cry one minute, then laugh and have fun the next. Let them help make decisions about what they feel comfortable with.

Give them something to remember the person by. It could be a memento or something like a stuffed animal made of their clothing.

Look at pictures of fun times with their lost loved one, allowing them to talk about their good times with them.

Give them opportunities to grieve in a way that is best for them. They may want you with them part of the time and want to be alone sometimes.

Be truthful within the realm they can understand.

Look for changes in their everyday behaviors and calmly discuss them.

Get them help if they need it. It may be talking to a close friend, family member, counselor, or religious advisor.

Make family roles clear. Do not let them be burdened with something they are unprepared for just because a member is gone.

(Hibbert, 2018)

Planning and Support Systems After the Loss of a Loved One

ARRANGEMENTS AND RESTRICTIONS
DURING THE PANDEMIC

Funerals are a regular staple after most deaths. They let the family and friends honor and remember their loved ones and receive support from family, friends, and acquaintances of their departed. Sometimes, the loved ones had opportunities before their death to make arrangements and take care of the costs of the funeral/burial while making known their actual wishes.

Other times, families opt for just graveside services because of cost, wishes of the deceased or other family members, or even if the person is very old and not many friends and family are left to come to the service. Other reasons could be because of the circumstances of the death or the situation of the deceased or their family members. Some funerals are held at churches if they have strong ties, while others are at the funeral home. Many years ago, wakes were held in people's homes, as well as the final service, and they were buried on family land or in a family cemetery on their farms.

In light of the COVID-19 pandemic, many governments had specific guidelines and policies on how funerals and burials had to be carried out to decrease the spread of the virus. In the United States, there were state and Centers for Disease Control (CDC) regulations (McCann, 2022). Quite a few issues and concerns arose because of these restrictions, and it had a tremendous effect on those who were grieving the loss of their loved ones by not enabling them to grieve as they wished. This could, in turn, hinder the COVID-19 grievers from obtaining awareness of and adjusting to the reality of the death. This was also the concern of several early career psychiatrists who shared their experiences during the pandemic. They hoped that the World Health Organization (WHO) perspectives might strengthen mental health care policies for the future (Adiukwu et al., 2020). So much of the healthy part of grieving is the support of others by assembling, talking, and receiving physical assurances in manners such as hugs (Neimeyer & Lee, 2021).

In a Massive Open Online Course (MOOC) delivered from Australia while so much of the world was shut down, published in 2020, authors tried to design a way for people to have actual natural conversations about death just as a regular part of life. Discuss how funerals, public morning, humor, and specific language about death were targeted. Out of 204 responses, several themes developed. They included the negative aspect of attending a funeral virtually and not being able to provide actual physical comfort to those who lost loved ones per physical distancing.

Other changes during the COVID-19 pandemic resulted in creative ways of mourning while still following guidelines and restrictions. Many funeral directors and even churches provided livestream services for those who could not go in person or, for safety reasons, did not wish to go in person. This became complicated when

Planning and Support Systems After the Loss of a Loved One

the issue of specific songs and music were used in the recordings, and copyright issues sometimes arose (McCann, 2022).

Religious Implications/Burial

Failure to have specific rituals performed for their family members as they were passing or afterward of religious beliefs also caused much agony during the COVID-19 pandemic. Survivors felt they were not doing what was needed for their loved ones before and after their deaths, and some feared for their whereabouts as a result (Wilson, n.d.). For example, those of the Catholic faith believe the last rites need to be given to the dying person in order for them to reach their preferred destination in the afterlife. This affects these believers in the United States and countries like Italy, where the Catholic faith is predominant.

In almost all countries, the traditional rituals that honored the deceased persons but also brought comfort to the mourners were reduced in size or banned (Wilson, n.d.). There were also times when family members could not be in contact with their loved ones, and local officials buried them, or they were cremated. It was reported that some were even put in mass graves as well, and within the Muslim culture, this is very much prohibited even in times as we experienced. Islamic rituals where the body of the deceased is prepared were also forbidden in Tunisia. Burying corpses in coffins also happened in Indonesia, where it is strictly not allowed in Islamic rituals (Adiukwu, 2022).

Because of the restrictions on grief rituals during the pandemic and the resulting long-lasting symptoms of grief afterward, a group of researchers from the Netherlands did a study on bereaved individuals from several different countries, the majority being Europeans who had lost a loved one prior to, or during the pandemic and found some interesting results.

In a study about experiences with funerals during the COVID-19 pandemic, 251 participants completed the survey online, and 232 qualified with the stipulations. Participants' ages ranged from 18-87 years, and the survey was available in several languages from several countries. Studies before the pandemic found no conclusive information about the relationships between funerals, rituals, and grief reactions. The findings were mainly that people who went to funerals had found them to be a comfort and that if they were a part of the planning, it helped them adjust better afterward (Rawlings, et. al., 2022)

The researchers wanted to examine how restrictions placed on these rituals might offer a take on their importance and if they show a different side to grief responses. For example, limiting numbers to a funeral could cause more family conflict, or if they felt they could not say goodbye because of the restrictions. Also, it was found that if they could go to the funeral, their grief would be less complicated (Bovero et al., 2021).

Using the 18-item Traumatic Grief Inventory self-report, participants reported how often they experienced the markers the previous month. There were five measures of the funeral service: funeral attendance, funeral evaluation, comfort, planning, and adverse events. Five aspects of grief rituals were measured: performance of collective rituals, performance of individual rituals, helpfulness of collective rituals, and helpful alternative rituals (Mietima-Veloop et al., 2021).

When looking at how COVID-19 impacted funeral and grief rituals, the authors Mietima-Veloop et. al. listed two items: "Did the restrictions due to COVID-19 have an impact on the experience of (1) the funeral and (2) grief rituals or activities after the funeral?" The results of this study found differences between levels of Education in the pre- and post-pandemic participants. Also found was the impact of restrictions on their funeral experience, which was very negative. The impact of restrictions on the experience of grief rituals was also harmful to the group of mainly Europeans who participated. It is also a reasonable assumption that these mourners realized that the restriction negatively impacted their experiences. However, they were so grateful for the funeral service as it was the best that could be done at that point. The questionnaire also had a comment section, and those surveys felt thankful because they got even a tiny amount of support and knew that circumstances were entirely different than usual. One mentioned that just lighting a candle was a comfort, and others surveyed were able to do alternative rituals that brought them comfort.

Many individuals taking the survey listed a large amount of Prolonged Grief (PG) symptoms even for several months afterward. PG symptoms also seemed to be relatively high for those who experienced an unexpected death, as well as if they had a close bond with the person who had passed. Further conclusions presented by the authors were that even though there were so many negative things that resulted from COVID-19, some positive aspects occurred. These included such things as people having closer connections because of what they experienced and being able to create some alternative rituals that were meaningful. They also concluded that people can be resilient despite the circumstances and how important it is to look at the great importance of funerals and rituals to those affected by grief.

Financial/Legal Responsibilities

Dealing with finances after the loss of a loved one is never easy. As mentioned earlier, it is beneficial if one has made the required pre-arrangements from both a financial and mental perspective for the survivors. While it is a hard topic to discuss, it doesn't have to be morbid. It can be meaningful to make your wishes known and a relief to family members that you prearranged this for them. Funeral directors are

Planning and Support Systems After the Loss of a Loved One

happy to sit down with you any time and discuss options and even set up payment plans for the services and products (Webster, 2020).

Other legal responsibilities after a loved one's death involve applying for the death certificate, which many funeral directors help with, and purchasing a plot and stone if not previously done. Additionally, the survivors will be working with a lawyer to settle estates. Getting one who is helpful, knowledgeable of estates, and affordable is vital. Of course, many legal issues are greatly improved if there is a Will, and the deceased's wishes are spelled out. The lawyer will also have to present the case to the court/judge and put a post in the local paper in case any outstanding payments need to be made on the deceased's account. These payments must also be confirmed within a specific period. Joint checking accounts make paying regular bills easier for the remaining spouse. Hospital bills can also be a concern, but some hospitals do not enforce full payment if the survivor is a wife whose husband passes (*Understanding Probate and Estate Administration*, n.d.).

Interestingly, while all these details are exhausting, they can be therapeutic in some ways because they give the survivor a sense of purpose. Legally, they must be done, so they do have to focus on the here and now and complete the assigned tasks. In some cases, estates must be divided as well as personal belongings, and at times, it can cause additional strain and tension in families (*Understanding Probate and Estate Administration*, n.d.). Unfortunately, it can be heartbreaking if family members disagree.

Like many processes during the COVID-19 pandemic, this was also more complicated. Things happened at a slower pace and were more painstaking. You also could not meet with people face to face when things were shut down, but those who were fortunate enough to do things by computer could do that—those who did not have those services readily available or did not know how were done much slower. However, a few new things were available that helped those unable to meet in person. One such convenience was using DocuSign for documents that needed to be processed with a signature when people could not be face-to-face.

COVID-19 PANDEMIC LONG-TERM IMPACT

Lack of Closure

It is hard to get good closure when a person is not able to do for their loved one what they wanted to and to grieve in the way in which they needed to. As previously mentioned, the pandemic put so many restrictions on grief rituals after the loss of a loved one. Not being able to gather as they wanted or at all after their loved one's death led to frustration. However, not being able to see their loved ones while they

Planning and Support Systems After the Loss of a Loved One

were in the hospital to give them the support and love they needed or speak to those giving them care regularly was awful. Knowing that the doctors were learning as they went in caring for their loved ones was distressing, and these physicians had extremely large caseloads to manage as well. Some people were not able to get the medicines they needed for just their regular needs, not to mention the ones they needed for fighting the COVID-19 virus, which was horrible on many fronts.

Social Media and Technology

We were bombarded with every detail, good and bad, on the news, Facebook, Twitter, Instagram, etc. People could call or text their condolences instead of physically showing up due to fear of COVID-19, which was helpful but also increased emotional distance between people. People could also attend/view ceremonies, funerals, etc., that they would not have been able to physically, which was good, but again added to the feeling of distance between mourners (González-Padilla & Tortolero-Blanco, 2020).

Telehealth has also become a great blessing because we now have access to care that we could not have previously. Students could also continue their Education via virtual classrooms and online courses to stay caught up in their studies. Remotely working from home became the norm for most. It was discovered that people could work effectively from home and not be perceived as shirking their responsibilities, which has continued. Many companies still allow employees to work remotely or in a hybrid capacity.

Post-Traumatic Stress Disorder, Grief, and COVID-19

Post-traumatic stress disorder (PTSD) is an anxiety disorder that can be a result of a traumatic event (Giannopoulou et al., 2021). Survivors might experience uncharacteristic feelings of stress, fear, anxiety, and nervousness—and this is perfectly normal. With PTSD, these feelings are extreme because they can cause a person to feel like they are constantly in danger and make it very difficult to function normally in their everyday life. Experiences of traumatic events and associations with PTSD and depression development in urban health care-seeking women.

While all survivors of traumatic events can react differently, there are a few main symptoms of PTSD (De Pasquale et al., 2022):

- Re-experiencing: Feeling like you are reliving the event through recurring, involuntary distressing memories like flashbacks, awful dreams, or even having intrusive thoughts

Planning and Support Systems After the Loss of a Loved One

- Avoidance: Either intentionally or subconsciously changing your behavior to avoid scenarios and places associated with the event or even losing interest in activities that you used to enjoy because they might activate overwhelming symptoms
- Cognitive and mood symptoms: People might have trouble recalling the event or have negative thoughts about themselves. They could also feel numb, guilty, worried, or even depressed and have trouble remembering the exact event. Cognitive symptoms could include out-of-body experiences or even a feeling that the world is inaccurate.
- Hyper-arousal: Being hypervigilant or feeling "on edge" all of the time, having difficulty sleeping, being easily startled, or prone to sudden outbursts of anger

Treatment of PTSD is essential because if it is left untreated, it can last for decades. It is not usually possible for them to "just get over it," and it can worsen over time, and can include psychiatric medications, cognitive-behavioral psychotherapy, or, in most cases, a combination of both (De Pasquale et al., 2022). Failure to deal with the issue of PTSD can cause much distress and disrupt normal social and work functions, which in turn causes problems in their relationships and the workplace.

POST-COVID STRESS DISORDER, PANDEMIC TRAUMA, AND STRESS EXPERIENCES

COVID-19 brought with it many issues. Not only physically but emotionally and economically as well. Much distress for people of all ages is seen in their feelings of fear, anger, worry, and even hurt. People are more anxious, depressed, tired, having trouble focusing, experiencing behavioral problems, and using some risky coping skills like substance abuse. There is so much grief from unexpected loss and threats of more loss from the virus, and just wondering how to go through their daily lives, as well as what is going to happen in the future. Just being in the middle of the pandemic, though, does not always fit perfectly into regular PTSD criteria (Bridgeland, et al., 2021).

There is, however, a current focus on putting a name to what people are dealing with because of the pandemic. The term Post-COVID Stress Disorder refers to the abundant responses and psychological consequences of the Covid-19 pandemic (Taxman et al., 2021). Dr. Caelan Soma, in an article for Starr Commonwealth (2021), listed several factors and types of stress that are seen as a result of the pandemic, as well as features that reflect the harmful consequences of accumulating stress and trauma.

These are:

Planning and Support Systems After the Loss of a Loved One

Protective Factors

- Social support
- Financial stability
- Healthcare Resources
- Safe workplace
- Wellness programs

Traumatic Stress

- Severe illness
- Hospitalization
- Witnessing death
- Death of a loved one
- Extreme exposure to COVID-19 details

General Stress

- COVID-19 exposure and quarantine
- Social isolation
- Employment and income loss
- Working from home with children
- Being a caregiver
- Making difficult decisions about health, Education, finances, etc.

It is important that as counselors we are knowledgeable of the different factors our clients may be dealing with as they try to manage their Post-COVID Stress Disorder, and come up with different strategist to assist them. Sometimes additional help is necessary and the following section will outline some options for us to suggest to our clients.

WHERE TO GET ADDITIONAL HELP

There are a number of was that counselors can help clients find the right place to seek out individuals and groups to help them along their grief journey.

- Local hospital (chaplains many times have grief support groups or offer counseling)
- Church (programs for those grieving)

Planning and Support Systems After the Loss of a Loved One

- Local school or university
- Local counseling offices
- Local funeral home
- Local senior center.
- Websites/Online support groups

WELLNESS AFTER LOSS

Finding hope and being hopeful for the future is of utmost importance. Clients may have questions about how they can accomplish this after the loss of their loved on. It is important as counselors to help them understand the importance of taking care of themselves physically, spiritually, mentally and socially.

Physical Wellness

After the loss of a loved one, there are usually people who will bring food to help the grieving family. This is a great help and often the only thing a person will eat because they are not thinking about cooking or feeding themselves in their time of loss. However, the food stops coming at some point, and a person needs to think about what they need. A healthy, balanced diet is essential to healing and overall health (Escapes, 2024).

Physical wellness also includes getting the proper amount of sleep. Many times, a person who is grieving either has trouble sleeping or wants to sleep all the time. Neither of which is best. Setting a regular time to go to bed, with regular rituals such as taking a warm bath, reading, brushing your teeth, drinking warm tea, etc., may help (Escapes, 2024). Moreover, if more is needed, a doctor can suggest a sleep aid to take regularly.

Getting regular exercise is also a great help after the loss of a loved one. It is proven that even minimal exercise forces the blood to flow all over the body and through the brain, which releases chemicals that are natural antidepressants and helpful in healing (Sharma, 2023). Even if a person starts slow, it is beneficial, and with another person, it can be therapeutic and helpful to keep one motivated.

Regular checkups with healthcare providers who will look after someone's physical well-being and prescribe medications and supplements are also necessary. They can also provide medications as needed for issues resulting from our loss.

Social Wellness

People need each other. It is proven that we are happier and healthier if we have good relationships with others. Sharing joys and sorrows is beneficial as they are multiplied and helpful. Others will usually reach out to a person who has experienced a loss, and even though things change with loss, we are social people. Even if one does not feel like going somewhere or engaging in an activity, one usually feels better after participating.

Being involved in activities that someone has previously enjoyed may be hard at first, but they will improve with little effort and time. Even exploring a new interest their loved ones were not interested in may bring new insight and friendships (Escapes, 2024).

Mental Wellness

Mental wellness can incorporate a couple of different avenues. One is that we all need someone to go to if we are distressed or have an issue we must resolve. Going to a doctor, counselor, or therapist who cares but is not in the middle of the situation can bring insight and a different perspective. These medical professionals can also give us healthy ways of coping with our loss and going forward with our lives. Participating in a support group is also a way to share with others going through the same thing. These people may be able to share insight into what is helping them get through this time, and it always feels good to know someone truly understands how we feel.

Mental wellness can also be enhanced by learning new things by reading, taking a class, or studying if a person is still in school. We are always young enough to learn something new, and stimulating our brains can promote healing.

Spiritual Wellness

We, as people, all have an innate desire to relate to a higher power or find a source of peace. Some people find solace in going to church, praying, reading scripture, and fellowshipping with others who are like-minded. Many enjoy religious music of different types. Some people find solace in meditation or even in spending time in nature. Some also find peace in participating in Yoga or Tai Chi activities. Regardless of what brings them peace, it is essential during grief to do what helps you as an individual.

Final points for Counselors when helping those who have lost loved ones:

Planning and Support Systems After the Loss of a Loved One

- Share with them that they do not need to be afraid to ask for help. Their friends and family may not know their needs, but they want to help. Whether it be a meal, helping with housework or yardwork, picking up or dropping off a child, running an errand, or even just stopping off for a short visit of small talk with coffee or tea.
- Try to help them dwell on what a blessing they had instead of what they lost.
- Help them figure out who they are without that person. They are still valuable and have a purpose.

DISCUSSION QUESTIONS

1. Did you experience grief during COVID-19 or another significant event? If so, how did that make things more difficult for you?
2. What is the socioeconomic climate in your area? How does it affect people dealing with loss/subsequent grieving?
3. How comfortable do you feel working with persons of different ages who experience loss/grief?
4. Would you feel comfortable counseling someone as they go through the arrangements they have to make after a family member has passed? For example, funeral planning and financial/legal issues?
5. How would you help a client get closure after their loss?
6. Do you have experience with PTSD either personally or in the counselor/client relationship? How comfortable are you with it, and how can you do better?

REFERENCES

Adiukwu, F., Kamalzadeh, L., Da Costa, M. P., Ransing, R., De Filippis, R., Pereira-Sánchez, V., Larnaout, A., González-Díaz, J. M., Eid, M., Syarif, Z., Orsolini, L., Ramalho, R., Vadivel, R., & Shalbafan, M. (2022). The grief experience during the COVID-19 pandemic across different cultures. *Annals of General Psychiatry*, 21(1), 18. 10.1186/s12991-022-00397-z35701763

Adler, M. G., & Fagley, N. S. (2004). Appreciation: Individual differences in finding value and meaning as a unique predictor of subjective Well-being. *Journal of Personality*, 73(1), 79–114. 10.1111/j.1467-6494.2004.00305.x15660674

Admin. (2022, May 5). *Factors that can lead to complicated grief.* GrieveWell. https://www.grievewell.com/for-supporters/factors-that-can-lead-to-complicated-grief/

American Counseling Association. (2014). *ACA Code of Ethics*. ACA. https://www.counseling.org/docs/default-source/default-document-library/ethics/2014-aca-code-of-ethics.pdf?sfvrsn=55ab73d0_1Bergman10.1186/s12904-017-0223-y

Bovero, A., Pidinchedda, A., Clovis, F., Berchialla, P., & Caretto, S. (2021). Psychosocial factors associated with complicated grief in caregivers during COVID-19: Results from a preliminary cross-sectional study. *Death Studies*, 1–10. 10.1080/07481187.2021.201914434957925

Bretscher, J., & Haugk, K. (n.d.). *The Gift of Empathy: Helping Others Feel Valued, Cared for, and Understood*. Stephen's Ministry.

Bridgland, M., Moeck, E., Green, D., Swain, T., Nayda, D., Matson, M., Hutchison, N. P., & Takarangi, M. K. T. (2021). Why the COVID-19 pandemic is a traumatic stressor. *PLoS One*, 16(1), 0240146. 10.1371/journal.pone.024014633428630

Chachar, A. S., Younus, S., & Ali, W. (2021). Developmental Understanding of Death and Grief Among Children During COVID-19 Pandemic: Application of Bronfenbrenner's Bioecological Model. *Frontiers in psychiatry*. 10.3389/fpsyt.2021.654584

Communicating with the Public. (n.d.). NFDA. https://nfda.org/covid-19/communicating-with-the-public

Complicated grief - Symptoms and causes. (2022). Mayo Clinic. https://www.mayoclinic.org/diseases-conditions/complicated-grief/symptoms-causes/syc-20360374

Cooper, M. (2023, May 3). *Manner of Death: Categories explained in simple terms*. LoveToKnow. https://www.lovetoknow.com/life/grief-loss/manner-death-categories-explained-simple-terms

Planning and Support Systems After the Loss of a Loved One

COVID-19 funeral assistance. (2024, January 18). FEMA.gov. https://www.fema .gov/disaster/historic/coronavirus/economic/funeral-assistance

De Pasquale, C., Conti, D., Dinaro, C., D'Antoni, R. A., La Delfa, E., & Di Nuovo, S. (2022). The COVID-19 Pandemic and Posttraumatic Stress Disorder: Emotional Impact on Healthcare Professions. *Frontiers in Psychiatry*, 13, 832843. 10.3389/ fpsyt.2022.83284335432014

Escapes, G. (2024, March 16). *Explore how grief impacts the body and offer strategies for managing these physical effects. — Grief Escapes.* Grief Escapes. https:// www.griefescapes.com/blog/the-physical-toll-of-grief-understanding-how-loss -impacts-your-body#:~:text=Grief%20is%20a%20natural%20response%20to%20 loss%2C%20but,support%20your%20overall%20well-being%20during%20this%20 challenging%20time

Esme. (2023, November 17). *Coping with Changed Relationships After the Death of Your Spouse.* ESME. https://esme.com/resources/bereavement/coping-with-changed -relationships-after-the-death-of-your-spouse

Gamino, L. A., Easterling, L. W., Stirman, L. S., & Sewell, K. W. (2000). Grief adjustment is influenced by funeral participation and the occurrence of adverse funeral events. *Omega*, 41(2), 79–92. 10.2190/QMV2-3NT5-BKD5-6AAV

Goncalves, J.Junior, Moreira, M. M., & Rolim Neto, M. L. (2020). Silent cries intensify the pain of the life that is ending: COVID-19 is robbing families of the chance to say a final goodbye. *Frontiers in Psychiatry*, 11, 570773. 10.3389/fp-syt.2020.57077333061924

González-Padilla, D. A., & Tortolero-Blanco, L. (2020). Social media influence in the COVID-19 Pandemic. *International Braz J Urol*, 46(suppl 1), 120–124. 10.1590/ s1677-5538.ibju.2020.s12132550706

Hibbert, C. (2018, April 10). *Siblings & Grief: 10 Things Everyone Should Know*, Dr. Christina Hibbert. https://www.drchristinahibbert.com/dealing-with-grief/ siblings-grief-10-things-everyone-should-know/

J. F. (2023, January 25). Death & Dying: How different cultures deal with grief and mourning. *Phys.org.* https://phys.org/news/2023-01-death-dying- culturesgrief. html#:~:text=Death%20and%20dying%3A%20How%20different%20cultures%20 deal%20with. %205%205.%20Sending%20on%20the%20spirit%20

Jackson-Cherry, L., & Erford, B. (2017). *Crisis assessment, intervention, and prevention* (3rd ed.). Pearson.

Kumar, R. M. (2021). The Many Faces of Grief: A Systematic Literature review of grief during the COVID-19 Pandemic. *Illness, Crisis, and Loss/Illness. Illness, Crises, and Loss*, 31(1), 100–119. 10.1177/105413732110380843660577

Lowej, R. B., & Aoun, S. M. (2020). Memorialization during COVID-10: Implications for the bereaved, service providers and policymakers. *Palliative Care and Social Practice*, 14, 1–9. 10.1177/2632352420980456

McCann, J. (2022, July 13). The long-term impact of COVID-19 on the funeral industry and funeral planning. *1800Flowers Petal Talk*. https://www.1800flowers.com/blog/everyday-moments/the-long-term-impact-of-covid-19-on-the-funeral-industry-and-funeral-planning/

Mitima-Verloop, H. B., Mooren, T., Kritikou, M. E., & Boelen, P. A. (2022). Restricted mourning: Impact of the COVID-19 pandemic on funeral services, grief rituals, and prolonged grief symptoms. *Frontiers in Psychiatry*, 13, 878818. 10.3389/fpsyt.2022.87881835711586

Mitima-Verloop, H. B., Mooren, T. T. M., & Boelen, P. A. (2021). Facilitating grief: An exploration of the function of funerals and rituals in relation to grief reactions. *Death Studies*, 45(9), 735–745. 10.1080/07481187.2019.168609031710282

Neimeyer, R. A., & Lee, S. A. (2021). Circumstances of the death and associated risk factors for severity and impairment of COVID-19 grief. *Death Studies*, 0, 1–10. 10.1080/07481187.2021.189645934019471

Nondenominational, C. I. I. A. (2020). *GriefShare Participant Workbook* (3rd ed.).

Rawlings, D., Miller-Lewis, L., & Tieman, J. (2022). Impact of the COVID-19 pandemic on funerals: Experiences of participants in the 2020 Dying2Learn Massive Open Online course. *Omega*, 003022282210752. 10.1177/00302228221075283351996622

Russ, V., Stopa, L., Sivyer, K., Hazeldine, J., & Maguire, T. (2022). The Relationship Between Adult Attachment and Complicated Grief: A Systematic Review. *Omega*, 003022282210831. 10.1177/00302228221083110356350229

Sharma, A. PhD. (2023, August 22). *Exercise and brain health*. Whole Brain Health. https://wholebrainhealth.org/exercise-and-brain-health/

Shear, M. K., Ghesquiere, A., & Glickman, K. (2013). Bereavement and complicated grief. *Current Psychiatry Reports*, 15(11), 406. 10.1007/s11920-013-0406-z24068457

Silverman, G. S., Baroiller, A., & Hemer, S. R. (2021). Culture and grief: Ethnographic perspectives on ritual, relationships and remembering. *Death Studies*, 45(1), 1–8. 10.1080/07481187.2020.185188533272138

Planning and Support Systems After the Loss of a Loved One

Taxman, J., Owen, G. & Essig, T. (2021). *Pandemic Trauma and Stress Experience (PTSE): Adapting Together.* APsaA Covid-19 Advisory Team.

Tucker, P., & Czapla, C. (2021). Post-COVID Stress Disorder: Another emerging consequence of the global pandemic. *The Psychiatric Times*, 38(1).

Understanding probate and estate administration. (n.d.). AgingCare https://www.agingcare.com/Articles/estate-administration-probate-after-death-in-family-153107.htm

University of Michigan. (2020). *Posttraumatic Stress Disorder during COVID-19.* U Michigan. https://medicine.umich.edu/dept/psychiatry/michigan-psychiatry-resources-covid-19/specific-mental-health-conditions/posttraumatic-stress-disorder-during-covid-19

Webster, L. C. (2022, August 26). *Help your family plan your funeral far in advance.* AARP. https://www.aarp.org/home-family/friends-family/info-2020/planning-your-own-funeral.html

Stay Safe Foundation. (n.d.). *What is PTSD – Stay Safe Foundation – a veteran / LEO 501C3 Non-Profit.* Stay Safe Foundation. https://staysafefoundation.org/What-Is-PTSD/

Wilson, J. F. (n.d.). *Death and dying: how different cultures deal with grief and mourning.* The Conversation. https://theconversation.com/death-and-dying-how-different-cultures-deal-with-grief-and-mourning-197299

Wolfelt, Ph. D., C. T. (n.d.). *Dealing with Families During the COVID-19 Pandemic.* International Cemetery, Cremation and Funeral Association. https://iccfa.com/wp-content/uploads/2022/03/COVID19_ICCFA_Families-Wolfelt.pdf

ADDITIONAL READING

Goodman, G. (2024). Stephen Ministry: Carrying each other's burdens. *Journal of Spirituality in Mental Health*, 1–23. 10.1080/19349637.2024.2343324

Initiative, C. (2015). *GriefShare Holiday Survival Guide* (3rd ed.).

Initiative, C. (2018). *GriefShare Loss of a Spouse Leader's guide.*

Ministries, S., McKay, W. J., & Haugk, K. C. (2000). *Stephen Ministry training manual.*

Nondenominational, C. I. I. A. (2020). *GriefShare Participant Workbook* (3rd ed.).

Rogers, J. (2009). *Grace for the widow*. B&H Publishing Group.

Sharma, A. PhD. (2023, August 22). *Exercise and brain health*. Whole Brain Health. https://wholebrainhealth.org/exercise-and-brain-health/

Tripp, P. D. (2005). *Grief: Finding Hope Again*. New Growth Press.

Wright, H. N. (2006). *Recovering from Losses in Life*. Revell.

Zonnebelt-Smeenge, S. J. R., EdD, & De Vries, R. C. (2019). *Getting to the other side of grief: Overcoming the Loss of a Spouse*. Baker Books.

Chapter 11
Role of Peer Support on Grief and Trauma Counseling During the Pandemic

Megha M. Nair
PES University, India

Adithi Priyadarshini Prabhu
PES University, India

Zidan Kachhi
https://orcid.org/0000-0002-8317-6356
PES University, India

ABSTRACT

Peer support happens when people assist one another with information, skills, emotional support, social support, or practical assistance. It is important to understand what peer support is, how it can help an individual, and why it should be encouraged and practiced. The chapter focuses on peer support, especially online peer support that was provided during the covid era for those going through grief and trauma. The chapter's goal is to gather as much research and data regarding peer support for grief and trauma counseling during the COVID-19 pandemic. It aims to enlighten the importance of peer groups and the types of peer group support that exist. The chapter will enable future counselors to understand the isolation aspect of grief and trauma and provide guidance to individuals to get the necessary peer support.

DOI: 10.4018/979-8-3693-1375-6.ch011

Copyright © 2024, IGI Global. Copying or distributing in print or electronic forms without written permission of IGI Global is prohibited.

GRIEF AND TRAUMA

Grief is often distinguished from bereavement and mourning. It is the anguish experienced after a significant loss, usually the death of a beloved person. (APA, 2018). Not every loss results in a deep sense of sorrow, and not every grieving process has a social appearance. Grief is often accompanied by physiological discomfort, separation anxiety, confusion, longing, obsessive past-focused thoughts, and fear of the future (APA, 2018). Irregular immune function, self-neglect, and suicidal ideation can make severe grief potentially fatal. Remorse for something done, regret for something lost, or anguish over an accident are some more ways to communicate grief. These are physical symptoms that affect the bereaved individual including poor eating, trouble sleeping, fatigue and low energy, physical discomfort, and weakened immunity. Sobbing fits, crying fits, or extreme bodily agitation are examples of more severe physical symptoms. A bad mood is the most common sign of grief (Zisook, Shear. et al, 2009). A wide range of emotions can be experienced, such as anxiety, depression, hopelessness, wrath, guilt, sadness, and loneliness. These feelings rarely happen at the same time and can manifest in related but separate stages. Grief can also cause a person's lifestyle to change; for instance, they may quit engaging in once-interesting activities, cease practicing self-care, or alter daily routines. Kubler Ross proposed a stage theory for grief, denying what has happened is a major effort made by the grieving individual during the initial stage of grieving, known as denial. They are purposefully unwilling to accept their loss in addition to not wanting to admit it. This then can lead to another phase, which is marked by intense feelings of resentment and contempt that materialize as fury and anger when the person is made to confront the loss after failing to stop it. When grief cannot be sufficiently eased by anger and the bereaved individual looks for ways to undo the loss in exchange for a sacrifice, usually with references to spirituality or religion, attempts at bargaining are made. If this doesn't work, the bereaved individual could become increasingly consumed with the death and experience remorse or hopelessness as they try to figure out how it could have been avoided. As a result of the person's internal battles with accepting their fate and loss, depression results. Fortunately, when the person stops trying to hide their feelings by bargaining, denial, etc., this seemingly hopeless period is followed, at least temporarily, by a true acceptance and letting go of the loss or at least, amnesty (Patrick Tyrrell; Seneca Harbergeret al, 2023).

Trauma is the term used to describe an emotional response to a terrible event, such as an accident, rape, or natural disaster. Shock and denial are typical reactions to an event. Long-term impacts can include unstable emotions, memories, strained relationships, and even physical complaints like headaches or nausea (American Psychology Association, 2018). There are mainly three types of traumas and they are acute, chronic, and complex trauma. Acute trauma occurs when there is an effect of a single tense or dangerous circumstance. Chronic trauma results from regular, extended exposure to very stressful circumstances. A few instances are child abuse, domestic violence, and bullying. Complex trauma is when one gets exposed to multiple traumatic events. Some of the symptoms for someone who is experiencing trauma could be trouble concentrating, overwhelming feelings, or trouble sleeping (all points north, Types of Trauma, 2022, November 18).

IMPACT OF COVID-19

The COVID-19 epidemic has claimed "bad deaths" as its victims (Arora & Bhatia, 2023). Among their distinguishing traits are physical discomfort, breathing problems, social isolation, psychological distress, and insufficient care. Grieving is now much harder than it was during previous pandemics due to the lack of coping resources. Grieving rituals, irregularity, lack of social support, and unclear prospects all deny bereaved people the essential opportunity to grieve healthily. Enhancing advanced care planning could make it easier to provide terminal patients with effective care. Virtual funeral services, internet counseling, phone conversations, and encouragement to stay in touch with the deceased can all be helpful to bereaving and mourning individuals. Unexpected human deaths have been connected to the coronavirus. The lack of ritualistic or spiritual support has impacted the quality of grief. During the COVID-19 pandemic, it is projected that there will be anticipated grieving reactions because most individuals become conscious of their death and fear losing loved ones to the virus (Wallace C. L et al, 2020). In the wake of the COVID-19 pandemic, family members expressed regret and expressed regret for abandoning a loved one in their final moments. As a result, they felt that in their capacity as the deceased's family members, they could not live up to the expectations and demands of others. "Survivor guilt," or the feeling that one made it through the disease but the deceased did not, can make grieving worse. Grieving and attending funerals are cultural reactions to loss. People were unable to participate in customary grieving rituals because of the pandemic. The government's travel restrictions, social exclusion, physical separation, and other measures exacerbated the grieving responses of those who had lost a loved one.

Cavicchioli, Meerrucci et al (2021) in their research stated that international action has been prompted by the novel coronavirus (SARS-CoV-2) and associated illness (COVID-19), which are having a serious impact on millions of people. Given the psychopathological outcomes of restrictive measures found during prior outbreaks, a thorough investigation was conducted to provide an evidence-based evaluation of the current COVID-19 quarantine's implications on mental health. Research that measured mental health indices (such as overall psychological distress, depressive symptoms, and PTSD symptoms) before, during, and following quarantine periods used to contain various epidemics (such as COVID-19, SARS, and MERS) was included in the review. A total of twenty-one different research projects produced eighty-two, 312 volunteers. Specifically, at least 20% of those placed under restricted measures to control pandemic illnesses reported having PTSD (21%) and depressive symptoms (22.69%), showing clinically high levels of psychological distress. In conclusion, about 20% of people in today's environment may begin to show signs of psychological issues that are clinically severe. In light of the COVID-19 quarantine guidelines in place, more study on mental health is required.

PEER SUPPORT

Peer support is the term for when people lend each other their skills, knowledge, emotions, social networks, or practical support. New treatments known as peer support services, or PSSs, have gained popularity recently in mental health systems throughout the world. It is believed that PSSs date back more than three centuries to the moral treatment era, albeit on an informal basis. The Mental Health Foundation (2020) defined peer support in mental health as "the help and support that people with lived experience of a mental illness or a learning disability can give to one another". There are various types of peer support, some of which are Peer support groups where there are gatherings where individuals who are facing similar challenges gather and talk about it amongst themselves. One-on-one peer support is when an individual seeks peer support from a trained supporter or mentor. Online communities where people can connect virtually with those who share similar challenges because they cannot get peer support in person. Telephone and helpline support, here there are trained peer support workers who are ready to listen and provide assistance through phone. Self-help groups are informal peer support where individuals facing challenges come together and talk without having a professional around.

Peer assistance can be provided in four different ways in long-term circumstances. Buddying or befriending someone without the support of peers rarely conveys self-management skills. Peer Assistance In this context, mentors actively support individuals in enhancing their capacity for self-regulation. A non-peer professional oversees the safe sharing of stories and helps peers support one another in a group environment. Peers are occasionally called in for sessions, and some of them work toward becoming peer-led organizations. Volunteer peers lead and facilitate peer-led support groups. These groups occasionally operate on their own, are connected to sizable nonprofits, and occasionally receive assistance from coordinators (Sartore, G.M. & Pourliakas, A).

Role of Peer Support on Grief and Trauma Counseling During Pandemic

According to research, peer support is advantageous for companies and the systems in which it is provided, as well as for the person providing the help and the person receiving it. Increased life expectancy, better physical and mental health, a better understanding of their condition, and enhanced self-management abilities are all possible benefits. Peer support workers may report higher levels of self-efficacy and self-esteem, lower rates of depression, and an overall better quality of life. Reduced healthcare costs, more acceptability among populations that are difficult to reach, additional service options, and enhanced cost-effectiveness can all be advantageous to organizations and systems. Peer support is a well-recognized, cost-effective, and simple-to-use mental health resource that benefits people of all backgrounds. The necessity of more easily available and less stigmatized mental health care is underscored by the lengthy wait times and many obstacles associated with seeking professional mental health services.

History of Peer Support

In practically every area of healthcare, peer support is becoming more widely acknowledged. Peer support for a range of illness conditions, groups, and locations is being increasingly supported by research in the health sciences. Policymakers consider peer support to be an effective strategy for increasing access to primary care, improving quality, engaging the community, and lowering health disparities. Most critically, more patients than ever are turning to their peers for assistance.

Peer support has deep origins in the histories of social change movements, self-help, psychotherapy, and survivor-led instincts. The origins of peer support can be traced to a psychiatric hospital in late eighteenth-century France, according to Yale School of Medicine Psychiatry Professor Larry Davidson. State facilities that were closed due to financial difficulties in the 1970s released patients without community assistance. Many of their communities did not want people with mental and behavioral health illnesses living in their towns, cities, or neighborhoods because of how stigmatized they were. They viewed past patients as unstable, dangerous people in the community. The peer movement had its beginnings at this point. These former patients helped one another and developed strong bonds since they had endured similar life situations. The need to hire recovered patients as hospital personnel was acknowledged by Jean Baptiste Pussin, the governor of Bicêtre Hospital in Paris. Peer staff members received recognition for their honesty and compassion towards the patients. A change in the mental health care paradigm that brought the era of "Moral therapy" was marked by hiring former patients (Patrick Tang, MPH). An examination of a Canadian asylum's patient record from 1870 to 1940 revealed multiple instances in which inmates provided official and unofficial support to other patients (Watson & Meddings, 2019). Most of the history of peer support help in a communal context is lost to history. This could be the result of the fact that grassroots self-help is elusive and difficult to describe. Peer support groups have been recognized in the field of addiction since the eighteenth century (Watson & Meddings, 2019). The most well-known of them is Alcoholics Anonymous (AA), which was established in Ohio, USA in 1935. AA is still very popular today and has been modified to address many addictions and mental health issues.

Robert Carkhoff and Charles Traux's efforts in 1965 brought peer support back to light when they found that mentally ill patients in a hospital setting might benefit from the assistance of lay counselors who had received specialized training. Emory Cowne introduced a "Community Mental Health Care" paradigm in 1967 that calls for the creation, application, and assessment of community interventions to be carried out by peers who are not professionals (Tang, n.d). Comparably, in Canada, the "Mental Patients Association (MPA)" was established in the early 1970s to enable people to support one another in preventing suicide during the weekends when access to resources is difficult (Watson & Meddings, 2019). Despite the gradual acceptance of the concept by the mental health establishment, the peer support movement gained popularity among consumers of mental health services. The mental health consumer or survivor movement is largely responsible for the rise in popularity, growth, and spread of peer support. Large state institutions were closing all over the country in the 1970s, depriving patients suffering from serious mental illness of appropriate transitional care. Simultaneously, patients receiving treatment in state mental health centers started protesting against systemic abuse and civil rights incidents. Following their discharge, ex-patients turned to independent peer and mutual support networks for relief, which aided in the empowerment of the person as well as the community (Tang, n.d).

Peer support would not exist today if it weren't for the pioneering work of Judi Chamberlin, Sally Zinman, and Howie the Harp, who established the nation's first peer-run organizations and laid the groundwork for current reforms in mental health services. Judi Chamberlin was a pioneer in the early peer support and psychiatric survivors' movement. Following a miscarriage, Judi Chamberlin willingly checked herself into a mental health facility in 1966. However, a psychiatrist discovered that she had schizophrenia after she had been placed in mental health facilities on several occasions voluntarily. As a result, she was placed in an involuntary five-month detention at Mt. Sinai Hospital in New York. During this time, Judi Chamberlin witnessed a wide range of mental abuses, including forced incarceration, overmedication, and regular isolation of patients who showed resistance—even when their protests were peaceful. Following her release, Judi Chamberlin went to Boston and became a member of the Mental Patients Liberation Front (MPLF), a group that pushed for changes to the law to better serve people with mental illnesses. At the vanguard of the psychiatric survivor movement were Judi Chamberlin and MPLF.

Role of Peer Support on Grief and Trauma Counseling During Pandemic

Judi Chamberlin was a co-founder of several of the nation's first drop-in facilities, all of which employed only peers and other former patients—that is, those with firsthand knowledge. Like many of today's drop-in centers, her early ones placed a strong emphasis on advocacy. (Hickney, W, 2022)

Following horrific mental abuse at the hands of her caregivers, Sally Zinman embarked on a lifetime of advocacy and action. She attributes her healing to returning to the natural world through gardening and reading, committing to advocacy work, and changing the mental health systems that had failed her. She has been a steadfast supporter of the rights of people with mental conditions throughout her career. Sally Zinman helped create the first state-wide peer-run organization in US history and continues to be an outspoken supporter of ending stigma. She has worked with many groups and engaged in consumer activism for many years during her career. She continues to emphasize the need to defend mental health rights and assist a community-based, whole-person approach to recovery and wellness. Howie the Harp, the renowned pioneer of the peer movement, identified as a peer. One of the first peer-led, consumer-run organizations in the US was founded with his assistance. In New York and California, Howie opened the first drop-in centers staffed by peer supporters. He dedicated his entire life and professional career to founding advocacy groups that would protect the rights of the homeless and underprivileged (Hickney, 2022).

Qualitative Rights Peer support services in India can be modeled after the Gujarat Project. The undertaking started in 2014. The goal of the initiative was to improve Gujarat's mental health policy. Additionally, the initiative innovated mental health care facilities by utilizing the WHO's Quality Rights framework and toolkit. Utilizing family and peer support groups was another project goal. To effectively share their experiences with others and offer recovery treatment, peer support volunteers received training (Pathare et al., 2019). The burden associated with mental illness is lessened by peer support services. To assist those with mental health issues, peer support providers are clearly showing some encouraging results and expanding quickly as a profession. The significance of peer support among troops was brought to light in the wake of World War I. Troops suffered from widespread trauma as a result of trench combat and the horrors of the battlefield. "Trench brotherhoods," or unofficial support groups among soldiers, were essential in assisting people in overcoming the psychological effects of combat. After being acknowledged, these peer support networks had an impact on the creation of official psychological services for veterans. The idea of "kizuna" (ties or connections) has historically played a crucial role in how Japanese society responds to natural disasters. Communities came together after calamities like the Great Kanto Earthquake of 1923 to help one another by sharing their losses and rebuilding experiences. This emphasis on group support in culture highlights the value of peer relationships in helping people recover from trauma and sorrow.

CULTURAL PERSPECTIVE OF PEER SUPPORT

The capacity to engage with individuals from different cultures and respectfully learn from them is known as cultural responsiveness. Cultural responsiveness in recovery refers to providing services that take into account and honor the client's cultural beliefs. Peer support workers need to acquire a sense of cultural competence to offer objective services to certain groups, including different minority groups, that also have comparable recovery experiences. To provide this service to clients, peer support workers need to be able to develop cultural competencies that lessen outside pressures like discrimination (Jorden & Hackket, 2019). A significant component of peer support work involves acknowledging, honoring, and respecting one's cultural background and opinions (Zheng et al., 2022). Cultural humility is the state of being open-minded, naturally interested, and willing to learn from and alongside individuals who have varied cultural backgrounds, beliefs, and values. Engaging in conversation with those who share a culture is one of the best ways to learn about it. This can be achieved by official and informal methods, such as reading books or articles, watching documentaries or movies, taking part in online forums, or just having conversations with peers or other community members. But learning about different cultures is a continuous process rather than a one-time thing. It takes continual and active labor to look for a variety of knowledge sources, reflect on your learning objectives, and challenge your assumptions.

It takes more than simply studying other cultures to boost peer support. Making adjustments to our behavior, communication style, and strategies for intervention to better suit our peers' needs and preferences is another way we may use this insight in our peer support work. Working with your peers, identifying approaches and solutions that are culturally relevant; respecting their personal space and boundaries; recognizing and appreciating their cultural assets; and using language, body language, and expressions suited to their culture are some ways to achieve this. Rather than aiming to become an expert in every culture, it is more necessary to admit our limitations and assumptions, be open to criticism, and adjust our voices and behavior accordingly. We reject preconceptions, presumptions, and judgments that could damage our relationship with our peers, cultural humility can help you develop mutual respect, trust, and understanding.

In Western nations, like those in North America and Europe, grieving is often viewed as a private and personal emotion. Individuals may be encouraged to talk openly about their emotions and, if required, seek professional help. Kübler-Ross's tiers of grieving; denial, anger, bargaining, despair, and acceptance are regularly mentioned in this context (Kübler-Ross, E. 1969).

Eastern societies, which include those in China or Japan, strongly value collectivism and the oneness of the family. Grieving may involve rituals and ceremonies that emphasize the kinship between ancestors and the circle of relative members. Maintaining family solidarity and honoring the deceased with memorial offerings or ancestor worship are common customs.

Indigenous cultures all around the world often have exclusive viewpoints on mourning and loss which are intricately entwined with cultural customs and religious beliefs. During the grieving process, rituals, ceremonies, and storytelling are important due to the fact they spotlight the connection between the dwelling, the lifeless, and the herbal global. There is a giant belief that ancestor spirits watch over and protect the living.

Examples of cultural views of peer assistance are cultural healing Practices, the one's peer help healing procedures include conventional recuperation tactics and rituals based totally on cultural viewpoints. For example, elders within the community must facilitate online rituals or recuperation circles with religious, cultural, and narrative components to assist members of the COVID-19-affected community in their efforts to get better, develop resilience, and locate choices. People can help each other, and share recollections, and artwork via annoying situations of cultural identification, discrimination, and acculturation through peer networks which may be founded on commonplace ethnic or non-secular histories. Muslim peer networks, for instance, can help folks who are suffering with their identification and faith or who are experiencing Islamophobia. Conventional Healing Circles: To promote resilience, restoration, and fashionable welfare, traditional healing circles draw at the teachings, customs, and practices of indigenous cultures. These circles normally include storytelling, drumming, rites, and a sense of connection to the earth and ancestors. Native American healing circles, for instance, may address ancient trauma and intergenerational healing of internal indigenous civilizations. Cultural arts like dance, track, visual arts, and storytelling are used by those communities as a method of expression, healing, and connection. Culturally primarily based arts-based sports foster resilience, nicely-being, and cultural identification, all contributing to an experience of network and belonging. These networks assist immigrants and refugees cope with acculturation-worrying situations, navigating immigration laws, and adapting to logo-new cultural surroundings. Peer help is available in various forms, which include language assistance, cultural orientation, emotional help, and practical help.

Cultural humility is a difficult concept to understand and put into practice. We may be put in difficult and novel situations, and we may make blunders or run into problems as a result. But instead of being failures, these difficulties and errors are chances for development. Embracing our limits, apologizing and making amends for any hurt caused, asking for help and direction from others, and being kind and understanding of both ourselves and our peers are some ways we might deal with them.

IMPACT OF PEER SUPPORT

Peer support is a basic but yet strong help and guidance for those going through any grief or trauma. The peer support could be given by anyone, it does not need to be healthcare professionals but the person's friend, family, or even someone who they do not know such as in online platforms.

Poremski, D., Kuek, et al (2022), conducted studies on the impact that their work has on the mental health of peer support experts. During their first year of employment, they spoke with ten peer support specialists in three interviews. A grounded theory approach was used to investigate how the individuals' health changed. The respondents' self-reported mental health did not change during the research. Nevertheless, the role helped the participants grow and gave them knowledge about their capabilities and circumstances. Even if they learned how to control their recuperation process without having to worry about relapsing, discussing their prior experiences could be challenging.

Higgins A, Hybholt L, Meuser OA, et al. (2022) conducted a study on Peer-Led Assistance for Suicide Loss Victims. The results showed that Peer support, empathy, and shared understanding all had a favorable effect on participants' levels of stigma, loneliness, and self-blame. In addition, they reported improvements in their sense of unity, hope, and self-worth as a result of helping others. The participants reported having improved coping strategies, problem-solving skills, and the capacity to grieve and change. The peer group gave members a way to normalize the loss within the framework of the mourning process, as well as to better understand their own and other people's experiences and memorialize the deceased—a vital stage in the grief process.

Peer Support provides opportunities for people to engage with others who share their identity, interests, or experiences, peer support helps people form social bonds. Fostering positive peer relationships can enhance people's overall well-being by reducing feelings of loneliness and isolation. Pfeiffer PN and Heisler M conducted a study in 2011 to ascertain the efficacy of peer support therapy for depression. A total of 869 participants participated in seven RCTs that contrasted peer assistance with standard treatment for depression. Peer support interventions worked better than usual therapy at reducing symptoms of depression. In seven RCTs with 301 participants in total, peer support and group cognitive behavioral treatment (CBT)

Role of Peer Support on Grief and Trauma Counseling During Pandemic

were compared. According to the evidence that is currently available, peer support initiatives help reduce symptoms of depression. (Pfeiffer PN and Heisler M, 2011)

PEER SUPPORT AND THE COVID-9 PANDEMIC

Numerous pandemic-associated elements contributed to the collective sorrow and grief experienced by way of those who lost cherished ones. An extensive variety of humans suffered the devastating loss of friends, circle of relatives, or coworkers due to COVID-19-associated ailments. Grieving has ended up extra severe and difficult due to the sudden nature of these deaths as well as restrictions on rituals and gatherings for burial services. Complicated Grief reactions can also be made worse using the occasions surrounding the COVID-19 fatalities, as well as by the lack of ability to say good-bye, the shortage of closure, and the confined entry to cherished ones while in the hospital.(Gesi C, Carmassi C, et al, 2020). Denial, fury, guilt, and choice are examples of continual and intense mourning signs that can have an unfavorable impact on someone's ability to revel in the ordinary and function properly. Hospitalized COVID-19 sufferers who have experienced trauma, first responders inside the clinical field, and others who have personally experienced the results of the pandemic can also showcase symptoms of their trauma, which include anxiety, hypervigilance, and intrusive thoughts. Exposure to doubtlessly deadly occasions, excessive pressure, or witnessing a top-notch deal of ache and loss can all bring about trauma (Treatment, C. F. S. A., 2014) Physical distance regulations, lockdowns, and quarantines are sometimes of the way social exclusion and loneliness have gotten worse, anxious trauma and the associated signs and symptoms. Feelings of loneliness and loss may be exacerbated by dropping in relationships, residing ways far away from cherished ones, and having fewer opportunities to shape exceptional connections. In addition to the standard assets of a guide, such as buddies, family, and networks, continuous help structures may emerge as unavailable or disrupted because of pandemic-associated challenges and fears. Addressing trauma and loss at the same time is probably challenging due to the fact there is not as an awful lot of social assistance available. It can also make them feel more impartial and enjoy existence more. Due to the pandemic's continuing individuality, there have been multiple cumulative losses, inclusive of a loss of employment, social relationships, and economic safety. The worries of trauma and loss will also be exacerbated through the ongoing uncertainty around the scope and consequences of the sickness. This ambiguity has the power to exacerbate anxiety, pessimism, and existential struggle.

Wallis E. Adams, E. Sally Rogers (n.d) did a study on the impact of the pandemic on peer support specialists. The findings from the study are that a significant number of peer support experts (57.1%) stated that more people have sought help since the pandemic's beginning. According to the responders, the individuals they support have had significantly more challenges since the pandemic. Increased isolation (91.5%), mental health symptoms (86.4%), drug use issues (67%), food shortages (63.5%), unstable housing (60.1%), the possibility of losing one's work (59.4%), and interpersonal/family violence (38.3%) are some of these challenges. It can help you feel better to talk to someone who is going through a similar circumstance and know that you are not alone in experiencing this, which is why peer support is so important while seeking grief and trauma counseling. Peers with similar backgrounds can provide a depth of empathy that may be difficult for others to match. As they have experienced similar things, they might be able to relate to the feelings, ideas, and difficulties that emerge. People who are grieving or getting over a terrible experience could think their emotions are odd or excessive. By assuring the person that these feelings are normal and essential to the healing process, peers can validate these feelings. Grief and tragedy both have a highly isolating effect. People may feel less alone and more a part of a community when they are aware that others have gone through and conquered struggles that are comparable to their own. Peers can offer helpful methods and strategies that have assisted them in overcoming trauma or loss. These can include techniques for managing intense emotions, stress-reduction plans, or self-care routines. Being surrounded by strong individuals who have endured hardship or loss can be an extremely effective source of resilience. It could give them hope and encourage them to think that they can succeed too. In peer support groups, people can open up about their feelings and thoughts without fear of rejection or criticism.

Peer support group participants might have a range of backgrounds, experiences, and cultures. This diversity can offer a range of perspectives and coping mechanisms, which can be helpful when choosing what will be most effective for each individual. People may feel more empowered to take an important part in the recovery process when they engage with peers. Their sense of control and influence over how they handle their pain or loss has grown. Robinson & Pond's (2019) study looked into whether bereaved people might gain from bereavement online peer support groups. A detailed review of both qualitative and quantitative literature was carried out. According to the qualitative survey, grieving users surely value the positive results that online peer support has shown. Being a member of an understanding community of individuals who have gone through similar losses to oneself, getting emotional support, sharing knowledge, restoring one's sense of self, and realizing how melancholy grows with time.

Suresh, Alam, & Karkossa, (2021) stated that the epidemic of the coronavirus (COVID-19) has had a significant impact on the general mental health of society. The frequency of anxiety, depression, and other mental health indicators has increased due to policies like forced lockdowns and physical segregation, even though these

Role of Peer Support on Grief and Trauma Counseling During Pandemic

indicators are generally declining. Peer support is the term for the social and emotional help that peers give to one another. It is a useful, yet neglected, mental health tool that can support you during these trying times. This study evaluated peer-reviewed literature released between October 2019 and March 2021 in an attempt to provide an overview of the pandemic's effects on mental health in society. It also offered advice on how peer assistance can help fulfill these needs. The epidemic has made mental health conditions worse in every nation. Peer support has been demonstrated to have generally positive effects on the mental health of a broad range of users and can be provided in several conveniently accessible methods. Peer support proved to be beneficial to improving mental health in general during the COVID-19 epidemic and could prove to be a successful strategy if similar situations occur in the future.

COVID-19 had a significant negative effect on people's mental health, especially during the isolation phase. Online peer support became useful since those who were alone needed someone to talk to. You will require help because it is very difficult to handle trauma and loss on your own. Talking to someone is a must for processing the trauma and loss because not doing so could cause a decline in one's mental health.

Peer support before COVID-19 existed was majorly in offline mode. It is not that there was no online peer support but it is that many were not aware of it. The importance of peer support is also now slowly being understood by everyone, not many understand the change and impact peer support can have on someone going through something and needs help and support. Many stereotypes are there that peer support is nothing but just talking to someone about what you are going through, yes that is one aspect of it but in peer support not only should one person just talk about what they are going through but also the other person should be actively listening and making sure that they give the feeling of understanding and that you are there for the person. Peer support before the pandemic often convened in physical spaces, such as community centers, hospitals, or houses of worship. These face-to-face interactions improved participants' trust and sense of community. Several peer support programs were led or moderated by competent individuals and arranged by predetermined protocols or models. These classes often included sharing sessions, group discussions, educational presentations, and skill-building exercises. Peer support groups were typically established locally to provide individuals with the opportunity to engage with others within their community. This targeted approach aided in fostering a sense of unity and inclusion among participants. The opportunity to receive emotional support and understanding from others who have experienced similar situations was one of the key benefits of peer support. Sentiments of shame and loneliness were lessened because of this validation.

After the pandemic, many peer support organizations moved to online forums, social media groups, and video conferencing because of rules that prohibited in-person gatherings. This modification upheld social distance rules while enabling ongoing assistance and interaction. For those who were previously unable to attend in-person meetings because of barriers like schedule conflicts, transportation issues, or mobility disabilities, virtual peer support initiatives are now more accessible. The internet format also attracted individuals from around the globe. Participants in virtual peer support were able to attend with more convenience and flexibility by doing so from the comfort of their homes. Participating in peer support activities is made easier for people with hectic schedules or caregiving duties because of this flexibility. Although virtual platforms expanded the reach of peer support, they also introduced challenges such as inadequate internet access, barriers to computer literacy, and concerns over privacy and security. Organizations had to deal with these problems to ensure equitable participation and access. A few peer support groups have experimented with novel methods of distribution, such as virtual reality environments, smartphone apps, and text-based aid services. These developments increased involvement and created new avenues for support and communication. Virtual peer support, which is increasingly integrated with traditional healthcare and mental health services, is being used by healthcare professionals to send patients to online support groups as part of treatment plans. This integration provided all-encompassing support for people's well-being and assisted in filling in gaps in care.

ONLINE AND OFFLINE PEER SUPPORT

Peer support used to be done offline in face-to-face groups, as opposed to the steadily increasing number of online groups on the Internet. Research demonstrates that peer support groups—both online and offline—have different advantages and disadvantages. Peer support groups, both online and offline, complement one another, according to Strand et al. (2020), and service consumers primarily view the combination of both as advantageous. The last ten years have seen an exponential increase in research and development on social media and online technology for health. One source of information on illnesses and how to treat them has been the internet. They link customers to physical resources where they can receive care. Researchers list several general benefits of online platforms, such as their ability to transcend time and space, represent user-driven environments, and allow for anonymity, in addition to benefits tailored specifically to the needs of individuals with serious mental illness, such as their ability to manage emotions and interpersonal skills that may otherwise be too much for them to handle in face-to-face interactions. When it comes to impromptu in-person meetings, online users have more control over the degree of involvement and interaction they choose to have with other users. Peer interactions on the internet can typically be beneficial, but it is also possible to come across online communities that encourage or enable self-harm and other

Role of Peer Support on Grief and Trauma Counseling During Pandemic

harmful or unhealthy behaviors. Online peer networks provide varied patient groups with a voice and a platform for self-expression, thereby challenging prevalent societal stigma and discrimination.

Concerns over poor mental health have grown as a result of the outbreak. Lockdowns and isolation have caused a significant portion of the population to undergo lockdowns and similar tactics implemented in numerous nations during the COVID-19 elevated levels of stress, anxiety, and despair, according to a recent survey (Suresh et al., 2021). The length of the quarantine, fear of getting the virus, impatience, boredom, lack of resources, and incomplete information are a few factors that may contribute to these unpleasant emotional states. People are staying inside, where they are unable to access conventional mental health care, as a result of lockdowns and social isolation. Peer support is an effective but often underutilized mental health tool that can be used to enhance mental health in situations such as these.

Peer support can enhance people's feelings of self-worth, social skills, optimism, and compassionate engagement. It is a safe, effective, and potentially transforming practice. This is demonstrated by the fact that peer support has been more widely available globally in the last few decades. Peer support's adaptability is one of its advantages. Peer support can be offered via a variety of channels and in a range of contexts. The feasibility of creating an online peer support group and its impact on well-being measurements were examined in the study by Drysdale et al. (2021). It was discovered that the post-test well-being scores of the online and in-person peer support groups were significantly higher than those of the control group and pre-test.

The viability of online peer help was confirmed by both quantitative results and qualitative accounts. Results after the condition demonstrated that, in terms of enhancing well-being, online and in-person peer support are equally helpful. The American Psychological Association in 2021 discussed the benefits of CHATogether, a freshly created online culturally-based support program. Researchers at Yale have published a new study that finds that this program functioned as a successful peer support model both during and after the COVID-19 outbreak. The CHATogether groups are made up of people who have similar experiences and challenges, and they support one another emotionally. People with comparable experiences and difficulties make up the CHATogether groups, and they assist one another emotionally.

It encouraged participants to employ constructive and creative activities as a means of coping with COVID-19 through social media outreach. Every week, the group convenes virtually, starting with individual check-ins. Next, in groups, participants role-play family conflict scenarios and discuss topics that have been brought to light by the COVID-19 pandemic, including the challenges Asian Americans face in navigating cross-cultural relationships, the academic demands of homeschooling, Black Lives Matter, and LGBTQ conflicts within Asian families. To resolve their internal problems and regain a sense of agency, members write skits based on their personal experiences (n.a., 2021).

Online peer assistance provides a level of anonymity that may promote openness and dialogue. Participation is possible without revealing one's identity, reducing stigma and fear related to judgment. There is a dearth of high-quality evidence about the efficacy or effectiveness of Internet support groups (ISGs) for depression, according to a systematic review conducted by Griffiths K. and colleagues on the topic of ISGs and depression (Banfield, Calear, Griffiths, 2009).

People with diverse experiences and backgrounds come together through online networks, which expands the pool of available help. This diversity fosters empathy, understanding, and the exchange of differing opinions. The research was conducted by Mo, P. K. H., and Coulson, N. S on exploring the communication of social support within virtual communities: A content analysis of messages posted to an online HIV/AIDS support group. The data indicated that emotional and informational support were the most often given forms of support in the messages, followed by esteem and network support. Practical aid was the least common form of assistance. The results suggest that this online support group is a popular forum for HIV/AIDS patients to offer social support to one another (Mo and Coulson, 2008). Online peer support ensures that people have constant access to support networks and can get help and encouragement outside of regular meeting times. With 24/7 access to online peer support networks, people can seek assistance whenever it's convenient for them. This flexibility ensures support when needed by accounting for varying schedules and time zones. Online peer assistance removes geographical barriers so that people can communicate with peers from anywhere. This accessibility could be quite useful for people who live far away or have mobility problems (Eysenbach, 2001).

Notably, there hasn't been enough focus on the impact that isolation and social distancing measures, such as lockdowns, have on people's mental health. While it is not a psychiatric or professional service, peer support can generally help enhance mental health. Despite lockdowns and quarantines, peer support is one resource that the community can readily offer to one another during the pandemic through freely accessible online channels.

INCLUSIVITY AND ACCESSIBILITY OF PEER SUPPORT GROUPS

Although peer support groups are accessible online and offline on all platforms, finding an offline group during the pandemic proved to be challenging. They had to endure suffering as a result of losing so many of their loved ones to the pandemic. Talking to family members or those who have gone through similar experiences

Role of Peer Support on Grief and Trauma Counseling During Pandemic

could offer them emotional support and a listening ear during their grief process. Online peer support from professionals is also available. One option is to receive counseling by video or over the phone. These choices allow clients to access services they might not have otherwise been able to due to time limits or location. According to the American Psychological Association, there are situations in which tele-mental health can be a suitable replacement for in-person care. When a client cannot meet in person or when the travel time and distance are crucial, peer assistance can be obtained through phone conversations or videos. The ability to choose from any type of peer support, from anywhere in the world, based on the level of support that best suits them is one positive aspect of this strategy.

In the same way that individuals can attend in-person groups, people can access online support groups. You can communicate with folks locally or worldwide because it's the internet. In group therapy, it might be useful. Being among others who are going through similar experiences to you makes you feel better. This could teach them that everyone experiences loss differently and reassure them that they are not grieving alone. Instead of getting one-on-one peer assistance, this type of platform is meant for people who would prefer to interact with other people going through a similar scenario. You feel more at peace when you realize that you are not the only one going through this. You would believe that you could help one another through difficult times and learn to cope with loss from one another.

RIGHT PLATFORM AND SAFE ENVIRONMENT

It's important to choose the right online peer support platform; make sure it's a reliable website and that it's being used for the intended purpose. You will be discussing and giving your account of what transpired, so it's critical to make sure that confidentiality is upheld and isn't recorded or utilized as content. It is crucial to make sure the counselor conducting the grief counseling session is a real one and not someone pretending to be one to receive payment, as only licensed counselors are allowed to offer counseling.

Peer support communities must be successful for users to feel safe and accepted, which is why trust is so important (Dellarocas, 2003). People in the community are more likely to trust a platform that has done its research and prioritizes user safety and privacy. People must be trusted for them to be open and truthful about their hardships and experiences. Creating an open online community and expressing oneself openly are advised. Peer interactions are necessary to allow ideas, advice, and help to freely flow. A secure and supportive environment is beneficial to users' mental and emotional well-being. When people feel comfortable and engage in techniques, the appropriate platforms are necessary to stop cyberbullying and harassment. When

253

urged, they are more likely to talk about their problems and ask for help. Rules, and moderation This ensures that the community will consistently be positive and productive. The whole experience for users is improved by a platform that is simple to use, offers pertinent functionality, and is straightforward to navigate. This may encourage more community members to engage and participate. An accessible platform encourages diversity by taking into account the varied requirements and backgrounds of its users.

A wider range of people are encouraged to participate as a result of this inclusiveness, strengthening the support system. An inclusive platform fosters diversity by taking into account the varied requirements and backgrounds of its users. Everyone can participate in a community where there is a platform accessible to persons with varying abilities. Examples of accessibility features include text-to-speech capabilities and many language selections. The community's operations are greatly influenced by the features, guidelines, and policies of the platform. Positive relationships are rewarded and negative behavior is penalized on a well-managed network. Selecting the appropriate platform sets the foundations for ongoing growth. As the community grows, maintaining a safe and encouraging atmosphere is crucial to preserving the advantages of the peer support system.

DIRECTIONS FOR ORGANIZING PEER SUPPORT GROUPS

A few things need to be taken into account before we set up a peer support session. Firstly, a description of the type of online support group that is being planned. This will assist us in planning the benefits that each group member will get. To decide what topics are appropriate, it is vital to describe the support group. The second step is that it is very important to choose the right platform to conduct the peer group session. It is highly recommended that the sessions of peer support be conducted through platforms like Webex. Other web-based services like Facetime, WhatsApp, or YouTube might not provide enough privacy or technological security, therefore using them is not preferred.

Steps to develop a peer support group:

1. Description of the Group: Write a summary of the kind of online support group you intend to organize. You could begin by outlining the support group's goals and mission. Finding current local, regional, or national groups that may influence your group can be facilitated by research. Establishing your support group under the umbrella of a bigger group organization, for example, might provide resources and help in starting a new support group. Your group may get more credibility by joining up with a large, well-known organization because of the

Role of Peer Support on Grief and Trauma Counseling During Pandemic

name recognition that this brings. It may also make it simpler for those in need of your support group services to find you (Hampton. C, n.d).

2. Timings of the group: Support groups can be long-running or restricted for certain periods. Since the medium of the sessions will be online, the support group can go on for longer periods when compared to an offline support group. Crises like divorce or grief are best suited for a short-term framework (one to two months). For chronic conditions like chronic illness, long-term support groups are appropriate (Hampton, C., n.d).

3. Nature of the group: Open support groups welcome new members at any time during the group's existence. This may also mean that family members, friends, and other acquaintances are invited to become members of the group. Closed groups can only be joined under certain circumstances (e.g., groups only for women) or for certain durations (e.g., the first three weeks). If you intend to work on a very specific issue and you would like the group to go through the process at the same time, you might want to consider creating a closed group. All support group styles, however, benefit greatly from open groups. You might want to think about forming a closed group if you intend to work on a particularly specific topic and want the group to go through the process at the same time. Open groups, however, work well for the majority of support group types. Pre-determining the nature of the support group helps to incorporate safety measures since the meetings happen online. Open groups pose more threat to confidentiality when it comes to online support group meetings, hence the organizer should be aware of the people who join and leave the group. The nature of the group will enable better goal-setting and communication within the group. Aim to keep a small number of people in each group. No more than ten or twelve people should make up a group. If the group membership is significantly larger, you may want to consider bringing in a co-facilitator. Group norms and individual expectations must be outlined in every support group. Ensuring that everyone in the group comprehends and abides by them is the facilitator's duty. (Hampton, C., n.d)

4. Time and Place: It is very important to choose the right platform to conduct the peer group session. It is highly recommended that the sessions of peer support be conducted through platforms like Webex. Other web-based services like Facetime, WhatsApp, or YouTube might not provide enough privacy or technological security, therefore using them is not preferred. Provide people with the choice of connecting via audio or video as part of confidentiality. Remind the people who are participating in the session to log in anonymously unless they choose for their names to appear (World Bank Group and IMF Staff, 2020).

5. Select a group leader or facilitator: Selecting the ideal leader for your support group is crucial. The facilitator or group leader initiates and ends the meetings, establishes the atmosphere for the conversation, teaches participants how to assist and listen to one another, and handles any issues that may arise. The talk should flow naturally in terms of conversation. Some strategies to accomplish this include asking members to participate and respond to one another, encouraging peers to listen to and support one another, and being aware of and prepared to provide resources and guidance when questions occur beyond the parameters of the support group. From time to time, group members may assume leadership roles or express their concerns in a way that is disruptive to the group dynamic. Facilitators need to handle disruptive behavior to maintain the smooth operation of the support group. Group facilitators may initially want to focus on the repair as a whole instead of just one participant. Referring to the group's pre-established guidelines can be helpful. If a participant in the group continues to behave disruptively, the facilitator may need to address the issue directly with them. The facilitator should have the ideal qualities like a flexible schedule, lots of energy, ability and support, and a desire to do the job (World Bank Group and IMF Staff, 2020).

6. Promote the support group: Promoting your online support is as crucial as conducting it. The promotion need not always be online, offline methods can also be beneficial to promote your support group. Make connections with local professionals and organizations. Distribute letters and, if available, fliers or pamphlets to the offices of neighborhood groups that deal with the issue your group is concerned about. Make sure the community information and referral hotlines in your city or county have information about your support group. Find out which organizations or agencies put out community or social service directories, and ask to have your group listed in the upcoming edition. If you provide the local press with information about your support group, they may be interested in writing stories about it, which will create interest. Share as much information as you can about your group with its members, and encourage them to notify others. Encourage participants to spread the word about the support group to others as soon as meetings begin. (Hampton, C., n.d)

CASES AND TESTIMONIALS ILLUSTRATING POSITIVE IMPACT

Peer support models and their application in different health systems have received a lot of attention and support in the last few years. Peer support approaches aim to leverage the power of peers and build upon it. According to Lloyd Evans and colleagues, peer-provided interventions had a marginally beneficial impact on

Role of Peer Support on Grief and Trauma Counseling During Pandemic

self-reported hope and recovery (White et al., 2020). Heisler (2006) talked about several case studies that demonstrated the beneficial effects of peer support groups. He discussed the importance that peer support models play in assisting individuals in managing their mental health about chronic illness.

Patients with diabetes who are at high risk could schedule group appointments at the Cleveland Veterans Affairs Medical Center. Members of the diabetes-specific group can help one another with common management challenges and exchange related knowledge. A clinical pharmacist, an internist, a nurse practitioner, and a health psychologist make up the medical team. Participants obtain information about the group from the clinic's medical director and primary care physician. The center tries to have the same group of patients and facilitators in each session to promote unity and interpersonal bonds.

60-75 percent of the patients usually attend any one conference. About 80% of patients whom a clerk calls before the meeting shows up. Group members develop short-term action plans and personal self-management goals for the behavioral goals with the assistance of the health psychologist in front of other patients. Each patient and a doctor or other health care provider have a brief one-on-one discussion about their goals before recording them in the chart. Before a patient leaves for their home, they are given a written action plan that includes specific, short-term behavioral approaches to help them reach their goals. The patients and group members discuss the objectives and lab values. If required, a staff member will change a patient's medication during a one-on-one consultation.

Project Dulce has improved participants' clinical outcomes. Project Dulce developed and assessed a culturally appropriate approach to improve diabetes treatment and results for neglected racial and ethnic groups. Referrals to the program come directly from primary care physicians and the county's low-income medical assistance program. The program combines peer-led self-management instruction with nurse case management. The results of one examination revealed significant improvements in triglycerides, total cholesterol, LDL cholesterol, diastolic blood pressure, and A1c within the group. A1c, total cholesterol, LDL cholesterol, and triglycerides were all considerably lower in the Project Dulce group after a year of treatment than in the control group. A1c checks twice a year, lipid panels, urine microalbumin-to-creatinine ratios, foot exams, and monofilament exams were all performed following the American Diabetes Association's (ADA) guidelines to the letter (Heisler, 2006).

The Significant Effect of Peer Support Groups on Mental Health and Overall Wellness

Richard J, Rebinsky R, Suresh R, et al (2022) conducted a Scoping review to evaluate the effects of peer support on the mental health of young adults. Peer support is positively correlated with improved mental health, which includes reduced anxiety, hopelessness, and loneliness as well as elevated happiness, self-esteem, and effective coping. Members of racial or sexual minorities, young people without children, and college students all appear to be impacted by this effect. Individual and group peer support appears to enhance mental health and confer advantages on those providing it. Compared to traditional mental health therapies, peer support appears to be a more practical and approachable means of enhancing the mental health of young adults. Future research projects should investigate the value of educating peer supporters as well as the various effects of peer support depending on how it is provided.

Peer support groups helped to provide support and assistance when mental health resources were not easily accessible and there was low satisfaction with the available resources. Concerning health and well-being, peer support has been recognized for more than 50 years as an effective alternate technique for professional intervention. According to Topping (2022), peer support programs are built on informal and naturalistic peer assistance to maximize the impact and equalize access to opportunities. Peer support sessions have been reported to show an increase in rehabilitation and lower rates of hospitalization. Discussions and conversations among individuals in peer support groups have reduced depression and suicidal thoughts, according to data examined by Topping (2022), participant satisfaction with therapy was higher and so were the abstinence rates among those who engaged in peer support groups and other treatment programs. Not only did the participants show a significant reduction in alcohol and drug use, but most of the organizers or mentors also maintained abstinence. The findings extend the benefits of peer support groups from those who receive them to those who offer them (Tracy and Wallace, 2016). Peer support groups have also been connected to lower infection rates in research on HIV risk behaviors among IUDs. One of the key things that support peer support programs positively mediated the relationship between distributive risk factors and interventions (Tracy and Wallace, 2016).

Group members are provided a platform where they can share coping mechanisms and methods that have helped them. Learning from those who have faced similar challenges may result in getting useful advice and accurate remarks. Peer support groups play a crucial role in reducing the stigma associated with mental health issues. Engaging in these open discussion forums fosters mutual understanding and reduces barriers among community members. Peer support groups offer a safe place where individuals can freely express themselves without fear of being judged. In this environment, group members are more inclined to trust one another and communicate openly. Peer support groups offer a unique and helpful form of assistance that improves other mental health treatments. Through the development of a sense of community, understanding, and mutual support, it improves the overall well-being of individuals overcoming various life challenges.

CONCLUSION

Peer support groups are essential in helping people facing difficulties feel like they belong and are understood. By creating a shared experience, they help people feel less alone and stigmatized. These frequently inexpensive clubs give their members a forum to empower themselves by working together to solve challenges. Unlike in professional partnerships, the group's special emotional bond, which is a result of their shared tragedy, offers a different kind of support. Members provide motivating role models by exchanging knowledge, advancements, and words of support. The fact that support groups provide a safe environment free from the perceived power dynamics of professional settings and allow people to talk about very personal matters is significant since it eventually lowers anxiety, boosts self-esteem, and improves general well-being.

DISCUSSION QUESTIONS

1. How can peer support groups be customized to address the various needs of the various COVID-19-affected communities, taking socioeconomic and cultural aspects into account?
2. For people coping with COVID-19-related grief and trauma, how might peer support supplement professional mental health services?
3. What are the main components of peer support that enable it to effectively manage grief and trauma in the context of the COVID-19 pandemic?
4. What effects have the move to online platforms had on the quality and availability of peer support for people going through grief and trauma during the pandemic?
5. In contrast to pre-pandemic eras, how has the COVID-19 pandemic affected grieving and trauma experiences differently?

Role of Peer Support on Grief and Trauma Counseling During Pandemic

REFERENCES

Ames, H. (2020, October 22). What to know about online grief counseling. *Media News Todaay.*

Arora, S., & Bhatia, S. (2023). Addressing grief and bereavement in the COVID-19 pandemic. *Illness, Crises, and Loss.* 10.1177/10541373221145536

Cavicchioli, M., Ferrucci, R., Guidetti, M., Canevini, M. P., Pravettoni, G., & Galli, F. (2021). *What will be the impact of the COVID-19 quarantine on psychological distress? Considerations based on a systematic review of pandemicadva outbreaks.*

Corrigan, P. W. (2016, April). Can peer support be effective online? *Epidemiology and Psychiatric Sciences,* 25(2), 127–128. 10.1017/S2045796015001079 26740342

Dellarocas, C. (2003). The digitization of word of mouth: Promise and challenges of online feedback mechanisms. *Management Science,* 49(10), 1407–1424. 10.1287/mnsc.49.10.1407.17308

Drysdale, M. T. B., McBeath, M. L., & Callaghan, S. A. (2021, October 11). The feasibility and impact of online peer support on the well-being of Higher Education Students. *The Journal of Mental Health Training, Education and Practice.*

Eysenbach, G. (2001). What is e-health? *Journal of Medical Internet Research,* 3(2), e20. 10.2196/jmir.3.2.e20 11720962

Gesi, C., Carmassi, C., Cerveri, G., Carpita, B., Cremone, I. M., & Dell'Osso, L. (2020, May 26). Complicated Grief: What to Expect After the Coronavirus Pandemic. *Frontiers in Psychiatry,* 11, 489. 10.3389/fpsyt.2020.00489 32574243

Griffiths, K. M., Calear, A. L., & Banfield, M. (2009). Systematic Review on Internet Support Groups (ISGs) and Depression (1): Do ISGs reduce depressive symptoms? *Journal of Medical Internet Research,* 11(3), e40. 10.2196/jmir.127019793719

Hampton, C. (n.d.). *Creating and facilitating peer support groups.* COMMUNI-TYTOOLBOX.

Heisler, M. (2006, December). *Building Peer Support Programs to Manage Chronic Disease: Seven Models for Success.* ResearchGate.

Hickney, W. (2022, November 3). *The Early Peer Support Movement - Colorado Mental Wellness Network.* Colorado Mental Wellness Network.

Higgins, A., Hybholt, L., Meuser, O. A., Eustace Cook, J., Downes, C., & Morrissey, J. (2022, March 15). Scoping Review of Peer-Led Support for People Bereaved by Suicide. *International Journal of Environmental Research and Public Health*, 19(6), 3485. 10.3390/ijerph1906348535329171

Jordan, M., & Hackett, J. T. (2019). NAADAC.

Leonard, J. (2020). What is trauma? What to know. n.a. (2021, May 3). Culturally based online peer support group brought mental health benefits during COVID-19. Medical Xpress - medical research advances and health news. n.a. (2022, February 18). Peer support. Mental Health Foundation. n.a. (2023, November 7). How can you learn about different cultures to improve your peer support? How to Learn About Different Cultures for Peer Support. n.a, (2022, November 18). The 3 different types of trauma | All Points North. All Points North.

Mo, P. K. H., & Coulson, N. (2008). Exploring the Communication of Social Support within Virtual Communities: A Content Analysis of Messages Posted to an Online HIV/AIDS Support Group. *Cyberpsychology & Behavior*, 11(3), 371–374. 10.1089/cpb.2007.011818537512

Naslund, J. A., Aschbrenner, K. A., Marsch, L. A., & Bartels, S. J. (2016, January 8). The Future of Mental Health Care. *Peer-to-peer support and social media: Epidemiology and Psychiatric Sciences*. Cambridge Core.

Pfeiffer, P. N., Heisler, M., Piette, J. D., Rogers, M. A., & Valenstein, M. (2011). Efficacy of peer support interventions for depression: A meta-analysis. *General Hospital Psychiatry*, 33(1), 29–36. 10.1016/j.genhosppsych.2010.10.00221353125

Poremski, D., Kuek, J. H. L., Yuan, Q., Li, Z., Yow, K. L., Eu, P. W., & Chua, H. C. (2022). The impact of peer support work on the mental health of peer support specialists. *International Journal of Mental Health Systems*, 16(1), 51. 10.1186/s13033-022-00561-836258206

Richard, J., Rebinsky, R., Suresh, R., Kubic, S., Carter, A., Cunningham, J. E. A., Ker, A., Williams, K., & Sorin, M. (2022, August 4). Scoping review to evaluate the effects of peer support on the mental health of young adults. *BMJ Open*, 12(8), e061336. 10.1136/bmjopen-2022-06133635926986

Robinson, C., & Pond, D. R. (2019, June 24). *Do online support groups for grief benefit the bereaved? systematic review of the quantitative and qualitative literature.* ScienceDirect.

Sartore, G. M., Pourliakas, A., & Lagioia, V. (2021, December). Peer support interventions for parents and carers of children with complex needs. *Cochrane Database of Systematic Reviews*.34923624

Shalaby, R. A. H., & Agyapong, V. I. O. (2020, June 9). Peer support in Mental Health: Literature Review. *JMIR Mental Health*, 7(6), e15572. 10.2196/1557232357127

Smith, W., PhD. (2023, October 2). *The Psychology of Grief: The 4 stages explained*. PositivePsychology.com.

Strand, M., Eng, L. S., & Gammon, D. (2020, May 29). *Combining online and offline peer support groups in community mental health care settings: a qualitative study of service users' experiences*. ResearchGate.

Suresh, R., Alam, A., & Karkossa, Z. (2021). Using peer support to Strengthen Mental Health During the COVID-19 Pandemic: A review. *Frontiers in Psychiatry*, 12, 12. 10.3389/fpsyt.2021.71418134322045

Tang, P. (n.d.). *A brief history of peer support: Origins: Peers for progress*. Peers For Progress A Brief History of Peer Support Origins Comments.

Topping, K. J. (2022, May 17). Peer education and peer counselling for Health and well-being: A review of Reviews. *International Journal of Environmental Research and Public Health*, 19(10), 6064. 10.3390/ijerph1910606435627601

Tracy, K., & Wallace, S. P. (2016, September 29). Benefits of peer support groups in the treatment of addiction. *Substance Abuse and Rehabilitation*, 7, 143–154. 10.2147/SAR.S8153527729825

Treatment, C. F. S. A. (2014). *Understanding the impact of trauma*. Trauma-Informed Care in Behavioral Health Services - NCBI Bookshelf.

Tyrrell, P., Harberger, S., Schoo, C., & Siddiqui, W. (2023, February 26). *Kubler-Ross Stages of Dying and Subsequent Models of Grief*. StatPearls - NCBI Bookshelf.

Wallace C. L., Wladkowski S. P., Gibson A., White P. (2020). Grief during the COVID-19 pandemic: Considerations for palliative care providers. Journal of Pain and Symptom Management. Wallis E. Adams, E. Sally Rogers,(n.d). THE IMPACT OF COVID-19 ON PEER SUPPORT SPECIALISTS: Findings from a National Survey. Center for Psychiatric Rehabilitation Boston University, Boston, MA Watson, E., & Meddings, S. (2019). *Peer support in Mental Health*. Google Books.

White, S., Foster, R., Marks, J., Morshead, R., Goldsmith, L., Barlow, S., Sin, J., & Gillard, S. (2020, November 11). *The effectiveness of one-to-one peer support in Mental Health Services: A systematic review and meta-analysis*. BioMed Central.

World Bank Group. (2020). *IMF Staff*. Peer Support Group Facilitator Guide. Public Documents.

Zheng, K., Spence, D. R., & Cusick, J. (2022, June 1). Honouring other cultures in peer work. Postsecondary Peer Support Training Curriculum.

Zisook, S., & Shear, K. (2009, June). Grief and bereavement: What psychiatrists need to know. *World Psychiatry; Official Journal of the World Psychiatric Association (WPA)*, 8(2), 67–74. 10.1002/j.2051-5545.2009.tb00217.x19516922

ADDITIONAL READING

Coping with Grief and Trauma During the Pandemic. (n.d.). *Anxiety and Depression Association of America*. ADAA.

Davidson, L., Chinman, M., Kloos, B., Weingarten, R., Stayner, D., & Tebes, J. K. (1999). Peer Support Among Individuals with Severe Mental Illness: A Review of the Evidence. *Clinical Psychology : a Publication of the Division of Clinical Psychology of the American Psychological Association*, 6(2), 165–187. 10.1093/clipsy.6.2.165

Henze, K. & Sweeny, P. (n.d.). *Part II of Peer Support Group Facilitation Skills: Dealing with Challenges in Groups*.

Jacobs, M., & Goodman, G. (1989). Psychology and self-help groups: Predictions on a partnership. *The American Psychologist*, 44(3), 536–545. 10.1037/0003-066 X.44.3.5362930056

Lloyd-Evans, B., Mayo-Wilson, E., Harrison, B., Istead, H., Brown, E., Pilling, S., Johnson, S., & Kendall, T. (2014). A systematic review and meta-analysis of randomised controlled trials of peer support for people with severe mental illness. *BMC Psychiatry*, 14(1), 39. 10.1186/1471-244X-14-3924528545

Paine, A., Suarez-Balcazar, Y., Fawcett, S., Jameson, L., & Embree, M. (1990). *Self-help leader's handbook: Leading effective meetings*. Research and Training Center on Independent Living.

Repper, J., & Carter, T. (2011). A review of the literature on peer support in mental health services. *Journal of Mental Health (Abingdon, England)*, 20(4), 392–411. 10.3109/09638237.2011.58394721770786

Stratford, A. C., Halpin, M., Phillips, K., Skerritt, F., Beales, A., Cheng, V., Hammond, M., O'Hagan, M., Loreto, C., Tiengtom, K., Kobe, B., Harrington, S., Fisher, D., & Davidson, L. (2019). The growth of peer support: An international charter. *Journal of Mental Health (Abingdon, England)*, 28(6), 627–632. 10.1080/096382 37.2017.134059328682640

Suresh R, Alam A, Karkossa Z. (2021). Using Peer Support to Strengthen Mental Health During the COVID-19 Pandemic: A Review. Front Psychiatry.

KEY TERMS AND DEFINITIONS

Bereavement: a period of mourning after a loss, especially after the death of a loved one

Bullying: the act of harassing, intimidating, or abusing others, especially habitually or from a perceived position of relative power

COVID-19 Pandemic: a potentially severe, primarily respiratory illness caused by a coronavirus and characterized by fever, coughing, and shortness of breath. In some people, the disease also damages major organs, such as the heart or kidneys

Cultural Humility: A personal lifelong commitment to self-evaluation and self-critique whereby the individual not only learns about another's culture, but one starts with an examination of her/his own beliefs and cultural identities.

Depression: a low mood or loss of pleasure or interest in activities for long periods

Empathy: the psychological identification with or vicarious experiencing of the emotions, thoughts, or attitudes of another

Grief: keen mental suffering or distress over affliction or loss; sharp sorrow; painful regret.

Mourning: the period or interval during which a person grieves or formally expresses grief, as by wearing black garments

Quarantine: a strict isolation imposed to prevent the spread of disease

Self Esteem: a realistic respect for or favorable impression of oneself; self-respect

Self-Efficacy: a strict isolation imposed to prevent the spread of disease

Trauma: when we experience very stressful, frightening, or distressing events that are difficult to cope with or out of our control.

Chapter 12
Self-Care Strategies for Grief Counselors and Caregivers

Ranjit Singha
https://orcid.org/0000-0002-3541-8752
Christ University, India

ABSTRACT

This chapter analyzes the significance of self-care within the bereavement counselling and caregiving fields, focusing on its capacity to avert burnout and sustain professional effectiveness. Alongside case studies demonstrating the successful application of self-care practices, this chapter examines techniques for efficient time management, establishing boundaries, and cultural sensitivity. Addressing practitioners' ethical obligations and emphasizing the need for continuous dedication to one's welfare are critical points of emphasis. Making self-care a priority cultivates resilience and enables professionals to deliver empathetic and enduring assistance to individuals requiring care.

INTRODUCTION

Within the volatile realm of bereavement counselling and caregiving, the importance of self-care becomes an essential cornerstone, promoting the development of resilience and maintaining the emotional strength of professionals (Moss et al., 2021). This chapter explores the critical significance of self-care for bereavement counsellors and caregivers, particularly emphasizing its profound influence on individual welfare and professional efficacy. It is impossible to overstate the crucial importance of self-care in the context of grief counselling and caregiving. As

DOI: 10.4018/979-8-3693-1375-6.ch012

Copyright © 2024, IGI Global. Copying or distributing in print or electronic forms without written permission of IGI Global is prohibited.

professionals navigate the depths of human suffering, they invariably encounter the raw intensity of the trauma and agony experienced by their clients. By observing the intricacies of grief, trauma, and loss, professionals internalize the psychological burden of the suffering of others, frequently at considerable personal expense.

Practitioners who fail to implement sufficient self-care protocols run the risk of experiencing the detrimental consequences of compassion fatigue, exhaustion, and vicarious trauma. A pervasive sense of emotional exhaustion, detachment, and inefficacy characterize burnout, eroding practitioners' motivation and engagement in their work. Prolonged exposure to the suffering of others induces compassion fatigue, characterized by a decline in empathy and compassion, ultimately culminating in emotional apathy and disconnection. Indirect exposure to traumatic events, known as vicarious trauma, can trigger symptoms akin to those experienced by trauma survivors (Forrest et al., 2020). These symptoms may consist of intrusive thoughts, nightmares, and hypervigilance. The consequences of unattended stress and emotional distress have a broader impact than just on the practitioners themselves; they permeate the therapeutic alliance and undermine the achievements of the clients. Burnout and compassion fatigue can compromise practitioners' capacity to provide empathetic and practical assistance, thereby deteriorating the standard of care and eroding the trust between the practitioner and the client. Practitioners who neglect their welfare risk reinforcing a recurring pattern of suffering in which their anguish intensifies the distress of those they attempt to assist (Mirutse et al., 2023).

In contrast, practitioners can strengthen their resilience and maintain their ability to offer empathetic assistance to needy individuals by making self-care an essential component of their professional conduct. Self-care comprises a wide range of activities, including social interaction, physical activity, mindfulness, and meditation, all of which contribute to the emotional, physical, and mental health of the individual engaging in the practice (Narasimhan et al., 2019). Practitioners develop the internal resources required to effectively navigate the intricacies of their roles with composure and proficiency by placing self-care as a top priority. Individuals acquire enhanced capabilities to establish and uphold healthy boundaries, advocate for their requirements, and seek assistance when required. By doing so, practitioners develop a therapeutic environment founded upon authenticity, empathy, and trust while demonstrating resilience and self-compassion for their clients (Jiang et al., 2021).

In the context of bereavement counselling and caregiving, the paramount significance of self-care resides in its ability to safeguard the humanity and integrity of professionals in the face of the inherent difficulties of their occupation. Practising self-compassion and healing entails upholding one's intrinsic value and dignity, as well as those one assists by prioritizing one's welfare (El-Osta et al., 2023). This statement underscores the intricate and diverse characteristics of these vocations, emphasizing the psychological strain and emotional obligations that are intrinsic

Self-Care Strategies for Grief Counselors and Caregivers

to assisting people through the complexities of grief and trauma. Acknowledging self-care as a fundamental aspect of successful practice, this chapter emphasizes promoting one's welfare to enable the most favourable results for clients (El-Osta et al., 2023). Addressing prevalent issues like compassion fatigue and burnout among bereavement counsellors and caregivers immediately is crucial. Extended periods spent in these occupations, entailing intense emotional encounters, have a detrimental impact on practitioners' mental, emotional, and physical health. Neglecting to confront exhaustion and compassion fatigue has far-reaching adverse effects that extend well beyond the individual practitioner. These effects compromise the quality of care and adversely affect client outcomes (Sweileh, 2020).

The COVID-19 pandemic has thrust self-care into the spotlight, emphasizing its critical role in maintaining physical, mental, and emotional well-being during times of uncertainty and stress. With the disruption of daily routines, heightened anxiety, and increased social isolation, individuals have turned to self-care practices as a means of coping and preserving their overall health. Burnout and compassion fatigue undermine the resilience and capacity of practitioners to assist those in need effectively. Emotional exhaustion, detachment, and diminished empathy hinder practitioners' capacity to engage authentically with their clients, compromising the therapeutic alliance and impeding the healing process. Furthermore, it is essential to note that exhaustion and compassion fatigue can affect the personal lives of practitioners, resulting in strained relationships, reduced job satisfaction, and an overall decline in quality of life (Silva et al., 2020). Implementing proactive measures immediately to mitigate the risks associated with compassion fatigue and exhaustion is paramount. Promoting a culture of self-care is crucial in bereavement counselling and caregiving to protect practitioners' mental and emotional well-being and enhance their ability to deliver empathetic and long-lasting assistance. Practitioners can improve the durability and resilience of their roles and reduce the adverse effects of stress and trauma by incorporating self-care into their daily routines (Mirutse et al., 2023).

Implementing practical strategies to foster a self-care culture may encompass routine self-evaluation to identify indications of compassion fatigue and exhaustion, setting limits on one's emotional involvement to prevent emotional overload, and, when necessary, seeking assistance from colleagues, superiors, or mental health practitioners. To further enhance emotional equilibrium and overall welfare, practitioners may also incorporate self-care practices into their daily schedules, including but not limited to mindfulness, meditation, physical activity, and relaxation methods (Haik et al., 2017). By placing self-care as a top priority, practitioners protect their mental and emotional well-being and improve their ability to offer empathetic and long-lasting assistance to individuals requiring support. By establishing a climate of self-care in bereavement counselling and caregiving, professionals demonstrate authenticity and resilience to their clients, promoting a setting conducive to recovery, development, and reciprocal assistance (Smith, 2017). This chapter aims to equip readers with practical resources and understandings to effectively manage the intricacies of their roles while maintaining resilience and effectiveness by conducting an in-depth analysis of self-care techniques specifically designed to address the unique difficulties bereavement counsellors and caregivers face.

UNDERSTANDING THE IMPACT OF GRIEF COUNSELING AND CAREGIVING

Upon further examination of the domains of grief counselling and caregiving, it becomes apparent that these vocations impose a significant psychological and emotional burden on their practitioners (Harrop et al., 2020). Participation in bereavement counselling and caregiving has a multitude of profound emotional and psychological consequences. Frequently, practitioners are confronted with the profound intensity of their clients' suffering as they navigate a labyrinth of grief, ire, and hopelessness. As individuals who bear witness to the profound depths of human suffering, bereavement counsellors and caregivers frequently experience a range of emotions, including helplessness, vicarious trauma, empathy, and compassion (Harrop et al., 2020). Furthermore, continuous exposure to profound emotional experiences may trigger a series of stressors and difficulties for individuals engaged in such practices. Grief counsellors and caregivers face various stressors that can negatively impact their health and professional effectiveness (Chen, 2019). Consistent client expectations for unwavering support and emotional exhaustion from prolonged exposure to others' suffering are among these stressors. Grief counsellors and caregivers frequently encounter the following obstacles: establishing and maintaining appropriate boundaries in therapeutic relationships, coping with the vicarious trauma that accompanies the suffering of others, and confronting the immense accountability that accompanies the provision of care and support during periods of profound vulnerability. Furthermore, professionals in the field of bereavement and trauma may encounter distinct obstacles due to the inherent unpredictability of these conditions; they must be flexible and resilient when confronted with unpredictability (Schachter & Holland, 2013). By recognizing and affirming the difficulties faced by professionals in the field, we can foster an environment that is resilient and supportive, enabling bereavement counsellors and caregivers to carry out their responsibilities with empathy, competence, and introspection.

Self-Care Strategies for Grief Counselors and Caregivers

SIGNS OF BURNOUT AND COMPASSION FATIGUE

In the rigorous domain of bereavement counselling and caregiving, professionals are susceptible to burnout and compassion fatigue, both of which have the potential to impair their overall welfare and professional effectiveness significantly. A pervasive feeling of emotional exhaustion, detachment, and ineffectiveness at work characterize burnout. Burnout can lead to depletion, disillusionment, and disillusionment among grief counsellors and caregivers, resulting in reduced motivation and engagement in their professional obligations. Additionally, individuals may manifest physical symptoms, including migraines, insomnia, and gastrointestinal problems, which highlights the comprehensive impact that burnout has on both the mind and body (Sweileh, 2020). Conversely, extended exposure to the distress of others leads to the development of compassion fatigue, characterized by a reduction in empathy and compassion. Individuals experiencing compassion fatigue may manifest symptoms such as emotional detachment, cynicism, and a reduced ability to empathize. Additional symptoms that may be observed include intrusive thoughts, nightmares, and an increased level of hypervigilance, which collectively demonstrate the psychological impact of vicarious trauma (Hui et al., 2023).

Self-awareness is crucial in protecting against the stealthy infiltration of compassion fatigue and exhaustion. By developing a heightened consciousness of their emotional and physical conditions, individuals can identify the indicators and manifestations of these phenomena, thereby equipping themselves to intervene proactively before their escalation. Furthermore, by cultivating self-awareness, professionals can set reasonable limits on themselves, place self-care as a top priority, and seek assistance when necessary; this promotes the longevity and resilience of their professional endeavours (Vincelette et al., 2019). By understanding the indicators of burnout and compassion fatigue and adopting a self-aware perspective, bereavement counsellors and caregivers can effectively manage the difficulties inherent in their professions while maintaining compassion, effectiveness, and longevity. By placing their welfare as a top priority, practitioners can foster a climate of self-preservation and fortitude, which will ultimately improve their ability to offer empathetic and enduring assistance to individuals requiring aid.

SETTING BOUNDARIES

Establishing effective boundaries is critical in bereavement counselling and caregiving to preserve personal well-being and professional efficacy. Both experienced and personal boundaries define the extent of the therapeutic alliance, protecting practitioners from the possible dangers of excessive engagement and boundary transgressions. Practitioners can create a secure and considerate atmosphere that promotes healing and development by clearly defining roles, responsibilities, and expectations. Furthermore, establishing boundaries fosters a perception of unambiguity and regularity, enabling professionals to manoeuvre through the intricacies of their positions with assurance and ethical conduct. Initiating the therapeutic relationship with explicit guidelines and expectations is one method for preserving healthy boundaries (Smith, 2016). By establishing the parameters of confidentiality, communication, and session frequency in concert, professionals can cultivate a sense of shared understanding and reciprocal regard between themselves and their clients.

Furthermore, individuals can develop self-awareness and mindfulness by tuning in to their requirements and limitations to know precisely when and how to establish boundaries effectively. The significance of boundaries in bereavement counselling and caregiving has been further emphasized and underscored amidst the COVID-19 pandemic. The exceptional conditions precipitated by the pandemic have presented unparalleled difficulties in upholding efficacious boundaries while aiding those undergoing bereavement and grief.

A noteworthy insight gained is the imperative nature of modifying boundaries to accommodate clients' changing requirements and situations in times of emergency. The COVID-19 pandemic has significantly disrupted conventional modes of interaction, including in-person sessions. As a result, professionals have begun to investigate alternative modes of support and communication, including teletherapy and virtual counselling. To preserve the integrity of the therapeutic relationship, practitioners have been compelled to establish explicit guidelines and expectations concerning the utilization of technology, confidentiality, and session protocols.

Furthermore, one of the most significant obstacles during the pandemic has been the blurring of professional and personal boundaries, which has been especially difficult for practitioners who may be coping with personal losses or crisis-related stressors. As a result of the heightened emotional intensity and demand for support, a greater consciousness of personal boundaries is required to avert compassion fatigue and exhaustion. Professionals have been compelled to prioritize self-care and set clear limits on their time commitments, burden, and emotional investment to safeguard their mental health and professional effectiveness.

Furthermore, the global health crisis has underscored the significance of adaptability and compassion when establishing limits. As a result of the uncertainties and disruptions brought about by the pandemic, clients may be experiencing increased levels of distress and vulnerability; therefore, practitioners must be sensitive to their particular needs and circumstances. By exhibiting empathy and versatility in modifying limits to account for these obstacles, professionals can cultivate an atmosphere of security and confidence within the therapeutic alliance. In general, the COVID-19 pandemic has brought to the forefront the significance of boundar-

Self-Care Strategies for Grief Counselors and Caregivers

ies in bereavement counselling and caregiving. It has also highlighted the need for self-awareness, adaptability, and clear communication to maintain effective boundaries when assisting those who are grieving and experiencing loss. Professionals can foster an environment conducive to client healing and development, despite the difficulties presented by the pandemic, by emphasizing boundary-setting and integrating it as a fundamental component of their approach.

In addition, self-care is an essential element in maintaining boundaries, as it allows professionals to restore their emotional resources and maintain their ability to deliver empathetic assistance. By deliberately allocating time for rejuvenation, rest, and relaxation, individuals can strengthen their capacity to maintain boundaries and handle the emotional challenges inherent in their positions without succumbing to compassion fatigue and exhaustion (Narasimhan et al., 2019). Keeping boundaries is an essential element of self-care. To cultivate a therapeutic milieu founded upon trust, respect, and integrity, bereavement counsellors and caregivers must place the utmost importance on establishing proper and transparent boundaries. By cultivating proactive communication, self-awareness, and self-care, professionals can effectively navigate the intricacies of their positions, enabling them to empower themselves to offer sustainable and empathetic assistance to individuals requiring support. In the rigorous domain of bereavement counselling and caregiving, professionals are susceptible to burnout and compassion fatigue, both of which have the potential to impair their overall welfare and professional effectiveness significantly. A pervasive feeling of emotional exhaustion, detachment, and ineffectiveness at work characterizes burnout. Burnout can lead to feelings of depletion and disillusionment among grief counsellors and caregivers, resulting in reduced motivation and engagement in their professional obligations. Additionally, individuals may manifest physical symptoms, including migraines, insomnia, and gastrointestinal problems, which highlights the comprehensive impact that burnout has on both the mind and body (Sweileh, 2020).

Self-awareness is crucial in protecting against the stealthy infiltration of compassion fatigue and exhaustion. By developing a heightened consciousness of their emotional and physical conditions, individuals can identify the indicators and manifestations of these phenomena, thereby equipping themselves to intervene proactively before their escalation. Furthermore, by cultivating self-awareness, professionals can set reasonable limits on themselves, prioritize self-care, and seek assistance when necessary, thereby promoting the longevity and resilience of their professional endeavours (Vincelette et al., 2019). By understanding the indicators of burnout and compassion fatigue and adopting a self-aware perspective, bereavement counsellors and caregivers can effectively manage the difficulties inherent in their professions while maintaining compassion, effectiveness, and longevity. Practitioners can foster a climate of self-preservation and fortitude by placing their welfare as a top priority, which will ultimately improve their ability to offer empathetic and enduring assistance to individuals in need.

SELF-CARE PRACTICES

Self-care should be a top priority for bereavement counsellors and caregivers to maintain their capacity to offer compassionate support to others as guardians of emotional health. Mindfulness and meditation are efficacious practices that foster the development of present-moment awareness and alleviate tension (Galante et al., 2023). Individuals can incorporate mindfulness practices into their daily schedules by allocating dedicated time for guided visualization, meditation, or deep breathing exercises. By grounding themselves in the current moment, individuals can develop a state of tranquillity and transparency in the face of the disorder that accompanies their responsibilities. This practice promotes fortitude and emotional equilibrium.

Likewise, moderate stretching, guided imagery, and progressive muscle relaxation are examples of relaxation techniques that can offer practitioners much-needed respite from the stresses and pressures of their profession. By consistently utilizing relaxation techniques, individuals can mitigate muscular tension, diminish anxiety, and foster holistic wellness. By integrating these strategies into their day-to-day operations, individuals can effectively reduce the detrimental consequences of stress and exhaustion (Wang et al., 2023).

Additionally, exercise and physical activity are crucial in fostering self-care among bereavement counsellors and caregivers. Consistently participating in physical activity improves physical health and yields significant mental and emotional welfare advantages. Engaging in physical activity such as vigorous walking, yoga, or group fitness classes can provide individuals with a sense of well-being and revitalization by stimulating their bodies and expelling stored energy. Furthermore, research reveals that physical activity triggers the production of endorphins, neurotransmitters that boost emotions of joy and relaxation. This additional support encourages individuals to engage in physical activity while confronting challenges (Sudeck et al., 2023). Fundamentally, through integrating self-care practices such as mindfulness, meditation, physical activity, and relaxation exercises, bereavement counsellors and caregivers can foster their welfare and maintain their ability to offer empathetic assistance to individuals requiring support. By placing self-care at the forefront of their professional agenda, practitioners can cultivate an environment within bereavement counselling and caregiving that promotes resilience, empathy, and sustainability.

Self-Care Strategies for Grief Counselors and Caregivers

NURTURING EMOTIONAL RESILIENCE

Professionals in bereavement counselling and caregiving must prioritize the development of emotional resilience to manage the significant challenges they encounter effectively. The development of emotional resilience commences with the practice of mindfulness and self-awareness. Practitioners can benefit from cultivating a profound comprehension of their emotional triggers, corresponding reactions, and adaptive strategies. Through introspection and empathy towards their innermost experiences, individuals can develop enhanced emotional intelligence and self-control, thereby equipping themselves to handle difficult circumstances with poise and dignity (Jiménez-Picón et al., 2021). Particularly for professionals in bereavement counselling and caregiving who are navigating unparalleled challenges and complexities in the line of work, there is a profound correlation between the development of emotional resilience and the COVID-19 pandemic.

Either for those experiencing grief and loss or for the professionals who are assisting them, the pandemic has precipitated an increase in emotional intensity and distress. Amidst the increased pressures and anxieties brought about by the pandemic, the development of emotional resilience assumes paramount importance. The COVID-19 pandemic has further emphasized the importance of mindfulness and self-awareness, which are fundamental practices that foster emotional resilience. To offer clients empathetic and practical support, practitioners must concurrently manage their emotional reactions to the crisis. Practicing mindfulness and developing self-awareness can provide individuals with a deeper understanding of their emotional triggers, reactions, and coping strategies. This enhanced understanding empowers individuals to confront difficult situations with more rationality and fortitude.

In addition, the pandemic has highlighted the significance of emotional intelligence in navigating uncertain and emotionally fraught situations. While managing their own emotional reactions to the ongoing crisis, practitioners must be attuned to their clients' subtle emotions and experiences. Practitioners can enhance their capacity to provide adequate support to individuals going through the bereavement process during such difficult times by fostering emotional intelligence, which consists of cultivating empathy, compassion, and self-control. Further, the pandemic underscores the necessity for adaptive coping mechanisms amid hardship. Although attentive to their self-care and well-being, practitioners must be capable of modifying their counselling and caregiving approaches to meet the changing circumstances and needs of their clients. Proficient individuals can surmount the complexities and uncertainties of the pandemic with enhanced adaptability and efficacy by cultivating resilience-building techniques and adaptive strategies. The COVID-19 pandemic has heightened the significance of emotional resilience. Practitioners of this practice can effectively navigate the substantial obstacles they face and offer enduring and

**Self-Care Strategies for Grief Counselors and Caregivers**

compassionate assistance to those bereaved and suffering during these unparalleled periods by emphasizing mindfulness, self-awareness, emotional intelligence, and adaptive coping mechanisms.

Furthermore, individuals can enhance their emotional resilience by cultivating a supportive social circle of mentors, peers, and supervisors. By soliciting advice and validation from reliable peers, professionals can gain invaluable insight and validation, enabling them to confront the intricacies of their positions with enhanced assurance and transparency. Furthermore, establishing relationships with individuals who have undergone comparable circumstances can cultivate a sense of unity and companionship, thereby alleviating feelings of seclusion and exhaustion (Baluszek et al., 2023). Emotion processing and management strategies are crucial for sustaining emotional resilience in challenging circumstances. Reflective supervision, journaling, and expressive arts therapy are all beneficial practices for practitioners to incorporate into their self-care regimens. By employing these methods, individuals can provide themselves with a secure and imaginative means of investigating and dealing with their emotions, thereby attaining understanding, perspective, and resolution regarding difficult circumstances (Li & Peng, 2022).

Additionally, practices such as loving-kindness, mindfulness-based techniques like mindfulness meditation and body scan exercises, among others, can be beneficial. Stress reduction and emotional regulation are both benefits of meditation. Individuals can enhance their emotional resilience and composure when confronted with challenging circumstances by developing an awareness of the present moment and accepting their inner experiences without judgment (Carroll et al., 2021). Fostering emotional resilience is a continuous process that demands unwavering devotion, self-compassion, and a resolve to individual development. Through the development of self-awareness, the promotion of supportive relationships, and the adoption of emotion processing and management techniques, individuals can nurture the internal reserves required to confront the challenges of bereavement counselling and caregiving in a manner characterized by dignity, sincerity, and fortitude.

SEEKING SUPPORT

Amidst the arduous and emotionally charged domains of bereavement counselling and caregiving, it is impossible to overstate the significance of requesting assistance from peers, mentors, and supervisors. Peer support is an essential element that assists professionals in managing the intricacies of their positions. Establishing connections with colleagues who have undergone comparable experiences cultivates a feeling of solidarity and camaraderie, affirming the emotions of practitioners while providing invaluable insights. Peer support networks facilitate the exchange of personal chal-

Self-Care Strategies for Grief Counselors and Caregivers

lenges, offer guidance, and obtain validation for practitioners, thereby cultivating a feeling of inclusion and camaraderie in the face of the profession's inherent isolation (Harrop et al., 2020). Similarly, seasoned professionals can provide invaluable counsel and direction to individuals grappling with bereavement counselling and caregiving challenges. Mentors provide practitioners with practical guidance, insight, and wisdom to assist them in navigating ethical dilemmas, professional obstacles, and opportunities for personal development. Professionals can enhance their professional growth and development by cultivating mentor-mentee connections and gaining access to the knowledge and experience of their predecessors (Jahani et al., 2022).

Additionally, supervision is essential for promoting practitioners' emotional health and professional development. By providing a structured environment for practitioners to reflect, receive feedback, and receive direction, supervisors assist practitioners in processing complex cases, identifying blind spots, and developing effective coping mechanisms. By engaging in consistent supervision sessions, professionals can enhance their understanding, self-assurance, and ability to bounce back from setbacks, thereby equipping themselves to adeptly and empathetically navigate the intricate complexities of bereavement counselling and caregiving (Kelly, 2023). Promoting a culture of candid dialogue about obstacles and sentiments is critical for cultivating an inclusive and supportive work environment. Organizations can create a psychologically secure environment that encourages professionals to seek assistance without fear of criticism or social disapproval by normalizing dialogues about exhaustion, stress, and emotional health.

Furthermore, by cultivating an environment that encourages candid dialogue, transparency, cooperation, and reciprocal assistance are elevated, thereby augmenting professionals' overall welfare and efficacy in the respective domains (Hunt et al., 2021). In grief counselling and caregiving, practitioners must prioritize self-care and professional development by actively pursuing peer, mentor, and supervisor support. Practitioners can foster connections, well-being, and resilience in the face of their work's arduous and noble nature by actively utilizing support networks and encouraging candid dialogue about difficulties and feelings.

TIME MANAGEMENT AND WORK-LIFE BALANCE

Proficient time management and healthy work-life balance are critical for practitioners in bereavement counselling and caregiving to safeguard their well-being and avert burnout. The foundation of effective time management strategies is establishing distinct priorities and objectives. Practitioners can optimize their time and resources by identifying and allocating them to their most critical responsibilities. By employing time-blocking techniques, to-do lists, and calendars, professionals can enhance their ability to manage their workload and guarantee adequate time for essential duties while reducing interruptions and diversions (Higgins et al., 2023). Furthermore, it is advantageous for practitioners to establish limits on their time and energy. By establishing time constraints on work hours, organizing periodic breaks, and designating specific periods for self-care and relaxation, professionals can prevent themselves from becoming overworked and vulnerable to exhaustion. Practitioners can maintain their capacity to offer compassionate assistance to those in need and recharge their energy reserves by prioritizing self-care and personal well-being (Higgins et al., 2023). Striking a balance between one's professional and personal lives necessitates deliberate exertion and the establishment of boundaries. Professionals can derive advantages from implementing measures to delineate work and personal life, such as designating specific areas for work and refraining from engaging in work-related correspondence outside of working hours. The ability of professionals to maintain a balance between their professional and personal lives has been profoundly affected by the COVID-19 pandemic, which has introduced distinct complexities and difficulties in delineating boundaries between these spheres.

A significant consequence of the pandemic has been the indistinct differentiation between professional and personal spheres, specifically for individuals who have adopted remote work arrangements. The erosion of the physical distinction between work and personal spheres has resulted from an increasing number of professionals now operating remotely, thereby complicating the task of delineating precise limits between these two areas.

Furthermore, due to the pandemic, work patterns and expectations have shifted, and many professionals are now confronted with increased burdens, heightened job insecurity, and extended work hours. In addition to the uncertainties associated with the pandemic, the demands of adjusting to remote work, handling domestic obligations, and managing household responsibilities have exacerbated the difficulty of balancing professional and personal commitments.

Additionally, professionals find it difficult to detach from their work beyond standard working hours due to the ubiquitous nature of technology and digital communication. Maintaining personal boundaries and scheduling time for relaxation and individual activities can be challenging due to the perpetual availability of emails, messages, and virtual meetings, which can induce a sense of being "on call." Additionally, the accessibility of customary support systems and resources for balancing professional and personal life, including childcare facilities, fitness centres, and social events, has been adversely affected by the pandemic. The absence of external assistance can exacerbate professionals' challenges in balancing their professional obligations and prioritizing their welfare. Notwithstanding these obstacles, the pandemic has additionally underscored the significance of establishing boundaries and prioritizing self-care to safeguard one's mental, physical, and emotional well-being.

Self-Care Strategies for Grief Counselors and Caregivers

As a result of being compelled to revaluate their work practices and routines, professionals are placing a greater emphasis on stress management, self-care, and work-life balance. Professions attempting to maintain a healthy work-life balance have faced formidable obstacles by the COVID-19 scourge. Nevertheless, by adopting strategies such as setting explicit limits, placing self-care as a top priority, and being flexible in the face of evolving conditions, individuals can surmount these obstacles and endeavour to attain a more sustainable and health-conscious equilibrium between their professional and personal responsibilities.

Furthermore, by implementing efficient time management strategies, individuals can enhance their efficiency and involvement in non-work-related activities by maximizing their productivity during working hours (Aeon et al., 2021). In addition, professionals can foster flexibility and adaptability in their strategies towards achieving harmonious work-life equilibrium. Acknowledging the potential for heightened professional obligations, practitioners can proactively modify their timetables and obligations to accommodate such variations while placing long-term emphasis on self-care and personal welfare (Thilagavathy & SN, 2021). Ensuring optimal time management and a harmonious work-life balance are critical factors in bereavement counselling and caregiving to prevent burnout and promote overall well-being. By adopting time management strategies, establishing limits on work obligations, and placing personal well-being and self-care at the forefront of their agendas, practitioners can cultivate resilience, equilibrium, and satisfaction in their professional and personal spheres.

CREATIVE OUTLETS AND HOBBIES

For grief counselling and caregiving professionals, creative pursuits and pastimes are indispensable for reducing stress and promoting health. Creative channels allow individuals to manifest their thoughts and feelings, navigate their emotions, and develop a state of mindfulness. Participating in artistic, musical, artisanal, or writing endeavours enables individuals to transform their feelings and sentiments into concrete manifestations, facilitating a process of emotional catharsis and discharge. Furthermore, creative expression can function as a means of exploration and self-discovery, allowing individuals to access their latent creativity and establish connections with facets of themselves that extend beyond their vocational personas. (Darewych, 2019).

Furthermore, research has demonstrated that participation in creative endeavours can facilitate relaxation and alleviate tension, providing individuals with a valuable respite from the rigours of their occupation. Active involvement in a creative pursuit can elicit a state of flow characterized by profound concentration and engagement, providing a momentary respite from the stresses and concerns of everyday existence. Engaging in creative endeavours, such as painting, performing a musical instrument, or gardening, provides individuals with a refuge that promotes self-expression and rejuvenation (Zhang et al., 2021).

To maintain equilibrium and wellness amidst the emotional challenges of bereavement counselling and caregiving, it is vital to discover happiness and satisfaction beyond the workplace. Participating in personal interests and recreational pursuits enables individuals to rejuvenate their energies, foster fervent convictions and interests, and cultivate meaningful connections with cherished ones. Practitioners can maintain their capacity to offer compassionate assistance to those in need and replenish their energy reserves by setting aside time for activities that bring them pleasure and fulfilment (Braja-Žganec et al., 2010). Engaging in creative pursuits and personal interests can significantly foster well-being and mitigate burnout risks in bereavement counselling and care professionals' giving. Individuals can promote resilience, equilibrium, and contentment in their professional and personal spheres by actively seeking out occasions for personal growth, unwinding, and pleasure beyond the workplace. Proficient time management and healthy work-life balance are critical for practitioners in bereavement counselling and caregiving to safeguard their well-being and avert burnout. The foundation of effective time management strategies is establishing distinct priorities and objectives. Practitioners can optimize their time and resources by identifying and allocating them to their most critical responsibilities. By employing time-blocking techniques, to-do lists, and calendars, professionals can enhance their ability to manage their workload and guarantee adequate time for essential duties while reducing interruptions and diversions (Higgins et al., 2023).

Furthermore, it is advantageous for practitioners to establish limits on their time and energy. By establishing time constraints on work hours, organizing periodic breaks, and designating specific periods for self-care and relaxation, professionals can prevent themselves from becoming overworked and vulnerable to exhaustion. Practitioners can maintain their capacity to offer compassionate assistance to those in need and recharge their energy reserves by prioritizing self-care and personal well-being (Higgins et al., 2023). Striking a balance between one's professional and personal lives necessitates deliberate exertion and the establishment of boundaries. Professionals can derive advantages from implementing measures to delineate work and personal life, such as designating specific areas for work and refraining from engaging in work-related correspondence outside of working hours.

Furthermore, by implementing efficient time management strategies, individuals can enhance their efficiency and involvement in non-work-related activities by maximizing their productivity during working hours (Aeon et al., 2021). In addition, professionals can foster flexibility and adaptability in their strategies to-

Self-Care Strategies for Grief Counselors and Caregivers

wards achieving harmonious work-life equilibrium. Acknowledging the potential for heightened professional obligations, practitioners can proactively modify their timetables and obligations to accommodate such variations while placing long-term emphasis on self-care and personal welfare (Thilagavathy & SN, 2021). Ensuring optimal time management and a harmonious work-life balance are critical factors in bereavement counselling and caregiving to prevent burnout and promote overall well-being. By adopting time management strategies, establishing limits on work obligations, and placing personal well-being and self-care at the forefront of their agendas, practitioners can cultivate resilience, equilibrium, and satisfaction in their professional and personal spheres.

SELF-CARE PLANS

In grief counselling and caregiving, practitioners must establish personalized self-care plans to maintain their capacity to offer empathetic support to others and prioritize their well-being. Initiating the creation of an individualized self-care strategy is introspection and evaluation. Practitioners can benefit by reflecting on their needs, strengths, and vulnerabilities and identifying areas of their lives that may require additional attention and support. A comprehensive understanding of individuals' self-care requirements and priorities can be attained by practitioners considering various factors such as physical health, emotional well-being, social connections, and leisure interests (Baker & Gabriel, 2021).

Practitioners can begin establishing objectives for self-care practices once they have identified their self-care requirements and priorities. By ensuring that goals are SMART (specific, measurable, achievable, pertinent, and time-bound), practitioners can monitor their advancement and adapt their approaches accordingly. Instances of self-care objectives consist of engaging in daily mindfulness meditation for ten minutes, exercising for thirty minutes three times per week, or organizing recurring social gatherings with close friends and family. Practitioners can benefit from identifying particular self-care activities and strategies following their requirements and preferences and establishing objectives. Potential activities to consider include leisure time in nature, meditation, journaling, creative expression, hobbies, or seeking assistance from peers, mentors, or mental health professionals. According to Sist et al. (2022), individuals can foster resilience and overall well-being by integrating various self-care activities into their daily schedules. Monitoring one's progress in self-care practices is critical to uphold accountability and sustain motivation. Practitioners can monitor and assess the efficacy of their self-care activities over time by employing a variety of instruments and methods. This may entail maintaining a journal dedicated to self-care, monitoring exercise or meditation sessions via a smartphone application, or arranging periodic check-ins with a reliable accountability companion. Practitioners can optimize their self-care strategies by consistently assessing their progress and reflecting on their experiences. This enables them to recognize recurring patterns, acknowledge accomplishments, and make necessary adjustments (El-Osta et al., 2023). Fundamentally, formulating personalized self-care strategies is a proactive and empowering undertaking that enables professionals to give precedence to their welfare and maintain their ability to offer empathetic assistance to others. Individuals can foster personal and professional resilience, equilibrium, and satisfaction by establishing objectives, identifying self-care endeavours, and monitoring progress in self-care practices.

CASE STUDIES AND PERSONAL STORIES

Case studies and personal anecdotes of bereavement counsellors and caregivers who have effectively integrated self-care practices provide practitioners with inspiration and valuable insights into prioritizing their well-being. The narratives mentioned above emphasize the profound impact that self-care can have and stress its critical role in maintaining fortitude and efficacy when confronted with difficult situations.

SH had several years of experience as a bereavement counsellor, during which time she assisted families and individuals grieving the loss of a loved one. As time passed, she became increasingly conscious of the emotional toll her profession was taking on her being; she found herself emotionally exhausted and inundated by the magnitude of her client's suffering. SH, intent on prioritizing self-care, initiated the implementation of various strategies to promote her overall wellness. She implemented systematic limitations on her work schedule, allocating consistent daily periods for rejuvenation and repose. In addition, she made time for pursuits that elicited happiness and satisfaction, including engaging in yoga, painting, and spending time immersed in the natural world. SH sought assistance from her supervisor and colleagues. In addition to engaging in self-care practices, she participated in routine supervision sessions to assist with processing complex cases and seeking advice when necessary. She also fostered a network of loved ones and acquaintances outside of work who offered her encouragement and emotional support. By placing a high value on her welfare, SH observed a substantial enhancement in her general disposition, vitality, and aptitude to manage the pressures of her occupation. With an enhanced sense of fortitude and stability, she was more adept at offering empathetic assistance to her clientele while upholding a harmonious equilibrium in her personal life.

For many years, DL has been providing care for individuals with chronic illnesses and disabilities. Although his occupation satisfied him, he frequently encountered difficulties managing his caregiving obligations to allocate time for personal de-

Self-Care Strategies for Grief Counselors and Caregivers

velopment. Motivated by a strong sense of individual responsibility, DL initiated integrating self-care activities into his daily schedule. Establishing a daily routine that included meditation and introspection enabled him to commence each day with tranquillity and equilibrium. In addition, he dedicated himself to consistent physical activity by organizing periods for strolls in natural surroundings and enrolling in yoga sessions.

Furthermore, DL prioritized emotional well-being by participating in caregiver support groups, requesting assistance from his colleagues, and attending to his physical health. As a result of these relationships, he gained a sense of solidarity, validation, and practical advice for managing burnout and stress. After DL began to prioritize self-care, he observed a significant improvement in his overall resilience and well-being. Having increased energy, concentration, and presence at work, he could attend to his requirements while providing empathetic assistance to his clients. By placing self-care as a top priority, DL could maintain his enthusiasm for providing care and derive more satisfaction from his position. The presented case studies underscore the profound impact of self-care on bereavement counsellors and caregivers. They illustrate how placing one's welfare as a top priority can increase fortitude, efficacy, and satisfaction within the assisting professions. By prioritizing self-care and drawing inspiration from the experiences of others, practitioners can develop the internal fortitude required to confront the difficulties of their positions with composure and perseverance.

ETHICAL CONSIDERATIONS

Professionals engaged in bereavement counselling and caregiving must uphold ethical obligations that benefit themselves and their clients. Self-care ethical considerations are of the utmost importance, as professionals must place their well-being at the forefront to provide ethical services and maintain their professional integrity. Practitioners must provide their consumers with competent and effective care. Professionals are obligated to uphold their physical, emotional, and psychological health to effectively and empathetically attend to the needs of their clients. Practitioners fulfil their ethical obligation to provide services of the utmost quality and effectiveness by placing self-care as a top priority (Abramson, 2021). Professionals have a moral obligation to protect their consumers from harm. Burnout, compassion fatigue, and vicarious trauma not only undermine the capacity of professionals to deliver sufficient care but also present possible hazards to the welfare of their clients. To uphold their ethical responsibility of protecting the well-being of their clients and averting injury, practitioners demonstrate a commitment to self-care and the mitigation of associated risks (Forrest et al., 2020).

Professionals are constrained by an ethical obligation to preserve their professional boundaries and adhere to ethical principles of behaviour. The importance of self-care cannot be overstated in this context, as professionals who disregard their welfare may be more vulnerable to violations of boundaries, breaches of confidentiality, and other ethical failings. By placing self-care as a top priority, practitioners ensure the integrity of the therapeutic relationship and demonstrate their commitment to ethical practice. It is the ethical responsibility of practitioners to participate in continuous professional development and engage in introspection actively. This entails prioritizing their personal growth and progress by incorporating self-care routines that enhance their physical, emotional, and psychological welfare. Practitioners can improve their ability to deliver sufficient care and maintain ethical principles by investing in their development and resilience (Fereidooni et al., 2024). Aspects of self-care that adhere to ethical standards are crucial for professionals engaged in bereavement counselling and caregiving. Practitioners satisfy their ethical responsibilities to deliver proficient, ethical, and effective care to their clients while preserving their professional standing and personal welfare when they place their well-being first. Maintaining ethical self-care is a moral obligation and a professional necessity, as it guarantees that the assisting professions adhere to the utmost standards of care and integrity.

CULTURAL SENSITIVITY IN SELF-CARE

Cultural sensitivity is a critical component of self-care, given that individuals from various cultural contexts may possess distinct viewpoints, customs, and personal health and wellness inclinations. Norms, values, and traditions of a particular culture profoundly affect self-care, influencing the beliefs and actions of individuals regarding their health and well-being. The definition of self-care can vary considerably among individuals due to factors such as ethnic background, religious affiliation, socioeconomic standing, and familial upbringing. As a result, professionals must acknowledge and value the wide range of self-care methodologies and cultural perspectives (Yamaguchi et al., 2017). Recognizing cultural variations in self-care entails acknowledging the absence of a universally applicable approach to overall wellness. Practitioners must embrace a culturally sensitive perspective that considers individuals from various cultural backgrounds' distinct requirements, inclinations, and situations. To gain insight into clients' cultural values and beliefs concerning self-care, engaging in candid conversations and working together to develop individualized self-care strategies consistent with their cultural environment (Mirfardi, 2023).

Self-Care Strategies for Grief Counselors and Caregivers

Professionals must exercise caution regarding potential cultural biases and stereotypes that could impact their understanding of self-care. Cultural humility should guide one's approach to self-care, as it recognizes the possible influence of cultural background on assumptions and interactions. To acquire knowledge from the extensive array of cultural customs and traditions, individuals should foster inquisitiveness, receptiveness, and reverence for varied viewpoints concerning welfare (Loue, 2022). Cultural considerations at the individual level: Professionals should be aware of more comprehensive sociocultural elements that could influence self-care behaviours within specific communities. This illustrates how systemic obstacles, including limitations in resource accessibility, social support systems, and healthcare provisions, can impact individuals' well-being perceptions and impede their ability to engage in self-care activities. Professionals must champion policies and practices that are culturally sensitive, aiming to rectify these disparities and advance the comprehensive welfare of every person, irrespective of their cultural heritage (Mirfardi, 2023). Cultural sensitivity holds excellent significance in self-care, given that people of various cultural origins may possess distinct viewpoints, customs, and inclinations concerning personal welfare. By recognizing and valuing cultural variations in self-care norms and beliefs, professionals can cultivate an environment that is more equitable and inclusive, thereby advocating for the comprehensive wellness of every individual.

DISCUSSION

The COVID-19 pandemic has thrust self-care into the spotlight, emphasizing its critical role in maintaining physical, mental, and emotional well-being during times of uncertainty and stress. With the disruption of daily routines, heightened anxiety, and increased social isolation, individuals have turned to self-care practices as a means of coping and preserving their overall health. The pandemic has catalyzed a shift in self-care practices, prompting individuals to adapt and innovate in response to new challenges. Traditional methods such as spa days or gym workouts may no longer be accessible or safe, leading people to explore alternative avenues such as virtual fitness classes, meditation apps, or DIY home spa treatments. This adaptability underscores the resilience of human nature and the capacity to find creative solutions even in the face of adversity. Despite its importance, the pandemic has also introduced barriers to self-care for many individuals. Economic hardships, caregiving responsibilities, and concerns about the virus may limit resources and time available for self-care activities.

Self-Care Strategies for Grief Counselors and Caregivers

Additionally, the blurring of boundaries between work and home life in remote work setups can make prioritizing self-care and establishing healthy routines challenging. Recognizing and addressing these barriers ensures equitable access to self-care resources and support. The pandemic has exacerbated mental health challenges for millions worldwide, underscoring the interconnectedness of mental health and self-care. Practices such as mindfulness, journaling, and seeking professional support have become essential tools for managing anxiety, depression, and other mental health conditions exacerbated by the pandemic. Prioritizing mental health needs is not only an act of self-care but also a critical component of resilience and adaptive coping during times of crisis. While self-care is often framed as an individual pursuit, the pandemic has highlighted the importance of community and collective well-being. Acts of kindness, mutual support, and solidarity have emerged as powerful forms of collective self-care, fostering resilience and social cohesion in the face of adversity. From neighbourhood support groups to online communities, the pandemic has demonstrated the strength of human connections in promoting wellness and healing. As the world navigates the ongoing challenges of the pandemic, prioritizing self-care remains paramount for individuals and communities. By fostering resilience, promoting holistic well-being, and cultivating a sense of agency in uncertain times, self-care is a foundational pillar for navigating the complexities of the pandemic and beyond. As we look ahead, integrating self-care into our daily lives and supporting equitable access to resources will be essential for building a healthier, more resilient future for all.

The COVID-19 pandemic has undeniably intensified the suffering experienced by individuals worldwide, and this heightened intensity of suffering has had a profound impact on practitioners and their clients alike. In navigating the labyrinth of grief, ire, and hopelessness, practitioners find themselves confronted with unprecedented levels of emotional distress and trauma among their clients. One significant aspect of the pandemic's impact on suffering is the sheer scale of loss experienced by individuals and communities. Whether it's the loss of loved ones to the virus itself, the loss of livelihoods due to economic disruptions, or the loss of normalcy and routine, the cumulative effect has been staggering. This profound sense of loss often manifests as grief, leaving individuals grappling with complex emotions and struggling to find meaning and solace in the face of such overwhelming circumstances.

Moreover, the prolonged pandemic has exacerbated feelings of frustration, anger, and helplessness. As restrictions continue and uncertainty persists, individuals may experience heightened levels of ire towards perceived injustices, whether directed at governmental responses, societal inequalities, or personal challenges exacerbated by the crisis. This anger and frustration can further intensify feelings of hopelessness and despair, creating a cycle of emotional distress that is difficult to break.

Self-Care Strategies for Grief Counselors and Caregivers

Additionally, the pandemic has exposed and exacerbated existing social and economic inequalities, disproportionately impacting already marginalized communities. Vulnerable populations, such as frontline workers, low-income individuals, and communities of colour, have borne the brunt of the pandemic's consequences, facing heightened levels of suffering due to systemic disparities in access to healthcare, economic resources, and social support networks. For practitioners, witnessing the profound intensity of their clients' suffering amid such widespread adversity can be emotionally taxing and morally challenging. The weight of bearing witness to so much pain and anguish can lead to burnout, compassion fatigue, and vicarious trauma, impacting their ability to provide adequate support and care for their clients. In response to these challenges, practitioners must prioritize self-care and seek out support networks to mitigate the impact of secondary trauma. Additionally, fostering resilience and adaptive coping strategies among clients becomes paramount, empowering them to navigate the complexities of their suffering and find pathways towards healing and recovery.

Ultimately, the impact of COVID-19 on the intensity of suffering experienced by individuals and communities cannot be understated. As practitioners continue to navigate this unprecedented landscape of grief, ire, and hopelessness, it becomes increasingly important to approach their work with compassion, empathy, and a commitment to promoting healing and resilience in the face of adversity.

In addition to understanding the indicators of burnout and compassion fatigue, bereavement counsellors and caregivers can implement various strategies to effectively manage the difficulties inherent in their professions while maintaining compassion, effectiveness, and longevity. First and foremost, self-awareness is critical. Practitioners must deeply understand their own emotional triggers, limitations, and coping mechanisms. This involves regularly checking in with themselves and acknowledging their professional and personal needs. By recognizing when they feel overwhelmed or emotionally drained, practitioners can take proactive steps to address these feelings before they escalate into burnout or compassion fatigue.

Furthermore, establishing healthy boundaries is essential for preserving emotional well-being. Practitioners must learn to limit their time, energy, and emotional investment in their work, ensuring they have the space and resources to recharge and replenish themselves. This may involve setting realistic expectations for workload, prioritizing self-care activities, and learning to say no when necessary.

Engaging in regular self-care practices is another crucial component of managing burnout and compassion fatigue. This can include exercise, meditation, journaling, spending time with loved ones, or pursuing hobbies and interests outside of work. By prioritizing their well-being, practitioners can replenish their reserves of compassion and resilience, enabling them to continue offering empathetic and enduring assistance to those in need. Additionally, seeking support from colleagues, supervi-

Self-Care Strategies for Grief Counselors and Caregivers

sors, or mental health professionals can provide valuable perspective and guidance during challenging times. Supervision and peer support groups offer opportunities for reflection, validation, and sharing experiences, fostering a sense of community and camaraderie among practitioners. Finally, maintaining a sense of purpose and meaning in their work can help practitioners weather their profession's inevitable ups and downs. By connecting with the more profound significance of their role in supporting individuals through the grieving process, practitioners can find motivation and fulfilment even in the face of adversity. Ultimately, by placing their welfare as a top priority, bereavement counsellors and caregivers can foster a climate of self-preservation and fortitude, improving their ability to offer empathetic and enduring assistance to individuals requiring aid. In doing so, they not only safeguard their well-being but also uphold the integrity and effectiveness of their profession.

Including case studies and personal anecdotes from bereavement counsellors and caregivers who have successfully incorporated self-care practices provides practitioners with inspiration and valuable insights into prioritizing their well-being in the face of the difficulties inherent in their fields. The narratives mentioned above underscore the significant influence that self-care can exert on one's personal welfare and professional effectiveness, thereby emphasizing its indispensable function in sustaining resilience and productivity in challenging circumstances.

Consider SH, an experienced bereavement counsellor who acknowledged the detrimental impact her vocation was having on her emotional state. SH implemented various strategies to enhance her overall wellness, with self-care taking precedence. These strategies encompassed setting systematic limitations on her work schedule, participating in activities that brought her joy, and requesting support from supervisors, colleagues, and loved ones. As a result of these endeavours, SH noticed a significant improvement in her overall attitude and capacity to handle the demands of her profession, which ultimately enabled her to provide more compassionate support to her clients while preserving a balanced personal life.

In a similar vein, DL, who provided care for individuals with chronic illnesses and disabilities, encountered difficulties in balancing his personal growth with his caregiving responsibilities. Nevertheless, through the implementation of self-care strategies, including engaging in physical activity and meditation and requesting assistance from caregiver support groups and colleagues, DL noticed substantial enhancements in both his resilience and overall state of being. By enhancing his work performance and demeanour, DL could attend to his personal requirements while offering compassionate support to his clients, which ultimately contributed to his heightened job satisfaction.

The case mentioned above studies highlight self-care's significant influence on bereavement counselors and caregivers. They illustrate how placing one's well-being as a top priority can improve resilience, effectiveness, and contentment in the helping

Self-Care Strategies for Grief Counselors and Caregivers

professions. By prioritizing self-care and deriving inspiration from the experiences of others, professionals can cultivate the internal resilience required to confront the challenges of their roles with poise and determination. This, in turn, will promote a more sustainable and health-conscious approach to their work.

The lessons derived from the COVID-19 pandemic have consistently emphasized the vital significance of self-care in the context of bereavement counselling and caregiving. This has established self-care as a foundational component that safeguards practitioners' well-being and professional efficacy.

An important insight gleaned from the pandemic is the increased importance of prioritizing self-care during periods of emergency. The unparalleled difficulties precipitated by the pandemic, encompassing heightened emotional intensity, prolonged tension, and increased uncertainty, have underscored the criticality for professionals to place their well-being first. The pandemic has brought to light that practitioners who neglect their self-care requirements cannot effectively assist others.

Furthermore, the global health crisis has underscored the interdependence of psychological, emotional, and physiological well-being. The ongoing exposure to intense emotional experiences and the stressors linked to the pandemic has emphasized the criticality for professionals to give precedence to their mental, emotional, and physical well-being. Self-care practices that attend to these dimensions of wellness have emerged as indispensable instruments for navigating the difficulties of the pandemic and maintaining professional efficacy.

Furthermore, the pandemic has highlighted the urgency for self-care practices to be flexible and adaptable. Due to the disruptions caused by lockdowns and social distancing measures to conventional forms of self-care, practitioners have been compelled to devise and investigate novel approaches to fostering their well-being. Virtual support groups, online mindfulness sessions, and creative endeavours have surfaced as advantageous resources for individuals striving to sustain their overall wellness in the face of the pandemic's difficulties.

In addition, the pandemic has highlighted the significance of support networks and community concerning self-care. Practitioners have sought solace, validation, and practical assistance from their peers, superiors, and close acquaintances throughout these trying times. Establishing and maintaining these connections has been critical in preserving fortitude and resilience amidst challenging circumstances. In general, the COVID-19 pandemic has underscored the paramount significance of self-care within the context of bereavement counselling and caregiving. It has provided invaluable insights into the interdependence of mental, emotional, and physical health, the need to adjust to evolving situations, and the utilization of support systems. By incorporating these insights into their daily work, professionals can foster resilience, maintain their professional efficacy, and persist in delivering

Self-Care Strategies for Grief Counselors and Caregivers

empathetic assistance to individuals requiring aid, notwithstanding the difficulties posed by a worldwide pandemic.

CONCLUSION

This chapter has examined the critical importance of self-care in bereavement counselling and caregiving, recognizing it as a fundamental element that contributes to practitioners' well-being and professional effectiveness. During our discourse, several significant insights and lessons have surfaced, underscoring the criticality of placing self-care as a top priority in these arduous vocations. We have previously emphasized the considerable influence that bereavement counselling and caregiving have on practitioners' mental, emotional, and physical health. Constant exposure to profound emotional encounters can trigger exhaustion, compassion fatigue, and vicarious trauma, underscoring the critical importance that professionals place on their well-being. Various self-care strategies and practices specifically designed to tackle the distinct obstacles encountered by professionals in these domains have been examined. A wide range of techniques, including engaging in creative pastimes, practising mindfulness and meditation, and other methods, are at practitioners' disposal to maintain their capacity to provide compassionate care while promoting their well-being.

Furthermore, we have placed significant emphasis on practitioners' ethical obligations concerning their self-care, acknowledging that maintaining the utmost standards of care and integrity is a professional imperative. Practitioners protect their health and efficacy, guarantee the welfare of their clients, and preserve the integrity of the therapeutic alliance by prioritizing their well-being. Significantly, we have duly recognized the culture of self-care, acknowledging that people of various cultural heritages may possess distinct viewpoints and customs, and practitioners must adopt a self-care approach that embodies cultural sensitivity and humility, demonstrating respect for the diverse traditions and experiences within the communities they serve. The chapter has emphasized the perpetual quality of self-care within bereavement counselling and caregiving contexts. Self-care should be understood as a continuous dedication to fostering one's overall health and resilience amidst persistent obstacles and pressures rather than a singular occurrence. By prioritizing self-care and fostering a culture of support and resilience, professionals can maintain their ability to offer sustainable and empathetic assistance to needy individuals. This, in turn, will improve the standard of care and overall welfare of both practitioners and clients.

Self-Care Strategies for Grief Counselors and Caregivers

DISCUSSION QUESTIONS:

1. How has the COVID-19 pandemic highlighted the importance of self-care in bereavement counselling and caregiving professions? What specific challenges have practitioners faced, and how have they adapted their self-care practices in response to them?

2. Reflecting on the case studies and personal anecdotes in this chapter, what are some common themes or patterns in how practitioners prioritize self-care? How do these examples illustrate the impact of self-care on professional effectiveness and personal well-being?

3. What are some potential barriers to implementing effective self-care practices in bereavement counselling and caregiving professions, and how can these barriers be addressed or overcome? How might supervisors and training programs support practitioners in prioritizing self-care?

4. Discuss the concept of boundary-setting in the context of self-care for bereavement counsellors and caregivers. How can practitioners establish healthy boundaries between their professional and personal lives to prevent burnout and compassion fatigue?

5. Explore the role of community and support networks in self-care for practitioners. How can colleagues, supervisors, and loved ones contribute to practitioners' well-being, and how can practitioners cultivate and nurture these relationships?

6. Reflecting on your own experiences and observations, what self-care practices have you found particularly effective in promoting your well-being as a counsellor or caregiver? How do you integrate these practices into your daily life, and how do they impact your professional effectiveness and personal fulfilment?

REFERENCES

Abramson, A. (2021). *The ethical imperative of self-care*. APA. https://www.apa.org. https://www.apa.org/monitor/2021/04/feature-imperative-self-care

Aeon, B., Faber, A., & Panaccio, A. (2021). Does time management work? A meta-analysis. *PLoS One*, 16(1), e0245066. 10.1371/journal.pone.024506633428644

Baker, C., & Gabriel, L. (2021). Exploring how therapists engage in self-care in times of personal distress. *British Journal of Guidance & Counselling*, 49(3), 435–444. 10.1080/03069885.2021.1885010

Baluszek, J. B., Brønnick, K., & Wiig, S. (2023). The relations between resilience and self-efficacy among healthcare practitioners in the context of the COVID-19 pandemic – a rapid review. *International Journal of Health Governance*, 28(2), 152–164. 10.1108/IJHG-11-2022-0098

Brajša-Žganec, A., Merkaš, M., & Šverko, I. (2010). Quality of life and leisure activities: How do leisure activities contribute to subjective well-being? *Social Indicators Research*, 102(1), 81–91. 10.1007/s11205-010-9724-2

Carroll, A., Sanders-O'Connor, E., Forrest, K., Fynes-Clinton, S., York, A., Ziaei, M., Flynn, L., Bower, J., & Reutens, D. C. (2021). Improving emotion regulation, well-being, and neuro-cognitive functioning in teachers: A matched controlled study comparing the mindfulness-based stress reduction and health enhancement programs. *Mindfulness*, 13(1), 123–144. 10.1007/s12671-021-01777-4

Chen, C. (2019). *Professional grief and burnout*. Springer. 10.1007/978-3-319-69892-2_1010-1

Darewych, O. (2019). *Positive arts interventions: Creative tools helping mental health students flourish*. Springer. 10.1007/978-3-030-20583-6_19

El-Osta, A., Sasco, E. R., Barbanti, E., Webber, I., Alaa, A., Karki, M., Bagkeris, E., Asmar, M. L. E., Almadi, M. A., Massoud, F., Alboksmaty, A., & Majeed, A. (2023). Tools for measuring individual self-care capability: A scoping review. *BMC Public Health*, 23(1), 1312. 10.1186/s12889-023-16194-637422637

Fereidooni, G. J., Ghofranipour, F., & Zarei, F. (2024). Interplay of self-care, self-efficacy, and health deviation self-care requisites: A study on type 2 diabetes patients through the lens of Orem's self-care theory. *BMC Primary Care*, 25(1), 48. 10.1186/s12875-024-02276-w38297225

Forrest, L. F., Abdurrahman, M., & Ritsma, A. (2020). Recognizing compassion fatigue, vicarious trauma, and burnout. Springer. 10.1007/978-3-030-45627-6_10

Galante, J., Grabovac, A., Wright, M., Ingram, D. M., Van Dam, N. T., Sanguinetti, J. L., Sparby, T., Van Lutterveld, R., & Sacchet, M. D. (2023). A framework for the Empirical investigation of Mindfulness Meditative Development. *Mindfulness*, 14(5), 1054–1067. 10.1007/s12671-023-02113-8

Haik, J., Brown, S., Liran, A., Visentin, D., Sokolov, A., Zilinsky, I., & Kornhaber, R. (2017). Burnout and compassion fatigue: Prevalence and associations among Israeli burn clinicians. *Neuropsychiatric Disease and Treatment*, 13, 1533–1540. 10.2147/NDT.S13318128670122

Harrop, E., Morgan, F., Longo, M., Semedo, L., Fitzgibbon, J., Pickett, S., Scott, H., Seddon, K., Sivell, S., Nelson, A., & Byrne, A. (2020). The impacts and effectiveness of support for people bereaved through advanced illness: A systematic review and thematic synthesis. *Palliative Medicine*, 34(7), 871–888. 10.1177/026 921632092053332419630

Harrop, E., Scott, H., Sivell, S., Seddon, K., Fitzgibbon, J., Morgan, F., Pickett, S., Byrne, A., Nelson, A., & Longo, M. (2020). Coping and well-being in bereavement: Two core outcomes for evaluating bereavement support in palliative care. *BMC Palliative Care*, 19(1), 29. 10.1186/s12904-020-0532-432164642

Higgins, J. P., Graziano, C., Froerer, C., Placide, R., Tavakoli, F., & Chu, A. (2023). Time management strategies for the new practitioner. *American Journal of Health-System Pharmacy*, 80(8), 483–486. 10.1093/ajhp/zxad00836626278

Hui, L. K., Garnett, A., Oleynikov, C., & Boamah, S. A. (2023). Compassion fatigue in healthcare providers during the COVID-19 pandemic: A scoping review protocol. *BMJ Open*, 13(5), e069843. 10.1136/bmjopen-2022-06984337258070

Hunt, D. F., Bailey, J., Lennox, B., Crofts, M., & Vincent, C. (2021). Enhancing psychological safety in mental health services. *International Journal of Mental Health Systems*, 15(1), 33. *Advance online publication.* 10.1186/s13033-021-00439-133853658

Jahani, L., Abolhassani, S., Babaee, S., & Omranifard, V. (2022). Effects of a compassion-based program on the grief experienced by caregivers of people who have dementia: A randomized controlled clinical trial. *BMC Nursing*, 21(1), 198. 10.1186/s12912-022-00980-535879751

Jiang, X., Topps, A. K., & Suzuki, R. (2021). A systematic review of self-care measures for professionals and trainees. *Training and Education in Professional Psychology*, 15(2), 126–139. 10.1037/tep0000318

Jiménez-Picón, N., Romero-Martín, M., Ponce-Blandón, J. A., Ramirez-Baena, L., Palomo-Lara, J. C., & Gómez-Salgado, J. (2021). The relationship between mindfulness and emotional intelligence as a protective factor for healthcare professionals: Systematic review. *International Journal of Environmental Research and Public Health*, 18(10), 5491. 10.3390/ijerph1810549134065519

Kelly, S. B. C. (2023). Supporting nursing, midwifery and allied health professional teams through restorative clinical supervision. *British Journal of Nursing*. https://www .britishjournalofnursing.com/content/professional/supporting-nursing-midwifery -and-allied-health-professional-teams-through-restorative-clinical-supervision

Li, Y., & Peng, J. (2022). Evaluation of expressive arts therapy on the resilience of university students in COVID-19: A network analysis approach. *International Journal of Environmental Research and Public Health*, 19(13), 7658. 10.3390/ ijerph1913765835805317

Loue, S. (2022). *Transformational learning through cultural humility*. Springer. 10.1007/978-3-031-11381-9_6

Mirfardi, A. (2023). The sociocultural and economic barriers to self-care culture for COVID-19 control in developing societies: The case of Iran. In *Contributions to Economics* (pp. 153–179). 10.1007/978-3-031-27886-0_6

Mirutse, A., Mengistu, Z., & Bizuwork, K. (2023). Prevalence of compassion fatigue, burnout, compassion satisfaction, and associated factors among nurses working in cancer treatment centres in Ethiopia, 2020. *BMC Nursing*, 22(1), 373. 10.1186/ s12912-023-01383-w37817139

Moss, S. J., Wollny, K., Poulin, T. G., Cook, D. J., Stelfox, H. T., Ordons, A. R. D., & Fiest, K. M. (2021). Bereavement interventions to support informal caregivers in the intensive care unit: A systematic review. *BMC Palliative Care*, 20(1), 66. 10.1186/s12904-021-00763-w33980242

Narasimhan, M., Allotey, P., & Hardon, A. (2019). Self-care interventions to advance health and well-being: A conceptual framework to inform normative guidance. *BMJ. British Medical Journal (Clinical Research Ed.)*. 10.1136/bmj.l688

Schachter, S. R., & Holland, J. C. (2013). Loss, grief, and bereavement: Implications for family caregivers and health care professionals of the mentally Ill. In *Caregiving* (pp. 145–160). Springer. 10.1007/978-1-4614-8791-3_8

Silva, V. S. E., Hornby, L., Almost, J., Lotherington, K., Appleby, A., Silva, A. R., Rochon, A., & Dhanani, S. (2020). Burnout and compassion fatigue among organ and tissue donation coordinators: A scoping review. *BMJ Open*, 10(12), e040783. 10.1136/bmjopen-2020-04078333323439

Sist, L., Savadori, S., Grandi, A., Martoni, M., Baiocchi, E., Lombardo, C., & Colombo, L. (2022). Self-care for nurses and midwives: Findings from a scoping review. *Healthcare (Basel)*, 10(12), 2473. 10.3390/healthcare1012247336553999

Smith, J. (2016). *Building and maintaining the therapeutic relationship*. Springer. 10.1007/978-3-319-49460-9_11

Smith, K. (2017). Self-care practices and the professional self. *Journal of Social Work in Disability & Rehabilitation*, 16(3–4), 186–203. 10.1080/1536710X.2017 .137223628876191

Sudeck, G., Thiel, A., & Strohacker, K. (2023). *Physical activity, subjective well-being and mental health*. Springer. 10.1007/978-3-031-03921-8_26

Sweileh, W. M. (2020). Research trends and scientific analysis of publications on burnout and compassion fatigue among healthcare providers. *Journal of Occupational Medicine and Toxicology (London, England)*, 15(1), 23. 10.1186/ s12995-020-00274-z32684943

Vincelette, C., Thivierge-Southidara, M., & Rochefort, C. M. (2019). Conceptual and methodological challenges of studies examining the determinants and outcomes of omitted nursing care: A narrative review of the literature. *International Journal of Nursing Studies*, 100, 103403. 10.1016/j.ijnurstu.2019.10340331629210

Wang, Z., Wang, F., Zhang, S., Liu, C., Feng, Y., & Chen, J. (2023). Effects of mindfulness-based interventions on stress, burnout in nurses: A systematic review and meta-analysis. *Frontiers in Psychiatry*, 14, 1218340. 10.3389/fp-syt.2023.121834037599884

Yamaguchi, A., Akutsu, S., Oshio, A., & Kim, M. S. (2017). Effects of cultural orientation, self-esteem, and collective self-esteem on well-being. *Psychological Studies*, 62(3), 241–249. 10.1007/s12646-017-0413-y

Zhang, M., Murphy, B. L., Cabanilla, A., & Yidi, C. (2021). Physical relaxation for occupational stress in healthcare workers: A systematic review and network meta-analysis of randomized controlled trials. *Journal of Occupational Health*, 63(1), e12243. 10.1002/1348-9585.1224334235817

ADDITIONAL READING

Cox, M. (2014). Racial and ethnic categories, U.S. census. In Cousins, L. (Ed.), *Encyclopedia of Human Services and Diversity* (Vol. 11, pp. 1101–1104). SAGE Publications, Inc., 10.4135/9781483346663.n472

Cox, M. (2020). Creating a Sense of Belonging for Black American Students. In Crosby-Cooper, T. (Ed.), *Implementing Culturally Responsive Practices in Education* (pp. 243–263). IGI Global., 10.4018/978-1-7998-3331-4.ch014

KEY TERMS AND DEFINITIONS

Burnout Prevention: Strategies and interventions to mitigate the physical, emotional, and psychological exhaustion associated with prolonged stress and overwork.

Caregiving: Providing physical, emotional, or practical assistance to individuals who cannot fully care for themselves due to illness, disability, or ageing.

Ethical Responsibilities: Obligations and duties to follow professional codes of conduct and moral principles, ensuring integrity and ethical practice.

Grief Counselling: Professional support and guidance provided to individuals coping with the loss of a loved one, aimed at facilitating healing and adaptation to loss.

Resilience: The ability to adapt and bounce back in adversity, maintaining emotional balance and well-being despite challenging circumstances.

Self-Care: Activities and practices undertaken to promote physical, emotional, and mental well-being, often personalized to an individual's needs and preferences.

Time Management: Organizing and prioritizing tasks and activities to utilize time and resources effectively, maximizing productivity and reducing stress.

Chapter 13
Support Sisters:
Life After COVID-19, Cancer, and Caregiving

Michelle R. Cox
https://orcid.org/0000-0002-2083-3582
Azusa Pacific University, USA

ABSTRACT

Those who lost loved ones to illness other than COVID-19 during the pandemic may have experienced feelings of confusion, isolation, and loneliness. Losing a spouse during the COVID-19 pandemic was a phenomenon. As society feared the coronavirus, some individuals fought deadly cancer diseases. Victims of cancer may not have received the proper and due medical care during the pandemic due to limited hospital beds, priority of care given to COVID-19 patients, or there may have been reduced medical staff. The author shares her personal story about her connection to group of women who met each other after the loss of their husbands to cancer during the COVID-19 pandemic. This chapter reviews the benefits of creating support groups after the COVID-19 pandemic, and counseling implications of how grief support counseling groups are proven to be compassionate, encouraging, resourceful, comforting, and life changing.

INTRODUCTION

From 2019 to 2021, the COVID-19 pandemic disrupted the entire world with an infection running rampant causing not only alarm and fear, but frustration with those who were fighting terminal illnesses. Some patients and their families had to compete with COVID-19 patients to obtain treatment or medical visits. Not only were there over 7 million deaths related to the deadly virus (Worldometer, 2024),

DOI: 10.4018/979-8-3693-1375-6.ch013

Copyright © 2024, IGI Global. Copying or distributing in print or electronic forms without written permission of IGI Global is prohibited.

but many patients also died of cancer during the COVID-19 pandemic. In fact, in 2020 over 10 million people died of cancer globally, according to the World Health Organization (WHO, 2022). My husband, Sammy, was diagnosed with pancreatic cancer in July 2020. It was the worst time to receive a cancer diagnosis. Due to COVID-19 restrictions on access to health services, including visits to the family doctor, cancer screening tests and visits to specialists, cancer patients were diagnosed at a more advanced stage during the pandemic (Rucinska & Nawrocki, 2022). My husband was a healthy man. He grew produce to avoid pesticides and exercised regularly, so we were in disbelief after receiving the cancer diagnosis, and in the middle of a worldwide pandemic.

I became the caregiver to my husband for the following 4 months after receiving his diagnosis. I felt as if I was in a whirlwind and didn't have the opportunity to process the cancer diagnosis. During those four months, we experienced challenges of receiving treatment for my husband due to competing attention with COVID-19 infected patients. After four months, my husband died from pancreatic cancer. The lack of attention given to non-COVID-19 infected patients added to my grief.

The purpose of this chapter is to share details of my own personal experience of loss during the COVID-19 pandemic while bringing awareness to the challenges experienced by caregivers, and share the value of grief support counseling groups in healing. Counseling implications to address issues experienced by caregiving clients who lost their loved ones to terminal illness during the COVID-19 pandemic are also presented.

THE COVID-19 PANDEMIC

Receiving a diagnosis of cancer during, or prior to, the COVID-19 pandemic required support not only from an experienced medical team, but also family members, particularly those who were caregivers. Hiring professional caregivers may not have been financially feasible for families, so was typical that caregivers were family members such as spouses or children.

Family physical presence is necessary to mitigate severe harms of isolation for patients who are suffering from terminal illnesses. However, COVID-19 caused a panic that changed how healthcare was provided which likely led to emotional harm of not just the patients, but also their family and caregivers. Hospital patients were isolated to protect them from infection by separating infectious people from uninfected people (Voo et al., 2020), but there were consequences to these restrictions. Caregiving was particularly challenging for those of us who were spouses, and who had to postpone grief of our significant loved ones as we cared for them through

Support Sisters

end-of-life without the same level of support that would have been received prior to or after the COVID-19 pandemic.

Caregiving Challenges

Caregivers, such as adult children, may have had no other option but to leave their personal homes and move in with terminally ill family members to provide necessary care day and night, risking possible COVID-19 exposure. Caregivers not only provided physical and emotional support for their loved ones, but they also experience their own change of life events as they watch their loved ones suffer. A diagnosis of a terminal illness of a loved one likely involves awareness of mortality, but it also elicits a need for empathy for the caregiver too, particularly if the caregiver is the spouse.

Hospital restrictions during the COVID-19 pandemic negatively impacted physical support, preventing patients from being accompanied by family members for treatments and hospital visitations. As a caregiver to my husband who was fighting a terminal illness during the COVID-19 pandemic, I had to quickly prepare for unexpected hospitalizations, and navigate medical care over the phone because restrictions wouldn't allow me to escort my husband, Sammy, to medical or hospital visits. One lesson learned was ensuring Sammy had his cell phone charger with him whenever he was admitted to the hospital because often hospital room phones were unreliable. Leaving messages for doctors or nurses to return phone calls for medical updates was formidable because often phone calls were not returned.

Healthcare Communication Decline

Communication issues were common at the height of the pandemic (Plunkett, 2021). We received inaccurate or untimely information which compounded my anxiety. Discharge instructions were sometimes lost in all of the chaos of the pandemic and I was even left without information provided by the hospital staff on how to care for my husband at home after he was discharged. Not receiving propre discharge information even led to a return to urgent care during the pandemic because I couldn't reach the discharge nurse of doctor.

Counseling Implications

The lives of caregivers are disrupted to care for a terminally ill loved family member. The professional work of some caregivers may have been placed on hold to support dying family members. Some caregivers may leave their own homes and moved in loved ones who needed round-the-clock care.

Support Sisters

There is no formal training for caregiving at home, and in most cases, caregivers did not know what to expect and are not prepared for the work. When caregivers are not allowed to accompany loved ones to their medical appointments are during hospital stays, the channel of communication is minimal if not non-existent. Hospital service managers and clinicians should be encouraged to make informed and optional exemptions when implementing isolation rules and visiting protocols for terminally ill patients and their families.

Miscommunication from physicians, nurses, social workers, and families heightened frustration and the stress of not seeing hospitalized loved ones during the pandemic (Plunkett et al., 2021). Proving critical care discharge instructions were sometimes forgotten by hospital staff (Horstman et al., 2017), could have exacerbated health issues and increased caregiver burden. Hospital social workers work within hospital settings to ensure patients and their families are supported, and have access to medical information than patient families. Hospital social workers and palliative care workers can equip caregivers with resources to support them in caregiving duties such as cleaning, home health care, transportation to medical visits, and preparation for end-of-life, and to reduce the caregiving burden. Counselors should encourage caregiving clients to seek out hospital social workers for assistance in response to hospital mishaps. Caring for a loved one can be burdensome to caregivers, particularly if there is a lack of experience in caregiving and without resources or instruction.

COVID-19 increased anxiety and reduced contact to healthcare providers, support systems, and sometimes family, which necessitate that oncology nurses serve as skilled communicators to help elicit patient's values and preferences for cancer care (Rosa et al., 2021). There is not only a need of information regarding primary care tasks; but caregivers should receive methods of reducing caregiver burdens and stressors, which can assist them in gaining control (Mathews, 2018). Additionally, caregivers also need time away from caregiving duties, so they should be encouraged to take breaks from caregiving at home, such as sleeping while the terminally ill patient sleeps, taking regular walks, or even reaching out to other family members or friends to relieve them on a regular basis.

GRIEF SUPPORT

As a counselor educator of more than 20 years, I taught group counseling skills and facilitated counseling groups, but the best lesson I have learned about support groups is from personal experience adjusting to life after the loss of my husband of almost 25 years.

Support Sisters

After Sammy died from pancreatic cancer during the COVID-19 pandemic, I felt lost, confused, sad, lonely, and discouraged. It was unexpected and he succumbed to the disease quickly, so I didn't have time to consider life without him. The palliative care team offered me support with the administration of medications as well as explanation of treatment.

Palliative Care

Sammy received treatment from a cancer treatment center, and we were connected to a palliative care team which provided support for pain management to patients. Throughout the struggles of caring for my husband during a worldwide pandemic, I reached out to the palliative care team often. The palliative care team provided me with support I needed to care for Sammy that I would not have otherwise received from other healthcare practitioners. Sammy died in the emergency room at a nearby hospital because the cancer treatment center was not local. When the palliative care team learned of his death, the entire team contacted me by phone through a video call while I was still at the hospital. I was comforted as they shared memories they had of my husband.

One member of the palliative care team continued to follow up with me for weeks after the death of my husband. She also provided me with an invitation to attend a grief support counseling group, which I considered.

Counseling Implications

It's common for widows and widowers to have cognitive processes that are utilized to reconstruct their identities after losing a spouse, which include disbelief, confusion, and disorientation. Many of these cognitive processes are linked to emotional processes such as anger, confusion, and depression (Jones et al., 2019). After the death of a spouse, a widow or widower may try to make sense of the loss, but it is particularly challenging for those who couldn't access support due to the COVID-19 pandemic.

The palliative care team plays an important role in the grief counseling process of loss to caregivers. Significant others to the deceased may feel the support from the palliative care team as more valuable than that from the grief counseling group (Näppä & Björkman-Randström, 2020). Access to palliative care teams became more significant during the COVID-19 pandemic (Rosa et al., 2021). Palliative care teams also prepare caregivers and family members for end-of-life, including hospice. Caregivers should be encouraged to reach out to the palliative care team for information about end-of-life and what should be expected throughout the process of end-of-life, as well as support after the death of the loved one.

Support Sisters

According to Elisabeth Kübler-Ross (1997) (a frontier on the topic of death and dying), the family's needs will change from the onset of the illness and continue in many forms until long after the death of the loved on occurs. The dying patient's problems come to an end, but the family's problems continue even after death. After the death of a spouse, the widow or widower must find new meaning to life with a significant and heart wrenching absence of the deceased through grief support.

COUNSELING AND THERAPY DURING BEREAVEMENT

I experienced challenges focusing on daily tasks because my thoughts were often interrupted with how he died in the hospital alone due to the COVID-19 hospital restrictions. I had to plan the memorial which was also impacted by COVID-19 restrictions. We were limited on the number of people who could attend the service. Some individuals were not given the option to hold a memorial, so I was grateful for to memorialize my husband, even if COVID-19 restricted. I felt as if I was experiencing post-traumatic stress disorder (PTSD) on top of grief during bereavement. I wasn't able to sleep and I kept thinking about my husband dying in the emergency room alone due to COVID-19 restrictions, and more hospital mishaps, which kept me from being with him. Sammy died in the hospital without loved ones at his bedside, and the thoughts were overwhelming. I became accustomed to caregiving around the clock and transitioned from caregiving to bereavement without an opportunity to process grief.

I experienced time differently after the death of my husband. Time felt like it was moving slow around me but the world appeared to move at a faster pace. Research shows present focus, blurring weekdays and weekdays together, and uncertainty about the future were common experiences that were reported during and after the COVID-19 pandemic (Holman et al., 2023), which was comforting for me because it confirmed the time distortion was not my imagination.

I kept thinking about receiving my husband's cancer diagnosis, and that I had to quickly shift from being a counselor educator to a caregiver. I created a routine of getting up in the middle of the night to give my husband pain medications, driving him to his chemotherapy treatments, nagging him about eating, educating myself about natural-remedies to fight cancer, and slept an average of 3 hours each night to give my husband pain medications around the clock. I had to do it all while working full-time as a college professor until I finally took a leave of absence. I was overwhelmed and didn't have the opportunity to prepare for my husband's end-of-life. When Sammy died, I had to transition from caregiver to bereaved spouse, and had to plan the memorial. Not until after the service ended, did I begin to process my grief. I didn't think I could survive the amount of emotional pain that I suffered.

Support Sisters

After the memorial service for my husband, I quickly transitioned back to being a counselor educator and knew I needed support so that I could emotionally support my adult children through their grief. I contacted my medical provider and requested therapy. Due to the COVID-19 restrictions, counseling was only offered by phone or video otherwise known as telemental health.

I was connected with a therapist named Vanessa who met with me weekly. When we initially met, she disclosed that I was her first client who grieved the loss of a spouse from cancer and I disclosed I was a counselor educator. Vanessa applied counseling skills and approaches within appropriate counseling frameworks. Our counseling sessions lasted for several months and looked forward to the mental space. I didn't need my therapist physically in the room with me, and I appreciated the convenience of the phone calls.

Although I found my individual therapy sessions helpful in processing my grief, I recognized and valued the need of support from others who were going through similar experiences. I had friends and family members who were widows, but no one else could relate to my experience of watching my husband suffer from cancer during the COVID-19 pandemic. I knew I needed support from various sources.

Counseling Implications

Grieving the loss of a family member, particularly a spouse, is a significant transition, but the effects of losing a spouse to a terminal disease during the COVID-19 pandemic can impact mental health so counseling professionals should assessed clients to determine if they suffer from psychological distress.

It has been reported that over 65% of a research sample 6 months into the COVID-19 pandemic experienced time speeding up or slowing down. During the first 6 months of the COVID-19 pandemic, distortions in time, otherwise known as Temporal Disintegration (TD), is very common and found to be associated with pre-pandemic mental health, lifetime stress and trauma exposure, and pandemic-related media exposure and stressors (Holman et al., 2023). TD may reflect the degree to which the pandemic disrupted daily routines, and is likely associated with poor mental health sequelae during the pandemic. Future research should examine whether TD is prospectively associated with mental health status in the context of coping with collective trauma. Knowing who is most vulnerable to experiencing TD may provide guidance for the allocation of mental health resources (Holman et al., 2023). Through counseling, TD may be identified as impacting clients' ability to manage time if it is distorted due to trauma from loss during the COVID-19 pandemic.

Trauma

Suffering the loss of a loved one has significant impact on the life of the survived spouse or significant other. Research has revealed strong positive links between loss and both anxiety and depressive symptoms, which is stronger for women, but may be buffered by the marital relationship. This is not to suggest that male surviving spouses have less meaningful relationships with the deceased. One possible explanation could relate to financial dependency on the loss of a husband of male significant other.

The association between loss and anxiety has been found to be attenuated at higher levels for the meaning in life for those who experienced loss and are not married compared to low levels of meaning and for those who are married individuals. Marriage also buffers the impact of loss on depressive symptoms. Cumulative pandemic-related loss is associated with anxiety and depressive symptoms. Additionally, it is suggested COVID-19 pandemic losses may have taken on more complicated mental health trajectories due to their repetitive, persistent, and highly emotional nature, such as the inability to say goodbye before the death of a loved one (Gold et al., 2023). These experiences could lead to other disorders such as post-traumatic stress disorder (PTSD).

According to the American Psychological Association (APA, 2023), post-traumatic stress disorder (PTSD) may develop in some people after extremely traumatic events such as a natural disaster and they relive the trauma through painful recollections that sometimes lead to experiencing physiological symptoms such as an exaggerated startle response, disturbed sleep, difficulty in concentrating or remembering, and guilt about surviving the trauma.

Complicated grief that can arise from the dysfunctional mourning process of the bereaved family members and can predict PTSD (Choi et al., 2023). Clinicians working with clients who suffered loss of a loved one to terminal illness should consider if the client is a good candidate for grief counseling or group counseling and should assess if other mental health issues such as PTSD warrant alternative treatments. If appropriate, connecting individuals who suffer from grief with individuals who experienced similar losses may be beneficial.

Types of Groups

Counseling professionals should determine which type of counseling is best for clients who suffer from grief. According to Worden (2008), grief counseling involves helping people facilitate uncomplicated or normal grief to adaptation to normal tasks of mourning loss in a reasonable time. Group therapy involves specialized techniques used to help people who suffer from complicated or abnormal grief.

Support Sisters

Groups may not be appropriate for everyone, and individuals are reluctant to join a group could disrupt the group if forced to join (Jacobs et al., 2016). However, in some cases, particularly when individuals who suffer loss can support one another, support groups can be beneficial.

According to the Association of Specialists in Group Work (ASGW), which is a national professional association that empowers professional clinicians with knowledge, skills, and resources in group work, there are four types of groups: task, psychoeducational, counseling, and therapy (ASGW, 2024). Task groups are assembled to accomplish a group task, psychoeducational groups promote growth and development, counseling groups alleviate personal and interpersonal problems or life transitions, and therapy groups address significant and persistent patterns of behavior (ASGW, 2024).

Bereaved family caregivers are likely overwhelmed with bereavement-related tasks, such as managing finances, and creating memorials, so there is a need for interventions to designed to reach a large body of individuals who can meet to support each other (Rolbiecki et al., 2020).

The function of a grief support counseling group is to share similar experiences with those who are also grieving. Members of groups gain input from others and learn more from listening than talking (Jacobs et al., 2016). Group members must transition from the experience of what they might consider normalcy with their loved ones, caregiving, and then grief. The loss of a spouse or partner has been shown to be significantly negatively correlated with having meaning in life (Näppä & Björkman-Randström, 2020). Social support, interpersonal learning and attachment, and meaning-making of loss are processes likely to impact grief support counseling group outcomes (Rice, 2015). Attending both individual grief counseling and grief support group counseling may also be beneficial to support clients who are grieving.

Distance delivered grief support groups should be considered for bereaved families and compares favorably to face-to-face groups (Supiano et al., 2021). Widows and widowers may benefit from grief particularly for those who are not ready for in-person meetings.

GRIEF SUPPORT COUNSELING GROUPS

During COVID-19 pandemic, some people were not comfortable with possible exposure to the COVID-19 infection. I was more comfortable meeting with a support group virtually, but I wasn't sure how effective a virtual grief support counseling group would be, but I was hopeful the group would provide me with the support I needed. I looked forward to other group members understanding my experience.

On the first night of the grief support counseling group, I noticed the group facilitator seemed younger than the rest of the group, and I wondered how much experience she had with grief. I couldn't imagine that she understood what I had experienced, but I was willing to give her a chance. The group facilitator introduced herself and shared her background. She admitted this was her first time leading an adult group, as her background was in supporting grieving children. She had a kind disposition during the first meeting, and I appreciated that she was structured. She provided each of us with curriculum which included a book and journal which was mailed to each of us in advance, and then she presented the rules of the group.

I expected a heterogenous group of both men and women, likely elderly, but hoping for middle aged people to have membership in the group. However, surprisingly, all of the group members were women ranging in age from the 30s to the 70s. The group was not only diverse in age, but also in culture. I am an advocate of diversity because it provides opportunities to learn about the diversity of worldviews. Our racial composition was diverse because Laura and Crystal were Latinas, Carol was White, and I was the Black woman in our group. The diversity of our group contributed to understanding how people of diverse populations can share common experiences regardless of race, ethnicity, culture, or age.

Counseling Implications

Virtual Groups

According to Holmgren (2023), online peer support in grief is a means of seeking support in its own right and has proven to be beneficial. The COVID-19 pandemic resulted in grief support counseling meetings held virtually. It wasn't popular to hold counseling meetings online at that time, but COVID-19 changed many common practices as people were forced to find alternative ways to communicate without exposure to the deadly virus. COVID-19 disrupted and complicated grief processes. It also challenged practices around supporting the bereaved (West et al., 2023). Grief support of any sort is helpful, but visually seeing the expressions of group members offer the ability to connect emotionally for family members as well as caregivers who were separated from their loved ones who were hospitalized during the COVID-19 pandemic. However, some individuals may prefer virtual counseling due to convenience and may be more comfortable with online meetings, which became more popular during the COVID-19 pandemic.

Support Sisters

Group Formats

There are several formats of grief counseling support groups which include (but are not limited to) face-to face groups, virtual groups, and online groups. Recruitment efforts should include talking with existing clients about their interest in face-to-face, online, or virtual support groups, as well as other resources that could further meet their needs. Some clients may prefer an emotional distance to processing their grief, or may have transportation issues; so virtual platforms might be more accessible to grief support counseling groups. Additionally, partnering with other agencies might prove beneficial due to a limited amount of online grief support services (Gibson et al., 2020). Partnering with other agencies also can increase the size of groups due to low participation rates, and can also provide a variety of meeting time options.

Best Practices of Virtual Groups

Creating affective grief support counseling groups virtually can be challenging and few studies currently exist on best practices in the facilitation of them. It's important to identify the type of group, the modalities through which they are offered, and how they relate to community needs. Specialists in group work should concisely state in writing the purpose and goals of the group (ASGW, 2024).

Online support groups may meet synchronously (meeting through a virtual platform in real time) even through discussion forums. Synchronous interaction allows participants to see each other through video as opposed to communication through threaded discussions which can occur any time of convenience.

Through Asynchronous online support communities, group members could support multiple conversation threads efficiently (Hartig & Viola, 2016). Conversations through discussion threads may provide convenience as members support one another through detailed responses.

Cultural Factors

It's important for counseling group facilitators to understand the cultural needs of the group members. While the delivery of online services differs contextually from face-to-face services, respect for cultural differences is still applicable in virtual counseling groups to avoid imposing cultural biases. According to ASGW (2024), group specialists are expected to promote socially and culturally diverse populations recognizing intersecting identity dimensions such as race, class, gender, sexuality, ability, and age, which support group facilitators role as change agents. They must also maintain awareness and sensitivity regarding both cultural and power differentiated meanings of confidentiality and privacy.

Group facilitators respect differing views towards disclosure of information, while striving for a shared understanding to which the group members can assent. Pre-screening participants can assist the facilitator in assessing each client's comfort with using tech services, familiarity with software, and how to navigate potential equipment challenges (Gibson et al., 2020), as well as identify cultural factors such as age and gender.

Ethical Considerations

It is important to inform group members of rules and parameters of the group. Setting group rules and expectations for groups have always been a common practice, but communicating rules and expectations with groups facilitated online, is extremely important.

When using online platforms of communication for grief counseling support groups, there is always the possibility of a confidentiality breach, and participants should be informed of these potential risks. Authorizations for information disclosure and consents for treatment or digital services should be obtained from participants.

Facilitators should plan for technology failures by providing alternate ways of making contact. (Gibson et al., 2020). Failing technology is inevitable so a good leader prepares the group in the beginning stages. For example, if a member loses internet connection during a meeting, the member should know to send a text message to the leader. The leader should also be prepared to receive messages during the group and inform group members of another member's loss of connection. It's also important to plan protocols for actions in cases of imminent crises, such as when a participant requires a private meeting off-line or if there is an issue of suicide risk (Gibson et al., 2020). Facilitators should provide clear guidance participants about these issues immediately at the onset of the group. Considerations include but are not limited to highlighting the importance of maintaining confidentiality in the virtual environment in which the group members are participating in the group process as well as the individual physical environments of origin, and ensuring that group members understand the associated limitations of confidentiality (ASGW, 2024).

Benefits of Virtual Groups

During the COVID-19 pandemic, meeting in person was not always available. Group members may not have felt comfortable in a blended group, or they may the time grief counseling process was offered may have been inconvenient (Näppä & Björkman-Randström, 2020). Online grief support counseling groups can be conveniently offered throughout the evenings or even on weekend, providing more accessibility, and proved to be impactful for grief support groups (Rice, 2015). In

Support Sisters

fact, research suggests the primary benefits of informal peer support were a shared understanding of grief, close companionship, and emotional strength, which was evident with the surviving sister's club which was formed after the 9-1-1 attack and proved to be affective for those wives (Richardson, 2016). Widows and widowers may express gratitude to communicate with others who experience the same type of loss and to understand how each other coped from it (Holmgren, 2023).

Discussions about death are not usually well received except amongst those who want to hear and share stories to share about the deceased. Online participants are more likely than face-to-face support community members to engage in sharing, especially when the subject is sensitive (Hartig & Viola, 2016). Online grief counseling support groups may prove to be beneficial for group members to share experiences such as how they supported their children after loss of a parent.

GRIEF SUPPORT COUNSELING GROUP PROCESSES

Although we were diverse in age and culture, members of my grief support counseling group shared a common enemy...Cancer. More specifically, we lost our significant others to cancer during the COVID-19 pandemic, which made the experience even more traumatic because we didn't have the physical support from family and friends, and weren't able to have arrange typical memorial services due to COVID-19 restrictions.

During the first session, the facilitator asked us about the event which led to the cancer diagnosis. In the four months that my husband suffered from the agony from cancer, I don't think anyone visited us except our adult children. The other members of the group shared similar experiences, and it was comforting that we could identify with each other's experiences. Our grief support counseling group shared how extended family and friends didn't see us up all night or rushing to emergency. They didn't observe mishaps from health care professionals or giving our loved one's pain medications around the clock. They didn't witness our loved ones growing weak and unable to walk or stand on their own because the cancer was killing them from the inside. People didn't see our pain, frustration, and fight for our spouses' lives. Our friends and family couldn't fully understand our experiences, and we shared that some family members expressed that we made them feel guilty when we shared how we felt about it. We were able to voice our frustration about the experiences with one another, which brought us some comfort knowing we weren't alone in these experiences.

During the following session, we were asked to share photos of our husbands while describing them. We each took a turn showing pictures of our husbands on the video call and told stories behind the photos. As someone who doesn't cry much in front of others, I found tears swelling in my eyes as I prepared to talk about Sammy. Sammy was my neighbor and I met him soon after he moved into the home directly across the street from mine. He was 11 years older than me, wise, patient, supportive, and a loving husband and father. I disclosed how I was attracted to him because of his walk, his gaze at me, and his self-confidence. Sammy and I were married for almost 25 years and he was my best friend. We enjoyed each other's company and people described us as the power couple. Sammy was also health conscientious, so we worked out gardened daily together. I shared that Sammy started experiencing pain in his gut for about three months before he saw a doctor about it. He changed his diet and even began taking natural herbs to settle his stomach. It was a shock to both of us when we received his diagnosis of pancreatic cancer in the midst of the COVID-19 pandemic, and he died 4 months after receiving the diagnosis. Pancreatic cancer causes a lot of pain, so I had to constantly administer opioid pain medications for 3 months. It is also a fast-spreading cancer, and we weren't prepared for him to succumb to the disease so quickly.

Laura, who was in her forties, lost her significant other, Tony, who she met 8 years prior to his death. Tony was 9 years younger than Laura and he was her lover and best friend. She met Tony through his sister and they planned to get married. However, Laura was separated from her husband and she never married Tony because her husband challenged the divorce. Her divorce wasn't finalized until after Tony's death, but Laura said Tony loved her as if they were married, so we always referenced Tony as her husband. She described him as positive and motivated people of all ages, particularly those who were suffering from cancer. Tony began having pain in his testicles and then pain in his back. He was diagnosed with stage four testicular cancer which later turned in to choriocarcinoma which is another fast-growing cancer which spread to Tony's lungs and brain. He was later placed in a chemically induced coma. Tony always made her laugh and increased her self-esteem.

Carol was in her seventies and described her husband Jerry as a man with a positive attitude, and was affectionately known as the "energizer bunny". The two of them traveled and spent time with children and grandchildren. She met him through a friend, and Jerry predicted they would be married even before he proposed to Carol. Jerry always made Carol feel important and he was comforting to Carol even during the time of his illness. The last 13 years of his life he suffered with multiple myeloma, which is a relatively rare cancer in which the white blood cells accumulate in bone marrow. Jerry had the cancer in his back and arms, and lost the ability to walk and talk. He went through remission several times after several forms of treatment, before he passed away. Carol shared she misses his hugs and the 9 kisses he gave her each day.

Support Sisters

Crystal was in her thirties and described her husband, Travis, as a leader and charismatic because others would gravitate to him. She also described him as her walking encyclopedia. She met Travis through her brother, and they attended college together. They shared a love for Disneyland, and Crystal described Travis as her best friend. Travis was about 7 years older than Crystal, and they were together for 12 years. Travis was diagnosed with esophageal cancer and suffered the disease for four years. He choked on his food a lot and experienced acid reflux for many years. Esophageal cancer is the 6th most common cause of cancer death (Mayo Clinic, 2022). The cancer spread to other parts of his body before he died. They had a daughter soon before he died.

We each cried as we reflected on our loved ones but we weren't uncomfortable with being vulnerable with each other as we shed tears. In fact, we understood each other's grief and supported each other with words of empathy and comfort. We all lost our husbands in the same month with the exception of Laura who lost Tony almost a year prior. We learned a lot from Laura's experiences such as first anniversary of Tony's death and witnessed how it impacted her grief. She prepared the rest of us for what we might experience during those significant upcoming anniversaries. Seeing how Laura survived a year of loss without Tony provided us with some level of hope.

One of the ladies shared something with the group that was thought provoking about our husbands. She said we lived the rest of "their" lives together. I pondered that statement. She was right. We spent the rest of Sammy's life together, but weren't going to spend the rest of "my" life together. The women in the grief support counseling group offered me comfort and we understood each other's pain more than anyone else could. Crystal often made us laugh through our sessions and also through our times together after our grief support counseling group concluded. Laughter seemed to help ease the pain for us. During our grief support counseling group, we laughed often as we shared funny stories about our deceased spouses.

I looked forward to our virtual meetings every Wednesday night. We were expected to complete the weekly reading and journaling prior to the following meeting. The book provided opportunity to reflect on an experience and allowed for journaling our feelings which I found helpful. I felt that the ladies were the only people who truly comprehended my pain of losing my best friend. Our grief was different from normal grief because it was complicated by reactions to a worldwide pandemic, and we didn't have the same access to medical care for our husbands as compared to those who received treatment prior to the COVID-19 pandemic. Some of us were not able to be by their side due to COVID-19 restrictions during treatments. We had to process the diagnosis while getting our husbands to their treatments, admitting them into the hospital for various medical emergencies, being caregivers at home, which seemed like a crash course on around the clock nursing. After the death of our husbands, we experienced additional grief and mourning when we hadn't completely processed the news of the terminal illness. We witnessed the trauma of grief complicated, particularly during a world pandemic.

Counseling Implications

Prior to establishing a grief support counseling group, facilitators should consider whether the group will time limited or homogeneous. They should also determine expectations such as the frequency of meetings, and if the online group will be offered as open versus closed groups (Gibson et al., 2020).

Shared Experience

In the case of grief support counseling groups, members should be selected based on a similar experience which may create empathy and cohesion of the group. Newcomers to grief support counseling groups have been found to describe: (1) the event of the loss; (2) their relationship with the deceased; (3) stories of the loss in which they share their uncontrollable emotional and physical states by emphasizing the unusual circumstances of their loss; and (4) depth of their connection with the deceased which provide an account for their grief (Varga & Paulus, 2014). Discussing these shared experiences may lead to validation of what they may have previously felt was abnormal to grief.

Use of Photos

Making meaning of one's caregiving and bereavement experiences can reduce post death distress, which can ultimately lead to more adaptive coping during bereavement, and can potentially reduce risk for complicated grief. Clinicians should work with bereaved caregiving clients in developing and sharing stories about their experiences while caregiving and during bereavement to make meaning of the experience. Using photos to help facilitate the sharing of stories in a safe and supportive group can not only foster meaning making, but can also increase social support (Rolbiecki et al., 2020). Photos of the deceased can be shared by the clients as they discuss the event of the photo and can support them in processing the loss. Photos can also be presented to the clients, if shared with the facilitator, as a memorial keepsake as the groups ends.

Support Sisters

Vulnerability

It's common for newcomers to grief support counseling groups to break the ice by discussing the event of the loss (Varga & Paulus, 2014). Grief support counseling groups may contribute to the development of a better understanding of each group members self-image and provides opportunities for support group members to process the stories of the death and make sense of them (Näppä & Björkman-Randström, 2020). Feelings of loneliness and isolation are common, and many times, the bereaved struggle with these feelings (Näppä & Björkman-Randström, 2020).

Grief support counseling groups give group members the tools to accept the loss they had suffered and recognize that life must go on (Näppä & Björkman-Randström, 2020), and require some level of vulnerability which can be accesses through sharing of the emotional and physical state of each member (Varga & Paulus, 2014). Members of grief support counseling groups benefit from opportunities to give, not just receive, assistance in the form of support, understanding, comfort, and suggestions about how to go on in life (Näppä & Björkman-Randström, 2020; Richardson, 2016). Through sharing of common experiences, and describing the event as well as their spouses, group members provide as well as receive support from one another.

Young widows experience unique challenges of losing social identity, making connections with few young people who understand what they are going through (Taylor & Robinson, 2016). Counselors working with young widows and widowers should provide empathy around this challenging experience. Humor is found to be an important coping strategy to allow young widows and widowers to laugh during trying times, even if it is about their deceased spouse (Taylor & Robinson, 2016).

BONDING THROUGH DEPTH OF CONNECTION

Discussing our unique experiences about caregiving and the death of our husbands during the COVID-19 pandemic was comforting. Eventually, we shared our phone information and I created a text group for us to communicate with each other outside of our group sessions. This created opportunities for each of us to support each other throughout the weeks.

During our grief support counseling group sessions, our facilitator asked us if we wouldn't mind merging with another group that was much smaller and heterogeneous. Because our group began to emotionally connect with one another, we didn't feel comfortable disrupting that process so we declined the request. Our bond began to develop and we looked forward to sharing and gaining comfort from one another, and we didn't allow anything to disrupt it.

Our support group ended after 8 weeks. The facilitator provided each of us with a sentimental gift engraved with photos of our husbands. Even after the support group ended, we continued to meet informally and virtually each week. We continued to share similar feelings of sadness, regrets, and loneliness every week in a video call. We even contacted our facilitator occasionally with updates on how we were progressing together.

The ladies and I texted each other through the weeks about shared of visitations from our husband that we felt we could only share with each other. We knew people outside of our group wouldn't understand the encounters that we experienced, and may have even thought we were crazy. But we understood the love that was manifested in the spirit of our loved ones. For example, I felt Sammy's presence of energy holding me in our bed one night, but I wasn't asleep. I also noticed his electric blanket automatically turning on, a couple of weeks after he passed away. I never used the electric blanket and it was where he left it. But one day, the light on the electric blanket control switch turned on. It was very strange because the blanket hadn't been used in months and wasn't even connected to the blanket. I recognize Sammy's sense of humor that day. He would have been the only one who could have switched it on to let me know he was there in spirit. I also found some comfort wearing his clothing to bed, hoping that I could smell his scent. One morning I woke up in his t-shirt and went to the bathroom sink to wash my face. After splashing the water on my face, a wet spot appeared on the shirt in the shape of a heart. I was so impressed that I took a picture in the mirror and shared it with my grief support counseling group. Most people would explain those stories as coincidences, but the ladies understood them as reminders that Sammy still loved me. Laura was thinking about Tony one day and gazed at a cloud formation in the form of a heart in the sky. She knew without a doubt that it was a romantic message of love in the sky from Tony and we all agreed. Crystal heard a song playing in her home which was a favorite of Travis's but the music began to play son its own. She also sensed it was Travis communicating to her to make her laugh. We felt comfortable sharing details of these encounters with each other.

Counseling Implications

Small grief support counseling groups can lead to intimacy and cohesiveness and promote mutual aid and support (Näppä & Björkman-Randström, 2020; Richardson, 2016). Groups may find comfort in continued communications even after the group ends. The role of social support in coping with stressors including grief, and the potential communication patterns that can assist in coping with the loss of a loved one, and allows widows to move at her own pace without judgment can make their experiences less traumatic (Huisman & Lemke, 2022).

Support Sisters

Encounters

After-Death-Communications (ADCs) are perceived as spontaneous contacts with living individuals by the deceased and are generally experienced as meaningful in a positive way. ADCs are associated with a reduction in fear of death, belief in life after death and that the deceased could communicate with the living, and increased reported spirituality (Penberthy et al., 2023). Whether or not group members are religious, they may find comfort in sharing experiences that bring them comfort knowing their loved ones are at peace and want them to be at peace as well.

ADJUSTMENTS TO LIFE AFTER THE DECEASED

We realized that family and friends did their best to support us, but we developed a unique bond from the loss of our loved ones during the COVID-19 pandemic that our family and friends couldn't understand. We continued regularly meet virtually to check on each other and discuss our walks through life without our significant others. We called or texted one another when we needed additional support. My support sisters and I shared how new experiences without our husbands.

Financial Concerns

I had a career as a professor and didn't have much time to research how I would financially maintain my household during Sammy's illness. I assumed his retirement and social security benefits would not be an issue. However, after his death, I quickly learned I was not old enough to receive his social security benefits. This was a surprise to me and I had to identify solutions to my financial predicament. I investigated my late husband's retirement which was not enough to make up the difference in my sole income and household expenses. My faith sustained me and I believe God covered me and my children financially, where Sammy no longer could.

Self-Challenges

The average age of a widow is 59, and at the age of 54 years old, I was even younger than the average widow. I considered myself a young widow and I spent most of my adult life married to my husband and we spend most of our time together. Sammy and enjoyed dining out, and restaurants were beginning to return to dining service in 2021. The thought of dining alone never really crossed my mind before Sammy died. I realized I had never dined alone in a restaurant. Sammy and I regularly had dinner at a Chinese French Bistro not far from our home. We dined there

Support Sisters

on a regular basis because his business office was located in the same building, and occasionally when I worked in the office with him, we would dine there. I decided to make reservations to dine there alone, after Crystal (who was in her 30's) shared how she dined alone on her wedding anniversary after her husband's death. She described how she dressed up for dinner as if she was going out with her husband, so I felt inspired and challenged to dine out alone.

As I entered low-lit restaurant, I noticed all of the couples dining together, but I expected it. The owner greeted me, and looked around for Sammy because she was accustomed to him accompanying me. Her eyes teared up and she offered her condolences after I told her Sammy passed away, and she quickly asked to take my order as if to shift away from the feelings of sadness. I text my grief support sisters while waiting for my dinner. Many encouraging words were text back as if they all were rooting for me. I also felt Sammy's encouragement in Spirit. The owner and my server went out of their way to make sure I received special attention. I didn't feel like I was dining alone and I felt a sense of accomplishment after dinner while walking to my car. I had to learn to live without Sammy.

We called ourselves "support sisters" because we grew to love each other as if we were sisters. My support sisters and I continued to lean on one another whenever we were overcome with sadness. We encouraged each other on Valentine's Day, our birthdays, our husbands' birthdays, and anniversaries through the group text by exchanging graphics and words of encouragement. If one of us needed someone to talk to, we dropped everything to respond. It was comforting to know that we could lean on one another, but most importantly, we understood each other's pain and experience.

A few months after our grief support counseling group ended, my support sisters and I decided to meet each other in person, so we planned a trip to San Diego. I looked forward to the trip, but was very nervous about it because we hadn't taken a trip for months due to the COVID-19 pandemic restrictions. In fact, vaccination became a concern with some us due to our various vaccination statuses. It would be the first trip that I had taken overnight without Sammy or our children. I felt this trip would be another opportunity to challenge myself in creating a new normal. Each of us took on different responsibilities for planning the trip from making spa reservations to identifying restaurants. We had very different diets so we had to find a restaurant that met each of our needs.

We decided to order head wreaths to wear in our own planned ceremony at the hotel to commemorate our husbands. We planned to throw flowers into the Pacific Ocean at sunset after saying a few loving words to our husbands on the boardwalk in back of the hotel. We each selected our own unique wreaths based on our favorite flowers or a flower that our husbands may have usually selected for us. People watched us as we proceeded outside the doors toward the boardwalk, tossing the

314

Support Sisters

flowers in the onto the ocean. Later that evening, we had dinner together and ended our evening at the hotel lounge. Some of the patrons recognized us on the boardwalk earlier that afternoon and told us we were "bad-asses". We grinned and agreed.

Romance

After almost a year after our husbands had passed away, we discussed dating. We were comfortable having these personal conversations with one another and likely would feel scrutinized if family members or friends didn't think it was appropriate for us to date. There has been a societal stigma about widows dating after the death of a spouse, but not necessarily towards widowers, suggesting stereotypical views based on gender. Some people believe it is honorable for a widow to remain unmarried for the rest of her life. However, it seems to be acceptable for widowers to remarry after the death of a spouse. Social stigmas regarding such new relationships may be lifting (Richardson, 2016). We ranged in age from the 30s to the 70s and recognized that we had a need for companionship.

Crystal, who was in her 30's, began dating before the rest of us and introduced us to dating applications. We all had a quick lesson in the functions of and types of dating applications from Crystal who was a millennial and had a better handle on the use of technology than the rest of us. Although dating applications became popular over the preceding 10 years, we didn't have experience with them because we were married.

After being married for over 25 years, I was out of touch with the way people connected. Dating through smart phone applications, and swiping left for no or to the right for yes, seemed inorganic to me. Carol, who was in her 70s, found meeting people within her social circles was more comfortable. We supported each other by understanding companionship needs that our family members could not provide us. I decided to sign up for a dating application. After being on the application for a couple of weeks, men tried to connect with me. I enjoyed connecting with one in particular. We messaged each other daily and even had a couple of video calls because he lived over 200 miles away. He had to leave out of the country for work and then notified me of a crisis that caused him to be stranded there. He later asked me if I could help him financially, and I knew at that moment he was scammer and I was almost a victim of catphishing which I learned is common for widows who are grieving and vulnerable.

Counseling Implications

It's possible widows and widows may have the desire to create new experiences after losing their spouses. After the loss of a spouse, individuals may lose friendships or social relationships may change or end. Friends of young or middle-aged widows may not offer much understanding of the loneliness and continued love for a deceased spouse. It's common for people to withdraw from new widows and widowers in fear of saying the wrong thing, but that just compounds the loneliness. However, younger and middle-aged widows and widowers may be able to tap into resilience that older widows and widowers might lack.

Social Networks

Connections with other widows and widowers may be helpful, and may also inform clinicians how to assist grieving spouses re-engage with others. Widows and widowers might benefit from guidance concerning connections with others who have a shared experience (whether online, offline, or both), and they may learn how to harness existing social networks to optimize received support (Morrigan et al., 2022).

Although studies show widows and widowers, who are satisfied with their marital relationships prior to the loss, some report their efforts to maintain connection with their spouses as part of their grief process (Jones et al., 2019). Clinicians should provide resources to social support and social engagement to help intersect the internal ways of dealing with the death of a spouse with forward or future-oriented attitudes, courageousness, strength, independence, or problem solving (Hendrickson et al, 2018).

Married couples might enjoy intimacy, date nights, and supporting one another through life's challenges. After the loss of a spouse, a widow or widower may find difficulty transitioning from marriage to being single and are faced with taking on those challenges alone. This transition can be daunting if the marriage was long-term.

For widows, safety becomes an added stressor as she attempts to adjust to the world without their husbands. The sense of coherence facilitates the widows' ability to face the challenges of daily life and develop strength to find balance and safety while redefining meaning in the loss, to affirm and rebuild the sense of self, to stay connected and involved with the community, and to engage in rebuilding their life routines (Høy & Hall, 2022). Adjustments to dining alone can feel overwhelming. Widows and widowers can find meaning in challenges to adjust to social activities without their spouses. Mental health professionals can assist in this process through applications of solutions focused therapy (SFT) which recognizes the client as the expert on their experience and focuses on client strengths. Application of solutions focused therapy can be applied to sessions and an affective example is through the

Support Sisters

new normal project. The new normal project if affective for individuals experiencing grief and invites clients to identify strengths to retain and potential solutions by identifying the components of their new normal in session and complete a creative project out of session (Vaterlaus, 2014). The client is given the tasks of not only identifying their goals of new normal, but encouraged to realize it as well. The components of the new normal generally fit into the categories of social, emotional, physical, mental, and spiritual (Vaterlaus, 2014). Through solutions focused therapy, widows and widowers are empowered to create a life project leading to their new normal.

Widows' efforts to move forward in their lives to possess characteristics like confidence, strength, and independence are the keys to women's experiences after the deaths of their husbands. Social support, engagement, and relationships were important factors related to the resilient responses of these widows (Hendrickson et al., 2018).

Dating and Remarriage

Feelings of the children may be a factor in a decision to reconnect with an old or new acquaintance, or to create a new romantic relationship or even friendship. Children often feel protective over the relationship that their parents had, without considering the loneliness that the survived parent experiences. Even if children support the survived parent in dating, it can be challenging because the forum of meeting people has drastically changed over the decades. For example, meeting people in the 1980s occurred at dances, clubs, or parties. Today, dating applications are the common medium for meeting people. A U.S. national survey reveals that 47% of Americans say dating is harder now than it was 10 years ago (Booth, 2024). In fact, a study showed online dating application users had significantly higher rates of psychological distress, anxiety, and depression (Holtzhausen et al., 2020). It's unknown how online dating might contribute to more distress on widows and widowers. Clinicians should prepare widows and widowers for the online dating world and protections from scams that search for those who are most vulnerable. Clients should be cautioned not to share personal information on dating applications about their widow status. They should also be prepared for the normalcy of being "left-swiped" on smartphone screens which could present feelings of rejection which could compound grief.

Experiencing a global pandemic could also impact the desire to establish a new romantic relationship after the loss of a spouse. When state and local governments ordered lockdowns, curfews, and stay-at-home orders, people became disconnected from each other. Socializing was limited for fear of being exposed to the COVID-19 virus. Not all widows or widowers have the desire to seek out new relationships. Some become comfortable in living alone or feel a continued commitment to the deceased spouse. Change is something that a majority of widows and widowers must embrace (Richardson, 2026). Widows and widowers may require support from clinicians to access peer support to adjust to the new landscape of dating.

Financial Adjustment

In many cultures, older women are financially dependent upon their husbands (Høy & Hall, 2022). Being a young widow presents unique challenges of financial security, sole parenting of young children or childless, unpreparedness, and lack of peer support. Some older widows and widowers have the benefit of receiving financial support from their deceased husbands from social security benefits. However, the U.S., the minimum age to receive social security benefits was 67 years of age for people born in 1962 or after in 2020, according to the United States Social Security Administration (SSA, 2024), so younger and middle-aged widows or widowers may be required to enter or return to the workforce after the death of their spouses to support themselves and/or their children.

If widows are young mothers without careers, they are in a challenging financial position to try to financially support themselves and their children while grieving and navigating life without the sole provider. Younger and middle-aged widows and widowers may be more open to challenging themselves to new experiences such as returning to or entering the workforce.

Mental health professionals should provide resources to widows and widowers about survivor benefits. Additionally, career counseling can be beneficial, offering direction to young or middle-aged widows who are displaced workers.

MOVING ON...NOT

Even three years after Sammy's death, it still seemed fresh. My support sisters and I shared the feeling that time felt like as if it were moving in slow motion, while the rest of the world moved at an extremely fast pace. Perhaps the change in my perception of time was different because I was in the whirlwind fighting for Sammy's life and when he passed away, the whirlwind came to a sudden stop. I see the world differently now, as if part of me died with him and I'm adjusting to partially being here on earth and partially being with Sammy in heaven. My memories help me realize that my life with him was real and not a figment of my imagination. Being in a world without him causes me to question reality and my memories keep me sane. It is a strange feeling, but I recognize that it is my new normal.

Support Sisters

I spoke to other widows and widowers who have shared with me their experiences even after many years of their spouses dying. Even those who remarried assured me that the grief doesn't end. They still carried love for their deceased spouses, while making room for the new spouses. They shared with me that they still feel an overwhelming sense of grief at times such as the anniversary of the deceased, or if a song is played. The new spouses also had to make room for them to grieve without feeling intimidated or inferior to the deceased. I learned widows and widowers must live with grief for the rest of their lives.

What NOT to Say to a Widow or Widower

My support sisters and I often discussed our relationships and shocking experiences with others who didn't understand what we were going through. We shared examples of things people would say to us that might anger us in our grief. But we also recognized that people are not perfect and sometimes say the wrong things. One of the statements that we started hearing after the first year of being widows was "you need to move on." Hearing this statement caused us to feel as if something was wrong with us because we didn't return to being the women we were prior to the death of our loved ones. Telling us to move on is like telling us to ignore the grief and pretend it didn't happen. We recognized our friends and family members loved us and didn't like seeing the sadness on our faces as we reflected on life without our loved ones. In some ways, I wondered if people selfishly wanted us to be the people we once were. Some widows and widowers stop socializing like they used to, and going to the movies or hanging out with other couples may no longer enjoyable.

Moving on is different from adjusting. Moving on suggests leaving our loved ones behind. We continued to love our husbands even after they passed away, so we would carry them with us. We had to adjust to a new world without them physically in it, but we would never forget them or move on without them. People expected us to return to being the people we once were, but that would not be possible because our husbands were a significant part of who we were. Without them, we were different. We had to find new meaning in life each day. We would wake up each morning and not feel the physical touch of our deceased spouses lying next to us. If we wanted advice, we could no longer turn to them for it. If we needed a hug, we didn't have our them to comfort us. If we wanted romance, our spouses could no longer provide it. We were constantly reminded of our deceased spouses and sometimes the memories could trigger emotional outbursts.

Years after the loss of our husbands, my support sisters and I continued to regularly connect virtually and text each other in between our meetings. My support sisters and I recognize that we weren't able to spend the rest of our lives with our husbands, but our husbands spent the rest of their lives with us.

Counseling Implications

Widow and widowers may not want to remove items that remind them of their deceased spouses. In fact, good memories can also bring comfort. Some people may not understand that each day is a struggle and required strength for adjustment. Days ahead would never be the same, so "moving on" was impossible. Adjusting was a more appropriate suggestion.

Widows report that friends often advise them to move forward, to stop moping or dwelling long before the widow(er) is prepared to do so. Research reveals informal peer support groups can flourish into lasting friendships (Richardson, 2016). Widows and their friends may have different understanding and expectations for communication and support after the initial period of grief as they engage in the process of mourning their loss (Huisman & Lemke, 2022). Clinicians should consider the development of social support systems for widows and widowers to provide support based on common experiences. Widows who desire to participate in social activities with other widows, not only highlight the importance of problem solving, but social engagement offers widows the opportunity to be social (Hendrickson et al., 2018). It's important, however, for widows and widowers initiate social engagement when they are ready.

When social support is constructed between individuals with a focus on the specific relationship, support is highly valued (Huisman & Lemke, 2022; Richardson, 2016). Clinicians should avoid suggesting widows and widowers "move-on". Forgetting and moving forward were linked with difficulties or challenges widows face after the death of their husbands. This is not to imply that forgetting and moving forward is the only trajectory to adjusting to widowhood, but dwelling on those memories should be avoided (Hendrickson et al., 2018). Sensitivity in messages communicated to grieving widows and widowers should be considered.

CONCLUSION

The COVID-19 pandemic left painful memories for caregivers, particularly spouses of individuals who died of terminal illnesses during the pandemic. Due to lockdowns, stay-at-home orders, and social distancing, caregivers who were responsible for ensuring their terminally ill loved ones, were restricted from providing the same level of care that they would have been provide prior to the pandemic. Loved ones had to compete for medical attention to those who were infected with COVID-19. Many patients who had terminal illnesses were not provided access to health services, cancer screenings, or chemotherapy treatments (Rucinska & Nawrocki, 2022). Some patients died alone, or without a proper goodbye, and caregivers were left

Support Sisters

with those tragic memories. Unfortunately, the COVID-19 pandemic is cemented in the memories of those who suffered traumatic loss during that horrific event.

Clinicians, therapists, and counselors must shift in how support those who grieve loss for those who battled diseases, such as cancer, during the pandemic. Grief support counseling groups can provide widows and widowers who suffered loss of a spouse during the COVID-19 pandemic because it provides opportunities to share similar experiences. Because losing a spouse during the COVID-19 pandemic is a phenomenon, the shared experiences through grief support counseling groups provides comfort to group members who have challenges in gaining understanding of the experience from family and friends. Grief support counseling groups can be offered online through a virtual platform, but the cultural makeup (ASGW, 2024), as well as ethical factors such as comfort level with technology, and limits of confidentiality should be considered (ASGW, 2024, Gibson et al., 2020).

Grief support counseling groups allow grieving widows and widowers who suffered loss during the COVID-19 pandemic opportunities to process their grief by describing the event which led to the death of their loved ones (Varga & Paulus, 2014, Taylor & Robinson, 2016).

Widows and widowers who lost their loved ones to terminal diseases such as cancer during the COVID-19 pandemic, share unique experiences such as: administering pain medications around the clock, hospital mishaps of loved ones being discharged without discharge instructions, absence as they died or restricted from holding a typical funeral service due to COVID-19 restrictions. These unique experiences can be shared within a grief support counseling group which could lead to long-term friendships due to the depth of the connections formed, and can be long term as they adjust to life without their spouses.

DISCUSSION QUESTIONS

1. Share the details of your own personal loss during the COVID-19 Pandemic
2. Describe restrictions that you or someone you know experienced in planning a funeral during the COVID-19 pandemic. How might those experiences impact the grief process?
3. What other types of homogeneous support groups might be needed for those who have experienced loss after the COVID-19 pandemic?
4. How might the use of a dating application while grieving loss of a spouse negatively impact the grief process?

REFERENCES

American Psychological Association (APA). (2023). *Posttraumatic stress disorder*. APA. https://www.apa.org/topics/ptsd

Association of Specialists in Group Work (ASGW). (2024). *Guiding principles for group work*. ASGW. https://asgw.org/wp-content/uploads/2021/07/ASGW-Guiding -Principles-May-2021.pdf

Booth, J. (2024). Dating statistics and facts in 2024. *Forbes*. https://www.forbes .com/health/dating/dating-statistics/

Choi, H., Cho, C., & Lee, H. (2023). Complicated grief, PTSD, and PTG in bereaved family: Moderating effect of resilience and family support. *Journal of Loss and Trauma*, 28(2), 145–160. 10.1080/15325024.2022.2084843

Gibson, A., Wladkowski, S. P., Wallace, C. L., & Anderson, K. A. (2020). Considerations for Developing Online Grief counseling Support Groups. *Journal of Social Work in End-of-Life & Palliative Care*, 16(2), 99–115. 10.1080/15524256.2020.1 74572732223368

Gold, A. I., Ryjova, Y., Corner, G. W., Rasmussen, H. F., Kim, Y., & Margolin, G. (2023). Loss during COVID-19: Moderating effects of meaning and romantic relationships on anxiety and depressive symptoms. *Psychological Trauma: Theory, Research, Practice, and Policy*. Advance online publication. 10.1037/tra000152637523301

Gračanin, A., Bylsma, L. M., & Vingerhoets, A. J. (2014). Is crying a self-soothing behavior? *Frontiers in Psychology*, 5(502). 10.3389/fpsyg.2014.0050224904511

Hartig, J., & Viola, J. (2016). Online Grief Support Communities. *Omega*, 73(1), 29–41. 10.1177/0030222815575698

Hendrickson, Z. M., Kim, J., Tol, W. A., Shrestha, A., Kafle, H. M., Luitel, N. P., Thapa, L., & Surkan, P. J. (2018). Resilience among Nepali widows after the death of a spouse: "That was my past and now I have to see my present.". *Qualitative Health Research*, 28(3), 466–478. 10.1177/1049732317739926529110564

Holman, E. A., Jones, N. M., Garfin, D. R., & Silver, R. C. (2023). Distortions in time perception during collective trauma: Insights from a national longitudinal study during the COVID-19 pandemic. *Psychological Trauma: Theory, Research, Practice, and Policy*, 15(5), 800–807. 10.1037/tra000132635925689

Holmgren, H. (2023). Is Online Peer Support Helpful in Widowhood? The Lived Experiences of Young Parents. *Illness, Crises, and Loss*, 31(3), 540–557. 10.1177/10541373221099411

Support Sisters

Holtzhausen, N., Fitzgerald, K., Thakur, I., Ashley, J., Rolphe, M., & Winona, S. (2020). Swipe-based dating applications use and its association with mental health outcomes: A cross-sectional study. *BMC Psychology*, 8(1), 22. 10.1186/s40359-020-0373-132127048

Horstman, M. J., Mills, W. L., Herman, L. I., Cai, C., Shelton, G., Qdaisat, T., Berger, D. H., & Naik, A. D. (2017). Patient experience with discharge instructions in postdischarge recovery: A qualitative study. *BMJ Open*, 7(2), e014842. 10.1136/bmjopen-2016-01484228228448

Høy, B., & Hall, E. O. C. (2022). "Take good care of yourself" An integrative review of older widows' self-care for health and well-being. *Journal of Women & Aging*, 34(1), 1–30. 10.1080/08952841.2020.175348432339070

Huisman, D. M., & Lemke, A. (2022). I Am This Widow: Social Support in Friendship After the Loss of a Spouse in Mid-Life. *Omega*, 86(1), 45–64. 10.1177/00302228209612313298534 6

Jacobs, E. E., Schimmel, C. J., Masson, R. L., & Harvill, I. L. (2016). *Group Counseling: Strategies and skills* (8th ed.). Cengage.

Jones, E., Oka, M., Clark, J., Gardner, H., Hunt, R., & Dutson, S. (2019). Lived experience of young widowed individuals: A qualitative study. *Death Studies*, 43(3), 183–192. 10.1080/07481187.2018.144513729498589

Kübler-Ross, E (1997). *On death and dying: What the dying have to teach doctors, nurses, clergy, and their own families* (reprint ed.). Scribner.

Mayo Clinic. (2022). *Esophageal cancer*. Mayo Clinic. https://www.mayoclinic.org/diseases-conditions/esophageal-cancer/symptoms-causes/syc-20356084

Morrigan, B., Keesing, S., & Breen, L. J. (2022). Exploring the Social Networks of Bereaved Spouses: Phenomenological Case Studies. *Omega*, 85(2), 268–284. 10.1177/00302228209444062 32698677

Näppä, U., & Björkman-Randström, K. (2020). Experiences of participation in grief counseling groups from significant others' perspectives; a qualitative study. *BMC Palliative Care*, 19(1), 1–10. 10.1186/s12904-020-00632-y32799845

National Institute of Health (NIH). (2022). *Mental Health*. NIH. https://COVID19.nih.gov/COVID-19-topics/mental-health

National Institute of Health (NIH). (2024). *Telemental Health*. NIH. https://www.nimh.nih.gov/sites/default/files/health/publications/what-is-telemental-health/what-is-telemental-health.pdf

Penberthy, J. K., Pehlivanova, M., Kalelioglu, T., Roe, C. A., Cooper, C. E., Lorimer, D., & Elsaesser, E. (2023). Factors Moderating the Impact of After Death Communications on Beliefs and Spirituality. *Omega*, 87(3), 884–901. 10.1177/003022 2821102916034240655

Plunkett, E., Broadbent, A., Fien, S., & Cardona, M. (2021). Impact of COVID-19 Social Distancing on the Quality of Dying: A Call for Discretionary Application of Rules. *Journal of Social Work in End-of-Life & Palliative Care*, 17(2-3), 132–136. 10.1080/15524256.2021.191592033956572

Rice, A. (2015). Common Therapeutic Factors in Grief counseling Groups. *Death Studies*, 39(3), 165–172. 10.1080/07481187.2014.94662725530427

Richardson, K. M. (2016). The surviving sisters club: Examining social support and posttraumatic growth among FDNY 9/11 widows. *Journal of Loss and Trauma*, 21(1), 1–15. 10.1080/15325024.2015.1024558

Rolbiecki, A. J., Oliver, D. P., Washington, K., Benson, J. J., & Jorgensen, L. (2020). Preliminary Results of Caregiver Speaks: A Storytelling Intervention for Bereaved Family Caregivers. *Journal of Loss and Trauma*, 25(5), 438–453. 10.1080/153250 24.2019.170798533335452

Rosa, W. E., Dahlin, C., Battista, V., Finlayson, C. S., Wisniewski, R. E., Greer, K., & Ferrell, B. R. (2021). Primary Palliative Care Clinical Implications: Oncology nursing during the COVID-19 pandemic. *Clinical Journal of Oncology Nursing*, 25(2), 119–125. 10.1188/21.CJON.119-12533739351

Rucinska, M., & Nawrocki, S. (2022). COVID-19 Pandemic: Impact on Cancer Patients. *International Journal of Environmental Research and Public Health*, 19(19), 12470. 10.3390/ijerph19191247036231769

Social Security Administration (SSA). (2024). *Survivors Benefits*. SSA.https://www .ssa.gov/pubs/EN-05-10084.pdf

Taylor, N. C., & Robinson, W. D. (2016). The Lived Experience of Young Widows and Widowers. *The American Journal of Family Therapy*, 44(2), 67–79. 10.1080/01926187.2016.1145081

Varga, M., & Paulus, T. (2014). Grieving Online: Newcomers' Constructions of Grief in an Online Support Group. *Death Studies*, 38(7), 443–449. 10.1080/07481 187.2013.78011224758214

Vaterlaus, J. M. (2014). New Normal Project: An intervention for grief and loss. *Journal of Family Psychotherapy*, 25(1), 78–82. 10.1080/08975353.2014.881699

Support Sisters

Voo, T. C., Senguttuvan, M., & Tam, C. C. (2020). During COVID-19: Physical, Virtual, and Surrogate. *Journal of Bioethical Inquiry*, 17(4), 767–772. 10.1007/s11673-020-10009-832840835

West, K., Rumble, H., Shaw, R., Cameron, A., & Roleston, C. (2023). Diarised Reflections on COVID-19 and Grief counseling: Disruptions and Affordances. *Illness, Crises, and Loss*, 31(1), 151–167. 10.1177/10541373211044069366605777

Worden, J. W. (2008). *Grief counseling and grief therapy: A handbook for the mental health practitioner* (4th ed.). Springer. 10.1891/9780826101211

World Health Organization (WHO). (2022). *Cancer*. WHO. https://www.who.int/news-room/fact-sheets/detail/cancer

Worldometer. (2024). *Coronavirus cases and deaths*. Worldometer. https://www.worldometers.info/coronavirus/

ADDITIONAL READING

Carolina, P., & Limonero, J. T. (2020). The relationship between the positive aspects of caring and the personal growth of caregivers of patients with advanced oncological illness. *Supportive Care in Cancer*, 28(7), 3007–3013. 10.1007/s00520-019-05139-831823055

Hathaway, C. A., Bloomer, A. M., Oswald, L. B., Siegel, E. M., Peoples, A. R., Ulrich, C. M., Penedo, F. J., Tworoger, S. S., & Gonzalez, B. D. (2022). Factors associated with self-reported social isolation among patients with cancer during the COVID-19 pandemic. *Health Psychology*, 41(4), 311–318. 10.1037/hea000117235324248

Kristensen, T., Elklit, A., & Karstoft, K.-I. (2012). Posttraumatic Stress Disorder after bereavement: Early psychological sequelae of losing a close relative due to terminal cancer. *Journal of Loss and Trauma*, 17(6), 508–521. 10.1080/15325024.2012.665304

Mah, K., Swami, N., Pope, A., Earle, C. C., Krzyzanowska, M. K., Rinat, N., Hales, S., Rodin, G., Breffni, H., & Zimmermann, C. (2022). Caregiver bereavement outcomes in advanced cancer: Associations with quality of death and patient age. *Supportive Care in Cancer*, 30(2), 1343–1353. 10.1007/s00520-021-06536-834499215

Matthews, B. L. (2018). Life of the Second-Order Patient: Factors Impacting the Informal Caregiver. *Journal of Loss and Trauma*, 23(1), 29–43. 10.1080/15325024.2017.1419800

Omid, S., Alarcon, S. V., Vega, E. A., Kutlu, O. C., Olga, K., Chan, J. A., Vera, K., Harz, D., & Conrad, C. (2022). COVID-19's Impact on Cancer Care: Increased Emotional Stress in Patients and High Risk of Provider Burnout. *Journal of Gastrointestinal Surgery*, 26(1), 1–12. 10.1007/s11605-021-05032-y34027579

Selman, L. E., Chao, D., Sowden, R., Marshall, S., Chamberlain, C., & Koffman, J. (2020). Bereavement Support on the Frontline of COVID-19: Recommendations for Hospital Clinicians. *Journal of Pain and Symptom Management*, 60(2), e81–e86. 10.1016/j.jpainsymman.2020.04.02432376262

Supiano, K. P., Koric, A., & Iacob, E. (2021). Extending our reach: Telehealth delivered grief support groups for rural hospice. *Social Work with Groups*, 44(2), 159–173. 10.1080/01609513.2020.1825153

Waldrop, D. P. (2007). Caregiver Grief in Terminal Illness and Bereavement: A Mixed-Methods Study. *Health & Social Work*, 32(3), 197–206. 10.1093/hsw/32.3.19717896676

KEY TERMS AND DEFINITIONS

Bereavement: The experience that occurs immediately after a loss and the required time to grieve the loss.

Caregiver: Family and/or friends who are responsible for at-home-care, support, and transportation for treatment of a love one.

Counseling Group: A group of individuals who meet regularly while led by a facilitator to resolve personal problems or life transitions.

COVID-19 Pandemic: A worldwide spread infectious disease that was named in 2019, leading to panic as well as social distancing in some areas. Millions deaths occurred across the world as a result.

Grief Support Group: A group of individuals who meet regularly, share a common experience of grief, and offer support to one another.

Mental Health Clinicians or Professionals: Counselors, therapists, social workers, who provide support, counseling, or therapy to clients, or educators in counselor preparation programs.

Terminal Illness: An illness or disease suffered by an individual which will lead to death

Compilation of References

Abramson, A. (2021). *The ethical imperative of self-care*. APA. https://www.apa.org. https://www.apa.org/monitor/2021/04/feature-imperative-self-care

Adegboro, J. S., Fadero, E. O., Momoh, D. M., & Adedugbe, B. O. (2020). Mitigating the adverse effects of lockdown during COVID-19 pandemic with home-based physical activities. *Educational Thought*, 10(1), 67–73.

Adiukwu, F., Kamalzadeh, L., Da Costa, M. P., Ransing, R., De Filippis, R., Pereira-Sánchez, V., Larnaout, A., González-Díaz, J. M., Eid, M., Syarif, Z., Orsolini, L., Ramalho, R., Vadivel, R., & Shalbafan, M. (2022). The grief experience during the COVID-19 pandemic across different cultures. *Annals of General Psychiatry*, 21(1), 18. 10.1186/s12991-022-00397-z35701763

Adler, M. G., & Fagley, N. S. (2004). Appreciation: Individual differences in finding value and meaning as a unique predictor of subjective Well-being. *Journal of Personality*, 73(1), 79–114. 10.1111/j.1467-6494.2004.00305.x15660674

Admin. (2022, May 5). *Factors that can lead to complicated grief*. GrieveWell. https://www.grievewell.com/for-supporters/factors-that-can-lead-to-complicated-grief/

Aeon, B., Faber, A., & Panaccio, A. (2021). Does time management work? A meta-analysis. *PLoS One*, 16(1), e0245066. 10.1371/journal.pone.024506633428644

Afuape, T., & Kerry Oldham, S. (2022). Beyond "solidarity" with Black Lives Matter: Drawing on liberation psychology and transformative justice to address institutional and community violence in young Black lives. *Journal of Family Therapy*, 44(1), 20–43. 10.1111/1467-6427.12369

Akinade, E. A. (2021). *Modern behaviour modification: Principles and practice*. Brightways Publishers.

Akinboye, J. O., Akinboye, D. O., & Adeyemo, D. A. (2016). Coping with stress in life and workplace. Stirling-Horden Publishers (Nig.) Ltd.

Alang, S. M. (2019). Mental health care among blacks in America: Confronting racism and constructing solutions. *Health Services Research*, 54(2), 346–355. 10.1111/1475-6773.1311530687928

Alexander, A., Fung, S., Eichler, M., Lehwald-Tywuschik, N., Uthayakumar, V., Safi, S.-A., Vay, C., Ashmawy, H., Kalmuk, S., Rehders, A., Vaghiri, S., & Knoefel, W. T. (2022). Quality of Life in Patients with Pancreatic Cancer before and during the COVID-19 Pandemic. *International Journal of Environmental Research and Public Health*, 19(6), 3731. 10.3390/ijerph1906373135329416

Alioto, A. G., Chadwell, M., Baran-Prall, J., Canelo, R., Casillas-Carmona, A. D. S., Gotham, H., Kurtz, L., Rivera, K., Wenger, P. J., & Wolf-Prusan, L. (2020). *Grief, Loss, and Bereavement Fact Sheet #5: Evidence-Based Treatments for Grief.* MHTTC Network. https://mhttcnetwork .org/sites/mhttc/files/2020-09/Fact%20Sheet%205%20EBT%20for%20Grief%2009082020_0.pdf

Ali, S., & Bloom, Z. D. (2019). Creative approaches to address online dating in counseling. *Journal of Creativity in Mental Health*, 14(1), 81–93. 10.1080/15401383.2018.1535922

Alvarenga, W. A., deMontigny, F., Zeghiche, S., Verdom, C., & Castanheira, L. (2021). Experience of hope: An exploratory research with bereaved mothers following perinatal death. *Women and Birth; Journal of the Australian College of Midwives*, 34(4), e426–e434. 10.1016/j. wombi.2020.08.01132950437

Alvis, L., Zhang, N., Sandler, I. N., & Kaplow, J. B. (2023). Developmental manifestations of grief in children and adolescents: Caregivers as key grief facilitators. *Journal of Child & Adolescent Trauma*, 16(2), 447–457. https://doi-org.proxy.library.ohio.edu/10.1007/s40653-021-00435-0. 10.1007/s40653-021-00435-035106114

Amdurer, T. (2019, March). *The caregiving conundrum.* CT Counseling. https://ct.counseling.org

American Cancer Society. (2024). *Cancer Facts and Figures.* ACS. https://www.cancer.org/ research/cancer-facts-statistics/all-cancer-facts-figures/2024-cancer-facts-figures.html

American Counseling Association (ACA). (2014). *2014 ACA Code of Ethics.* ACA. https://www .counseling.org/Resources/aca-code-of-ethics.pdf

American Counseling Association. (2014). *2014 ACA code of ethics.* ACA. https://www.counseling .org/docs/default-source/default-document-library/2014-code-of-ethics-finaladdress.pdf

American Counseling Association. (2014). *ACA Code of Ethics.* ACA. https://www.counseling .org/docs/default-source/default-document-library/ethics/2014-aca-code-of-ethics.pdf?sfvrsn= 55ab73d0_1Bergman10.1186/s12904-017-0223-y

American Counseling Association. (2014). *ACA code of ethics.* ACA. https://www.counseling .org/resources/aca-code-of-ethics

American Psychiatric Association. (2022). *Diagnostic and Statistical Manual of Mental Disorders, Fifth Edition, Text Revision (DSM-5-TR).* American Psychiatric Association Publishing. https:// www.psychiatry.org/psychiatrists/practice/dsm

American Psychological Association (APA). (2017). *Stress in America: The state of our nation.* APA. https://www.apa.org/news/press/releases/2017/11/lowest-point

Compilation of References

American Psychological Association (APA). (2022). *Increased need for mental health care strains capacity*. APA. https://www.apa.org/news/press/releases/2022/11/mental-health-care-strains

American Psychological Association (APA). (2023). *Posttraumatic stress disorder*. APA. https://www.apa.org/topics/ptsd

American Psychological Association (APA). (2023a). *Trauma*. APA. https://www.apa.org/topics/trauma

American Psychological Association (APA). (2024). *Grief*. APA. https://www.apa.org/topics/grief#:~:text=Grief%20is%20the%20anguish%20experienced,and%20apprehension%20about%20the%20future

American Psychological Association. (n.d.). *Grief: Coping with the loss of your loved one*. American Psychological Association. https://www.apa.org/topics/families/grief

American School Counseling Association. (2022). *2022 ASCA code of ethics*. ASCA. https://www.schoolcounselor.org/About-School-Counseling/Ethical-Responsibilities/ASCA-Ethical-Standards-for-School-Counselors-(1)

Ames, H. (2020, October 22). What to know about online grief counseling. *Media News Todaay*.

Anderson, L. A., O'Brien Caughy, M., & Owen, M. T. (2022). "The Talk" and Parenting While Black in America: Centering Race, Resistance, and Refuge. *The Journal of Black Psychology*, 48(3–4), 475–506. 10.1177/00957984211034294

Ang, C. S. (2023). Life Will Never be the Same: Experiences of Grief and Loss among Older Adults. *Current Psychology (New Brunswick, N.J.)*, 42(15), 12975–12987. 10.1007/s12144-021-02595-6

Aoun, S. M., Breen, L. J., White, I., Rumbold, B., & Kellehear, A. (2018). What sources of bereavement support are perceived helpful by bereaved people and why? Empirical evidence for the compassionate communities approach. *Palliative Medicine*, 32(8), 1378–1388. 10.1177/026921631877499529754514

APA. (2022). *Grief*. APA. https://www.apa.org/topics/grief

Applewhite, A. (2020). *The chair rocks: A manifesto against ageism*. Celedon Books.

Ardelt, M. (2020). Can wisdom and psychosocial growth be learned in university courses? *Journal of Moral Education*, 49(1), 30–45. 10.1080/03057240.2018.1471392

Árnason, A. (2007). "Fall apart and put yourself together again": The anthropology of death and bereavement counselling in Britain. *Mortality*, 12(1), 48–65. 10.1080/13576270601088335

Arno, P. S., Levine, C., & Memmott, M. M. (1999). The economic value of informal caregiving. *Health Affairs (Project Hope)*, 18(2), 182–188. 10.1377/hlthaff.18.2.18210091447

Arora, S., & Bhatia, S. (2023). Addressing grief and bereavement in the COVID-19 pandemic. *Illness, Crises, and Loss*. 10.1177/10541373221145536

329

Asgari, M., Ghasemzadeh, M., Alimohamadi, A., Sakhael, S., Killikelly, C., & Nikfar, E. (2023). Investigation into grief experiences of the bereaved during the covid-19 pandemic. *Omega*, 0(0), 1–20. 10.1177/00302228231173075537184963

Assadi, F. (2023). Understanding the Childhood Grief: What Should We Tell the Children? *International Journal of Preventive Medicine*, 14(1), 1–3. https://doi-org.proxy.library.ohio.edu/10.4103/ijpvm.ijpvm_371_22. 10.4103/ijpvm.ijpvm_371_2237855003

Association of Specialists in Group Work (ASGW). (2024). *Guiding principles for group work*. ASGW. https://asgw.org/wp-content/uploads/2021/07/ASGW-Guiding-Principles-May-2021.pdf

Attig, T. (2010). *How we grief: Relearning the world* (Revd. Ed.). Oxford University Press.

Baker, C., & Gabriel, L. (2021). Exploring how therapists engage in self-care in times of personal distress. *British Journal of Guidance & Counselling*, 49(3), 435–444. 10.1080/03069885.2021.1885010

Baluszek, J. B., Brønnick, K., & Wiig, S. (2023). The relations between resilience and self-efficacy among healthcare practitioners in the context of the COVID-19 pandemic – a rapid review. *International Journal of Health Governance*, 28(2), 152–164. 10.1108/IJHG-11-2022-0098

Barnett, J. E., & Homany, G. (2022). The new self-care: It's not all about you. *Practice Innovations (Washington, D.C.)*, 7(4), 313–326. 10.1037/pri0000190

Beaunoyer, E., Hiracheta Torres, L., Maessen, L., & Guitton, M. J. (2020). Grieving in the Digital Era: Mapping online support for grief and bereavement. *Patient Education and Counseling*, 103(12), 2515–2524. 10.1016/j.pec.2020.06.01332591255

Beauregard, C. (2020). Being in between Exploring cultural bereavement and identity expression through drawing. *Journal of Creativity in Mental Health*, 15(3), 292–310. 10.1080/15401383.2019.1702131

Becker, E. (1997). *The denial of death*. Free Press Paperbacks.

Beer, T. (2020). November's grim COVID-19 totals: More than 4.3 million infections and 37,000 Americans killed. *Forbes*.https://www.forbes.com/sites/tommybeer/2020/12/01/novembers-grim-COVID-19-totals-more-than-43-million-infections-and-37000-americans-killed/?sh=2b94405f6acb

Blair, M., & Perry, B. (2017). Family caregiving and compassion fatigue: A literature review. Perspectives. *The Journal of Gerontological Nursing Association*, 38(2), 14–19.

Blueford, J. M., Diambra, J. F., & Wheat, L. S. (2022). Counselor preparedness to counsel grieving clients: Insights and implications. *Death Studies*, 46(10), 2413–2423. 10.1080/07481187.2021.195664434308795

Booth, J. (2024). Dating statistics and facts in 2024. *Forbes*. https://www.forbes.com/health/dating/dating-statistics/

Compilation of References

Botha, F., & Dahmann, S. C. (2023). Locus of control, self-control, and health outcomes. *SSM - Population Health*, 25, 101566. 10.1016/j.ssmph.2023.10156638077246

Bottomley, , Burke, L. A., & Neimeyer, R. A. (2017). Domains of social support that predict bereavement distress following homicide loss. *Omega*, 75(1), 3–25. 10.1177/00302228156122 8228395645

Bovero, A., Pidinchedda, A., Clovis, F., Berchialla, P., & Caretto, S. (2021). Psychosocial factors associated with complicated grief in caregivers during COVID-19: Results from a preliminary cross-sectional study. *Death Studies*, 1–10. 10.1080/07481187.2021.201914434957925

Braitman, L. (2023). *"What Looks Like Bravery" explains how achievement can't protect us from grief. interview.* NPR.

Brajša-Žganec, A., Merkaš, M., & Šverko, I. (2010). Quality of life and leisure activities: How do leisure activities contribute to subjective well-being? *Social Indicators Research*, 102(1), 81–91. 10.1007/s11205-010-9724-2

Braude, S., & Dwarika, V. (2020). Teachers' experiences of supporting learners with attention-deficit hyperactivity disorder: Lessons for professional development of teachers. *South African Journal of Childhood Education*, 10(1). 10.4102/sajce.v10i1.843

Breen, L. J., Kawashima, D., Joy, K., Cadell, S., Roth, D., Chow, A., & Macdonald, M. E. (2022). Grief literacy: A call to action for compassionate communities. *Death Studies*, 46(2), 425–433. 10.1080/07481187.2020.173978032189580

Bretscher, J., & Haugk, K. (n.d.). *The Gift of Empathy: Helping Others Feel Valued, Cared for, and Understood.* Stephen's Ministry.

Bridgland, M., Moeck, E., Green, D., Swain, T., Nayda, D., Matson, M., Hutchison, N. P., & Takarangi, M. K. T. (2021). Why the COVID-19 pandemic is a traumatic stressor. *PLoS One*, 16(1), 0240146. 10.1371/journal.pone.024014633428630

Brinkmann, S. (2020). Learning to grieve: A preliminary analysis. *Culture and Psychology*, 26(3), 469–483. 10.1177/1354067X19877918

Brooke, S. L., & Miraglia, D. A. (2015). *Using the creative therapies to cope with grief and loss.* Charles C. Thomas Publisher, LTD.

Brown, J. C. (2021). *An epidemic of violence. Fatal violence against transgender and gender non-conforming people in the United States in 2020.* Human Rights Campaign. https://reports .hrc.org/an-epidemic-of-violence-fatal-violence-against-transgender-and-gender-non-confirming -people-in-the-united-states-in-2020?_ga=2.185816937.1993557673.1707439958-2145036884 .1707439958

Brown, L. J., Bond, M. J., & Topa, G. (2019). The pragmatic derivation and validation of measures of adaptive and maladaptive coping styles. *Cogent Psychology*, 6(1), 1568070. 10.1080/23311908.2019.1568070

Brubaker, J. R., Hayes, G. R., & Mazmanian, M. (2019). Orienting to networked grief. *Proceedings of the ACM on Human-Computer Interaction, 3*(CSCW), (pp. 1–19). ACM. 10.1145/3359129

Bui, E., Mauro, C., Robinaugh, D. J., Skritskaya, N. A., Wang, Y., Gribbin, C., Ghesquiere, A., Horenstein, A., Duan, N., Reynolds, C., Zisook, S., Simon, N. M., & Shear, M. K. (2015). The Structured Clinical Interview For Complicated Grief: Reliability, Validity, and Exploratory Factor Analysis. *Depression and Anxiety, 32*(7), 485–492. 10.1002/da.2238526061724

Burke, C., Hampel, S., Gholson, K., Zhang, P., & Rufkhar, B. (2021). COVID-19 family support team: Providing person and family centered care during the COVID-19 pandemic. *Journal of Social Work in End-of-Life & Palliative Care, 17*(2–3), 158–163. 10.1080/15524256.2021.192 212634057887

Burns, M., Griese, B., King, S., & Talmi, A. (2020). Childhood bereavement: Understanding prevalence and related adversity in the United States. *The American Journal of Orthopsychiatry, 90*(4), 391–405. 10.1037/ort000044231999137

Byrne, D., Overbaugh, K., Czekanski, K., Wilby, M., Blumenfeld, S., & Laske, R. A. (2020). Assessing undergraduate nursing students' attitudes toward the dying in an end-of-life simulation using an ACE.S unfolding case study. *Journal of Hospice and Palliative Nursing : JHPN : the Official Journal of the Hospice and Palliative Nurses Association, 22*(2), E11–E12. 10.1097/ NJH.0000000000000062631977535

Cardany, A. B. (2018). Mitigating death anxiety: Identifying music's role in terror management. *Psychology of Music, 46*(1), 3–17. 10.1177/0305735617690600

Carkhuff, R. R. (2019). *The art of helping in the 21ˢᵗ century* (10th ed.). Human Resource Development Press, Inc.

Carroll, A., Sanders-O'Connor, E., Forrest, K., Fynes-Clinton, S., York, A., Ziaei, M., Flynn, L., Bower, J., & Reutens, D. C. (2021). Improving emotion regulation, well-being, and neuro-cognitive functioning in teachers: A matched controlled study comparing the mindfulness-based stress reduction and health enhancement programs. *Mindfulness, 13*(1), 123–144. 10.1007/s12671-021-01777-4

Carter, R. T. (2007). Racism and psychological and emotional injury: Recognizing and assessing race-based traumatic stress. *The Counseling Psychologist, 35*(1), 13–105. 10.1177/0011000006292033

Castano, E., Leidner, B., Bonacossa, A., Nikkah, J., Perrulli, R., Spencer, B., & Humphrey, N. (2011). Ideology, fear of death and death anxiety. *Political Psychology, 32*(4), 601–621. 10.1111/j. 1467-9221.2011.00822.x

Castrellón, L. E., Fernández, É., Reyna Rivarola, A. R., & López, G. R. (2021). Centering loss and grief: Positioning schools as sites of collective healing in the era of COVID-19. *Frontiers in Education, 6*, 636993. Advance online publication. 10.3389/feduc.2021.636993

Compilation of References

Cavicchioli, M., Ferrucci, R., Guidetti, M., Canevini, M. P., Pravettoni, G., & Galli, F. (2021). *What will be the impact of the COVID-19 quarantine on psychological distress? Considerations based on a systematic review of pandemicadva outbreaks.*

Center for Disease Control and Prevention (CDC). (2021). *Racism and Health.* CDC. https:// www.cdc.gov/minorityhealth/racism-disparities/index.html

Center for Disease Control and Prevention (CDC). (2021). *Racism and Health.* CDC. https://www .cdc.gov/minorityhealth/racism-disparities/index.html10.1007/s00520-022-07468-7

Centers for Disease Control and Prevention. (2021). *Distribution of COVID-19 deaths and populations, by jurisdiction, age, and race and Hispanic origin.* CDC. https://data.cdc.gov/NCHS/ Distribution-of-COVID-19-Deathsand-Populations-by/jwta-jxbg.

Chachar, A. S., Younus, S., & Ali, W. (2021). Developmental Understanding of Death and Grief Among Children During COVID-19 Pandemic: Application of Bronfenbrenner's Bioecological Model. *Frontiers in psychiatry.* 10.3389/fpsyt.2021.654584

Chandrasekara, W. S. (2016). Help-seeking attitudes and willingness to seek psychological help: Application of the theory of planned behaviour. *International Journal of Management. Accounting and Economics*, 3(4), 232–245.

Chen, C. (2019). *Professional grief and burnout.* Springer. 10.1007/978-3-319-69892-2_1010-1

Choi, H., Cho, C., & Lee, H. (2023). Complicated grief, PTSD, and PTG in bereaved family: Moderating effect of resilience and family support. *Journal of Loss and Trauma*, 28(2), 145–160. 10.1080/15325024.2022.2084843

Chronister, J., Castruita Rios, Y., & Rumrill, S. (2021). Crisis and trauma counseling and intervention. *Certified Rehabilitation Counselor Examination Preparation.* 10.1891/9780826158253.0005

Coenen, C. (2024). *Seasons of grief.* Jessica Kingsley Publishers.

Cohen, F., Solomon, S., Maxfield, M., Pyszczynski, T., & Greenberg, J. (2004). Fatal Attraction: The effects of mortality salience on evaluations of charismatic, task oriented, and relationship-oriented leaders. *Psychological Science*, 15(12), 846–851. 10.1111/j.0956-7976.2004.00765.x15563330

Collaborative for Academic, Social, and Emotional Learning (CASEL). (2003). Safe and sound: *An educational leader's guide to edidence based social and emotional learning programs.* Chicago, IL: CASEL.

Communicating with the Public. (n.d.). NFDA. https://nfda.org/covid-19/communicating-with -the-public

Complicated grief - Symptoms and causes. (2022). Mayo Clinic. https://www.mayoclinic.org/ diseases-conditions/complicated-grief/symptoms-causes/syc-20360374

Cook, A., Spinazzola, J., Ford, J., Lanktree, C., Blaustein, M., Cloitre, M., & Van der Kolk, B. (2005). Complex trauma. *Psychiatric Annals*, 35(5), 390–398. https://sites.northwestern.edu/cans/files/2022/08/Complex-trauma-in-children.pdf. 10.3928/00485713-20050501-05

Cooper, M. (2023, May 3). *Manner of Death: Categories explained in simple terms.* LoveToKnow. https://www.lovetoknow.com/life/grief-loss/manner-death-categories-explained-simple-terms

Corrigan, P. W. (2016, April). Can peer support be effective online? *Epidemiology and Psychiatric Sciences*, 25(2), 127–128. 10.1017/S204579601500107926740342

Costa, A. C. D. S., Menon, V., Phadke, R., Dapke, K., Miranda, A. V., Ahmad, S., Essar, M. Y., & Hashim, H. T. (2022). Mental health in the post COVID-19 era: Future perspectives. *Einstein (Sao Paulo, Brazil)*, 20, eCE6760. 10.31744/einstein_journal/2022CE676035584448

COVID-19 funeral assistance. (2024, January 18). FEMA.gov. https://www.fema.gov/disaster/historic/coronavirus/economic/funeral-assistance

Cox, J. M., Toussaint, A., Woerner, J., Smith, A., & Haeny, A. M. (2023). *Coping while Black: Comparing coping strategies across COVID-19 and the killing of Black people.* NCBI. https://www.ncbi.nlm.nih.gov/pmc/articles/PMC10132418/

Cox, M. R., Bledsoe, S., & Bowens, B. (2017). Challenges of Teacher Diversity Training. *The International Journal of Diversity in Education*, 17(2), 1–15. 10.18848/2327-0020/CGP/v17i02/1-15

Dang, S., Looijmans, A., Lamura, G., & Hagedoorn, M. (2024). Perceived life balance among young adult students: A comparison between caregivers and non-caregivers. *BMC Psychology*, 12(1), 1–12. 10.1186/s40359-023-01500-z38185676

Darewych, O. (2019). *Positive arts interventions: Creative tools helping mental health students flourish.* Springer. 10.1007/978-3-030-20583-6_19

Davis, E. S., Norton, A., & Chapman, R. (2020). Counselors'-in-training perceptions of using music for theoretical conceptualization training. *Journal of Creativity in Mental Health*, 15(4), 443–456. 10.1080/15401383.2020.1731041

De Maria, M., Ferro, F., Vellone, E., Ausili, D., Luciani, M., & Matarese, M. (2022). Self-care of patients with multiple chronic conditions and their caregivers during the COVID-19 pandemic: A qualitative descriptive study. *Journal of Advanced Nursing*, 78(5), 1431–1447. 10.1111/jan.1511534846083

De Pasquale, C., Conti, D., Dinaro, C., D'Antoni, R. A., La Delfa, E., & Di Nuovo, S. (2022). The COVID-19 Pandemic and Posttraumatic Stress Disorder: Emotional Impact on Healthcare Professions. *Frontiers in Psychiatry*, 13, 832843. 10.3389/fpsyt.2022.83284335432014

DeGruy. (2017). *Dr. Joy DeGruy: Post Traumatic Slave Syndrome.* DeGruy. https://www.joydegruy.com/

Dekker, N. L. (2023). Anticipatory grief in dementia: An ethnographic study of loss and connection. *Culture, Medicine and Psychiatry*, 47(3), 701–721. 10.1007/s11013-022-09792-335767160

Compilation of References

Dellarocas, C. (2003). The digitization of word of mouth: Promise and challenges of online feedback mechanisms. *Management Science*, 49(10), 1407–1424. 10.1287/mnsc.49.10.1407.17308

DeMuth, M., Taggi-Pinto, A., Miller, E. G., & Alderfer, M. A. (2020). Bereavement accommodations in the classroom: Experiences and opinions of school staff. *The Journal of School Health*, 90(3), 165–171. 10.1111/josh.1287031957037

Devere, R. (2017). *Music and dementia: An overview.* Practical Neurology. https://www.practicalneurology.com

Dick, A. S., & Mueller, U. (2018). *Advancing developmental science: Philosophy, theory, and method.* Psychology Press.

Diolaiuti, F., Marazziti, D., Beatino, M. F., Mucci, F., & Pozza, A. (2021). Impact and consequences of COVID-19 pandemic on complicated grief and persistent complex bereavement disorder. *Psychiatry Research*, 300, 113916. 10.1016/j.psychres.2021.11391633836468

Disabato, D. J., Aurora, P., Sidney, P. G., Taber, J. M., Thompson, C. A., & Coifman, K. G. (2022). Self-care behaviors and affect during the early stages of the COVID-19 pandemic. [Supplemental]. *Health Psychology*, 41(11), 833–842. 10.1037/hea000123936107666

Djelantik, A. A., Robinaugh, D. J., Kleber, R. J., Smid, G. E., & Boelen, P. A. (2019). Symptomatology following loss and trauma: Latent class and network analyses of prolonged grief disorder, posttraumatic stress disorder, and depression in a treatment-seeking trauma-exposed sample. *Depression and Anxiety*, 37(1), 26–34. 10.1002/da.2288030724427

Doerrfeld, C. (2018). *The rabbit listened.* Scallywag Press.

Douglas, R. D., Alvis, L. M., Rooney, E. E., Busby, D. R., & Kaplow, J. B. (2021). Racial,\ ethnic, and neighborhood income disparities in childhood posttraumatic stress and grief: Exploring indirect effects through trauma exposure and bereavement. *Journal of Traumatic Stress*, 34(5), 929–942. 10.1002/jts.2273234643296

Drabwell, L., Eng, J., Stevenson, F., King, M., Osborn, D., & Pitman, A. (2020). Perceptions of the use of alcohol and drugs after sudden bereavement by unnatural causes: Analysis of online qualitative data. *International Journal of Environmental Research and Public Health*, 17(3), 677. 10.3390/ijerph1703067731972984

Drysdale, M. T. B., McBeath, M. L., & Callaghan, S. A. (2021, October 11). The feasibility and impact of online peer support on the well-being of Higher Education Students. *The Journal of Mental Health Training, Education and Practice.*

Dubi, M., Powell, P., & Gentry, J.E. (2017). *Trauma, ptsd, grief & loss.* Pesi Publishing & Media.

Duncan, D. A. (2020). Death and dying: A systematic review into approaches used to support bereaved children. *Review of Education*, 8(2), 452–479. 10.1002/rev3.3193

335

Dwyer, M. L., Alt, M., Brooks, J. V., Katz, H., & Poje, A. B. (2021). Burnout and Compassion Satisfaction: Survey Findings of Healthcare Employee Wellness During COVID-19 Pandemic using ProQOL. *Kansas Journal of Medicine*, 14, 121–127. 10.17161/kjm.vol141517134084270

Dyregrov, A., Dyregrov, K., & Lytje, M. (2020). Loss in the family – A reflection on how schools can support their students. *Bereavement Care*, 39(3), 95–101. 10.1080/02682621.2020.1828722

Eisma, M. C., & Tamminga, A. (2020). Grief before and during the COVID-19 pandemic: Multiple group comparisons. *Journal of Pain and Symptom Management, 60*(6). https://doi.org/10.1016/j.jpainsymma.2020.10.004

Eisma, M. C., de Lang, T. A., & Boelen, P. A. (2020). How thinking hurts: Rumination, worry, and avoidance processes in adjustment to bereavement. *Clinical Psychology &amp. Psychotherapy (Chicago, Ill.)*, 27(4), 548–558. 10.1002/cpp.244032969670

Eisma, M. C., Franzen, M., Paauw, M., Bleeker, A., & aan het Rot, M. (2021). Rumination, worry and negative and positive affect in prolonged grief: A daily diary study. *Clinical Psychology &amp. Psychotherapy (Chicago, Ill.)*, 29(1), 299–312. 10.1002/cpp.263534170063

Ekwelundu, C. A. (2022). Effect of assertiveness training technique on bullying behaviour of secondary school students in Anambra State, Nigeria. *European Journal of Soil Science*, 7(2), 118–131. 10.46827/ejsss.v7i2.1230

El-Osta, A., Sasco, E. R., Barbanti, E., Webber, I., Alaa, A., Karki, M., Bagkeris, E., Asmar, M. L. E., Almadi, M. A., Massoud, F., Alboksmaty, A., & Majeed, A. (2023). Tools for measuring individual self-care capability: A scoping review. *BMC Public Health*, 23(1), 1312. 10.1186/s12889-023-16194-637422637

Emanuel, L., Johnson, R., & Taromino, C. (2017). Adjusting to a Diagnosis of Cancer: Processes for Building Patient Capacity for Decision-Making. *Journal of Cancer Education*, 32(3), 491–495. 10.1007/s13187-016-1008-326960311

Escapes, G. (2024, March 16). *Explore how grief impacts the body and offer strategies for managing these physical effects. — Grief Escapes.* Grief Escapes. https://www.griefescapes.com/blog/the-physical-toll-of-grief-understanding-how-loss-impacts-your-body#:~:text=Grief%20is%20a%20natural%20response%20to%20loss%2C%20but,support%20your%20overall%20well-being%20during%20this%20challenging%20time

Eslami, A. A., Rabiei, L., Afzali, S. M., Hamidizadeh, S., & Masoudi, R. (2016). The effectiveness of assertiveness training on the levels of stress, anxiety, and depression of high school students. *Iranian Red Crescent Medical Journal*, 18(1), e21096. 10.5812/ircmj.2109626889390

Esme. (2023, November 17). *Coping with Changed Relationships After the Death of Your Spouse.* ESME. https://esme.com/resources/bereavement/coping-with-changed-relationships-after-the-death-of-your-spouse

Eysenbach, G. (2001). What is e-health? *Journal of Medical Internet Research*, 3(2), e20. 10.2196/jmir.3.2.e2011720962

Compilation of References

Feder, S., Smith, D., Griffin, H., Shreve, S. T., Kinder, D., Kutney, L. A., & Ersek, M. (2021). "Why couldn't I go in to see him?" Bereaved families' perceptions of end-of-life communication during COVID-19. *Journal of the American Geriatrics Society*, 69(3), 587–592. 10.1111/jgs.1699333320956

Fee, A., Hanna, J., & Hasson, F. (2023). Pre-loss grief experiences of adults when someone important to them is at end-of-life: A qualitative systematic review. *Death Studies*, 47(1), 30–44. 10.1080/07481187.2021.199893534751635

Fereidooni, G. J., Ghofranipour, F., & Zarei, F. (2024). Interplay of self-care, self-efficacy, and health deviation self-care requisites: A study on type 2 diabetes patients through the lens of Orem's self-care theory. *BMC Primary Care*, 25(1), 48. 10.1186/s12875-024-02276-w38297225

Finzi-Dottan, R., & Berckovitch Kormosh, M. (2018). The spillover of compassion fatigue into marital quality: A mediation model. *Traumatology*, 24(2), 113–122. 10.1037/trm0000137

Flesia, L., Adeeb, M., Waseem, A., Helmy, M., & Monaro, M. (2023). Psychological Distress Related to the COVID-19 Pandemic: The Protective Role of Hope. *European Journal of Investigation in Health, Psychology and Education*, 13(1), 67–80. 10.3390/ejihpe1301000536661755

Flint, G. A., Lammers, W., & Mitnick, D. G. (2014). Emotional freedom techniques. *Journal of Aggression, Maltreatment &amp. Journal of Aggression, Maltreatment & Trauma*, 12(1–2), 125–150. 10.1300/J146v12n01_07

Folkman, S., & Lazarus, R. S. (1980). An analysis of coping in a middle-aged community sample. *Journal of Health and Social Behavior*, 21(3), 219. 10.2307/21366177410799

Folkman, S., & Lazarus, R. S. (1988). The relationship between coping and emotion: Implications for theory and research. *Social Science &amp. Medicine*, 26(3), 309–317. 10.1016/0277-9536(88)90395-43279520

Forrest, L. F., Abdurrahman, M., & Ritsma, A. (2020). Recognizing compassion fatigue, vicarious trauma, and burnout. Springer. 10.1007/978-3-030-45627-6_10

Fowler, K. L. (2008). The wholeness of things: Infusing diversity and social justice into death education. *Omega*, 57(1), 53–91. 10.2190/OM.57.1.d18507327

Fracasso, C. L., Krippner, S., & Friedman, H. L. (2020). *Holistic Treatment in Mental Health: A Handbook of Practitioners' Perspectives*. McFarland.

Frazer Consultants. (2020, August 17). *Grief theories series: Rando's six R process of mourning*. Frazer Consultants. https://web.frazerconsultants.com/grief-theories-series-randos-six-r-process-of-mourning/

Freire, P. (2000). *Pedagogy of the oppressed* (30th anniversary ed.). Continuum.

Galante, J., Grabovac, A., Wright, M., Ingram, D. M., Van Dam, N. T., Sanguinetti, J. L., Sparby, T., Van Lutterveld, R., & Sacchet, M. D. (2023). A framework for the Empirical investigation of Mindfulness Meditative Development. *Mindfulness*, 14(5), 1054–1067. 10.1007/s12671-023-02113-8

Gamino, L. A. (2017). ADEC at 40: Second half of life wisdom for the future of death education and counseling. *Death Studies*, 41(3), 188–195. 10.1080/07481187.2017.128933128151061

Gamino, L. A., Easterling, L. W., Stirman, L. S., & Sewell, K. W. (2000). Grief adjustment is influenced by funeral participation and the occurrence of adverse funeral events. *Omega*, 41(2), 79–92. 10.2190/QMV2-3NT5-BKD5-6AAV

Garcia, R. B. (2021). Using grief support groups to support bereaved students. *Supporting Bereaved Students at School*, 115-129. 10.1093/med:psych/9780190606893.003.0009

Garcia, G. (2019). *Listening to my body: A guide to helping kids understand the connection between their sensations (what the heck are those?) and feelings so that they can get better at figuring out what they need.* Skinned Knee Publishing.

Garcia-Rada, X., Sezer, O., & Norton, M. I. (2019). Rituals and Nuptials: The Emotional and Relational Consequences of Relationship Rituals. *Journal of the Association for Consumer Research*, 4(2), 185–197. 10.1086/702761

Gasiorowska, A., Zaleskiewicz, T., & Kesebir, P. (2018). Money as existential anxiety buffer: Exposure to money precents mortality reminder from leading to increased death thoughts. *Journal of Experimental Social Psychology*, 79, 394–409. 10.1016/j.jesp.2018.09.004

Gerwig, G. (Director.) (2023). *Barbie* [Film]. Warner Brothers Pictures.

Gesi, C., Carmassi, C., Cerveri, G., Carpita, B., Cremone, I. M., & Dell'Osso, L. (2020, May 26). Complicated Grief: What to Expect After the Coronavirus Pandemic. *Frontiers in Psychiatry*, 11, 489. 10.3389/fpsyt.2020.0048932574243

Ghezeljeh, T. N., Seyedfatemi, N., Bolhari, J., Kamyari, N., & Rezaei, M. (2023). Effects of family-based dignity intervention and expressive writing on anticipatory grief in family caregivers of patients with cancer: A randomized controlled trial. *BMC Psychiatry*, 23(1), 220. 10.1186/s12888-023-04715-x37005577

Gibson, A. F. (2021). Exploring the impact of COVID-19 on mobile dating: Critical avenues for research. *Social and Personality Psychology Compass*, 15(11), e12643. 10.1111/spc3.1264334899975

Gibson, A., Wladkowski, S. P., Wallace, C. L., & Anderson, K. A. (2020). Considerations for Developing Online Grief counseling Support Groups. *Journal of Social Work in End-of-Life & Palliative Care*, 16(2), 99–115. 10.1080/15524256.2020.174572732223368

Gibson, M. J., & Houser, A. (2007). Valuing the invaluable: A new look at the economic value of family caregiving. *Issue Brief (Public Policy Institute (American Association of Retired Persons))*, (IB82), 1–12.17612038

Compilation of References

Gladding, S. T. (2020). *The creative arts in counseling* (6th ed.). American Counseling Association.

Glad, K. A., Stensland, S., Czajkowski, N. O., Boelen, P. A., & Dyb, G. (2022). The longitudinal association between symptoms of posttraumatic stress and complicated grief: A random intercepts cross-lag analysis. *Psychological Trauma: Theory, Research, Practice, and Policy*, 14(3), 386–392. 10.1037/tra000108734398627

Goicoechea, T., & Lahue, K. (2021). Case studies in pediatric music therapy during COVID-19. *Music Therapy Perspectives*, 39(2), 126–132. 10.1093/mtp/miab009

Gökler-Danışman, I., Yalçınay-İnan, M., & Yiğit, İ. (2017). Experience of grief by patients with cancer in relation to perceptions of illness: The mediating roles of identity centrality, stigma-induced discrimination, and hopefulness. *Journal of Psychosocial Oncology*, 35(6), 776–796. 10.1080/0 7347332.2017.134038928609249

Gold, A. I., Ryjova, Y., Corner, G. W., Rasmussen, H. F., Kim, Y., & Margolin, G. (2023). Loss during COVID-19: Moderating effects of meaning and romantic relationships on anxiety and depressive symptoms. *Psychological Trauma: Theory, Research, Practice, and Policy*. Advance online publication. 10.1037/tra000152637523301

Golshiri, P., Mostofi, A., & Rouzbahani, S. (2023). The effect of problem-solving and assertiveness training on self-esteem and mental health of female adolescents: A randomized clinical trial. *BMC Psychology*, 11(1), 106. 10.1186/s40359-023-01154-x37032337

Goncalves, J.Junior, Moreira, M. M., & Rolim Neto, M. L. (2020). Silent cries intensify the pain of the life that is ending: COVID-19 is robbing families of the chance to say a final goodbye. *Frontiers in Psychiatry*, 11, 570773. 10.3389/fpsyt.2020.57077333061924

González-Padilla, D. A., & Tortolero-Blanco, L. (2020). Social media influence in the COVID-19 Pandemic. *International Braz J Urol*, 46(suppl 1), 120–124. 10.1590/s1677-5538.ibju.2020. s12132550706

Gori, A., Topino, E., & Caretti, V. (2021). The impact of Covid-19 Lockdown on perceived stress: The role of Defence Mechanisms and coping strategies. *Journal of Contingencies and Crisis Management*, 30(4), 379–390. 10.1111/1468-5973.12380

Gračanin, A., Bylsma, L. M., & Vingerhoets, A. J. (2014). Is crying a self-soothing behavior? *Frontiers in Psychology*, 5(502). 10.3389/fpsyg.2014.0050224904511

Grauf-Grounds, C., & Rivera, P. M. (2020). The ORCA-stance as a practice beyond cultural humility. In C. Grauf-Grounds, T Schermer Sellers, S. Edwards, H.S. Cheon, D. MacDonald, S. Whitney & P. Rivera. (Eds.). *A practice beyond cultural humility: How clinicians can work more effectively in a diverse world* (pp. 8-25). Routledge.

Greenberg, J., Pyszczynski, T., Solomon, S., Rosenblatt, A., Veeder, M., Kirkland, S., & Lyon, D. (1990). Evidence of terror management II: The effects of mortality salience on reactions to those who threaten or bolster the cultural worldview. *Journal of Personality and Social Psychology*, 58(2), 308–318. 10.1037/0022-3514.58.2.308

Greiner, C. M., Park, J., & Goldstein, S. E. (2022). Teacher trainees' experiences with and beliefs about responding to students' challenging life events. *Teaching and Teacher Education*, 111, 103603. 10.1016/j.tate.2021.103603

Griffiths, K. M., Calear, A. L., & Banfield, M. (2009). Systematic Review on Internet Support Groups (ISGs) and Depression (1): Do ISGs reduce depressive symptoms? *Journal of Medical Internet Research*, 11(3), e40. 10.2196/jmir.127019793719

Gross, R. (2015). *The nature and experience of grief. In understanding grief: An introduction* (1st ed.). Routledge. 10.4324/9781315727936

Guise, R. (2015). *Study guide for the national marriage and family licensing exam.* Family Solutions Institute.

Haik, J., Brown, S., Liran, A., Visentin, D., Sokolov, A., Zilinsky, I., & Kornhaber, R. (2017). Burnout and compassion fatigue: Prevalence and associations among Israeli burn clinicians. *Neuropsychiatric Disease and Treatment*, 13, 1533–1540. 10.2147/NDT.S13318128670122

Hall, M. E. L., Shannonhouse, L., Aten, J., McMartin, J., & Silverman, E. (2020). The varieties of redemptive experiences: A qualitative study of meaning-making in evangelical Christian cancer patients. *Psychology of Religion and Spirituality*, 12(1), 13–25. 10.1037/rel0000210

Hammond, L. C., & Gantt, L. (1998). Using art in counseling: Ethical considerations. *Journal of Counseling and Development*, 76(3), 271–276. 10.1002/j.1556-6676.1998.tb02542.x

Hampton, C. (n.d.). *Creating and facilitating peer support groups.* COMMUNITYTOOLBOX.

Hanauer, C., Telaar, B., Rosner, R., & Doering, B. K. (2024). The efficacy of psychosocial interventions for grief symptoms in bereaved children and adolescents: A systematic review and meta-analysis. *Journal of Affective Disorders, 350*, 164–173. https://doi-org.proxy.library.ohio.edu/10.1016/j.jad.2024.01.063

Hannon, M. D., White, E. E., & Fleming, H. (2023). Ambivalence to action: Addressing systemic racism in counselor education. *Counselor Education and Supervision*, 62(2), 108–117. Advance online publication. 10.1002/ceas.12264

Han, S., Riddell, J. R., & Piquero, A. R. (2023). Anti-Asian American Hate Crimes Spike During the Early Stages of the COVID-19 Pandemic. *Journal of Interpersonal Violence*, 38(3-4), 3513–3533. 10.1177/08862605221107056356572 78

Hanson, W. (2002). *The next place.* Walden House Press.

Harasymchuk, C., Walker, D. L., Muise, A., & Impett, E. A. (2021). Planning date nights that promote closeness: The roles of relationship goals and self-expansion. *Journal of Social and Personal Relationships*, 38(5), 1692–1709. 10.1177/0265407521100043634121791

Harrichand, J., & Herlihy, B. (2019). Grief and loss: When the professional becomes personal. *Counseling Today*.

Compilation of References

Harrop, E., Morgan, F., Longo, M., Semedo, L., Fitzgibbon, J., Pickett, S., Scott, H., Seddon, K., Sivell, S., Nelson, A., & Byrne, A. (2020). The impacts and effectiveness of support for people bereaved through advanced illness: A systematic review and thematic synthesis. *Palliative Medicine*, 34(7), 871–888. 10.1177/0269216320920533332419630

Harrop, E., Scott, H., Sivell, S., Seddon, K., Fitzgibbon, J., Morgan, F., Pickett, S., Byrne, A., Nelson, A., & Longo, M. (2020). Coping and well-being in bereavement: Two core outcomes for evaluating bereavement support in palliative care. *BMC Palliative Care*, 19(1), 29. 10.1186/s12904-020-0532-432164642

Hartig, J., & Viola, J. (2016). Online Grief Support Communities. *Omega*, 73(1), 29–41. 10.1177/0030222815575698

Hathaway, C. A., Bloomer, A. M., Oswald, L. B., Siegel, E. M., Peoples, A. R., Ulrich, C. M., Penedo, F. J., Tworoger, S. S., & Gonzalez, B. D. (2022). Factors associated with self-reported social isolation among patients with cancer during the COVID-19 pandemic. [Supplemental]. *Health Psychology*, 41(4), 311–318. 10.1037/hea000117235324248

Hay, A., Howell, J. A., Rudaizky, D., & Breen, L. J. (2022). Experiences and support needs of bereaved students in higher education. *Omega*, 003022282210965. 10.1177/0030222822109656535549940

Heidegger, M. (2008). *Being and Time*. Harper Perennial Modern Classics.

Heisler, M. (2006, December). *Building Peer Support Programs to Manage Chronic Disease: Seven Models for Success*. ResearchGate.

Henderson, D. A., & Gladding, S. T. (1998). The creative arts in counseling: A multicultural approach. *The Arts in Psychotherapy*, 25(3), 183–187. 10.1016/S0197-4556(98)00011-2

Hendrickson, Z. M., Kim, J., Tol, W. A., Shrestha, A., Kafle, H. M., Luitel, N. P., Thapa, L., & Surkan, P. J. (2018). Resilience among Nepali widows after the death of a spouse: "That was my past and now I have to see my present.". *Qualitative Health Research*, 28(3), 466–478. 10.1177/1049732317739265291 10564

Hibbert, C. (2018, April 10). *Siblings & Grief: 10 Things Everyone Should Know*, Dr. Christina Hibbert. https://www.drchristinahibbert.com/dealing-with-grief/siblings-grief-10-things-everyone-should-know/

Hickney, W. (2022, November 3). *The Early Peer Support Movement - Colorado Mental Wellness Network*. Colorado Mental Wellness Network.

Hidalgo, I. (2021). Spiritual coping and its effects on children's grief, personal growth, and mental health 2-24 months after the death of a parent, grandparent, or sibling. *Journal of Pediatric Healthcare*, 36(2), 212. .10.1016/j.pedhc.2021.07.003

Higgins, A., Hybholt, L., Meuser, O. A., Eustace Cook, J., Downes, C., & Morrissey, J. (2022, March 15). Scoping Review of Peer-Led Support for People Bereaved by Suicide. *International Journal of Environmental Research and Public Health*, 19(6), 3485. 10.3390/ijerph1906348535329171

Higgins, J. P., Graziano, C., Froerer, C., Placide, R., Tavakoli, F., & Chu, A. (2023). Time management strategies for the new practitioner. *American Journal of Health-System Pharmacy*, 80(8), 483–486. 10.1093/ajhp/zxad00836626278

Hobson, J., & Morrison-Saunders, A. (2013). Reframing teaching relationships: From student-centered to subject centered learning. *Teaching in Higher Education*, 18(7), 773–783. 10.1080/13562517.2013.836095

Hoehn-Velasco, L., Balmori de la Miyar, J. R., Silvario-Murillo, A., & Sherajum, M. F. (2023). *Marriage and divorce during a pandemic: the impact of the COVID-19 pandemic on marital formation and dissolution in Mexico*. NCBI. https://www.ncbi.nlm.nih.gov/pmc/articles/PMC10088673/

Holman, E. A., Jones, N. M., Garfin, D. R., & Silver, R. C. (2023). Distortions in time perception during collective trauma: Insights from a national longitudinal study during the COVID-19 pandemic. *Psychological Trauma: Theory, Research, Practice, and Policy*, 15(5), 800–807. 10.1037/tra000132635925689

Holmgren, H. (2023). Is Online Peer Support Helpful in Widowhood? The Lived Experiences of Young Parents. *Illness, Crises, and Loss*, 31(3), 540–557. 10.1177/10541373221099411

Holm, M., Alvariza, A., Furst, C. J., Ohlen, J., & Arestedt, K. (2019). Psychometric evaluation of the anticipatory grief scale in a sample of family caregivers in the context of palliative care. *Health and Quality of Life Outcomes*, 17(1), 42. 10.1186/s12955-019-1110-430837000

Holtzhausen, N., Fitzgerald, K., Thakur, I., Ashley, J., Rolfe, M., & Pit, S. W. (2020). Swipe-based dating applications use and its association with mental health outcomes: A cross-sectional study. *BMC Psychology*, 8(1), 22. 10.1186/s40359-020-0373-132127048

Hooyman, N. R., Kramer, B. J., & Sanders, S. (2021). *Living through loss: Interventions Across the Life Span*. Columbia University Press.

Horowitz, J. M. (2022, April 14). *More than half of Americans in their 40s are "sandwiched" between an aging parent and their own children*. Pew Research Center. https://www.pewresearch.org/short-reads/2022/04/08/more-than-half-of-americans-in-their-40s-are-sandwiched-between-an-aging-parent-and-their-own-children/

Horstman, M. J., Mills, W. L., Herman, L. I., Cai, C., Shelton, G., Qdaisat, T., Berger, D. H., & Naik, A. D. (2017). Patient experience with discharge instructions in postdischarge recovery: A qualitative study. *BMJ Open*, 7(2), e014842. 10.1136/bmjopen-2016-01484228228448

Høy, B., & Hall, E. O. C. (2022). "Take good care of yourself" An integrative review of older widows' self-care for health and well-being. *Journal of Women & Aging*, 34(1), 1–30. 10.1080/08952841.2020.175348432339070

Hui, L. K., Garnett, A., Oleynikov, C., & Boamah, S. A. (2023). Compassion fatigue in healthcare providers during the COVID-19 pandemic: A scoping review protocol. *BMJ Open*, 13(5), e069843. 10.1136/bmjopen-2022-06984337258070

Compilation of References

Huisman, D. M., & Lemke, A. (2022). I Am This Widow: Social Support in Friendship After the Loss of a Spouse in Mid-Life. *Omega*, 86(1), 45–64. 10.1177/00302228209612313298534

Hu, K., Godfrey, K., Ren, Q., Wang, S., Yang, X., & Li, Q. (2022). The impact of the COVID-19 pandemic on college students in USA: Two years later. *Psychiatry Research*, 315, 114685. 10.1016/j.psychres.2022.11468535872401

Hunt, D. F., Bailey, J., Lennox, B., Crofts, M., & Vincent, C. (2021). Enhancing psychological safety in mental health services. *International Journal of Mental Health Systems*, 15(1), 33. *Advance online publication.* 10.1186/s13033-021-00439-133853658

Hussain, S. (2023). *Hamza attends a funeral*. Kube Publishing.

Iglewicz, A., Shear, M. K., Reynolds, C. F.III, Simon, N., Lebowitz, B., & Zisook, S. (2019). Complicated grief therapy for clinicians: An evidence-based protocol for Mental Health Practice. *Depression and Anxiety*, 37(1), 90–98. 10.1002/da.2296531622522

J. F. (2023, January 25). Death & Dying: How different cultures deal with grief and mourning. *Phys.org.* https://phys.org/news/2023-01-death-dying- culturesgrief.html#:~:text=Death%20 and%20dying%3A%20How%20different%20cultures%20deal%20with. %205%205.%20Sending%20on%20the%20spirit%20

Jackson-Cherry, L., & Erford, B. (2017). *Crisis assessment, intervention, and prevention* (3rd ed.). Pearson.

Jacob, G., Faber, S. C., Faber, N., Barlett, A., Quimet, A. J., & Williams, M. T. (2022). A systematic review of Black People coping with racism: Approaches, analysis, and empowerment. *Perspectives on Psychological Science*, 7(5), 482–495. 10.1177/17456916221100509360006823

Jacobs, E. E., Schimmel, C. J., Masson, R. L., & Harvill, I. L. (2016). *Group Counseling: Strategies and skills* (8th ed.). Cengage.

JAG Institute. (2023). *Annual report indicating increased rate of childhood bereavement*. JAG Institute.

JAG Institute. (2023). *Annual report indicating increased rate of childhood bereavement*. JAG Institute. *https://www.prweb.com/releases/jag-institute-releases-annual-report-indicating-increased-rate-of-childhood-bereavement-876461466.html*

Jahani, L., Abolhassani, S., Babaee, S., & Omranifard, V. (2022). Effects of a compassion-based program on the grief experienced by caregivers of people who have dementia: A randomized controlled clinical trial. *BMC Nursing*, 21(1), 198. 10.1186/s12912-022-00980-535879751

James, R. (2017). *Crisis intervention strategies* (8th ed.). Centage Learning.

Jankauskaite, G., O'Brien, K. M., & Yang, N. (2021). Assessing knowledge and predicting grief counseling skills among university counseling center therapists. *The Counseling Psychologist*, 49(3), 458–484. 10.1177/0011000020983525

343

Jeffreys, S. (2011). *Helping grieving people: When tears are not enough* (2nd ed.). Routledge. 10.4324/9780203856154

Jiang, X., Topps, A. K., & Suzuki, R. (2021). A systematic review of self-care measures for professionals and trainees. *Training and Education in Professional Psychology*, 15(2), 126–139. 10.1037/tep0000318

Jiménez-Picón, N., Romero-Martín, M., Ponce-Blandón, J. A., Ramirez-Baena, L., Palomo-Lara, J. C., & Gómez-Salgado, J. (2021). The relationship between mindfulness and emotional intelligence as a protective factor for healthcare professionals: Systematic review. *International Journal of Environmental Research and Public Health*, 18(10), 5491. 10.3390/ijerph1810549134065519

Jodry, J., & Reid, M. (2020). Acting theory applied to counseling: Stanislavski continues to contribute to psychic healing. *Journal of Creativity in Mental Health*, 15(2), 223–234. 10.1080/15401383.2019.1683110

Jones, E., Oka, M., Clark, J., Gardner, H., Hunt, R., & Dutson, S. (2019). Lived experience of young widowed individuals: A qualitative study. *Death Studies*, 43(3), 183–192. 10.1080/0748 1187.2018.144513729498589

Jong, J. (2021). Death anxiety and religion. *Current Opinion in Psychology*, 40, 40–44. 10.1016/j. copsyc.2020.08.00432942111

Jordan, M., & Hackett, J. T. (2019). NAADAC.

Joseph, A. O., Fagbamila, O. D., & Joseph, A. A. (2021). COVID-19 pandemic preventive guidelines and protocols: How does this affect the Yoruba funeral rites in Nigeria? *International Journal of Modern Anthropology*, 2(16), 570–585. 10.4314/ijma.v2i16.3

Joy, C., Staniland, L., Mazzucchelli, T. G., Skinner, S., Cuddeford, L., & Breen, L. J. (2024). What bereaved children want to Know About Death and Grief. *Journal of Child & Family Studies*, 33(1), 327–337. 10.1007/s10826-023-02694-x

Kaplow, J. B., Layne, C. M., Pynoos, R. S., & Saltzman, W. (2023). *Multidimensional grief therapy: A flexible approach to assessing and supporting bereaved youth*. Cambridge University Press. 10.1017/9781316422359

Kaplow, J. B., Saxe, G. N., Putnam, F. W., Pynoos, R. S., & Lieberman, A. F. (2006). The long–term consequences of early childhood trauma: A case study and discussion. *Psychiatry*, 69(4), 362–375. 10.1521/psyc.2006.69.4.36217326730

Karaman, M. A., Eşici, H., Tomar, İ. H., & Aliyev, R. (2021). COVID-19: Are school counseling services ready? Students' psychological symptoms, school counselors' views, and solutions. *Frontiers in Psychology*, 12, 647740. 10.3389/fpsyg.2021.64774033868121

Karpouza, E., & Emvalotis, A. (2019). Exploring the teacher student relationship in graduate education a constructivist grounded theory. *Teaching in Higher Education*, 24(2), 121–140. 10.1080/13562517.2018.1468319

Compilation of References

Kaus, K. J. (2022). *Death Anxiety: A Quantitative Exploration of Professional Counselors Experiences* [Doctoral dissertation, Minnesota State University, Mankato]. Cornerstone: A Collection of Scholarly and Creative Works for Minnesota State University, Mankato. https://cornerstone.lib.mnsu.edu/etds/942/

Kelly, S. B. C. (2023). Supporting nursing, midwifery and allied health professional teams through restorative clinical supervision. *British Journal of Nursing*. https://www.britishjournalofnursing.com/content/professional/supporting-nursing-midwifery-and-allied-health-professional-teams-through-restorative-clinical-supervision

Kennedy, C. J., Gardner, F., & Farrelly, C. (2020). Death, dying and bereavement: Considering compassion and empowerment. *Pastoral Care in Education*, 38(2), 138–155. 10.1080/02643944.2020.1725905

Khanipour-Kencha, A., Jackson, A. C., & Bahramnezhad, F. (2022). Anticipatory grief during COVID-19: A commentary. *British Journal of Community Nursing*, 27(3), 114–117. 10.12968/bjcn.2022.27.3.11435274970

Khoury, B., Barbarin, O., Gutiérrez, G., Klicperova-Baker, M., Padakannaya, P., & Thompson, A. (2022). Complicated grief during COVID-19: An international perspective. *International Perspectives in Psychology: Research, Practice, Consultation*, 11(3), 214–221. 10.1027/2157-3891/a000055

Kierkegaard, S. (1981). *The concept of anxiety*. Princeton University Press. 10.1515/9781400846979-002

Kierkegaard, S. (1983). *The sickness unto death*. Princeton University Press.

Kirchberg, T. M., & Neimeyer, R. A. (1991). Reactions of beginning counselors to situations involving death and dying. *Death Studies*, 15(6), 603–610. 10.1080/07481189108252548?10115708

Kirchberg, T. M., Neimeyer, R. A., & James, R. K. (1998). Beginning counselors' death concerns and empathic responses to client situations involving death and grief. *Death Studies*, 22(2), 99–120. 10.1080/074811898201623?10182421

Knewstubb, B. (2016). The learning-teaching nexus: Modelling the learning-teaching relationship in higher education. *Studies in Higher Education*, 41(3), 525–540. 10.1080/03075079.2014.934802

Ko, H., & Lee, S. M. (2021). Effects of Imbalance of Self- and Other-Care on Counselors' Burnout. *Journal of Counseling and Development*, 99(3), 252–262. 10.1002/jcad.12372

Konigsberg, R. D. (2011). *The truth about grief: The myth of its five stages and the new science of loss*. Simon & Schuster.

Konings, F., Sumter, S., & Vandenbosch, L. (2023). It's not You, it's Me: Experiences with Ghosting on Mobile Dating Applications and Belgian Emerging Adults' Self-Esteem. *Sexuality & Culture*, 27(4), 1328–1351. 10.1007/s12119-023-10065-3

345

Kosloff, S., Greenberg, J., Weise, D., & Solomon, S. (2009). The effects of mortality salience on political preferences: The roles of charisma and political orientation. *Journal of Experimental Social Psychology*, 46(1), 139–145. 10.1016/j.jesp.2009.09.002

Kossek, E. E. (2016). Managing work–life boundaries in the digital age. *Organizational Dynamics*, 45(3), 258–270. 10.1016/j.orgdyn.2016.07.010

Kristensen, T., Elklit, A., & Karstoft, K.-I. (2012). Posttraumatic Stress Disorder after bereavement: Early psychological sequelae of losing a close relative due to terminal cancer. *Journal of Loss and Trauma*, 17(6), 508–521. 10.1080/15325024.2012.665304

Kübler-Ross, E (1997). *On death and dying: What the dying have to teach doctors, nurses, clergy, and their own families* (reprint ed.). Scribner.

Kübler-Ross, E. (1997). *On death and dying: What the dying have to teach doctors, nurses, clergy, and their own families (reprint ed.).*

Kubler-Ross, E. (1970). *On death and dying.* Collier Books/Macmillan Publishing Co.

Kumar, R. M. (2021). The Many Faces of Grief: A Systematic Literature review of grief during the COVID-19 Pandemic. *Illness, Crisis, and Loss/Illness. Illness, Crises, and Loss*, 31(1), 100–119. 10.1177/10541373211038084436605776

Kumpasoglu, G. B., Eltan, S., Merdan-Yilidiz, E. D., & Batigun, A. D. (2020). Mediating the role of life satisfaction and death anxiety in the relationship between dark triad and social media addiction. *Personality and Individual Differences*, 172, 1–8.

Lawrence, S. T. (2019). *The grieving child in the classroom: A guide for school-based professionals.* Routledge. 10.4324/9780429055515

Leigh, O. K. T., Clemons, K., Robertson, A., Placeres, V., Gay, J., Lopez, P. C., Mason, E. C., Ieva, K. P., Lane, E. M. D., & Saunders, R. (2023). Antiracist school counseling: A consensual qualitative study. *Journal of Counseling and Development*, 101(3), 310–322. 10.1002/jcad.12477

Lenes, E., Swank, J., & Nash, S. (2015). A qualitative exploration of a music experience within a counselor education sexuality course. *Journal of Creativity in Mental Health*, 10(2), 216–231. 10.1080/15401383.2014.983255

Leonard, J. (2020). What is trauma? What to know. n.a. (2021, May 3). Culturally based online peer support group brought mental health benefits during COVID-19. Medical Xpress - medical research advances and health news. n.a. (2022, February 18). Peer support. Mental Health Foundation. n.a. (2023, November 7). How can you learn about different cultures to improve your peer support? How to Learn About Different Cultures for Peer Support. n.a, (2022, November 18). The 3 different types of trauma I All Points North. All Points North.

Leung, T., Schmidt, F., & Mushquash, C. (2023). A persona history of trauma and experience of secondary traumatic stress, vicarious trauma, and burnout in mental health workers: A systematic literature review. [Supplemental]. *Psychological Trauma: Theory, Research, Practice, and Policy*, 15(Suppl 2), S213–S221. 10.1037/tra000127735511539

Compilation of References

Levkovich, I., & Elyoseph, Z. (2021). "I don't know what to say": Teachers' perspectives on supporting bereaved students after the death of a parent. *Omega*, 86(3), 945–965. 10.1177/003 02228219936243358258

Levy, B. (2022). *Breaking the age code: How your beliefs about aging determine how long and how well you live*. William Morrow & Co.

Li, C., Tang, N., Yang, L., Zeng, Q., Yu, T., Pu, X., Wang, J., & Zhang, H. (2023). Effect of caregiver burden on anticipatory grief among caregivers of elderly cancer patients: Chain mediation role of family functioning and resilience. *Frontiers in Psychology*, 13, 1020517. 10.3389/fpsyg.2022.102051736704702

Liew, C. H., & Servaty-Seib, H. L. (2019). College students' feedback on a student bereavement leave policy. *Journal of Student Affairs Research and Practice*, 57(1), 55–68. 10.1080/19496591.2019.1614940

Lima, T. M. F., Costa, A. F. D., Lopes, M. C. B. T., Campanharo, C. R. V., Batista, R. E. A., Fernandes, H., & Okuno, M. F. P. (2023). Factors related to burden and self-care for hypertension in family caregivers. *Cogitare Enfermagem, 28.*https://doi.org/10.1590/ce.v28i0.92871

Linder, L., Lunardini, M., & Zimmerman, H. (2024). Supporting Childhood Bereavement Through School-Based Grief Group. *Omega*, 89(2), 741–758. https://doi-org.proxy.library.ohio.edu/10.1177/00302228221082756. 10.1177/00302228221082756135357962

Lipp, N., & O'Brien, K. M. (2020). Bereaved college students: Social support, coping style, continuing bonds, and social media use as predictors of complicated grief and posttraumatic growth. *Omega*, 85(1), 178–203. 10.1177/00302228209419523264785

Liu, Z., Heffernan, C., & Tan, J. (2020). Caregiver burden: A concept analysis. *International Journal of Nursing Sciences*, 7(4), 438–445. 10.1016/j.ijnss.2020.07.01233195757

Li, Y., & Peng, J. (2022). Evaluation of expressive arts therapy on the resilience of university students in COVID-19: A network analysis approach. *International Journal of Environmental Research and Public Health*, 19(13), 7658. 10.3390/ijerph1913765835805317

Long, S., Benoist, C. & Weidner, W. (2023). *World Alzheimer's report 2023*. Alzheimer's Disease International. World-Alzheimer-Report-2023.pdf (alzint.org)

Loue, S. (2022). *Transformational learning through cultural humility*. Springer. 10.1007/978-3-031-11381-9_6

Lowej, R. B., & Aoun, S. M. (2020). Memorialization during COVID-10: Implications for the bereaved, service providers and policymakers. *Palliative Care and Social Practice*, 14, 1–9. 10.1177/2632352420980456

Lund, P. C. (2020). Deconstructing grief: A sociological analysis of prolonged grief disorder. *Social Theory & Health*, 19(2), 186–200. 10.1057/s41285-020-00135-z

Lynch, S. H., Shuster, G., & Lobo, M. L. (2018). The family caregiver experience - examining the positive and negative aspects of compassion satisfaction and compassion fatigue as caregiving outcomes. *Aging & Mental Health, 22*(11), 1424–1431. 10.1080/13607863.2017.136434428812375

Määttä, K., & Uusiautti, S. (2012). Seven Rules on Having a Happy Marriage Along With Work. *The Family Journal (Alexandria, Va.), 20*(3), 267–273. 10.1177/1066480712448997

MacArthur, N. D., Kirby, E., & Mowll, J. (2022). Bereavement affinities: A qualitative study of lived experiences of grief and loss. *Death Studies, 47*(7), 836–846. 10.1080/07481187.2022.213504436327234

Magee, B. (1997). *The philosophy of Schopenhauer.* Clarendon Press. 10.1093/0198237227.001.0001

Magin, Z. E., David, A. B., Carney, L. M., Park, C. L., Gutierrez, I. A., & George, L. S. (2021). Belief in god and psychological distress: Is it the belief or certainty of the belief? *Religions, 12*(9), 757. 10.3390/rel12090757

Mah, K., Swami, N., Pope, A., Earle, C. C., Krzyzanowska, M. K., Rinat, N., Hales, S., Rodin, G., Breffni, H., & Zimmermann, C. (2022). Caregiver bereavement outcomes in advanced cancer: Associations with quality of death and patient age. *Supportive Care in Cancer, 30*(2), 1343–1353. 10.1007/s00520-021-06536-834499215

Mansoori, J., Khodabakhshi-Koolaee, A., Falsafinejad, M. R., & Kashani Vahid, L. (2023). Bereavement for a loved person: A look at the opinions and process of coping with grief in the covid-19 ERA. *Practice in Clinical Psychology, 11*(3), 223–238. 10.32598/jpcp.11.3.746.4

Marinho, J. D. S., Batista, I. B., Nobre, R. A. D. S., Guimarães, M. S. A., Dos Santos-Orlandi, A. A., Brito, T. R. P., Pagotto, V., Saidel, M. G. B., Fusco, S. F. B., Maia, F. O. M., Corona, L. P., & Nunes, D. P. (2022). Burden, satisfaction caregiving, and family relations in informal caregivers of older adults. *Frontiers in Medicine, 9*, 1059467. 10.3389/fmed.2022.105946736619643

Martin, J. (2015). *The 7 psychological stages of chronic pain.* Pain News Network. www.painnewsnetwork.org

Maynard, K. K. (1991). *Thomas Hardy's tragic poetry.* University of Iowa Press.

Mayo Clinic. (2022). *Esophageal cancer.* Mayo Clinic. https://www.mayoclinic.org/diseases-conditions/esophageal-cancer/symptoms-causes/syc-20356084

Mayo Foundation for Medical Education and Research. (2022, December 13). *Complicated grief.* Mayo Clinic. https://www.mayoclinic.org/diseases-conditions/complicated-grief/symptoms-causes/syc-20360374

McCann, J. (2022, July 13). The long-term impact of COVID-19 on the funeral industry and funeral planning. *1800Flowers Petal Talk.* https://www.1800flowers.com/blog/everyday-moments/the-long-term-impact-of-covid-19-on-the-funeral-industry-and-funeral-planning/

Compilation of References

McCoyd, J. L., Goldblatt, H. E., Hennessy, K., & Akincigil, A. (2023). Revising ruling discourses: The griefwork evidence-to-practice gap and the mental health workforce. *Death Studies*, 47(10), 1–10. 10.1080/07481187.2023.217115936695284

McKinney, R., & Britton, P. J. (2021). Coming alongside supervisees: Introducing the skillset of companioning to counselor supervision. *Journal of Counselor Practice*, 12(1), 23–46. 10.22229/com1212021

McMahon, E. M., Corcoran, P., O'Regan, G., Keely, H., Cannon, M., Carli, V., Wasserman, C., Hadlaczky, G., Sarchiapone, M., Apter, A., Balazs, J., Balint, M., Bobes, J., Brunner, R., Cozman, D., Haring, C., Iosue, M., Kaess, M., Kahn, J. P., & Wasserman, D. (2017). Physical activity in European adolescents and associations with anxiety, depression and well-beign. *European Child & Adolescent Psychiatry*, 26(1), 111–122. 10.1007/s00787-016-0875-927277894

Meagher, D. K. (2001). School based grief crisis management programs. *What Will We Do? Preparing a School Community to Cope with Crises, 2nd Edition*. 10.2190/WW2C3

Meichenbaum, D., & Myers, J. (2016). Checklist of Strategies for Coping with Grief. In R.A. Neimeyer (Ed.). *Techniques of grief therapy (Vol. 2): Assessment and interventions*. Routledge

Meichsner, F., & Wilz, G. (2018). Dementia caregivers' coping with pre-death grief: Effects of a CBT-based intervention. *Aging & Mental Health*, 22(2), 218–225. 10.1080/13607863.2016.124742827792398

Menzies, R. E., & Menzies, R. G. (2020). Death anxiety in the time of COVID-19: Theoretical explanations and clinical implications. *Cognitive Behaviour Therapist*, 13, e19. 10.1017/S1754470X2000021534191938

Menzies, R. E., & Menzies, R. G. (2021). *Mortals: How the fear of death shaped human society*. Allen & Unwin.

Menzies, R. E., Neimeyer, R. A., & Menzies, R. G. (2020). Death anxiety, loss, and grief in the time of COVID-19. *Behaviour Change*, 37(3), 111–115. 10.1017/bec.2020.10

Meyers, L. (2014). *Advocacy in action*. CT Counseling. https://ct.counseling.org/2014/04/advocacy-in-action/

Midgley, C., Lockwood, P., & Thai, S. (2022). *Can the social network bridge social distancing? Social media use during the COVID-19 pandemic*. Research Gate. https://www.researchgate.net/publication/363794377_Can_the_social_network_bridge_social_distancing_Social_media_use_during_the_COVID-19_pandemic

Mikocka-Walus, A., Stokes, M., Evans, S., Olive, L., & Westrupp, E. (2021). Finding the power within and without: How can we strengthen resilience against symptoms of stress, anxiety, and depression in australian parents during the COVID-19 pandemic? *Journal of Psychosomatic Research*, 145, 110433. 10.1016/j.jpsychores.2021.11043333812660

Minor, A. J., Moody, S. J., Tadlock-Marlo, R., Pender, R., & Person, M. (2013). Music as a medium for cohort development. *Journal of Creativity in Mental Health*, 8(4), 381–394. 10.1080/15401383.2013.857928

Mirfardi, A. (2023). The sociocultural and economic barriers to self-care culture for COVID-19 control in developing societies: The case of Iran. In *Contributions to Economics* (pp. 153–179). 10.1007/978-3-031-27886-0_6

Mirutse, A., Mengistu, Z., & Bizuwork, K. (2023). Prevalence of compassion fatigue, burnout, compassion satisfaction, and associated factors among nurses working in cancer treatment centres in Ethiopia, 2020. *BMC Nursing*, 22(1), 373. 10.1186/s12912-023-01383-w37817139

Mitchell, H.-R., Kim, Y., Llabre, M. M., & Ironson, G. (2022). Four-symptom model of medical-related posttraumatic stress among adult cancer patients. [Supplemental]. *Health Psychology*, 41(7), 492–501. 10.1037/hea000118735587888

Mitima-Verloop, H. B., Mooren, T. T. M., & Boelen, P. A. (2021). Facilitating grief: An exploration of the function of funerals and rituals in relation to grief reactions. *Death Studies*, 45(9), 735–745. 10.1080/07481187.2019.168609031710282

Mitima-Verloop, H. B., Mooren, T., Kritikou, M. E., & Boelen, P. A. (2022). Restricted mourning: Impact of the COVID-19 pandemic on funeral services, grief rituals, and prolonged grief symptoms. *Frontiers in Psychiatry*, 13(0), 878818. 10.3389/fpsyt.2022.87881835711586

Mo, P. K. H., & Coulson, N. (2008). Exploring the Communication of Social Support within Virtual Communities: A Content Analysis of Messages Posted to an Online HIV/AIDS Support Group. *Cyberpsychology & Behavior*, 11(3), 371–374. 10.1089/cpb.2007.011818537512

Morais, F. L. T., Fachini da Costa, A., Barbosa, T. L. M. C., Vancini, C. C. R., Assayag, B. R. E., Fernandes, H., & Pinto Okuno, M. F. (2023). Factors related to burden and self-care for hypertension in family caregivers. *Cogitagre Enfermagem*, 28, 1-12. https://doi.org/10.1590/ce.v28i.0.92871

Morell-Velasco, C., Fernández-Alcántara, M., Hueso-Montoro, C., & Montoya-Juárez, R. (2020). Teachers' perception of grief in primary and secondary school students in Spain: Children's responses and elements which facilitate or hinder the grieving process. *Journal of Pediatric Nursing*, 51, e100–e107. 10.1016/j.pedn.2019.12.01631928803

Moreno-Colom, S., Borràs Català, V., Cruz Gómez, I., & Porcel López, S. (2023). The Experience of Remote Work during Lockdown in Catalonia: A Gender Perspective. *Revista Española de Investigaciones Sociológicas*, 183, 77–98. 10.5477/cis/reis.183.77

Morrigan, B., Keesing, S., & Breen, L. J. (2022). Exploring the Social Networks of Bereaved Spouses: Phenomenological Case Studies. *Omega*, 85(2), 268–284. 10.1177/00302228209440 6232698677

Mosse, E. (2024). *Grieving and Ritualizing Marriage Death: The Garden as Outer World Companion and Inner World Landscape* [Dissertation].

Compilation of References

Moss, S. J., Wollny, K., Poulin, T. G., Cook, D. J., Stelfox, H. T., Ordons, A. R. D., & Fiest, K. M. (2021). Bereavement interventions to support informal caregivers in the intensive care unit: A systematic review. *BMC Palliative Care*, 20(1), 66. 10.1186/s12904-021-00763-w33980242

Mueser, K. T., Gottlieb, J. D., Xie, H., Lu, W., Yanos, P. T., Rosenberg, S. D., Silverstein, S. M., Duva, S. M., Minsky, S., Wolfe, R. S., & McHugo, G. J. (2015). Evaluation of cognitive restructuring for post-traumatic stress disorder on people with severe mental illness. *The British Journal of Psychiatry*, 206(6), 501–508. 10.1192/bjp.bp.114.14792625858178

Mundell, E. (2024). *Grief affects the body, not just the mind*. Healthday. https://www.healthday.com/a-to-z-health/mental-health/grief-affects-the-body-not-just-the-mind

Munley, P. H., & Johnson, P. D. (2003). Theory and practice: Ernest Becker: A vital resource for counseling psychology. *Counselling Psychology Quarterly*, 16(4), 363–372. 10.1080/09515070310001636779

Munshi, L., Evans, G., & Razak, F. (2021). The case for relaxing no-visitor policies in hospitals during the ongoing COVID-19 pandemic. *CMAJ : Canadian Medical Association Journal = Journal de l'Association Medicale Canadienne, 193*(4), E135–E137. https://doi.org/10.1503/cmaj.202636

Najafi, K., Farahani, A. S., Rassouli, M., Majd, H. A., & Karami, M. (2022). Emotional upheaval, the essence of anticipatory grief in mothers of children with life threatening illnesses: A qualitative study. *BMC Psychology*, 10(1), 196. 10.1186/s40359-022-00904-735953867

Näppä, U., & Björkman-Randström, K. (2020). Experiences of participation in grief counseling groups from significant others' perspectives; a qualitative study. *BMC Palliative Care*, 19(1), 1–10. 10.1186/s12904-020-00632-y32799845

Narasimhan, M., Allotey, P., & Hardon, A. (2019). Self-care interventions to advance health and well-being: A conceptual framework to inform normative guidance. *BMJ. British Medical Journal (Clinical Research Ed.)*. 10.1136/bmj.l688

Naslund, J. A., Aschbrenner, K. A., Marsch, L. A., & Bartels, S. J. (2016, January 8). The Future of Mental Health Care. *Peer-to-peer support and social media: Epidemiology and Psychiatric Sciences*. Cambridge Core.

National Institute of Health (NIH). (2022). *Mental health*. NIH. https://COVID-19.nih.gov/COVID-19-topics/mental-health

National Institute of Health (NIH). (2022). *Mental Health*. NIH. https://COVID19.nih.gov/COVID-19-topics/mental-health

National Institute of Health (NIH). (2024). *Telemental Health*. NIH. https://www.nimh.nih.gov/sites/default/files/health/publications/what-is-telemental-health/what-is-telemental-health.pdf

National Research Council (US) Committee on the Role of Human Factors in Home Health Care. (2010). *The Role of Human Factors in Home Health Care: Workshop Summary*. Washington (DC): National Academies Press (US). https://www.ncbi.nlm.nih.gov/books/NBK210048/

Neff, K. D. (2023). Self-compassion: Theory, method, research, and intervention. *Annual Review of Psychology*, 74(1), 193–218. 10.1146/annurev-psych-032420-03104735961039

Neimeyer, R. A., & Lee, S. A. (2021). Circumstances of the death and associated risk factors for severity and impairment of COVID-19 grief. *Death Studies*, 0, 1–10. 10.1080/07481187.2021.189645934019471

Newhouse, L. (2021, March 1). Is crying good for you? *Harvard Medical School Blog*. https://www.health.harvard.edu/blog/is-crying-good-for-you-2021030122020

Ngamasana, E. L., Zarwell, M., Eberly, L., & Gunn, L. H. (2024). Difference in the physical and mental health of informal caregivers pre- and post-COVID-19 National Emergency Declaration in the United States. *SSM - Population Health*, 25, 101609. 10.1016/j.ssmph.2024.10160938313872

Nondenominational, C. I. I. A. (2020). *GriefShare Participant Workbook* (3rd ed.).

Nwosu, N., Enajedu, E. E., Itobore, U. A., & Ncheke, D. C. (2022). Effect of cognitive restructuring intervention on emotional adjustment of sample divorcees in Nsukka Education Zone of Enugu State, Nigeria. *International Journal of Education, Learning and Development*, 10(8), 18–26. 10.37745/ijeld.2013vo10n8pp1826

Nystul, M. S. (2019). *Introduction to counselling: An art and science perspective* (6th ed.). Cognella Academic Publishing.

O'Connor, M.-F., & Seeley, S. H. (2022). Grieving as a form of learning: Insights from neuroscience applied to grief and loss. *Current Opinion in Psychology*, 43, 317–322. 10.1016/j.copsyc.2021.08.01934520954

Ogunleye, T. (2021). Effective grief management: The role of the professional counsellor. In T. D. O. Adewuyi, B. K. Odu., & K. Olagunju (Eds.), *Topical issues in socio-personal guidance and counselling* (68-74). Brightways Publishers.

Oh, S. K., Yoo, K. H., & Owlett, J. (2021). Focusing on the "public" in public relations: The importance of person-centred messages (PCMs) in crisis communication on Twitter. *Journal of International Crisis and Risk Communication Research*, 4(1), 93–128. 10.30658/jicrcr.4.1.4

Ohuakanwa, C. E. (2015). Operant conditioning techniques in behaviour modification. In Uwaoma, N. C., & Chima, I. M. (Eds.), *Behaviour modification: Modern principles and practices* (pp. 124–146). Gabtony Prints Ltd.

Olatomide, O. O. (2019). Counselling for social reformation in Nigeria: The place of traditional moral values as viewed by Obafemi Awolowo University students. In A. Mburza & Emenike, E. H. (Eds.), *Critical considerations on social transformation and national healing for professional practicing counsellors in Nigeria* (pp. 1-14). Counselling Association of Nigeria (CASSON).

Olatomide, O. O. (2021). Socio-physiological adjustment strategies of retirees during the Coronavirus pandemic in Ondo State, Nigeria. *Rivers State Journal of Professional Counselling*, 1(1), 101–117.

Compilation of References

Omid, S., Alarcon, S. V., Vega, E. A., Kutlu, O. C., Olga, K., Chan, J. A., Vera, K., Harz, D., & Conrad, C. (2022). COVID-19's Impact on Cancer Care: Increased Emotional Stress in Patients and High Risk of Provider Burnout. *Journal of Gastrointestinal Surgery*, 26(1), 1–12. 10.1007/s11605-021-05032-y34027579

Orbay, I., Baydur, H., & Ucan, G. (2022). Compassion Fatigue in Informal Caregivers of Children with Cancer; a Section from Turkey. *Social Work in Public Health*, 37(8), 729–743. 10.1080/19371918.2022.208583735658822

Ozguc, S., Serin, E. K., & Tanriverdi, D. (2024). Death anxiety associated with coronavirus (COVID-19) disease: A systematic Review and Meta Analysis. *Omega*, 88(3), 823–856. 10.1177/00302228211050050334622711

Page, D. (2023, July 31). *What is The sandwich generation? experts explain this unique type of caregiving*. Care.com. https://www.care.com/c/what-is-the-sandwich-generation/

Pamela, N., Alberth, A. G., Tell, E. J., & Jansen, T. (2023). Policies to Sustain Employment Among Family Caregivers: The Family Caregiver Perspective. *Journal of Applied Gerontology*, 42(1), 3–11. 10.1177/0733464822112563536114013

Parker, E. T., III. (2024). What's lost in dismantling DEI offices? *Inside Higher Ed.* https://www.insidehighered.com/opinion/views/2024/02/19/whats-lost-dismantling-dei-offices-opinion#

Parray, W. M., & Kumar, S. (2022). The effect of assertiveness training on behaviour, self-esteem, stress, academic achievement and psychological wellbeing of students: A quasi-experimental study. *Industrial Research/Development*, 2(2), 83–90. 10.11648/j.r.d.20220302.13

Pathak, E. B., Garcia, R. B., Menard, J. M., & Salemi, J. L. (2021). Out-of-Hospital COVID-19 Deaths: Consequences for Quality of Medical Care and Accuracy of Cause of Death Coding. *American Journal of Public Health. American Journal of Public Health*, 111(S2, Supplement 2), S101–S106. 10.2105/AJPH.2021.30642834314208

Patinadan, P. V., Tan-Ho, G., Choo, P. Y., & Ho, A. H. Y. (2022). Resolving anticipatory grief and enhancing dignity at the end-of-life: A systematic review of palliative interventions. *Death Studies*, 46(2), 337–350. 10.1080/07481187.2020.172842632079501

Penberthy, J. K., Pehlivanova, M., Kalelioglu, T., Roe, C. A., Cooper, C. E., Lorimer, D., & Elsaesser, E. (2023). Factors Moderating the Impact of After Death Communications on Beliefs and Spirituality. *Omega*, 87(3), 884–901. 10.1177/00302228211029160342406552

Pew Research Center. (2022). *At least four-in-ten U.S. adults have faced high levels of psychological distress during the COVID-19 pandemic*. Pew Research Center. https://www.pewresearch.org/short-reads/2022/12/12/at-least-four-in-ten-u-s-adults-have-faced-high-levels-of-psychological-distress-during-covid-19-pandemic/

Pew Research Center. (2023). *Key findings about online dating in the U.S.* Pew Research Center. https://www.pewresearch.org/short-reads/2023/02/02/key-findings-about-online-dating-in-the-u-s/

Pfeiffer, P. N., Heisler, M., Piette, J. D., Rogers, M. A., & Valenstein, M. (2011). Efficacy of peer support interventions for depression: A meta-analysis. *General Hospital Psychiatry*, 33(1), 29–36. 10.1016/j.genhosppsych.2010.10.00221353125

Phillips, L. (2023). A closer look at the mental health provider shortage. *Counseling*. https://www.counseling.org/publications/counseling-today-magazine/article-archive/article/legacy/a-closer-look-at-the-mental-health-provider-shortage

Pincus, R., Hannor-Walker, T., Wright, L., & Justice, J. (2020). COVID-19's effect on students: How school counselors rise to the rescue. *NASSP Bulletin*, 104(4), 241–256. 10.1177/0192636520975866

Plant, B. (2022). Living posthumously: From anticipatory grief to self-mourning. *Mortality*, 27(1), 38–52. 10.1080/13576275.2020.1810650

Plato, . (1975). *Phaedo* (Gallop, D., Trans.). Clarendon Press.

Plunkett, E., Broadbent, A., Fien, S., & Cardona, M. (2021). Impact of COVID-19 Social Distancing on the Quality of Dying: A Call for Discretionary Application of Rules. *Journal of Social Work in End-of-Life & Palliative Care*, 17(2-3), 132–136. 10.1080/15524256.2021.191592033956572

Poremski, D., Kuek, J. H. L., Yuan, Q., Li, Z., Yow, K. L., Eu, P. W., & Chua, H. C. (2022). The impact of peer support work on the mental health of peer support specialists. *International Journal of Mental Health Systems*, 16(1), 51. 10.1186/s13033-022-00561-836258206

Price, M. J., Wachsmuth, L. P., Ferguson, K. A., Robbins-Welty, G. A., Riordan, P. A., Pieper, C. F., & Galanos, A. (2021). Grief in medical students: The short and long-term impacts on health and well-being. *The American Journal of Hospice & Palliative Care*, 39(2), 196–204. 10.1177/10499091211011172233910376

Prigerson, H. G., Maciejewski, P. K., Reynolds, C. F.III, Bierhals, A. J., Newsom, J. T., Fasiczka, A., Frank, E., Doman, J., & Miller, M. (1995). Inventory of complicated grief: A scale to measure maladaptive symptoms of loss. *Psychiatry Research*, 59(1–2), 65–79. 10.1016/0165-1781(95)02757-28771222

Prigerson, H. G., Shear, M. K., & Reynolds, C. F.III. (2022). Prolonged grief disorder diagnostic criteria—Helping those with maladaptive grief responses. *JAMA Psychiatry*, 79(4), 277. 10.1001/jamapsychiatry.2021.420135107569

Pyszczynski, T., Solomon, S., & Greenberg, J. (2015). Thirty years of terror management theory: From genesis to revelation. In Olson, J. M., & Zanna, M. P. (Eds.), Vol. 52, pp. 1–70). Advances in Experimental Social Psychology. Academic Press.

Quinlan, K. M. (2016). How emotion matters in four key relationships in teaching and learning in higher education. *College Teaching*, 64(3), 101–111. 10.1080/87567555.2015.1088818

Rajic, I., Genc, A., & Batic-Ocovaj, S. (2023). Relationships between bereavement support strategies and empathy dimensions. *Primenjena Psihologia*, 16(2), 229–267. 10.19090/pp.v16i2.2449

Compilation of References

Ratcliffe, M., & Byrne, E. A. (2021). The interpersonal and social dimensions of emotion regulation in grief. *Cultural, Existential and Phenomenological Dimensions of Grief Experience*, (pp. 84-98). Taylor & Francis. 10.4324/9781003099420-8

Ratts, M. J. (2009). Social justice counseling: Toward the development of a fifth force among counseling paradigms. *The Journal of Humanistic Counseling, Education and Development*, 48(2), 160–172. 10.1002/j.2161-1939.2009.tb00076.x

Ravi, A., Gorelick, J., & Pal, H. (2021). Identifying and Addressing Vicarious Trauma. *American Family Physician*, 103(9), 570–572.33929175

Rawlings, D., Miller-Lewis, L., & Tieman, J. (2022). Impact of the COVID-19 pandemic on funerals: Experiences of participants in the 2020 Dying2Learn Massive Open Online course. *Omega*, 003022282210752. 10.1177/00302228221075528335199622

Rice, A. (2015). Common Therapeutic Factors in Grief counseling Groups. *Death Studies*, 39(3), 165–172. 10.1080/07481187.2014.94662725530427

Richard, J., Rebinsky, R., Suresh, R., Kubic, S., Carter, A., Cunningham, J. E. A., Ker, A., Williams, K., & Sorin, M. (2022, August 4). Scoping review to evaluate the effects of peer support on the mental health of young adults. *BMJ Open*, 12(8), e061336. 10.1136/bmjopen-2022-06133635926986

Richardson, K. M. (2016). The surviving sisters club: Examining social support and posttraumatic growth among FDNY 9/11 widows. *Journal of Loss and Trauma*, 21(1), 1–15. 10.1080/15325024.2015.1024558

Roberts, A. R. (2015). Building the past and present to the future of crisis intervention and crisis management. In Roberts, A. R. (Ed.), *Crisis intervention handbook: Assessment, treatment and research* (pp. 3–34). Oxford University Press.

Robinson, C., & Pond, D. R. (2019, June 24). *Do online support groups for grief benefit the bereaved? systematic review of the quantitative and qualitative literature*. ScienceDirect.

Rogalla, K. B. (2020). Anticipatory grief, proactive coping, social support, and growth: Exploring positive experiences of preparing for loss. *Omega*, 81(1), 107–129. 10.1177/00302228187 6146129516784

Rolbiecki, A. J., Oliver, D. P., Washington, K., Benson, J. J., & Jorgensen, L. (2020). Preliminary Results of Caregiver Speaks: A Storytelling Intervention for Bereaved Family Caregivers. *Journal of Loss and Trauma*, 25(5), 438–453. 10.1080/15325024.2019.170798533335452

Rolls, L., & Payne, S. A. (2007). Children and young people's experience of UK childhood bereavement services. *Mortality*, 12(3), 281–303. 10.1080/13576270701430585

Rosa, W. E., Dahlin, C., Battista, V., Finlayson, C. S., Wisniewski, R. E., Greer, K., & Ferrell, B. R. (2021). Primary Palliative Care Clinical Implications: Oncology nursing during the COVID-19 pandemic. *Clinical Journal of Oncology Nursing*, 25(2), 119–125. 10.1188/21. CJON.119-12533739351

Rosenblatt, P. C. (2017). Researching grief: Cultural, relational, and individual possibilities. *Journal of Loss and Trauma*, 22(8), 617–630. 10.1080/15325024.2017.1388347

Rosenfeld, E. K. (2018). *The fire that changed the way we think about grief*. The Harvard Crimson.

Rucinska, M., & Nawrocki, S. (2022). COVID-19 Pandemic: Impact on Cancer Patients. *International Journal of Environmental Research and Public Health*, 19(19), 12470. 10.3390/ijerph19191247036231769

Ruíz, F. M. D., Fernández, M. I. M., Granero, M. J., Hernández, P. J. M., Correa, C. M., & Fernández, S. C. (2021). Social acceptance of death and its implication for end-of-life care. *Journal of Advanced Nursing*, 77(7), 3132–3141. 10.1111/jan.1483633755231

Runkle, J. D., Sugg, M. M., Yadav, S., Harden, S., Weiser, J., & Michael, K. (2023). Real-time mental health crisis response in the United States to COVID-19: Insights from a national text-based platform. *Crisis*, 44(1), 29–40. 10.1027/0227-5910/a00082634674553

Russ, V., Stopa, L., Sivyer, K., Hazeldine, J., & Maguire, T. (2022). The Relationship Between Adult Attachment and Complicated Grief: A Systematic Review. *Omega*, 003022282210831. 10.1177/00302228221083311035635029

Salisbury, H. (2021). Helen Salisbury: Dealing with covid trauma and grief. *BMJ (Clinical Research Ed.)*, n649. 10.1136/bmj.n64933687946

Sallnow, L., & Paul, S. (2015). Understanding community engagement in end-of-life care: Developing conceptual clarity. *Critical Public Health*, 25(2), 231–238. 10.1080/09581596.2014.909582

Sandhu, T., & Singh, H. (2021). Counselor Burnout during COVID-19: Predictive Role of Cognitive Emotion Regulation. *Indian Journal of Positive Psychology*, 12(3), 258–262.

Saradha, I., Sasikala, T., & Rathinasabapathy, B. (2020). A study to evaluate the effectiveness of Assertiveness Training Programme (Atp) to impart assertive behaviour among adolescents. *Journal of Positive School Psychology*, 6(6), 5054–5061.

Sartore, G. M., Pourliakas, A., & Lagioia, V. (2021, December). Peer support interventions for parents and carers of children with complex needs. *Cochrane Database of Systematic Reviews*.34923624

Sawyer, J. S. (2024). Grief and bereavement beliefs and their associations with death anxiety and complicated grief in a U.S. college student sample. *Death Studies*, 1–12. Advance online publication. 10.1080/07481187.2024.234993338713539

Schachter, S. R., & Holland, J. C. (2013). Loss, grief, and bereavement: Implications for family caregivers and health care professionals of the mentally III. In *Caregiving* (pp. 145–160). Springer. 10.1007/978-1-4614-8791-3_8

Scheinfeld, E., Gangi, K., Nelson, E. C., & Sinardi, C. C. (2022). Please scream inside your heart: Compounded loss and coping during the COVID-19 pandemic. *Health Communication*, 37(10), 1316–1328. 10.1080/10410236.2021.188641333586557

356

Compilation of References

Schulz, R., Hebert, R., & Boerner, K. (2008). Bereavement after caregiving. *Geriatrics*, 63(1), 20–22.18257616

Schulz, R., & Sherwood, P. R. (2008). Physical and mental health effects of family caregiving. *The American Journal of Nursing*, 108(9, Suppl), 23–27. 10.1097/01. NAJ.0000336406.45248.4c18797217

Schussler, D. L., Oh, Y., Mahfouz, J., Levitan, J., Frank, J. L., Broderick, P. C., Mitra, J. L., Berrena, E., Kohler, K., & Greenberg, M. T. (2020). Stress and well-being: A systematic case study of adolescents' experiences in a mindfulness-based program. *Journal of Child and Family Studies*, 30(2), 431–446. 10.1007/s10826-020-01864-5

Schwartz, H. L. (2019). *Connected teaching: Relationship, power and mattering in higher education*. Stylus Publishing.

Scott, S., Sheperis, D., Simmons, R. T., & Rush-Wilson, T. (2016). *Faith as a cultural variable: Implications for counselor training*. Research Gate. https://www.researchgate.net/publication/309098355_Faith_as_a_Cultural_Variable_Implications_for_Counselor_Training

Seligman, L., & Reichenberg, L. W. (2015). *Theories of counselling and psychotherapy; Systems, strategies, and skills* (4th ed.). Pearson.

Selman, L. S. R. F. (2020, April 17). How coronavirus has transformed the grieving process. *The Conversation.*https://theconversation.com/how-coronavirus-has-transformed-the-grieving-process-136368

Selman, L. E., Chao, D., Sowden, R., Marshall, S., Chamberlain, C., & Koffman, J. (2020). Bereavement Support on the Frontline of COVID-19: Recommendations for Hospital Clinicians. *Journal of Pain and Symptom Management*, 60(2), e81–e86. 10.1016/j.jpainsymman.2020.04.02432376262

Serlin, I. A., & Criswell, E. (2014). Humanistic psychology and women: A critical historical perspective. In Schneider, K. J., Fraser Pierson, J., & Bugental, F. T. (Eds.), *The Handbook of Humanistic Psychology: Theory, Research, and Practice* (pp. 27–40). SAGE Publications, Incorporated.

Shalaby, R. A. H., & Agyapong, V. I. O. (2020, June 9). Peer support in Mental Health: Literature Review. *JMIR Mental Health*, 7(6), e15572. 10.2196/1557232357127

Sharma, A. PhD. (2023, August 22). *Exercise and brain health*. Whole Brain Health. https://wholebrainhealth.org/exercise-and-brain-health/

Shear, M. K., Ghesquiere, A., & Glickman, K. (2013). Bereavement and complicated grief. *Current Psychiatry Reports*, 15(11), 406. 10.1007/s11920-013-0406-z24068457

Shukla, A., Choudhari, S. G., Gaidhane, A. M., & Quazi Syed, Z. (2022). Role of Art Therapy in the Promotion of Mental Health: A Critical Review. *Cureus*, 14(8). Advance online publication. 10.7759/cureus.2802636134083

Silva, V. S. E., Hornby, L., Almost, J., Lotherington, K., Appleby, A., Silva, A. R., Rochon, A., & Dhanani, S. (2020). Burnout and compassion fatigue among organ and tissue donation coordinators: A scoping review. *BMJ Open*, 10(12), e040783. 10.1136/bmjopen-2020-04078333323439

Silverman, G. S., Baroiller, A., & Hemer, S. R. (2020). Culture and grief: Ethnographic perspectives on ritual, relationships and remembering. *Death Studies*, 45(1), 1–8. 10.1080/074811 87.2020.185188533272138

Singh, H., Haghayegh, A. T., Shah, R., Cheung, L., Wijekoon, S., Reel, K., & Sangrar, R. (2023). A qualitative exploration of allied health providers' perspectives on cultural humility in palliative and end-of-life care. *BMC Palliative Care*, 22(92), 1–14. 10.1186/s12904-023-01214-437434238

Sist, L., Savadori, S., Grandi, A., Martoni, M., Baiocchi, E., Lombardo, C., & Colombo, L. (2022). Self-care for nurses and midwives: Findings from a scoping review. *Healthcare (Basel)*, 10(12), 2473. 10.3390/healthcare1012247336553999

Skalski, S., Konaszewski, K., Dobrakowski, P., Surzykiewics, J., & Lee, S. A. (2022). Pandemic grief in Poland: Adaptation of a measure and its relationship with social support and resilience. *Current Psychology (New Brunswick, N.J.)*, 41(10), 7393–7401. 10.1007/s12144-021-01731-633935472

Skritskaya, N. A., Mauro, C., Olonoff, M., Qiu, X., Duncan, S., Wang, Y., Duan, N., Lebowitz, B., Reynolds, C. F.III, Simon, N. M., Zisook, S., & Shear, M. K. (2017). Measuring maladaptive cognitions in complicated grief: Introducing the typical beliefs questionnaire. *The American Journal of Geriatric Psychiatry*, 25(5), 541–550. 10.1016/j.jagp.2016.09.00327793576

Smith, J. (2016). *Building and maintaining the therapeutic relationship*. Springer. 10.1007/978-3-319-49460-9_11

Smith, W., PhD. (2023, October 2). *The Psychology of Grief: The 4 stages explained*. Positive-Psychology.com.

Smith, K. (2017). Self-care practices and the professional self. *Journal of Social Work in Disability & Rehabilitation*, 16(3–4), 186–203. 10.1080/1536710X.2017.137223628876191

Social Security Administration (SSA). (2024). *Survivors Benefits*. SSA.https://www.ssa.gov/pubs/EN-05-10084.pdf

Solomon, S., Greenberg, J., & Pyszczynski, T. (2004). The cultural animal: Twenty years of terror management theory and research. In Greenberg, J., Pyszczynski & Koole, S. (Eds.), *Handbook of experimental psychology*. (pp. 13-34). Guilford Press.

Solomon, S., Greenberg, J., & Pyszczynski, T. (2016). *The worm at the core: On the role of death in life*. Penguin.

Sprang, G., Ford, J., Kerig, P., & Bride, B. (2019). Defining secondary traumatic stress and developing targeted assessments and interventions: Lessons learned from research and leading experts. *Traumatology*, 25(2), 72–81. 10.1037/trm0000180

Stanley, T. (2020). Yoga nidra for releasing grief. *Yoga Journal*, (317), 44–45.

Compilation of References

Statz, T. L., Kobayashi, L. C., & Finlay, J. M. (2023). 'Losing the illusion of control and predictability of life': Experiences of grief and loss among ageing US adults during the COVID-19 pandemic. *Ageing and Society*, 43(12), 2821–2844. 10.1017/S0144686X21001872

Stay Safe Foundation. (n.d.). *What is PTSD – Stay Safe Foundation – a veteran / LEO 501C3 Non-Profit*. Stay Safe Foundation. https://staysafefoundation.org/What-Is-PTSD/

Stevens, E. K., Aziz, S., Wuensch, K. L., & Walcott, C. (2024). Caregivers of children with special healthcare needs: A quantitative examination of work-family culture, caregiver burden, and work-life balance. *Journal of Child and Family Studies*, 33(5), 1365–1377. 10.1007/s10826-024-02822-1

Stilos, K. K., & Wynnychuk, L. (2021). Self-care is a must for health care providers caring for the dying. *Canadian oncology nursing journal Revue canadienne de nursing oncologique, 31*(2), 239–241.

Strand, M., Eng, L. S., & Gammon, D. (2020, May 29). *Combining online and offline peer support groups in community mental health care settings: a qualitative study of service users' experiences*. ResearchGate.

Substance Abuse and Mental Health Services Administration. Department of Health & Human Services, Tips for Survivors: Coping with grief after a disaster or traumatic event (2017). Rockville, Md.

Sudeck, G., Thiel, A., & Strohacker, K. (2023). *Physical activity, subjective well-being and mental health*. Springer. 10.1007/978-3-031-03921-8_26

Sunde, A. (2021). When Schools Go Dark, School Counselors Shine: School Counseling during a Global Pandemic. Brief. *ERIC*, 1-15. https://eric.ed.gov/?id=ED613589

Suomala Folkerds, A. (2019). *Death: A qualitative content analysis of counseling journals, 1986-2016* [Doctoral dissertation, Minnesota State University, Mankato]. Cornerstone: A Collection of Scholarly and Creative Works for Minnesota State University, Mankato. https://cornerstone.lib.mnsu.edu/etds/942/

Suomala Folkerds, A., & Coursol, D. H. (2023). An Examination of Death in Premier Counseling Journals. *The Interactive Journal of Global Leadership and Learning, 2*(3).

Supiano, K. P., Luptak, M., Andersen, T., Beynon, C., Lacob, E., & Wong, B. (2022). If we knew then what we know now: The preparedness experience of pre-loss and post-loss dementia caregivers. *Death Studies*, 46(2), 369–380. 10.1080/07481187.2020.173101432093533

Suresh, R., Alam, A., & Karkossa, Z. (2021). Using peer support to Strengthen Mental Health During the COVID-19 Pandemic: A review. *Frontiers in Psychiatry*, 12, 12. 10.3389/fpsyt.2021.71418134322045

Sussex Publishers. (2020). Covid Stress Syndrome: What it is and why it matters. *Psychology Today*. https://www.psychologytoday.com/au/blog/experimentations/202007/covid-stress-syndrome-what-it-is-and-why-it-matters

Sutton, G. W., Arnzen, C., & Kelly, H. L. (2016). Christian counseling and psychotherapy: Components of clinician spirituality that predict type of Christian intervention. *Journal of Psychology and Christianity*, 35(3), 204–214.

Sweileh, W. M. (2020). Research trends and scientific analysis of publications on burnout and compassion fatigue among healthcare providers. *Journal of Occupational Medicine and Toxicology (London, England)*, 15(1), 23. 10.1186/s12995-020-00274-z32684943

Szuhany, K. L., Malgaroli, M., Miron, C. D., & Simon, N. M. (2021). Prolonged Grief Disorder: Course, Diagnosis, Assessment, and Treatment. *Focus - American Psychiatric Publishing*, 19(2), 161–172. 10.1176/appi.focus.2020005234690579

Tang, S., & Chow, A. Y. M. (2021). *Rumination in Bereavement.* Springer International Publishing. https://doi-org.huary.kl.oakland.edu/10.1007/978-3-030-22009-9_1027

Tang, P. (n.d.). *A brief history of peer support: Origins: Peers for progress.* Peers For Progress A Brief History of Peer Support Origins Comments.

Tang, S., & Ziang, Z. (2021). Who suffered most after deaths due to COVID-19? Prevalence and correlates of prolonged grief disorder in COVID-19 related bereaved adults. *Globalization and Health*, 17(1), 1–9. 10.1186/s12992-021-00669-533573673

Tanhan, F. (2014). An analysis of factors affecting teachers' irrational beliefs. *Educational Sciences: Theory & Practice*, 14(2), 465–470. 10.12738/estp.2014.2.1724

Tan, J., & Andriessen, K. (2021). The experiences of grief and personal growth in University students: A qualitative study. *International Journal of Environmental Research and Public Health*, 18(4), 1899. 10.3390/ijerph1804189933669340

Taxman, J., Owen, G. & Essig, T. (2021). *Pandemic Trauma and Stress Experience* (PTSE): *Adapting Together.* APsaA Covid-19 Advisory Team.

Taylor, N. C., & Robinson, W. D. (2016). The Lived Experience of Young Widows and Widowers. *The American Journal of Family Therapy*, 44(2), 67–79. 10.1080/01926187.2016.1145081

Taylor, S., Landry, C. A., Paluszek, M. M., Rachor, G. S., & Asmundson, G. J. G. (2020). Worry, avoidance, and coping during the COVID-19 pandemic: A comprehensive network analysis. *Journal of Anxiety Disorders*, 76, 102327. 10.1016/j.janxdis.2020.10232733137601

Tempski, P., Danila, A. H., Arantes-Costa, F. M., Siqueira, M. A., Torsani, M. B., & Martins, M. A. (2020). The COVID-19 pandemic: Time for medical teachers and students to overcome grief. *Clinics (São Paulo)*, 75, e2206. 10.6061/clinics/2020/e220632756822

Terry, M. L., Bivens, A. J., & Neimeyer, R. A. (1996). Comfort and empathy of experienced counselors in client situations involving death and loss. *Omega*, 32(4), 269–285. 10.2190/WJ89-KCTY-DBWG-8QTX

Tervalon, M. and Murray-García, J. (1998). *Cultural Humility Versus Cultural Competence.*

Compilation of References

Tervalon, M., & Murray-García, J. (1998, May). Cultural Humility Versus Cultural Competence: A Critical Distinction in Defining Physician Training Outcomes in Multicultural Education. *Journal of Health Care for the Poor and Underserved*, 9(2), 117–125. 10.1353/hpu.2010.0233

The Center for Prolonged Grief. (n.d.). *Overview*. Center for Prolonged Grief. https://prolongedgrief .columbia.edu

Thomassen, A. G., Johnsen, B. H., Hystad, S. W., & Johnsen, G. E. (2022). Avoidance coping mediates the effect of hardiness on mental distress symptoms for both male and female subjects. *Scandinavian Journal of Psychology*, 63(1), 39–45. 10.1111/sjop.1278234676897

Thorson-Olesen, S. J., Meinertz, N., & Eckert, S. (2019). Caring for Aging Populations: Examining Compassion Fatigue and Satisfaction. *Journal of Adult Development*, 26(3), 232–240. 10.1007/s10804-018-9315-z

Tiech Fire, N., Gvion, Y., Alkalay, S., & Zalsman, G. (2022). The "Forgotten grievers": The impact of pupil suicide on post-trauma and grief symptoms in school staff. *International Journal of Environmental Research and Public Health*, 19(19), 12160. 10.3390/ijerph191912160362314464

Tillich, P. (1952). *The courage to be*. Yale University Press.

Topping, K. J. (2022, May 17). Peer education and peer counselling for Health and well-being: A review of Reviews. *International Journal of Environmental Research and Public Health*, 19(10), 6064. 10.3390/ijerph1910606435627601

Tracy, K., & Wallace, S. P. (2016, September 29). Benefits of peer support groups in the treatment of addiction. *Substance Abuse and Rehabilitation*, 7, 143–154. 10.2147/SAR.S8153527729825

Treatment, C. F. S. A. (2014). *Understanding the impact of trauma*. Trauma-Informed Care in Behavioral Health Services - NCBI Bookshelf.

Treglia, D., Cutuli, J. J., Arasteh, K., & Bridgeland, J. (2023). Parental and other caregiver loss due to COVID-19 in the United States: Prevalence by race, state, relationship, and child age. *Journal of Community Health*, 48(3), 390–397. 10.1007/s10900-022-01160-x36515763

Tucker, P., & Czapla, C. (2021). Post-COVID Stress Disorder: Another emerging consequence of the global pandemic. *The Psychiatric Times*, 38(1).

Tuna, B., & Avci, O. H. (2023). Qualitative analysis of university counselors' online counseling experiences during the covid-19 pandemic. *Current Psychology (New Brunswick, N.J.)*, 42(10), 8489–8503. Advance online publication. 10.1007/s12144-023-04358-x37193098

Tureluren, E., Claes, L., & Andriessen, K. (2022). Help-seeking behavior in bereaved university and college students: Associations with grief, mental health distress, and personal growth. *Frontiers in Psychology*, 13, 963839. 10.3389/fpsyg.2022.96383935992443

Tyrrell, P., Harberger, S., Schoo, C., & Siddiqui, W. (2023, February 26). *Kubler-Ross Stages of Dying and Subsequent Models of Grief*. StatPearls - NCBI Bookshelf.

Understanding probate and estate administration. (n.d.). AgingCare https://www.agingcare.com/ Articles/estate-administration-probate-after-death-in-family-153107.htm

University of Michigan. (2020). *Posttraumatic Stress Disorder during COVID-19.* U Michigan. https://medicine.umich.edu/dept/psychiatry/michigan-psychiatry-resources-covid-19/specific -mental-health-conditions/posttraumatic-stress-disorder-during-covid-19

Updated National Survey Trends in Telehealth Utilization and Modality. (2023). Office of the Assistant Secretary for Planning and Evaluation, U. S. Department of Health and Human Services. https://aspe.hhs.gov/sites/default/files/documents/7d6b4989431f4c70144f209622975116/ household-pulse-survey-telehealth-covid-ib.pdf

Valliani, K., & Mughal, F. B. (2022). Human emotions during COVID-19: A lens through Kubler-Ross Grief theory. *Psychological Trauma: Theory, Research, Practice, and Policy*, 14(2), 247–249. 10.1037/tra000106434323565

van Schaik, T., Brouwer, M. A., Knibbe, N. E., Knibbe, H. J., & Teunissen, S. C. (2022). The effect of the COVID-19 pandemic on grief experiences of bereaved relatives: An overview review. *Omega*, 003022282211438. 10.1177/00302228221143861136453639

Varga, M. A., Lanier, B., Biber, D., & Stewart, B. (2021). Holistic grief effects, mental health, and counseling support in bereaved college students. *The College Student Affairs Journal*, 39(1), 1–13. 10.1353/csj.2021.0000

Varga, M., & Paulus, T. (2014). Grieving Online: Newcomers' Constructions of Grief in an On-line Support Group. *Death Studies*, 38(7), 443–449. 10.1080/07481187.2013.78011224758214

Varga, S., & Gallagher, S. (2020). Anticipatory-vicarious grief: The anatomy of a moral emotion. *The Monist*, 103(2), 176–189. 10.1093/monist/onz034

Vaterlaus, J. M. (2014). New Normal Project: An intervention for grief and loss. *Journal of Family Psychotherapy*, 25(1), 78–82. 10.1080/08975353.2014.881699

Vincelette, C., Thivierge-Southidara, M., & Rochefort, C. M. (2019). Conceptual and methodological challenges of studies examining the determinants and outcomes of omitted nursing care: A narrative review of the literature. *International Journal of Nursing Studies*, 100, 103403. 10.1016/j.ijnurstu.2019.10340331629210

Voo, T. C., Senguttuvan, M., & Tam, C. C. (2020). Family Presence for Patients and Separated Relatives during COVID-19: Physical, Virtual, and Surrogate. *Journal of Bioethical Inquiry*, 17(4), 767–772. 10.1007/s11673-020-10009-832840835

Waldrop, D. P. (2007). Caregiver Grief in Terminal Illness and Bereavement: A Mixed-Methods Study. *Health & Social Work*, 32(3), 197–206. 10.1093/hsw/32.3.19717896676

Compilation of References

Wallace C. L., Wladkowski S. P., Gibson A., White P. (2020). Grief during the COVID-19 pandemic: Considerations for palliative care providers. Journal of Pain and Symptom Management. Wallis E. Adams, E. Sally Rogers,(n.d). THE IMPACT OF COVID-19 ON PEER SUPPORT SPECIALISTS: Findings from a National Survey. Center for Psychiatric Rehabilitation Boston University, Boston, MA Watson, E., & Meddings, S. (2019). *Peer support in Mental Health.* Google Books.

Wallace, C. L., Wladkowski, S. P., Gibaon, A., & White, P. (2020). Grief during the COVID-19 pandemic: Considerations for palliative care providers. *Journal of Pain and Symptom Management, 60*(1), Article e70-e76. 10.1016/j.jpainsymman.2020.04.012

Walsh, F. (2020). Loss and resilience in the time of Covid-19: Meaning making, hope, and transcendence. *Family Process*, 59(3), 898–911. 10.1111/famp.1258832678915

Walsh, K. (2022). *Grief and loss: Theories and skills for the helping professions* (3rd ed.). Waveland Press, Inc.

Wang, J., Batanova, M., Ferris, K. A., & Lerner, R. M. (2016). Character development within the relational developmental systems Metatheory: A view of the issues. *Research in Human Development*, 13(2), 91–96. 10.1080/15427609.2016.1165932

Wango, G., & Gwiyo, L. M. (2021). When death strikes early as often will: How counsellors and schools can support grieving pupils and students. *Improving Schools*, 26(1), 39–53. 10.1177/1365480221996847

Wang, Z., Wang, F., Zhang, S., Liu, C., Feng, Y., & Chen, J. (2023). Effects of mindfulness-based interventions on stress, burnout in nurses: A systematic review and meta-analysis. *Frontiers in Psychiatry*, 14, 1218340. 10.3389/fpsyt.2023.121834037599884

Washington, D. (2019). *Fall Forward.* Commencement address at University of Pennsylvania.

Wass, H. (2004). A perspective on the current state of death education. *Death Studies*, 28(4), 289–308. 10.1080/07481180490043231515129687

Watkins, M. (2012). Revolutionary Leadership: From Paulo Freire to the Occupy Movement. Journal for Social Action in Counseling and Psychology. *Journal for Social Action in Counseling and Psychology*, 4(2), 1–22. 10.33043/JSACP.4.2.1-22

Watson, D. L., & Tharp, R. G. (2014). *Self-directed behaviour: Self-modification for personal adjustment* (10th ed.). Centage Learning.

Webster, L. C. (2022, August 26). *Help your family plan your funeral far in advance.* AARP. https://www.aarp.org/home-family/friends-family/info-2020/planning-your-own-funeral.html

West, K., Rumble, H., Shaw, R., Cameron, A., & Roleston, C. (2023). Diarised Reflections on COVID-19 and Grief counseling: Disruptions and Affordances. *Illness, Crises, and Loss*, 31(1), 151–167. 10.1177/10541373211044069366605777

Wheat, L. S., Matthews, J. J., & Whiting, P. P. (2022). Grief content inclusion in CACREP-accredited counselor education programs. *The Journal of Counselor Preparation and Supervisor*, 15(2). https://digitalcommons.sacredheart.edu/jcps/vol15/iss2/14

White, S., Foster, R., Marks, J., Morshead, R., Goldsmith, L., Barlow, S., Sin, J., & Gillard, S. (2020, November 11). *The effectiveness of one-to-one peer support in Mental Health Services: A systematic review and meta-analysis*. BioMed Central.

Williams, J., Howett, N., & Shorter, G. W. (2023). What roles does physical activity play following the death of a young person? A qualitative investigation. *BMC Public Health*, 23(1), 210. 10.1186/s12889-022-14542-636721110

Wilson, J. F. (n.d.). *Death and dying: how different cultures deal with grief and mourning*. The Conversation. https://theconversation.com/death-and-dying-how-different-cultures-deal-with-grief-and-mourning-197299

Wilson, J.F. (2023). Death and dying: How different cultures deal with grief and mourning. *The Conversation.* https:theconversation.com/death-and-dying-how-different-cultures-deal-with-grief-and-mourning-197299

Wilson, D. M., Darko, E. M., Kusi-Appiah, E., Roh, S. J., Ramic, A., & Errasti-Ibarrondo, B. (2022). What exactly is "complicated" grief? A scoping research literature review to understand its risk factors and prevalence. *Omega*, 86(2), 471–487. 10.1177/003022282097730533259275

Wladkowski, S. P., Wallace, C. L., & Gibson, A. (2002). Theoretical Exploration of Live Discharge from Hospice for Caregivers of Adults with Dementia. *Journal of Social Work in End-of-Life & Palliative Care*, 16(2), 133–150. 10.1080/15524256.2020.174535132223695

Wojtkowiak, J., Lind, J., & Smid, G. E. (2021). Ritual in therapy for prolonged grief: A scoping review of ritual elements in evidence-informed grief interventions. *Frontiers in Psychiatry*, 11, 623835. 10.3389/fpsyt.2020.62383533613334

Wolfelt, Ph. D., C. T. (n.d.). *Dealing with Families During the COVID-19 Pandemic*. International Cemetery, Cremation and Funeral Association. https://iccfa.com/wp-content/uploads/2022/03/COVID19_ICCFA_Families-Wolfelt.pdf

Wolfelt, A. (2021). *Nature heals: Reconciling your grief through engaging with the natural world*. Companion Press.

Wolfelt, A. (2021). *The understanding your grief support group guide: Starting and leading a bereavement support group*. Companion Press.

Worden, J. W. (2018). *Grief counseling and grief therapy: A handbook for the mental health practitioner* (5th ed.). Springer. 10.1891/9780826134752

World Bank Group. (2020). *IMF Staff*. Peer Support Group Facilitator Guide. Public Documents.

World Health Organisation (2018). *International classification of diseases for mortality and morbidity statistics* (11th Revision). WHO.

Compilation of References

World Health Organization (WHO). (2022). *Cancer*. WHO. https://www.who.int/news-room/fact-sheets/detail/cancer

World Health Organization (WHO). (2024, March 31). *WHO COVID-19 dashboard*. WHO.

Worldometer (2024). *Coronavirus cases and deaths*. Worldometer. https://www.worldometers.info/coronavirus/

Worldometer. (2024). *Coronavirus cases and deaths*. Worldometer. https://www.worldometers.info/coronavirus/

Wosket, V. (1999). *The therapeutic use of self: Counselling practice, research, and supervision*. Taylor & Frances/Routledge.

Yalom, I. D. (1980). *Existential Psychotherapy*. Basic Books.

Yalom, I. D. (2008). *Staring at the Sun*. Jossey-Bass.

Yamaguchi, A., Akutsu, S., Oshio, A., & Kim, M. S. (2017). Effects of cultural orientation, self-esteem, and collective self-esteem on well-being. *Psychological Studies*, 62(3), 241–249. 10.1007/s12646-017-0413-y

Yan, Y., Hou, J., Li, Q., & Yu, N. X. (2023). Suicide before and during the COVID-19 pandemic: A systematic review with meta-analysis. *International Journal of Environmental Research and Public Health*, 20(4), 3346. 10.3390/ijerph2004334636834037

Zalli, E. (2024). Grief and resilience: Finding strength and growth through the grieving process. *Norwegian Journal of Development of the International Science*, 128, 48–55. 10.5281/zenodo.10817324

Zanville, N., Cohen, B., Gray, T. F., Phillips, J., Linder, L., Starkweather, A., Yeager, K. A., & Cooley, M. E. (2021). The oncology nursing society rapid review and research priorities for cancer care in the context of COVID-19. *Oncology Nursing Forum*, 48(2), 131–145. 10.1188/21. ONF.131-14533600397

Zeglin, R. J., Niemela, D. R., Rosenblatt, K., & Hernandez-Garcia, J. (2019). Using photovoice as a counselor education pedagogical tool: A pilot. *Journal of Creativity in Mental Health*, 14(2), 258–268. 10.1080/15401383.2019.1581116

Zeigler-Hill, V., & Shackelford, T. K. (2020). *Encyclopedia of personality and individual differences*. Springer. 10.1007/978-3-319-24612-3

Zhang, M., Murphy, B. L., Cabanilla, A., & Yidi, C. (2021). Physical relaxation for occupational stress in healthcare workers: A systematic review and network meta-analysis of randomized controlled trials. *Journal of Occupational Health*, 63(1), e12243. 10.1002/1348-9585.1224334235817

Zheng, K., Spence, D. R., & Cusick, J. (2022, June 1). Honouring other cultures in peer work. Postsecondary Peer Support Training Curriculum.

Zisook, S., & Shear, K. (2009, June). Grief and bereavement: What psychiatrists need to know. *World Psychiatry; Official Journal of the World Psychiatric Association (WPA)*, 8(2), 67–74. 10.1002/j.2051-5545.2009.tb00217.x19516922

About the Contributors

Michelle R. Cox, PhD, has been teaching in APU's School Counseling and School Psychology program since 2003, and has several years of experience as an educational counselor. She was an associate counselor for Victor Valley College for 16 years, and prior to that was the first CalWorks Counselor at Chaffey College, assisting in the development of the Workforce Preparation program in which she provided educational and vocational counseling and educational planning to students receiving CalWorks assistance. She was a part-time instructor for the University of La Verne, teaching in the Educational Counseling program. Cox also has 9 years of experience as a vocational rehabilitation counselor, helping clients who have suffered injuries and require services to return to suitable and gainful employment. She established her own career counseling service, providing job-seeking skills to clients, as well as assistance in the completion of professional résumés. Cox is active in the community, having served as a member and president of the Adelanto School District Board of Education, School Site Council member for Morgan Kincaid Preparatory School, Snowline Joint Unified School District Multicultural Committee member, and substitute teacher for several school districts. Her research focuses on cultural issues related to schooling, and systemic oppression experienced by Black American students.

***

Diane H. Coursol, Ph.D. is a Professor in Counseling at Minnesota State University, Mankato. She has been a counselor educator for 37 years and currently teaches the Practicum, Internship, Assessment, Diagnosis and Treatment Planning, Technology and Counseling Skills courses in the masters and doctoral programs at Minnesota State University, Mankato. Dr. Coursol has worked in a variety of settings, including hospital, private practice, and agency settings.

Emily Horton is an assistant professor of counseling at the University of Houston Clear Lake. She received her master's degree in clinical mental health counseling from West Virginia University and a Ph.D. in Counselor Education and Supervision from the University of Texas at San Antonio. She is a Licensed Professional Counselor and Registered Play Therapist who specializes in providing counseling to children and adolescents. Prior to coming to UHCL, she served as the director of a 16-bed residential eating disorder treatment center for adolescents. She has had the honor of working in various clinical settings, including private practices, non-profits, and college counseling centers. Her research primarily focuses on play therapy, eating disorders and body image, and perinatal mental health. She has been published in several peer-reviewed professional journals and has presented numerous presentations at international, national, regional, state, and local conferences.

Zidan Kachhi is a counselling psychologist and an assistant professor. He has authored two books and published various papers in peer reviewed journals.

About the Contributors

Joetta Harlow Kelly is an Assistant Professor of School Counseling with the School of Education at Campbellsville University in the school's graduate program and is a licensed counselor. She served in ministry for many years, has taught both Art and PE, and managed MSU's Wellness Center, teaching there as well. She also teaches classes in First Aid/CPR/AED and was a swim instructor for many years. Joetta has degrees from Campbellsville, Murray State University and Western Kentucky University, and has written and/or illustrated 13 children's books. She lives in Murray, Kentucky and enjoys spending time and traveling with her friends and family which includes her 3 children, their spouses, her 5 grand girls and her little yorkie. Writing the chapter for this book was particularly meaningful as she lost her husband during Covid and seeks to minister to others going through loss, just as she was blessed to be ministered to.

Amy Maturen is dually licensed as a Marriage and Family Therapist as well as a Mental Health Counselor in the state of Florida. She earned her Ph.D. in Counselor Education and Supervision along with her Masters Degree in Marriage and Family Counseling from Capella University. She is certified in Play Therapy and Mindfulness. She serves as the Clinical Director of Lutheran Counseling Services in Winter Park, Florida while also providing counseling services to individuals, couples and families. Her specialties include chronic illness, caretakers, and grief. She has two years of experience as an Adjunct Professor in the Counseling Department of Mid-America Christian University in Oklahoma working with Masters level students and recently began as an Adjunct at Walden University. In addition to teaching, she has been a University Supervisor at MACU for over a year mentoring and guiding students in their fieldwork experience prior to graduation. She continues to focus her research on chronic illness and grief.

Diana McCullough is a retired Army veteran with over 10 years of service. Diana is an Adjunct and a Community Social Worker who works with the Intellectual or Developmental Disability (I/DD) population. She comes with a bachelor's degree in social work from Fayetteville State University (FSU) and a Masters in Rehabilitation Counseling, with a minor in Clinical Mental Health from Winston Salem State University (WSSU). Diana is currently in the third year of her doctoral program in Psychology seeking to explore forced-choice identity among biracial individuals. Her professional and lived experiences have shaped her dedication to dismantling systemic oppression within higher educational institutions and counseling settings. She has been published recently in a peer-reviewed professional book and has presented numerous presentations at international, state, and local conferences.

Megha M Nair is a 2nd year B. Sc Psychology (Hons) student, studying in PES University, Bengaluru, India.

Onijuni Olufemi Olatomide had a B.Ed in Guidance and Counselling from Ondo State University, Ado-Ekiti (now Ekiti State University, Ado-Ekiti), and bagged an M.Ed degree in Guidance and Counselling from Adekunle Ajasin University, Akungba-Akoko, Ondo State. He later bagged a Ph.D in Counselling Psychology from Obafemi Awolowo University, Ile-Ife, Osun State – all in Nigeria. He had taught across levels of Nigerian educational institutions, namely primary, secondary, and tertiary. He had practised as a Counsellor both from the school system, and outside of the school system. In each of these levels, he had practised as school Counsellor to students and staff alike. Much earlier, he had practised as an Assistant Counsellor in Guidance and Counselling Specialist Clinic, Kaduna, Kaduna State before bagging his second and third degrees. Dr. Olatomide, Onijuni Olufemi joined the services of Obafemi Awolowo University, Ile-Ife, in 2010 as an Assistant Lecturer, and is presently a Senior Lecturer in the Department of Educational Foundations and Counselling, Faculty of Education in the Institution. He is currently the Coordinator of students' Counselling Practicum exercise. Dr. Olatomide, Onijuni Olufemi has over 35 publications in reputable national and international journal outlets. Also, he is a reviewer to some recognised publication outlets – both within and without Nigeria. His research interests areas are in older workers' employment and retirees.

Adithi Priyadarshini Prabhu, is a 2rd year BSc. Psychology (Hons) student, studying in PES University, Bengaluru, India.

About the Contributors

Tobi Russell received her Doctorate in Counselor Education from Oakland University, her Master of Science degree in clinical psychology from Eastern Michigan University and received a Master of Arts degree in counseling from Oakland University. Dr. Russell has a child and adolescent specialization, is a certified advanced alcohol and drug counselor as well as a certified clinical supervisor in addictions in the state of Michigan. She is a board-certified expert in traumatic stress. She counsels individuals from age 7 and up dealing with depression, anxiety, grief and loss, substance abuse, PTSD/trauma, self-injury, eating disorders, and childhood adjustment to stressors. Dr. Russell has worked in residential facilities, outpatient agencies and has owned her own private practice in Michigan since 2011. Dr. Russell is currently a fixed-term remote faculty at Central Michigan University in the Department of Counseling. She was a lecturer at Oakland University for 14 years and an adjunct professor at Baker College for 5 years. Dr. Russell is a member of the American Counseling Association. In her spare time, she enjoys arts and crafts, reading and spending time with family including her Maine Coon cat, Roxie.

Ranjit Singha is a Doctorate Research Fellow at Christ (Deemed to be University) and holds the prestigious American Psychological Association (APA) membership. With a strong background in Research and Development, he has significantly contributed to various fields such as Mindfulness, Addiction Psychology, Women Empowerment, UN Sustainable Development Goals, and Data Science. With over 15 years of experience in Administration, Teaching, and Research, both in Industry and Higher Education Institutions (HEI), Mr Ranjit has established himself as a seasoned professional. Mr Ranjit is dedicatedly involved in research and teaching endeavours, primarily focusing on mindfulness and compassion-based interventions. His work in these areas aims to promote well-being and foster positive change in individuals and communities.

Aaron Suomala Folkerds is an assistant professor of graduate counseling at Minnesota State University-Moorhead and the chaplain/wellness coordinator at the Moorhead Police Department in Moorhead, MN. He has a Master of Divinity Degree (M.Div) from The Lutheran School of Theology at Chicago (LSTC), a Master of science degree (MS) in mental health counseling and a doctoral degree (Ed.D.) in counselor education and supervision from MN State University-Mankato. He is an ordained Lutheran pastor in the Evangelical Lutheran Church in America (ELCA), a Nationally Registered Emergency Medical Technician (NREMT) and a Licensed Marriage and Family Therapist in MN (LMFT).

Kimberly Tharpe, PhD. received her doctorate in 2023 in Performance Psychology. As a school counselor, she has served at each developmental level of education, inclusive of elementary, middle school, high school, as well as university/college levels. She has served in the school community as an instructor at Azusa Pacific University within the School Counseling and Psychology Department for over 23 years. Dr. Tharpe has served in several counseling arenas such as, vocational rehabilitation, adolescent group home facilities, K-12 educational settings, crisis counseling, college and career counseling, motivational counseling as well as university counseling positions. She continues to advocate for school counselors within local Union Negotiation teams. Dr. Tharpe aims to protect and serve students in the K-12 settings as well as advocate for School Counselors in conjunction with ASCA standards and recommendations.

Index

A

Active listening 46, 132, 154, 155, 159, 160, 166, 167, 210, 211

Aggravating Words 112, 114, 115, 123, 124, 127

anxiety 1, 2, 3, 4, 5, 6, 9, 10, 11, 13, 20, 28, 35, 37, 40, 42, 46, 48, 57, 58, 59, 60, 61, 62, 63, 64, 65, 66, 67, 70, 71, 72, 73, 74, 75, 79, 80, 88, 90, 96, 98, 100, 101, 102, 106, 107, 109, 122, 125, 129, 130, 133, 134, 136, 147, 150, 156, 158, 177, 183, 189, 198, 217, 221, 226, 238, 247, 248, 251, 258, 259, 263, 267, 272, 283, 284, 297, 298, 302, 317, 322

B

Bereaved 6, 7, 13, 15, 17, 18, 25, 29, 86, 91, 109, 110, 112, 113, 114, 115, 116, 117, 118, 119, 120, 121, 122, 123, 124, 125, 126, 127, 128, 129, 130, 131, 140, 148, 153, 158, 159, 162, 164, 166, 168, 169, 172, 173, 174, 176, 177, 178, 179, 180, 181, 182, 183, 184, 185, 186, 187, 188, 189, 190, 191, 192, 193, 194, 195, 196, 197, 201, 206, 223, 234, 238, 239, 248, 261, 274, 291, 300, 302, 303, 304, 310, 311, 322, 323, 324

bereavement 8, 15, 16, 17, 25, 27, 30, 31, 67, 75, 77, 79, 81, 88, 91, 93, 106, 107, 108, 109, 110, 113, 114, 116, 118, 119, 124, 125, 126, 127, 128, 129, 131, 137, 138, 139, 140, 147, 148, 151, 156, 163, 164, 171, 172, 173, 176, 177, 178, 179, 181, 183, 184, 191, 193, 194, 195, 196, 197, 198, 200, 201, 213, 217, 233, 234, 238, 248, 260, 263, 264, 265, 266, 267, 268, 269, 270, 271, 272, 273, 274, 275, 277, 278, 279, 280, 281, 282, 285, 286, 287, 288, 289, 291, 292, 300, 303, 310, 325, 326

Burnout Prevention 294

C

cancer 6, 12, 13, 14, 16, 20, 22, 23, 25, 26, 27, 28, 47, 52, 53, 54, 55, 65, 102, 213, 292, 295, 296, 298, 299, 300, 301, 307, 308, 309, 320, 321, 323, 324, 325, 326

caregiver 10, 13, 16, 22, 27, 28, 29, 30, 31, 34, 37, 38, 39, 40, 41, 46, 47, 51, 54, 56, 86, 87, 129, 130, 140, 146, 147, 164, 169, 202, 203, 204, 205, 206, 208, 209, 211, 212, 213, 214, 228, 281, 286, 289, 296, 297, 298, 300, 324, 325, 326

caregiver burden 38, 39, 54, 56, 202, 203, 212, 214, 298

Caregiving 10, 13, 15, 16, 17, 22, 31, 37, 38, 53, 87, 108, 202, 203, 204, 205, 206, 207, 208, 209, 210, 211, 212, 213, 250, 265, 266, 267, 268, 269, 270, 271, 272, 273, 274, 275, 277, 278, 279, 280, 281, 282, 283, 286, 287, 288, 289, 292, 294, 295, 296, 297, 298, 300, 303, 310, 311

Catharsis 119, 122, 127, 277

children 3, 4, 5, 7, 9, 18, 19, 38, 39, 43, 44, 51, 54, 69, 86, 90, 107, 118, 120, 128, 129, 130, 131, 132, 133, 135, 136, 137, 138, 139, 140, 141, 142, 144, 146, 147, 148, 158, 159, 162, 165, 171, 172, 173, 180, 185, 186, 187, 194, 195, 203, 204, 213, 214, 216, 220, 221, 228, 232, 258, 262, 296, 297, 301, 304, 307, 308, 313, 314, 317, 318

choices 69, 100, 245, 253

comfort 18, 66, 76, 84, 113, 161, 166, 206, 219, 222, 223, 224, 250, 306, 307, 309, 311, 312, 313, 319, 320, 321

Complicated Grief 13, 15, 18, 22, 25, 26, 27, 62, 75, 81, 88, 92, 93, 95, 106, 107, 108, 109, 115, 131, 173, 178, 206, 232, 234, 247, 260, 302, 304, 310, 322 coping 11, 14, 18, 24, 46, 47, 48, 49, 50, 54, 56, 79, 80, 81, 82, 84, 85, 86, 88, 99, 106, 107, 108, 109, 111, 113, 114, 116, 121, 122, 135, 137, 140, 149, 153, 156, 157, 159, 160, 161, 162, 163, 166, 169, 170, 173, 180, 181, 189, 197, 198, 200, 207, 208, 217, 218, 227, 230, 233, 239, 246, 248, 251, 258, 259, 263, 267, 268, 270, 273, 274, 275, 283, 284, 285, 291, 294, 301, 310, 311, 312

Coping strategies 14, 24, 79, 81, 107, 114, 160, 161, 162, 169, 181, 218, 246, 273, 285

Counseling 1, 2, 3, 9, 10, 11, 14, 15, 18, 19, 21, 22, 23, 24, 27, 28, 29, 30, 32, 50, 51, 52, 53, 56, 59, 64, 65, 66, 67, 68, 70, 72, 73, 75, 76, 77, 95, 97, 128, 130, 137, 139, 148, 150, 151, 153, 154, 157, 159, 164, 166, 169, 170, 171, 172, 174, 202, 209, 210, 212, 219, 228, 229, 231, 232, 237, 239, 248, 253, 260, 268, 295, 296, 297, 298, 299, 300, 301, 302, 303, 304, 305, 306, 307, 309, 310, 311, 312, 314, 316, 318, 320, 321, 322, 323, 324, 325, 326

Counseling group 299, 303, 304, 305, 307, 309, 310, 311, 312, 314, 321, 326

counselor burnout 2, 19, 21, 29, 32

counselor education 1, 3, 26, 32, 55, 74, 77, 138

COVID 1, 2, 3, 4, 5, 6, 8, 9, 10, 11, 12, 13, 14, 15, 16, 17, 19, 20, 22, 23, 24, 25, 26, 27, 28, 29, 30, 31, 32, 33, 41, 42, 43, 44, 50, 54, 55, 59, 71, 75, 79, 80, 81, 84, 85, 87, 103, 104, 107, 108, 109, 110, 115, 120, 125, 126, 129, 139, 140, 146, 147, 150, 152, 170, 171, 172, 173, 174, 179, 195, 197, 198, 200, 204, 212, 213, 215, 220, 221, 222, 223, 224, 225, 226, 227, 228, 231, 232, 233, 234, 235, 237, 239, 240, 245, 247, 248, 249, 251, 259, 260, 261, 262, 264, 267, 270, 273, 276, 277, 283, 284, 285, 287, 289, 290, 291, 292, 295, 296, 297,

298, 299, 300, 301, 302, 303, 304, 306, 307, 308, 309, 311, 313, 314, 317, 320, 321, 322, 323, 324, 325, 326

COVID-19 1, 2, 3, 4, 5, 6, 8, 9, 10, 11, 12, 13, 14, 15, 16, 17, 19, 20, 22, 23, 24, 25, 26, 27, 28, 29, 30, 31, 32, 33, 41, 42, 43, 44, 50, 54, 55, 59, 71, 75, 79, 80, 81, 84, 85, 87, 103, 104, 107, 108, 109, 115, 120, 125, 126, 129, 139, 140, 147, 150, 170, 171, 172, 173, 174, 179, 195, 197, 198, 200, 212, 213, 215, 220, 221, 222, 223, 224, 225, 226, 227, 228, 231, 232, 233, 234, 235, 237, 239, 240, 245, 247, 248, 249, 251, 259, 260, 261, 262, 264, 267, 270, 273, 276, 277, 283, 284, 285, 287, 289, 290, 291, 292, 295, 296, 297, 298, 299, 300, 301, 302, 303, 304, 306, 307, 308, 309, 311, 313, 314, 317, 320, 321, 322, 323, 324, 325, 326

COVID-19 pandemic 1, 2, 3, 4, 5, 6, 8, 9, 10, 11, 12, 13, 15, 16, 17, 19, 20, 22, 23, 24, 25, 26, 27, 28, 29, 30, 31, 33, 42, 54, 55, 79, 81, 103, 109, 115, 120, 125, 126, 129, 150, 170, 174, 179, 195, 197, 198, 200, 212, 221, 222, 223, 225, 227, 232, 233, 234, 235, 237, 239, 251, 259, 260, 262, 264, 267, 270, 273, 276, 283, 284, 287, 289, 290, 291, 295, 296, 297, 299, 300, 301, 302, 303, 304, 306, 307, 308, 309, 311, 313, 314, 320, 321, 322, 324, 325, 326

Crisis 9, 20, 29, 88, 107, 117, 118, 126, 127, 172, 173, 176, 177, 179, 189, 192, 196, 198, 200, 201, 233, 234, 270, 273, 284, 287, 315

Cultural Humility 57, 59, 64, 69, 70, 73, 76, 244, 245, 264, 283, 292

Cultural perspective 244

Culture and Grief 174, 234

D

Death Anxiety 57, 58, 59, 60, 61, 62, 63, 64, 65, 66, 67, 70, 71, 72, 73, 74, 75

E

Emotional Hazards 177, 196, 201

emotions 8, 30, 38, 39, 47, 49, 56, 67, 79, 83, 92, 93, 97, 99, 101, 102, 111, 118, 119, 121, 130, 131, 132, 133, 142, 156, 158, 159, 160, 161, 163, 164, 165, 166, 169, 185, 192, 193, 204, 206, 207, 208, 209, 210, 215, 217, 218, 219, 238, 240, 244, 248, 250, 264, 268, 272, 273, 274, 277, 284

Empathy 46, 76, 126, 154, 159, 200, 205, 206, 210, 211, 232, 246, 248, 252, 264, 266, 267, 268, 269, 270, 272, 273, 285, 297, 309, 310, 311

Ethical Responsibilities 282, 294

F

feelings 5, 7, 10, 15, 17, 18, 19, 37, 38, 39, 40, 41, 44, 46, 47, 48, 50, 56, 66, 69, 78, 79, 80, 81, 82, 83, 84, 87, 89, 90, 96, 97, 98, 99, 100, 101, 102, 103, 105, 111, 114, 118, 119, 122, 123, 133, 134, 136, 139, 143, 147, 148, 153, 154, 156, 157, 158, 159, 160, 161, 163, 164, 167, 168, 169, 181, 185, 186, 187, 188, 189, 205, 206, 208, 209, 210, 211, 215, 216, 217, 226, 227, 238, 239, 246, 247, 248, 251, 271, 274, 275, 277, 284, 285, 295, 309, 311, 312, 314, 317

Follow-up 192, 201

G

Grief 1, 2, 3, 7, 8, 10, 11, 12, 13, 14, 15, 16, 17, 18, 22, 23, 25, 26, 27, 29, 30, 31, 32, 33, 34, 35, 36, 37, 38, 39, 40, 41, 42, 43, 44, 45, 46, 47, 48, 49, 50, 51, 52, 53, 54, 55, 56, 62, 65, 66, 67, 68, 69, 70, 71, 72, 73, 74, 75, 77, 78, 79, 80, 81, 82, 83, 84, 85, 86, 87, 88, 89, 90, 91, 92, 93, 94, 95, 96, 97, 98, 99, 100, 101, 102, 103, 104, 105, 106, 107, 108, 109, 110, 111, 112, 113, 114, 115, 116, 117, 118, 119, 120, 121, 122, 123, 124, 125, 126, 127, 128, 129, 130, 131, 132, 133, 134, 135, 136, 137, 138, 139, 140, 142, 143, 144, 146, 147, 148, 149, 150, 151, 152, 153, 154, 155, 156, 157, 158, 159, 160, 161, 162, 163, 164, 165, 166, 167, 169, 170, 171, 172, 173, 174, 175, 176, 177, 178, 179, 180, 181, 182, 183, 185, 189, 190, 191, 193, 195, 196, 197, 198, 199, 200, 201, 202, 203, 204, 206, 207, 208, 209, 210, 211, 212, 215, 216, 217, 218, 219, 220, 221, 223, 224, 225, 226, 227, 228, 230, 231, 232, 233, 234, 235, 236, 237, 238, 239, 246, 247, 248, 253, 255, 259, 260, 261, 262, 263, 264, 265, 266, 267, 268, 269, 270, 271, 273, 275, 277, 279, 284, 285, 290, 291, 292, 294, 295, 296, 298, 299, 300, 301, 302, 303, 304, 305, 306, 307, 309, 310, 311, 312, 314, 316, 317, 319, 320, 321, 322, 323, 324, 325, 326

Grief and Loss 49, 55, 66, 69, 70, 100, 106, 108, 163, 165, 166, 167, 198, 202, 204, 206, 208, 209, 210, 211, 212, 273, 324

Grief Avoidance Behavior 78, 80, 81, 89, 90

Grief Counselling 126, 201, 265, 268, 275, 277, 279, 294

grief support group 128, 136, 138, 140, 303, 326

grief support groups 96, 128, 134, 137, 172, 228, 303, 306, 326

group counseling 298, 302, 303, 323

H

History 8, 11, 33, 34, 35, 57, 115, 185, 190, 212, 241, 242, 243, 262

hope 7, 8, 12, 14, 15, 25, 35, 36, 37, 41, 48, 56, 71, 98, 110, 121, 125, 136, 212, 229, 236, 246, 248, 257, 309

I

Inclusivity and Accessibility 252

insight 150, 165, 230, 244, 270, 274, 275, 282, 287

Intervention 10, 11, 14, 15, 29, 30, 47, 49, 50, 53, 54, 95, 96, 101, 117, 118, 127, 129, 130, 131, 133, 142, 148, 151, 162, 164, 166, 167, 172, 177, 178, 179, 184, 189, 190, 191, 192, 198, 199, 200, 201, 209, 217, 233, 244, 258, 324

L

Loss 2, 3, 6, 7, 8, 10, 13, 14, 15, 16, 17, 18, 19, 27, 29, 32, 33, 34, 35, 36, 37, 38, 39, 40, 41, 43, 44, 45, 46, 47, 48, 49, 50, 52, 53, 54, 55, 56, 65, 66, 67, 68, 69, 70, 71, 74, 75, 76, 77, 78, 79, 80, 81, 82, 83, 84, 86, 87, 88, 89, 90, 91, 92, 94, 95, 96, 97, 98, 100, 101, 102, 104, 105, 106, 108, 110, 111, 113, 115, 116, 117, 118, 119, 120, 122, 123, 125, 127, 129, 131, 133, 134, 135, 136, 137, 138, 140, 143, 145, 147, 150, 151, 159, 161, 162, 163, 164, 165, 166, 167, 169, 170, 171, 172, 176, 177, 179, 180, 181, 185, 187, 188, 191, 193, 194, 195, 196, 197, 198, 202, 204, 206, 208, 209, 210, 211, 212, 215, 216, 217, 218, 219, 221, 222, 224, 225, 227, 228, 229, 230, 231, 232, 233, 234, 235, 236, 238, 239, 245, 246, 247, 248, 249, 253, 260, 264, 266, 271, 273, 280, 284, 292, 294, 295, 296, 298, 299, 301, 302, 303, 306, 307, 309, 310, 311, 312, 313, 316, 317, 319, 320, 321, 322, 323, 324, 325, 326

M

Mental health 1, 2, 3, 5, 6, 8, 9, 10, 11, 12, 15, 19, 20, 21, 22, 23, 24, 27, 28, 29, 30, 31, 32, 36, 41, 42, 43, 46, 54, 72, 73, 74, 75, 76, 77, 80, 87, 91, 92, 93, 99, 101, 104, 105, 107, 109, 122, 126, 128, 129, 130, 131, 137, 140, 150, 151, 171, 174, 183, 184, 189, 198, 201, 205, 207, 212, 213, 222, 235, 239, 240, 241, 242, 243, 246, 248, 249, 250, 251, 252, 253, 257, 258, 259, 260, 261, 262, 263, 264, 266, 267, 270, 279, 284, 286, 290, 291, 293, 301, 302, 316, 318, 323, 325, 326

mental health professional 32

ministry 232, 235

P

pre-loss 47, 53, 55, 56

proactive coping 54, 56

Prolonged Grief Disorder 7, 8, 87, 88, 90, 91, 95, 96, 105, 106, 108, 109, 110, 111, 115, 126, 150, 158, 173

R

Rehabilitative Counsellor 115, 122, 127, 179, 183, 184, 185, 186, 189, 190, 191, 192, 195, 196, 201

relationships 3, 4, 8, 18, 26, 66, 70, 73, 75, 82, 83, 86, 87, 94, 95, 110, 126, 131, 149, 150, 153, 154, 155, 157, 160, 166, 170, 174, 200, 203, 216, 223, 227, 230, 233, 234, 238, 244, 246, 247, 251, 254, 267, 268, 274, 281, 289, 302, 315, 316, 317, 319, 322

resilience 11, 28, 46, 50, 54, 56, 98, 110, 116, 126, 128, 150, 153, 154, 155, 156, 157, 159, 160, 166, 167, 200, 205, 207, 208, 245, 248, 265, 266, 267, 268, 269, 271, 272, 273, 274, 275, 277, 278, 279, 280, 281, 282, 283, 284, 285, 286, 287, 288, 290, 292, 294, 316, 322

S

sadness 16, 18, 32, 37, 38, 39, 44, 50, 77, 78, 85, 88, 90, 130, 133, 156, 158, 163, 167, 177, 201, 204, 206, 207, 219, 238, 312, 314, 319

School Counselor 137, 157, 159, 164, 166, 168, 170

schools 2, 11, 88, 136, 138, 147, 148, 151, 154, 167, 170, 171, 172, 174, 175

Self-Care 19, 20, 21, 22, 24, 25, 32, 96, 202, 203, 207, 209, 210, 211, 212, 213, 214, 238, 248, 265, 266, 267, 268, 269, 270, 271, 272, 273, 274, 275, 276, 277, 278, 279, 280, 281, 282, 283, 284, 285, 286, 287, 288, 289, 290, 291, 292, 293, 294, 323

Self-Care for Caregivers 211

self-efficacy 52, 56, 241, 264, 290

Social Supports 112, 113, 114, 115, 116, 117, 119, 120, 122, 123, 124, 127, 176, 177, 178, 180, 181, 182, 183, 184, 187, 188, 192, 193, 194, 195, 196, 201

sorrow 7, 46, 91, 238, 244, 247, 264

Strategies 4, 11, 14, 15, 24, 57, 60, 67, 68, 69, 70, 79, 81, 102, 107, 108, 114, 126, 129, 130, 146, 147, 151, 153, 154, 156, 157, 159, 160, 161, 162, 167, 169, 170, 181, 186, 198, 199, 200, 201, 206, 207, 208, 211, 218, 233, 244, 246, 248, 256, 265, 267, 272, 273, 274, 275, 277, 278, 279, 280, 282, 285, 286, 288, 291, 294, 323

suffer 2, 11, 35, 184, 194, 297, 301, 302, 303

support groups 10, 22, 96, 104, 128, 129, 130, 131, 134, 137, 150, 155, 161, 172, 219, 228, 229, 240, 242, 243, 248, 249, 250, 251, 252, 253, 254, 255, 257, 258, 259, 260, 261, 262, 281, 284, 286, 287, 295, 298, 303, 305, 306, 307, 320, 321, 322, 326

supportive care 27, 325

T

Teachers 44, 88, 126, 137, 146, 147, 148, 149, 150, 152, 153, 154, 155, 157, 159, 160, 161, 162, 163, 164, 167, 170, 171, 173, 174, 215, 290

Terror Management Theory 57, 59, 62, 63, 75, 76

Therapeutic Effect 97, 112, 113, 120, 123, 124, 127

therapy 18, 20, 21, 23, 30, 36, 47, 49, 51, 76, 95, 96, 97, 98, 99, 100, 101, 102, 107, 108, 111, 126, 166, 172, 175, 190, 201, 210, 217, 241, 246, 253, 258, 274, 292, 300, 301, 302, 303, 316, 317, 324, 325, 326

Time Management 265, 275, 277, 278, 279, 290, 291, 294

traumatic loss 321

U

understanding 15, 49, 59, 62, 64, 66, 67, 69, 70, 78, 83, 85, 95, 104, 114, 120, 125, 131, 139, 140, 146, 147, 148, 149, 152, 153, 155, 157, 161, 162, 168, 170, 193, 200, 204, 206, 207, 208, 209, 219, 225, 232, 233, 235, 241, 244, 246, 248, 249, 252, 258, 259, 262, 268, 269, 270, 271, 273, 274, 275, 279, 283, 285, 303, 304, 306, 307, 311, 315, 316, 320, 321

Y

Yoruba 120, 127, 195, 198, 201

Publishing Tomorrow's Research Today

IGI Global
www.igi-global.com

Uncover Current Insights and Future Trends in
Education
with IGI Global's Cutting-Edge Recommended Books

Print Only, E-Book Only, or Print + E-Book.
Order direct through IGI Global's Online Bookstore at www.igi-global.com or through your preferred provider.

ISBN: 9781668493007
© 2023; 234 pp.
List Price: US$ **215**

ISBN: 9798369300749
© 2024; 383 pp.
List Price: US$ **230**

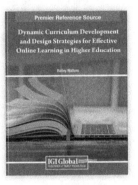

ISBN: 9781668486467
© 2023; 471 pp.
List Price: US$ **215**

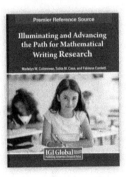

ISBN: 9781668465387
© 2024; 389 pp.
List Price: US$ **215**

ISBN: 9781668475836
© 2024; 359 pp.
List Price: US$ **215**

ISBN: 9781668444238
© 2023; 334 pp.
List Price: US$ **240**

Do you want to stay current on the latest research trends, product announcements, news, and special offers?
Join IGI Global's mailing list to receive customized recommendations, exclusive discounts, and more.
Sign up at: www.igi-global.com/newsletters.

Scan the QR Code here to view more related titles in Education.

www.igi-global.com | Sign up at www.igi-global.com/newsletters | facebook.com/igiglobal | twitter.com/igiglobal | linkedin.com/igiglobal

Ensure Quality Research is Introduced to the Academic Community

Become a Reviewer for IGI Global Authored Book Projects

  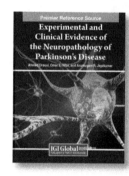 

The overall success of an authored book project is dependent on quality and timely manuscript evaluations.

Applications and Inquiries may be sent to:
development@igi-global.com

Applicants must have a doctorate (or equivalent degree) as well as publishing, research, and reviewing experience. Authored Book Evaluators are appointed for one-year terms and are expected to complete at least three evaluations per term. Upon successful completion of this term, evaluators can be considered for an additional term.

If you have a colleague that may be interested in this opportunity, we encourage you to share this information with them.

Publishing Tomorrow's Research Today
IGI Global's Open Access Journal Program
Including Nearly 200 Peer-Reviewed, Gold (Full) Open Access Journals across IGI Global's Three Academic Subject Areas: Business & Management; Scientific, Technical, and Medical (STM); and Education

Consider Submitting Your Manuscript to One of These Nearly 200 Open Access Journals for to Increase Their Discoverability & Citation Impact

| Web of Science Impact Factor **6.5** | Web of Science Impact Factor **4.7** | Web of Science Impact Factor **3.2** | Web of Science Impact Factor **2.6** |

JOURNAL OF Organizational and End User Computing

JOURNAL OF Global Information Management

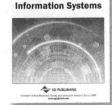
INTERNATIONAL JOURNAL ON Semantic Web and Information Systems

JOURNAL OF Database Management

Choosing IGI Global's Open Access Journal Program Can Greatly Increase the Reach of Your Research

Higher Usage
Open access papers are 2-3 times more likely to be read than non-open access papers.

Higher Download Rates
Open access papers benefit from 89% higher download rates than non-open access papers.

Higher Citation Rates
Open access papers are 47% more likely to be cited than non-open access papers.

Submitting an article to a journal offers an invaluable opportunity for you to share your work with the broader academic community, fostering knowledge dissemination and constructive feedback.

Submit an Article and Browse the IGI Global Call for Papers Pages

We can work with you to find the journal most well-suited for your next research manuscript.
For open access publishing support, contact: journaleditor@igi-global.com

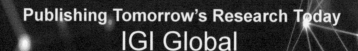

Printed in the USA
CPSIA information can be obtained
at www.ICGtesting.com
LVHW080534170924
791295LV00005B/411